Image and Remembrance

Image and Remembrance

Representation and the Holocaust

Edited by Shelley Hornstein and Florence Jacobowitz

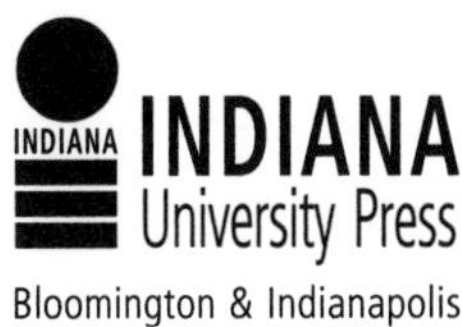

Bloomington & Indianapolis

This book is a publication of

Indiana University Press
601 North Morton Street
Bloomington, IN 47404-3797 USA

http://iupress.indiana.edu

Telephone orders 800-842-6796
Fax orders 812-855-7931
Orders by e-mail iuporder@indiana.edu

The paper used in this publication meets the minimum requirements of American National Standard for Information Sciences—Permanence of Paper for Printed Library Materials, ANSI Z39.48-1984.

Manufactured in the United States of America

Library of Congress Cataloging-in-Publication Data

Image and remembrance : representation and the Holocaust / edited by Shelley Hornstein and Florence Jacobowitz.
p. cm.
Includes bibliographical references and index.
ISBN 0-253-34188-4 (alk. paper) — ISBN 0-253-21569-2 (pbk. : alk. paper)
1. Holocaust, Jewish (1939–1945), in art. 2. Arts, Modern—20th century. I. Hornstein, Shelley. II. Jacobowitz, Florence, date
NX650.H57 I46 2003
700'.458—dc21

2002004061

1 2 3 4 5 08 07 06 05 04 03

In memory of
Shimon and Rela Jacobowitz
and
Ruth Hornstein

Contents

Part IV National Expressions of Remembrance

Acknowledgments

We wish to acknowledge the Social Sciences and Humanities Research Council and the Atkinson Faculty of Liberal and Professional Studies at York University for their generous support. The grants they awarded us made the realization of this project possible.

This book is, in many ways, the culmination of a larger project, which included a newly designed course and a series of guest lectures on a number of topics related to the themes addressed in this anthology. The Deutscher Akademischer Austasch Dienst honored us with the first team-teaching award in German studies at York University for a newly designed course we offered titled "Culture, Memory, and Resistance: Representation and the Holocaust in Visual Art and Film," and we are grateful for the opportunity to have taught it. We wish to thank Howard Adelman, the Harry Crowe Memorial Fund, Matthew Teitelbaum, and the Art Gallery of Ontario for generously supporting a talk by Eric Michaud; Dov Goldstein of the Design Exchange, Detlef Mertins and the School of Architecture at the University of Toronto, and Doina Popescu and the Goethe Institut for a lecture by Daniel Libeskind; and the Holocaust Remembrance Committee of Toronto, the French Consulate General, and, at York University, the Centre for Jewish Studies and the Dean's Office of the Atkinson Faculty for their generous support of a screening of Claude Lanzmann's *A Visitor from the Living,* which was followed by a discussion with the filmmaker. The community's overwhelming response to these events underscored the need for this kind of discussion.

We thank our graduate students Sharona Adamowicz, Kate Bride, Josh Heumann, Lee Rodney, and Jason Shron for their help and commitment to the concerns of this project. Sharona and Kate were with us the longest on this project; we are especially indebted to them for their diligence and dedication, and the wonderful dispositions with which they are graced. Thanks, as well, to Hazel O'Loughlin-Vidal for her conscientious efforts in preparing the manuscript for publication, and to Howard Buckstein for producing the index.

Our contributors were enthusiastic about the project from its inception. We would like to thank them all for their participation in this act of remembrance.

Finally, we thank our families: Sam, Lara, Ari, and Elias Rabinovitch, and Jim, Shimon, Yonah, and Nina Diamond. Their love and support is deeply appreciated.

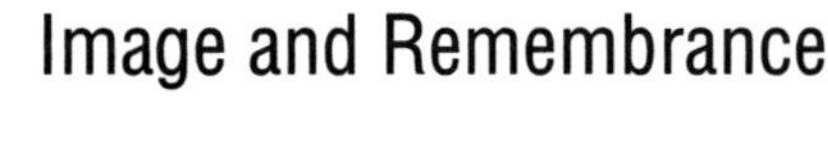

Image and Remembrance

Introduction | SHELLEY HORNSTEIN AND FLORENCE JACOBOWITZ

> On many occasions, we survivors of the Nazi concentration camps have come to notice how little use words are in describing our experiences. Their "poor reception" derives from the fact that we now live in a civilization of the image, registered, multiplied, televised, and that the public, particularly the young, is ever less likely to benefit from written information. . . . [I]n all of our accounts, verbal or written, one finds expressions such as "indescribable," "inexpressible," "words are not enough," "one would need a language for . . ." This was, in fact, our daily thought; language is for the description of daily experience, but here it is another world, here one would need a language "of this other world," a language born here.
>
> —Primo Levi[1]

This collection of essays on art and the Holocaust began as a commemorative endeavor based on the belief that a collection of critical writing can itself be a form of memorialization. A book, like a work of visual art, a film, or a monument, is a place that can inspire thought, reflection, learning, debate, and mourning. Remembering is looking at the past from the present; therefore, this book is intended as a site where the activity of commemoration is evoked. We have chosen to look at some of the ways in which artists give form to issues surrounding the Holocaust and its far-reaching devastation, which still resonates.

Our approach to this volume is inspired by the Jewish imperative to remember, *zachor,* which, as Yosef Yerushalmi suggests, is marked by activity, or the *act* of remembering.[2] We see engagement with this text as an active practice rather than a passive one, and reading as an act of criticism that can initiate remembrance. While this is an anthology of art criticism, it is also a way of acknowledging the continuing relevance of the past in contemporary life. A range of artists have increasingly felt an urgent need to document and give expression to testimony, experience, and memory of the Holocaust. While their reasons are diverse, certainly part of their urgency is due to the aging of the survivor population and the increasing loss of firsthand testimony, which is irreplaceable. We are inviting our readers, therefore, to consider this volume as something more than a work of scholarship to be archived.

Again, we hope this volume, like a monument, will be visited by a broad community. To that end, we have assembled a diverse range of contributions with the intention of opening up ideas that are prevalent and have become pressing.

Since this is a commemorative volume, our intention is to reach beyond the confines of academic discourse, which has a tendency to create its own language and speak only to its constituents. We hesitated to take on this subject for fear of contributing another academic volume to what might arguably be seen as a growing Holocaust industry. We share the concerns that have been voiced regarding the recent allure of the academic study of the Holocaust, which risks becoming a transient fashion, soon to be replaced by the next. Instead, we argue for recognizing that Holocaust studies must be a sustained and committed activity rooted in the imperative to remember. We recognize the contradictions involved in this project: in order to talk about representation and the Holocaust, one is obliged to address a variety of debates which have introduced new terms, such as "postmemory" (Marianne Hirsch),[3] allusive "realism" (Saul Friedlander),[4] and "Holocaust effect" (Ernst van Alphen),[5] as a means of navigating through the complexities of the subject. At the same time, we are uneasy entrenching academic discourse that risks containing and closing off all further discussion and disenfranchising the general public. Each of these contributions must struggle with the terminology that has already taken root regarding how representation of the Holocaust is possible; however, in this volume we remain committed to sorting through the complexities of these debates while avoiding a shift of significance from the subject to the lexicon that scholars have introduced surrounding issues of representation.

Much of the artwork and critical practice is motivated by the sense of urgent need to resist erasure and inscribe memory. A collection of essays which encourages reflection contributes to an ongoing cultural process of memorialization to keep history vital. Traditionally, cultural memory is not preserved through recorded history but rather through collective activities which vivify memory. As Nora has argued, *lieux de mémoire* (sites of memory) are modern responses to this dilemma. Lieux de mémoire, he suggests, "are fundamentally vestiges, the ultimate embodiments of a commemorative consciousness that survives in a history which, having renounced memory, cries out for it."[6] Jewish historiographic practice is informed by activities which concretize the act of remembering and resist forgetting. What our book attempts to acknowledge is that one cultural form, art, moves freely between history and memory. Many have argued that this is precisely why artistic practice is suspect when it addresses the Holocaust. The debates surrounding issues of representation are underpinned by the suggestion that a form of discourse is bounded by what can be imagined. It is limited by knowledge that is imaginable and is shaped by preexisting schemas. To acknowledge that the Holocaust was an unprecedented catastrophe of inconceivable proportion suggests that it defies representation. This concept of representation assumes that one can only represent what it is possible to conceive; that language is limited by what is known and that events that test these limits and exceed them demand a new language.

We are suggesting, rather, that the problem of realism and representation and the related questions it raises concerning authenticity are not insurmountable. To begin, realism as an aesthetic style or form is complex and too often is reduced to simplistic perceptual verisimilitude, re-creating what is perceived as reality. The assumption is that the audience cannot make the distinction between reality and represented reality and will ultimately be duped into believing that what they see is real. Representation has always been recognized as the active play between creating a fictional work and making reference to a real event. There are various degrees of transparency and flexibility within forms of realist representation; a number of artists working within realism produce works which accommodate allusiveness and critical distance and signal their status as constructions.

The subject of the Holocaust demands a firm grounding in truth and facticity regarding the events that took place. Although we acknowledge the problem of "dramatic license," or the pleasure of the happy ending often implicit in certain forms of narrative art, artists have used imaginative forms successfully to represent the Holocaust. Art Spiegelman's *Maus* is a case in point. It renders the real as both history and autobiography through the stylistic forms of "commix," which traditionally remain in the realm of fictional entertainment. Yet Spiegelman never relinquishes his task of exploring veracity with a meticulous attention to detail, fortifying his father's memories with accurate renderings of the events remembered: for example, of life in hiding during the first stages of persecution and entrapment, and later of the camps. Spiegelman respects the sanctity of his subject matter and uses the form of commix without diminishing the profundity or the commitment to historical accuracy of the catastrophic history being remembered and recounted. Clearly, as an artist, Spiegelman feels himself responsible to his task. He inserts himself into the narrative and agonizes over the choices he must make to represent the events told, as this passage demonstrates:

> Some part of me doesn't want to draw or think about Auschwitz. I can't visualize it clearly, and I can't BEGIN to imagine what it felt like.[7]

Spiegelman's struggle reflects the ethical framework that informs his project. Rather than begin with a fixed theoretical position—is it possible to talk about the Holocaust through existing conventions of representation?—we have chosen to begin this discussion by inviting contributions that respond to artwork and film that confirm, like *Maus,* the possibility of addressing the Holocaust through art. Each of these contributions recognizes and addresses a variety of critical concerns, such as the questions of beauty and pleasure (and even entertainment) inherent to any discussion of aesthetics. At the same time, these essays evidence the role aesthetics plays in providing an arena for expression otherwise unseen and unspoken in more traditional forms of historiographic practice. There is value in acknowledging the reluctance to represent the Holocaust (the idea that one cannot and even should not represent the magnitude of annihilation), but focusing on whether representation is possible or appropriate at all after Auschwitz deflects from the complex and layered nature of the subject of the Holocaust. Artists have addressed many aspects, in addition to the question of representation, that explore the use of images in the practice of remembrance.

This volume, therefore, is not designed to be a comprehensive overview of art and the Holocaust. The structure of the collection reflects some of the fundamental concerns that continue to inform the urgency and necessity to remember. The volume is structured in four thematic parts that address rememoration and its various expressions in art. We begin with "Commemoration and Sites of Mourning" because the volume is intended to act as a commemorative text. We recognize that a memorial place allows public and private reflection. The reader is invited to enter this memorial space and contemplate these ideas in an open framework. We want to elicit the reader's engagement with the material; the categories we propose, therefore, are signposts to various points of entry. In addition, "Commemoration and Sites of Mourning," which begins with the response of selected artists, sets an elegiac tone for the remainder of the collection. The contributions here explore the nature of memorial art and site-specific monuments to collective memory. These essays address the relationship between the work and its public reception, which can extend beyond the local context of a site.

"Personal Responses and Familial Legacies" investigates the work of second-generation artists, children of survivors, struggling with issues of memory and identity. The realm of the familial informs these works as artists inscribe themselves within the context of their histories. "Memento Mori: Atrocity and

Aesthetics" takes on the challenges of image-making, beauty, and form, given the interdiction against visualizing and aestheticizing the unimaginable. This section addresses some iconic complexities concerning explicit images and responses to atrocity. Finally, "National Expressions of Remembrance" opens up the politics of place and commemoration to conclude that a site is never neutral and history and national agendas are at all times political.

We had many choices as to how to group the contributions in this book, since there are necessary connections and crossovers. We did not want to group the essays according to technique or medium (painting, architecture, film), which is more typical of a traditional visual arts collection. Here, questions of representation, the delicacy of the subject matter, the necessity of ethical choices, and the urgency that underlies much of this work demand the reconception of familiar schemas. Hence, this volume acts as a place for rethinking these issues, reconsidering the processes of art-making and its cultural significance.

Given the subject matter and our desire to make this volume a place of reflection that intentionally does not offer a redemptive, concluding chapter, there is no narrative structure, with a problem established at the outset and resolved at the end. Instead, our project is a grouping of modules that invite the reader to raise questions and consider process as well as content. For this reason we also want the reader to approach each contribution without the reductiveness characteristic of glosses in a typical introduction. We prefer to create a place of openness so that the reader is at liberty to select freely. We have therefore decided not to give a synopsis of each contribution, which risks simplifying carefully laid out arguments. In addition, such summaries diminish the reader's engagement with the material, which we are encouraging. Instead, we wish to point out, more generally, some recurring themes and concerns that traverse this commemorative volume.

Initially, we invited contributors to consider a selection of themes regarding questions of representation in visual art and film that would act as a guideline. These included public and private mourning, displacement and identity, considerations of topography and site-specific work, commemorative art and the shaping of collective memory, expressions of trauma and loss, witnessing and testimony, and expressions of personal memory in biography, memoir, and journal. Although the responses were diverse, a number of issues were repeatedly expressed, suggesting their centrality to this volume. Salient among them is the notion of shaping or spatializing absence. Given the devastation of the Holocaust, artists feel the need to mark loss tangibly and visually in a variety of ways: for example, Daniel Libeskind's "voids" in the Jewish Museum in Berlin, Shimon Attie's slide projections of lost Jewish culture onto Berlin facades, the use of holograms in the Jewish Museum in Vienna to suggest an invisible presence of loss. Acknowledging absence leads one to mourn the unfathomable projected loss of potential Jewish life and culture.

The theme of witnessing in art opens up the consideration of trauma and memory; how does one retrieve testimony that is embedded in the traumatic experience of unprecedented events? One artist, Claude Lanzmann, approaches this problem in *Shoah* through a strategy of reenactment. The problem of articulating traumatic testimony is not limited to first-generation survivors, but continues to have repercussions on the second and third generations, who have inherited their parents' legacy.

As this collection addresses questions of representation, it follows that many of our contributors raise the problem of what it means to aestheticize the Holocaust. In addition to having commemorative value, the art raises complex issues of how aesthetics functions, and why there is a stronger response to some works than to others. The clearly influential works by artists such as Lanzmann, Spiegelman, Boltanski, and Libeskind have become paradigms. These artists' works are negotiating and challenging the complex boundaries between aesthetics, ethics, politics, and history in groundbreaking ways. The role of criticism in this collection is to open up these questions.

Notes

1. Primo Levi, "Preface," in *Rivisitando i lager,* exhibition catalogue (Milan, Italy: Idea, 1985). We would like to thank Roberto and Yvonne Perin for their translation of Levi's piece for this volume.

2. Yosef Hayim Yerushalmi, *Zachor: Jewish History and Jewish Memory* (Seattle: University of Washington Press, [1982] 1996), 5ff.

3. Marianne Hirsch, *Family Frames: Photography, Narrative, and Postmemory* (Cambridge, Mass.: Harvard University Press, 1997).

4. Saul Friedlander, ed., *Probing the Limits of Representation: Nazism and the "Final Solution"* (Cambridge, Mass.: Harvard University Press, 1992).

5. Ernst van Alphen, *Caught by History: Holocaust Effects in Contemporary Art, Literature, and Theory* (Stanford, Calif.: Stanford University Press, 1997).

6. Pierre Nora, ed., *Realms of Memory: Rethinking the French Past,* trans. Arthur Goldhammer, vol. 1 (New York: Columbia University Press, 1996), 6.

7. Art Spiegelman, *Maus: A Survivor's Tale,* vol. 2 (New York: Pantheon, [1986] 1991), 46.

Part I

Commemoration and Sites of Mourning

1 *Shoah* as Cinema | FLORENCE JACOBOWITZ

> I will have spent my life trying to understand the function of remembering which is not the opposite of forgetting but rather its lining. We do not remember. We rewrite memory much as history is rewritten. How can one remember thirst?
>
> —Chris Marker, *Sans Soleil* (1982)

Claude Lanzmann's film *Shoah* is acclaimed for its invention of a form of cinematic discourse that activates the imagination to evoke the unimaginable in a manner uniquely its own. *Shoah*'s style is revelatory and its diegesis is, in many ways, completely original. From its choice of concentration (the process of the annihilation of European Jewry) to its methodology (the development of a dialectical style which juxtaposes and counterpoints words [*paroles*]: testimonies with places [*lieux*]: present-day shots of cities, towns, forests, train stations, rivers, and the sites of former concentration camps), *Shoah* invents a form of cinema appropriate to its intentions.

Viewing *Shoah* is like entering a site of memorialization; it is a monument to the murdered, and its tone is elegiac and mournful. It becomes a memorial space where the relationship between past and present is contemplated and, like memorials, it addresses not only what should be remembered but how, and the way a work of art can contribute to the inscription of historical testimony and public memory. *Shoah* is prefaced by a quotation from Isaiah, "and I will give them an everlasting name," and as this quotation suggests, the film is dedicated to naming, remembering, and giving a voice to those unjustly silenced and rendered invisible. This dedication at the outset underlines that *Shoah* is first and foremost for the victims of Nazi atrocities. Like many recent memorial artworks,[1] *Shoah* constructs itself around an absence, a void, the annihilated, and tries to make absence felt. The mystery at the heart of *Shoah* is the unimpeded and efficient bureaucratic process whereby trainloads of people arriving in Treblinka, Chelmno, or Auschwitz disappeared every few hours and how this process continued, unabated, for years. *Shoah* concentrates on the logistics of transportation, the collection of personal effects, waiting areas, means of killing, burial procedures. It is also obsessed with the elusive and the ephemeral, that which defies testimony: the terrifying moments that preceded death, the time of death. Who saw these people last, what did the conditions of transportation feel like, where were they asked to wait, what was the weather like that day, who heard them scream? The act of making testimony come alive, traces, solidified by corroboration, transforms memory into evidence and truth. Lanzmann's rememorative work is highly politicized: the point is not to invite a distanced contemplation of an event in the past but to experience the presentness of its repercussions and the consistence of attitudes that contributed to its taking place. The crime of genocide that haunts *Shoah* is a trauma that refuses to be relegated to history.

Shoah is a film that is difficult to identify in terms of genre. It seems clearer to assert what it is not. Lanzmann has proclaimed it not a documentary because of its refusal to exploit archival footage (which would present it as a document of the past) to illustrate or represent.[2] Many have distinguished *Shoah* from what has become the emblematic narrative film about the Holocaust, Spielberg's *Schindler's List,* for reasons that are too many to enumerate here.[3] Less because of its use of fictional strategies—*Shoah* relies heavily on cinematic conventions characteristic of fiction—most notably in its refusal to offer a redemptory narrative conclusion or to relate the near eradication of European Jewry through a narrative of salvation at the hands of a German gentile. What *Shoah* isn't is easier to ascertain than what it is: it is part testament, part essay, part drama, part travelogue, part journal, part lamentation.

Without detracting from the film's originality, it is useful to think about *Shoah* in relation to a postwar body of films created in response to the devastation of the war and to the moral and existential crisis left in its wake. Roberto Rossellini was amongst the first to reconceive cinematic realism and to present a personal response to a social moment, evident in the titles of works like *Germania anno zero* (1947) or *Europa 51* (1952). In France, the Left Bank group which included Alain Resnais, Chris Marker, and Georges Franju also produced politicized films which contemplate how a culture remembers, how time is mutable, how history is inscribed and whose interests it serves. Their works are radically original, yet they share a number of characteristics, including the director's felt presence (a personal position) and an understanding that it is the nature of the cinema to both register physical reality and mobilize the inner reality of the imagination. All of these directors made films which address the problem of memory and the significance of remembrance. *Viaggio in Italia* (1953) is emblematic of Rossellini's modernist reconception of cinematic realism as an essay on postwar life. It is, in part, a documentary (and travelogue) on Naples, Italian culture and mores, and an essay on a culture's attitude toward death and memorialization and how this is integrated into present everyday life. It is, in part, a documentary on Rossellini's then wife Ingrid Bergman, a Swede foreign to Mediterranean life, who confronts an expressive culture from which she feels estranged.[4] It is, as well, a fictional narrative about a couple, the Joyces, and the dissolution of their marriage. By stripping them of the habits, routines, and familiarity of home, their visit to Italy exposes their incompatibility. In many ways Rossellini's tactics are not far from Lanzmann's—he creates the conditions that will provoke an authentic response. Bergman's genuine sense of estrangement from a culture foreign to her is, in many ways, what drives the narrative and contributes to its distinctive realism. The film traverses the borders which distinguish document from fiction, public from private, objective reality from subjective consciousness.

Viaggio in Italia is also a meditation on how the language of film works. Toward the end of the film, there is a sequence in which all these concerns coalesce. The Joyces are invited to visit Pompeii, where archeologists pour a plastic cast of the space left by two bodies, caught in an embrace at the moment of death. It is an extraordinary scene; as Katharine Joyce (Ingrid Bergman) witnesses the reconstruction of a couple at the moment of their death, she breaks down, overwhelmed. The plaster cast gives absence a shape and a form, producing a material vestige from a catastrophe. It rehumanizes an event that is beyond the imagination and insists on its presentness. The revelation of the personal still speaks to a contemporary moment, its pathos and trauma erasing time. Katharine's poignant response, "Life is so short," underlines this. Earlier in the film she visits museums, catacombs, and memorial sites; this is another stark expression of rememoration and mortality, and its directness frightens her. In a sense Rossellini is signaling that all cinema is like this—film, like the still photograph, captures an imprint of the real and forever signals an absence.[5] Cinematic images, like photographs, are memento mori and are, therefore, inherently elegiac. The power of the cinema (which eclipses photography) is that its semblance of presentness and of suspended time, and its rendering of duration and dimensions in space (imparted through techniques like camera movement and the long take), connect the past and the present, signaling not only what was but what is, condensing and collapsing time.

Alain Resnais's postwar meditations on memory and absence are different from Rossellini's (and Lanzmann's) in style and approach, but they do share some of the same preoccupations. *Nuit et brouillard [Night and Fog]* (1955) was a work commissioned by the Comité d'histoire de la Seconde Guerre Mondiale, one that was to commemorate the liberation of the camps. Resnais's strategy of juxtaposing and linking the events of the past, represented by black and white archival images and a chronological progression to the present, presented in color in relentless tracking shots around the ruins of a concentration camp, foregrounds the problem of forgetting, of burying history in the past. The theme of *Night and Fog* is Resnais's insistence that we look directly, that we confront evidence of the atrocities committed in these camps. As the camera records a torn concrete ceiling in a gas chamber, we are told this is "le seul signe . . . mais il faut le savoir . . ." [the only sign . . . but one must know it . . .]. Resnais is challenging the limits of permissibility—what can be publicly discussed in a commissioned work of commemoration, made only ten years after the liberation of the camps. Resnais had already made a number of films which address how a culture writes its history;[6] *Toute la mémoire du monde* (1956), which followed *Night and Fog,* continues to explore these concerns in its critique of (and protest against) the manner in which the past, culture, and memory are controlled, catalogued, and entombed in the Bibliothèque Nationale. Georges Franju's *Hôtel des invalides* (1951) and *Le sang des bêtes* (1949) are poetic protests against the way society builds monuments and tourist sites to atrocities, sanctifying destruction, or how horror is masked in the heart of a civilized city, in a slaughterhouse.

This is a somewhat lengthy digression, but it is relevant to think about *Shoah* in relation to a body of work that began thinking about ways of adequately speaking and memorializing, and the contribution cinema makes to this cultural process. These filmmakers thought about representation and catastrophe and the need to speak personally and accountably. *Shoah* is closer to this tradition than to a diverse group of contemporary documentaries premised on the postmodernist rejection of the idea that an image can refer to objective truth. These documentaries employ fictional strategies and stylization to distinguish themselves from traditional documentaries that aim for a self-effacing objective rendering of the real. They reinforce the postmodern notion that truth is relative, a construction contingent upon the limitations of subjective perspective and prevailing ideologies.[7] Cinema is considered yet another reflection in the simulacrum, mistaken for reality.

Linda Williams's "Mirrors without Memories: Truth, History, and the New Documentary" places *Shoah* squarely among a series of these postmodern documentaries that emerged in the '80s, such as Errol Morris's *The Thin Blue Line* (1988).[8] These films are compared in terms of style—they use strategies borrowed from fiction filmmaking and are self-reflexive—and approaches—their directors intervene to unearth events related to a traumatic past which continue to reverberate in the present. *Shoah*'s demonstration of the repetition in the present of attitudes and actions consistent with those in the past are evident in scenes like the one on the church steps in Chelmno, where Polish antisemitism and the resulting silencing of the Jew, Srebnik, dramatically unfold before the camera. The problem is that within the postmodern schema one can "reveal the seduction of lies" (20), but truth remains "relative," "contingent," never "guaranteed" or "absolute." The truth of the past may be hard to fathom and difficult to retrieve, but this does not mean that a coherent notion of the past cannot be guaranteed. Lanzmann recognizes the significance of making his case in the present, speaking to a contemporary audience; testimony is collected in the present, and Lanzmann establishes that the crime of the *Shoah* is one that takes place—that persists and continues to have repercussions. Lanzmann is equally clear that the truth of the past is knowable; the film's objective is to demonstrate, collect evidence, create the conditions that will allow deeply felt testimony to surface. *Shoah* is not ambiguous in its position regarding who is accountable, and in this sense the film differs from Resnais's universalist cry near the conclusion of *Night and Fog*—"Alors, qui est responsable?" [Who, then, is responsible?]. *Shoah* determines who is responsible, which might be why the Polish government tried to obstruct its airing on French television. *Shoah* in not hesitant or diplomatic. Polish antisemitism is registered full-force in a contemporary setting. The German officials' denial of accountability, the indifference of witnessing townspeople, the trauma of the victims of Nazi brutality (still evident in the present) corroborate historical truth. *Shoah* is grounded in a coherent, immutable truth; it just refuses to suggest that the Holocaust was an event that ended in 1945.

Postmodern readings that question the ability to identify stable, unconditional truths dangerously undermine the political import of memorialization and historiographic practice. *Shoah*'s insistent registration of corroborative evidence is an act of resistance to obliteration, forgetting, revision, a counterattack against an act of destruction that was masked and ignored. Lanzmann, like Raul Hilberg, presents the indisputable historical details that illustrate the systematized process of the destruction of European Jewry—the logistics of transportation, bureaucratic procedures, etc.—but *Shoah* also explores experiential detail (and here the cinema becomes particularly useful): what it may have felt like to await imminent death in the "funnel" in Treblinka, or to be working in the "special detail" in Auschwitz and meet a friend or relative whom you know will soon be killed. *Shoah* is also a history of private feelings. This is part of the paradoxical nature of eyewitness testimony, which draws from memory and is tinged with personal recollection. It is still evidence, but it has to be corroborated to be legally acceptable, and the film's capturing of reenacted testimony counters the fallibility of memory. Although rooted in the subjective, it can still substantiate objective truth. *Shoah* is, for this reason, much closer in spirit to the personal postwar documentaries that commented on the films' relationship to a reality which could be identified and addressed.

MONTAGE

Le film fait travailler l'imagination.

—Claude Lanzmann[9]

According to Lanzmann, a provisional title for *Shoah* was *Le lieu et la parole,*[10] which refers to the film's methodology of juxtaposing and linking places shot in the present with the witnesses' testimony of events that took place during the war. The combination of landscape and descriptive telling evokes the viewer's imaginative participation in what is being narrated or told. This results in an image which can be visualized without being represented. Lanzmann illustrates this concept by telling of a letter he received in which someone wrote, "C'est la première fois que j'entends le cri d'un enfant dans une chambre à gaz" [This is the first time that I hear a child's cry in a gas chamber].[11] This results from the viewer's imaginative participation; an image or sound that is not directly represented in the film is experienced nonetheless. Lanzmann calls it a hallucinated image. Gertrud Koch notes this aspect of *Shoah* and argues that it is integral to the way the film evokes the unimaginable without recourse to direct representation: "whenever something is narrated, an image (*Vorstellung*) is presented, the image of something which is absent. The image, the imaginary—and here Lanzmann is a loyal Sartrean—is the presence of an absence which is located outside the spatiotemporal continuum of the image."[12]

Shoah depends upon montage and audience identification for its impact. In many ways, the film illustrates aspects of Lev Kuleshov's experiments with montage in the '20s. In one of the most famous of these experiments, a shot of a well-known actor's face (Ivan Mozhukin) is intercut with various things—a bowl of soup, a baby, a dead woman. Although the same shot of the actor's face is used each time, the audience reads it differently; linked with a bowl of soup the face expresses hunger, yet next to the dead body it seems sad. The experiment suggests that the audience constructs a spatial relationship between the face and the object, in the imagination. This implies a process of viewer identification—viewers bridge the cuts with their participation and personal engagement through empathetic identification. Hitchcock understood this process well—not everything need be represented; the viewer's imaginative involvement through montage and identification can be far more potent than mimetic representation. This doesn't necessarily imply a passive spectator being pulled by an emotional response. One can be detached and still intellectually aware and engaged; however, cinema plays on the viewer's inclination to identify with a character and share imaginatively and empathetically in the human experience being presented. In *Shoah,* one can, through montage, imagine spatial relations as well as temporal bridges. A shot of Ruth

Elias in Israel, describing her arrival at Auschwitz, cut to a present-day shot of a train moving forward to the gates of the camp allows one to imaginatively create a spatial link as well as a temporal one. The sequence in which Filip Müller recollects his resolution to enter the gas chamber and die with those of the Czech family camp intercuts his image with a panning shot of the model of the gas chamber in Auschwitz; although this model is not a place (it is the closest the film comes to a figurative representation of a gas chamber in the past), one can imaginatively interpolate oneself into his narrative and imagine the scene clearly. It moves beyond illustration; editing alters reality and creates another reality, and the viewer provides the imaginative bridges that efface the cut, as well as spatial and temporal difference. One is aware that the shots of present-day witnesses and locations are not directly illustrative of the past, but one also, simultaneously, suspends disbelief, providing the imaginative bridge. This is because montage works in conjunction with character development, mise-en-scène, stylistic conventions, and tone, which intensify the invitation for the viewer's engagement and imaginative involvement.[13]

CHARACTERS

The testimonies that *Shoah* elicits and documents are those of witnesses established as characters. Lanzmann refers to them as "personnages,"[14] protagonists, aware of the fictional strategies from which he draws. They are more than neutral subjects, becoming the film's cast, with distinctive voices and identifiable characteristics. The central protagonists are reintroduced at various points along the 9½-hour journey (and the film should be viewed, if not as a whole, in no more than two parts), and the viewer is expected to get to know them. Sometimes a voice begins speaking offscreen over an image of a location and only later does the speaker appear visually. *Shoah* plays with the complexities of viewer identification; one must actively piece together voice and image and read gestures, facial expressions, hesitations as being as significant as what is spoken, particularly as the testimony reenacted is often traumatic. At the same time this level of testimony sets up a degree of intimacy, underlined through stylistic techniques like the close-up or the slow zoom into a face, which heighten the intimacy between viewer and character and the tendency toward identification. This intimacy is further intensified through the witnesses' individuality, established in shots in which they are associated with particular settings and by their distinctive manners and voices. They materialize as protagonists, which opens up the possibility of identification. Abraham Bomba, for example, is vividly realized and immediately identifiable: his clipped, measured, determined speech, his patterned shirt graphically offsetting the blue of the Mediterranean, the motorboat nearby all create an indelible image of Bomba in the present, interviewed in Tel Aviv.

Repetition allows a character to become familiar, and as the image changes, the voice leads viewers into the imaginative reconstruction of the character's testimony.

Many of *Shoah*'s key protagonists become memorable in this way. Filip Müller's soft-spoken, gentle voice marks his testimony, as does his look of suppressed alarm and disbelief as he describes the atrocities he saw. Rudolf Vrba's urbane sophistication, underlined by Lanzmann's frequently shooting him against the background of the New York skyline, becomes familiar and recognizable. Vrba's style—his wry, analytical testimony, characterized by caustic comments like "the Germans are a sporty nation, . . . yes, *immer laufen*" to describe the Nazis' sadistic practice of *laufschritt,* forcing new arrivals to Auschwitz to run off the trains while being beaten—soon becomes identifiable. Simon Srebnik looks older than his forty-seven years, and yet at times his face communicates the teenager he was—describing his recollection of the pyres in the fields of Chelmno, he remarks, "the flames reached the sky."

Lanzmann's Jewish survivors are the film's heroes just as the Germans and Poles, guilty of a range of crimes from indifference to cruelty, are its antagonists. Bernard Cuau's description of the cast as a varied group of "menteurs, criminels, saints, crucifiés, amnésiques" [liars, criminals, saints, the crucified, amnesiacs] is correct.[15] If there ever was a doubt about the complicity of the Sonderkommandos, the special details, *Shoah* vindicates them by registering their helplessness, their humanity and suffering.[16] Farmers whose land abutted Treblinka, such as Czeslaw Borowi, and the inhabitants of Grabow, peering out from behind shuttered windows (many in homes appropriated from Jewish townspeople they were only too happy to see leave), are almost stereotypes, overstated and heightened in their dress (which appears little changed from the past), demeanor, and quickly revealed antisemitism. Comments like "All Poland was in the hands of the Jews," or a Chelmno villager's reminiscence that Srebnik "looked ripe for the coffin," or Borowi's description of "Jew" (Yiddish) as "ra-ra-ra," or Mrs. Michelson's disingenuous response after being told that four hundred thousand Jews were killed outside Chelmno ("I knew it had a four in it . . . sad, sad, sad"), or the Grabow inhabitants' description of the pretty Jewesses to whom the Poles liked to make love are so characteristic that had they been scripted in a fiction they would almost appear overstated. The clinical detachment of Franz Suchomel, an SS *Unterscharführer* (he is introduced as such in the film, as if the title will perpetually remain his role and identity), is almost antithetical to the traumatic testimony of Müller and the other victims. He easily, emotionlessly, with workmanlike thoroughness describes in steady detail the gruesome killing process in Treblinka. His flat testimony is only briefly animated when he passionately sings the Treblinka "cheer." Even a more subtle witness like the former courier of the Polish government in exile, Jan Karski, stiff and proper, now a professor residing in the

United States and filmed against his bookcases, is a fully articulated character. The complexity of his character is evident in his demeanor as well as in telling comments, as when he likens the Jewish Bund leader to a Polish nobleman (clearly impressed) and then notes how when he enters the Warsaw ghetto he reverts back to being a Jew from the ghetto ("Apparently, this was his nature"). Even Adam Czerniakow becomes a character presented in absentia, vivified through his diary, brought to life by Raul Hilberg's dignified presentation of his testimony. One becomes engaged with these characters, one begins to identify with and insert oneself into their narratives.

MISE-EN-SCÈNE

Shoah's mise-en-scène is central to the film, as it provides a visual landscape for the oral testimony presented. In many ways Lanzmann, filming in 1975, was still able to capture a country largely unchanged from the '40s. The station at Treblinka, the locomotives, the horse-drawn buggies, the houses of Grabow and Wlodawa, the verdant countryside around Chelmno, the Narew River all seem frozen in time. The sites of former concentration camps evoke an elegiac tone; for example, the site of Treblinka is marked by Franciszek Duszenko and Adam Haupt's memorial of jagged tombstone-like rocks which underline its identity as a cemetery. Suchomel's clinical description of, for example, the funnel, the "road to Heaven" where Jewish internees awaited death, set against the contemporary images of Treblinka as memorial site, generates great pathos. Auschwitz, preserved as a haunted ruin of its former self, works in a similar way, in conjunction with the testimony of former internees whose memories reactivate it as a presence brought to life. Contemporary cities associated with individual survivors, such as New York, Tel Aviv, Geneva, and Berlin, help intensify a sense of diversity lost in the concept of the extermination of European Jewry. At times mise-en-scène is used conceptually, as in the shots of the industrialized Ruhr that are used to illustrate how the killing process was conceived and executed in terms of a manufacturing system. At other times mise-en-scène is used theatrically, as when Bomba's testimony is staged in the barber shop, or when the elderly couple are seen dancing in a ballroom (which might be the *Klu,* a dancehall and point of deportation for many Berlinese Jews). Even the church in Chelmno, filmed on a festive day when a religious procession is taking place, replete with children strewing petals, provides a surreal juxtaposition, almost set-like, to illustrate the centuries of religious and racial intolerance, persecution, and violence.

Trains and train stations are central to *Shoah,* in part because of the film's preoccupation with practical, logistical detail (millions of Jews were transported by train to their death, and conductors drove them, villagers watched them go by, German officials planned their busy routes and charged them for their travel), in part because the Sonderkommando's existence depended on their arrival, and in part because the metaphor of the journey envelops the film's structure. *Shoah* is a film that travels in time, taking one back to the scene of the crime.

STRUCTURE AND TONE

> Le film est un film rond, circulaire, et il faut le terminer comme il a commencé.
>
> —Claude Lanzmann[17]

The structure and sensibility of *Shoah* are circular, enclosed, like the world of film noir or a film like Marker's *La jetée* (1962), where the revelation of the mystery returns the protagonist full circle to the point of his death. It is a film permeated with helplessness and defeat, reiterated in the many shots of trains all headed toward Auschwitz, Birkenau, or Treblinka. Lanzmann has talked about his preoccupation with questions like "At which moment did it start to be too late?" and his efforts to convey to viewers the Jews' complete and utter entrapment.[18] It was immediately too late and there was no way out. This is a crucial theme in *Shoah.* It contests Hannah Arendt's idea of sheep to the slaughter, of victim passivity. There was nothing that could effectively alter their fate. Neither informing the outside world nor attempting to organize resistance within the camps (as attested by Müller, Vrba, and Karski) could effect change. When the "special detail" workers informed incoming Jews of their fate, their acts only seemed to escalate the suffering, or contributed to increased slaughter and cruelty, evidenced in Filip Müller's account of the 1943 torture and murder of a woman and a worker in the "special detail" for their attempts to inform the group of their impending death. Müller testifies that such a warning generally "was of no use and made the victims' last moments even harder to bear." The feeling of being trapped, frozen, or dead is described by a number of witnesses, including Bomba and Srebnik. Witnessing atrocity became the norm and reacting was complicated by a lack of context—it was impossible to fully comprehend events because one lacked the schemas, the categories needed to place what was happening; it was so entirely unprecedented.

The overwhelming sense of doom, communicated thematically, is underscored by style. The world of *Shoah* is as closed and sealed as the fate of the victims it mourns. The film's final chapter, which explores the battle of resistance in the Warsaw ghetto, does not present the uprising as being in any sense redemptive of the vast annihilation *Shoah* documents. Instead, it is presented as a microcosm of the devastation that took place in Europe. The ghetto is described by Simcha Rottem ("Kajik") as an isolated place, cut off from the outside world. The starvation in the ghetto was a strategy used in the process of elimination. Dr. Grassler, the deputy to the Nazi commissioner of the Warsaw ghetto, defends himself as having been responsible for maintaining the ghetto's labor force and thus as having preserved life. Lanzmann challenges this defense, correctly unmasking what the ghetto was—a form of death camp, as corroborated by Simcha Rottem, Itzhak Zuckermann, and Jan Karski, a Polish outsider, a passerby who witnessed the atrocious conditions of the ghetto.

Lanzmann comments that the tone of the film is "le ton de l'échec," the tone of defeat, as is characteristic of film noir (he cites the 1944 *Assurance sur la mort* (*Double Indemnity*) as an example[19]), correctly identifying its atmosphere and ethos. It presents a closed, unfathomable world where defeat is the only possible conclusion. Rottem's testimony of hearing a woman's voice calling from the rubble, a person he couldn't find or save, and his sense of being the last Jew perfectly express the film's sensibility. *Shoah* is not about the handful who survived, it is about the annihilation of European Jewry. There was no salvation, and from the moment of deportation it was "too late."

STYLE AND TECHNIQUE

As a filmmaker working on a shoestring budget who was prioritizing the transmission of testimony, Lanzmann found his attention to style necessarily dominated by practical circumstances, like having to reload his single camera every eleven minutes. Nevertheless, he uses certain techniques expressively to contribute to the film's formalist quality. A number of discernible stylistic techniques are repeatedly used in *Shoah.* One is the slow circular panoramic shot (which doesn't always complete the circle, but moves in an arc) around a landscape; another is the slow zoom in and out; yet another is the steady tracking or traveling shot. Often these slow, steady movements (or, in the case of the zoom, implied movement) counterpoint the emotional content of the testimony, and this in part helps the viewer maintain a cerebral detachment and balances the kind of inside/outside relationship the viewer has with the material. The slow repetitive movement, accompanied by voiceover or silence, contributes to the hallucinatory quality of the film's diegesis—its temporal otherness, its sense of being both of the present and of the past. At times a jarring hand-held camera is used, for example in the shots taken in the ruins of the former gas chamber and crematoria at Birkenau, and this underlines the trauma of the testimony it accompanies. The tracking shots are sometimes subjective, heightening viewer identification: visualizing, for example, the sense of personal entry to a camp that the testimony describes. The tracking movements also serve to reiterate the train/journey motif so central to the film. These movements approaching a site or moving away from one mimic the idea of traveling via memory. At times, slow, steady movement combined with the long take imparts the sense of duration and real time, underscoring the presentness of felt time that the cinema imparts and the sense of lived continuity so essential to Lanzmann's project. A long take pulling into Treblinka, for example, illustrates a subjective sense of real time. These long takes have a mournful quality; little happens, instead they are meditative and contribute a sense of lamentation. Lengthy silent takes of snowy ruins and frozen fields or the shot of a slow pan over mounds of luggage give a visual shape to absence, as if the landscape or leftover objects can also be incorporated as testimony. At times corroborative testimonies (such as those of Ruth Elias and Rudolf Vrba) are linked via a continuous pan over the landscape, which visually underlines the idea that factual evidence is strengthened and confirmed through the testimony of two eyewitnesses.

THE *CAMÉRA-STYLO:* THE AUTEUR WRITES[20]

Lanzmann's presence in his film is as significant as that of his cast. His role is varied; he acts as a catalyst eliciting a response, as a metteur-en-scène staging a scene, as a journalist reporting, and as a prosecutor cross-examining his witness. He is neither neutral nor objective—Lanzmann takes a position with the victims, not for humanity, not for the liberators, but for the dead. He insists on getting as close as possible to the experience of being interned and trapped. He foregrounds his ethics—he insists on recording precious testimony, however painful the process. "You have to do it. I know it's very hard. I know and apologize," he tells Bomba. Lanzmann films the van where Suchomel is being illicitly and secretly taped, despite his promise of anonymity. The means are justified, exposed as an act of resistance to the masking of a crime. Lanzmann is confrontational, demanding that witnesses remember. It is almost as if, by interjecting himself, he acts and articulates his protest. He aggressively demands of a reluctant, self-effacing bartender in a beerhall, Joseph Oberhauser, "Mr. Oberhauser! Do you remember Belzec? No memories of Belzec? Of the overflowing graves? You don't remember?" In the analogy of the world of film noir, the policier, the revenge Western, his presence in the film and his return to the scene of the crime, reactivate and unlock what has been suppressed and become part of the film's diegesis. This may leave Lanzmann subject to criticism for being intrusive or narcissistic. His stance is, I believe, an expression of the idea that the director makes his personal voice, his mark, felt. The film is not an objective work; Lanzmann's position is presented with a forthright intensity (as is the filmmaker's right). This is a story about a closed, doomed trajectory of utter destruction; the Jews of Europe were abandoned and had no choices once the process of entrapment began.

> He said that in the nineteenth century mankind had come to terms with space, and that the great question of the twentieth was the coexistence of different concepts of time. (Chris Marker, *Sans Soleil* [1982])

The opening of *Shoah* succinctly illustrates the film's style and formal logic; a hallucinatory timelessness[21] is invoked in the opening shots. The opening title text introduces the director's personal voice: "I found him [Srebnik] in Israel and persuaded that one-time boy singer to return with me to Chelmno." Here time past and present are condensed and coexist, and we see the return of the repressed (Srebnik was shot in the head and miraculously survived, and his spectral reappearance defies reality). Before the titles end water sounds can be heard, and the first image is a long take; it is a slow tracking shot, from the shore, of a boat passing by. Srebnik sits motionless as the boat glides effortlessly through the water in silence, propelled by the rhythmic motions of a man standing and poling. The image is lush, verdant, and almost pastoral, and the serenity it evokes is entirely antithetical to the opening titles' introduction of death, torture, and incarceration. A voice begins singing a song about a "little white house which lingers in my memory," dreamt about each night; Polish voices (belonging to persons unseen) begin to comment, describing the memories evoked by the reappearance of the man and the song on the river. "He was thirteen and a half years old. . . ." The second long take is marked by a change in camera position; it is now in the boat and the shot is a medium close-up of Srebnik's face. The slow movement continues, now a result of the boat's even passage through the water. Srebnik repeats the verse of his song and after a moment or two of silence, a woman's voice comments that hearing him again has caused her to "relive what happened." The comment is accompanied by a slow zoom into a tight close-up of Srebnik's face.

These two long takes immediately activate the temporal collapse so central to the film—the sense of a continuous present held in the memory of the boy singing on the river. The boy is chained and doomed, ignored by the villagers who witness the event and remain silent (until this reappearance). These shots introduce the elegiac tone of the film, imparting an overwhelming sense of lost possibilities and sorrow. The dialectic created between the words, the site, and the reenactment depends on the cinema's fusion of reality and the imagination and the alternate state of perception the cinema invokes. We enter this commemorative site and engage with history in an entirely new way.

Notes

1. Other examples of this effort include Esther Shalev and Jochen Gerz's sinking monument; Rachel Whiteread's casts of the space occupied by objects, as in the inverted bookcase motif of the Vienna memorial; Daniel Libeskind's "void" in the Jewish Museum, Berlin; Shimon Attie's photographic projections over the sites of eradicated communities; and Boltanski's mounds of clothing, candles, and imagery in installations like "Canada" (1998).

2. He has done so on numerous occasions: see, for example, "Seminar with Claude Lanzmann, 11 April 1990," *Yale French Studies,* no. 79 (1991), 96.

3. See Yosefa Loshitzky, ed., *Spielberg's Holocaust: Critical Perspectives on* Schindler's List (Bloomington: Indiana University Press, 1997).

4. For an elaborated discussion of this, see Robin Wood's "Rossellini" and "Ingrid Bergman on Rossellini" in *Film Comment,* July 1974, 6–11 and 12–15. See as well

Florence Jacobowitz's "Rewriting Realism: Bergman and Rossellini in Europe, 1949–1955," *Cineaction* 41, 23–33.

5. In many ways this scene is remarkably analogous to Rachel Whiteread's work with plaster casts of the space inside or around the absent object, and the elegiac sensibility imparted by these castings. They are comparable to a photographic negative in the way they bridge presence and absence.

6. This theme is addressed in *Les Statues Meurent Aussi* (1953), co-directed with Chris Marker.

7. In the introduction to *Probing the Limits of Representation: Nazism and the "Final Solution"* (Cambridge, Mass.: Harvard University Press, 1992), Saul Friedlander rightly notes the problems of applying postmodern theory to discussions of the Holocaust: "[P]ostmodern thought's rejection of the possibility of identifying some stable reality or truth beyond the constant polysemy and self-referentiality of linguistic constructs challenges the need to establish the realities and truths of the Holocaust" (4–5).

8. Linda Williams, "Mirrors without Memories: Truth, History, and the New Documentary," *Film Quarterly* 46 (spring 1993), 9–21.

9. "The film makes the imagination work" ("Le lieu et la parole: Entretien avec Claude Lanzmann réalisé par Marc Chevrie et Hervé Le Roux," *Les cahiers du cinéma,* no. 374 [July–August 1985], 20).

10. Ibid., 19.

11. Ibid., 20.

12. Gertrud Koch, "The Aesthetic Transformation of the Image of the Unimaginable: Notes on Claude Lanzmann's *Shoah," October,* no. 48 (spring 1989): 21.

13. Viewer identification remains one of the greatly undertheorized areas of film criticism. The psychoanalytic model, which stresses forms of visual pleasure such as voyeurism, and the rationales of "suture" theory are overly simplified explanations of viewer involvement in narrative fiction, and they flatten the complexities of how identification works and the levels of intellectual awareness and emotional engagement that can work simultaneously. Directors like Sirk, Lang, and Ophuls understood how one can produce a form of Brechtian "epic" cinema within Hollywood without relinquishing identification with a character's position of entrapment, alienation, etc. See Andrew Britton's "Metaphor and Mimesis—*Madame de," Movie,* no. 29/30 (summer 1983), 91–107, for an elaboration of realism and viewer identification.

14. "Il y a trois catégories de personnages dans le film" [There are three categories of characters in the film] ("Le lieu," 20).

15. Bernard Cuau, "Dans le cinéma une langue étrangère," in *Au sujet de* Shoah: *Le film de Claude Lanzmann,* Bernard Cuau et al. (Paris: Belin, 1990), 14.

16. Lanzmann contrasts "the deep humanity, the compassion of the Jews of the *Sonderkommando* towards the people who were about to die with the gesture of the Poles (the throat slitting gesture), which I am utterly convinced is not a gesture of warning" ("Seminar with Claude Lanzmann," 86).

17. "The film is rounded, circular, and it must end the way it began" ("Le lieu," 22).

18. "Seminar with Claude Lanzmann," 89.

19. "Le lieu," 23.

20. The term *le caméra-stylo,* the camera pen, was coined by Alexandre Astruc in an essay in which he wrote that the cinema has become "a form in which and by which an artist can express his thoughts, however abstract they may be, or translate his obsessions exactly as he does in a contemporary essay or novel. That is why I would like to call this new age of cinema the age of caméra-stylo." This essay greatly influenced the postwar New Wave critics turned filmmakers (James Monaco, *The*

New Wave: Truffaut, Godard, Chabrol, Rohmer, Rivette [New York: Oxford University Press, 1976], 5).

21. Lanzmann makes this point in "Shoah: Un contre-mythe," an article included in the film's press kit: "Le film que je réalise est un contre-mythe, c'est-à-dire une enquête sur le présent de l'Holocauste ou à tout le moins sur un passé dont les cicatrices sont encore si fraîchement et si vivement inscrites dans les lieux et dans les consciences qu'il se donne à voir dans une hallucinante intemporalité" [The film that I am directing is a 'counter-myth,' that is to say an inquiry into the actuality of the Holocaust or, at the very least, of a past whose scars are still so freshly and vividly inscribed in the places and in the consciences that it is seen as a hallucinatory timelessness].

2 Second-Sight

Shimon Attie's Recollection | BEREL LANG

Shimon Attie's representations of the Holocaust are as distinctive ontologically as they are aesthetically. Under the rubric of the *Finstere Medine* [The dark district], he projects onto the buildings of what in the 1930s was a predominantly Jewish section of Berlin, the Scheunen Quarter, the images of those buildings with all the signs of the life that then inhabited them: the bearded faces, the Hebrew lettering on shop windows. All these are superimposed as images on buildings that are now almost entirely "Judenrein" [free of Jews], some of them postwar constructions, others the very ones photographed in the 1930s—but, of course, also with a great difference. So the projected images of the past rest on the actuality of the present, and Attie leaves the projected images there for a Berlin audience to see for a short time, but also photographs them for the permanent record that we, far from Berlin, are able to examine.[1] The question, then, of *where* Attie's artworks are is more difficult than it normally is, applied to more conventional art like paintings or poems. But we have at least the photographic record of his installations—and the photographs themselves, however we classify them among the genres of art, speak in their own and distinctive voice.

To be sure, as photographs of photographs, they offer the difficult combination of a Platonic nightmare and an artist's dreamworld. It is tempting, then, to turn to Attie's own statements about his work for clues on how to read it; that is, to understand his visual (and vivid) images in the terms he himself sets.

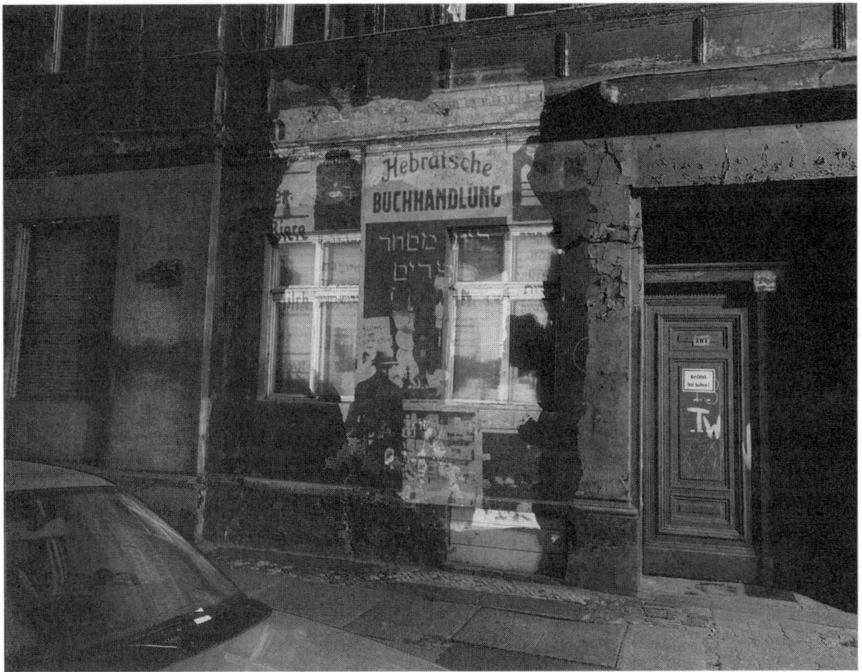

2.1 Shimon Attie, *Almstadtstrasse 43,* slide projection of former Hebrew bookstore (then Grenadierstrasse 7, 1930), Berlin, 1992, on-location installation and chromogenic photograph. Courtesy Jack Shainman Gallery, New York City.

But this, of course, is just what the "intentional fallacy" is meant to warn us against, as it urges us to do what most viewers (at least until they become critics) would spontaneously do anyway; that is, to look at art's images in the present, *their* present, quite apart from what the artist—whose words, apart from his art, are only words—tells us that he sees or what we should be seeing.[2]

We have, then, to make our own way here, although admittedly only as we are willing to assume the fact of the Holocaust as the causal clue required even to begin to understand Attie's visual projections and installations. In his photographic reconstructions, Attie engages a number of important general issues set in motion by the very conception of "Holocaust images" or "Holocaust art," with its provocative consequences for the relations between form and content, the aesthetic and the ethical, the particular (or historical) and the universal (that is, the aesthetic *or* the ethical). I can here only point to certain implications of these relations for (and from) the concept of Holocaust art, indicating why they are important for aesthetic theory and how they take shape in Attie's remarkably imaginative work.

I hasten to add that in this context, the phrase "remarkably imaginative" is meant only in part as laudatory; indeed, I shall be proposing here, as I have elsewhere, that certain subjects or occasions of art may benefit from less rather than from more imagination, or, to put the matter even more bluntly, that art may itself at times be a menace to art. And more specifically, that certain vectors coming out of Attie's work verge on this danger, the more precariously because we encounter them not very far from the apex of his work's power. The same tendencies, I believe, disclose the anatomy more generally of the moral and historical burden of art—specifically of Holocaust art, but in the end, of art as such.

In an earlier essay about the distinctive demands on and responses of Holocaust representation, I paraphrased a line by Walter Pater, saying that "[a]ll Holocaust literature aspires to the condition of history."[3] This gloss was meant to suggest that imaginative writing about the Holocaust often, even typically, eschews standard literary devices or figures in favor of historical ones—purporting to present factual narratives which are not factual at all, splicing actual juridical testimony into fictional frames, appealing to historical genres like the diary or letter or memoir but as imagined rather than historical means, in poetry violating literary convention not only to be unconventional but to be un-poetic, and in the medium of film disguising its virtuoso powers under the more severe constraints of the documentary (a small example of this last point is Spielberg's conceit in *Schindler's List* of using black and white film rather than color).

There is, it seems to me, nothing mysterious or even subtle about this historicizing impulse. For the representation of moral enormity on the scale of genocide, artistic sensibility and imagination might well defer to the weight of history and its "story." It seems obvious that artists would, should, hardly think of the ideal of beauty in their address to the subject of the Holocaust. Even so far as concerns the representation of evil or cruelty, history as it emerges transformed after the "Final Solution" has proved to be every bit as inventive as the artistic imagination ever was; the historical record shows that its own creators, the Nazis themselves, required time and strenuous effort before they realized exactly what it was they were creating in the "artifact" of genocide. And it follows from such considerations that, given the moral pressure exerted by this subject—perhaps not uniquely but extraordinarily—the usual risks run by art in imaginatively heightening or revising perception, in taking the aesthetic turn, increase substantially.

All these factors might be good reasons for regarding photography, Attie's basic instrument, as a privileged medium in taking the Holocaust as a subject for art. For to whatever extent one emphasizes the creative or aesthetic process of photography, its distinctive and certainly disproportionate referentiality in comparison to other visual or, for that matter, literary arts is evident. Admittedly, the schools or movements that have been categorized under the generic title of "realism" have surfaced in virtually all the arts, in literature and even in music as well as in painting. But when Roland Barthes in *Camera Lucida* characterizes the photograph as not a "copy" but an "emanation," he invokes (I think convincingly) something more basic than the terms of only one more artistic trope or genre: "It is often said," he writes, "that it was the painters who invented photography. . . . I say: no, it was the chemists. . . . The photograph is literally an emanation of the referent. From a real body, which was there, proceed radiations which ultimately touch me, who am here."[4] And indeed certain photographs and documentary clips from the Holocaust have become standard (I'm tempted to say, rigid) designators of the Holocaust in a way paralleled by very few of its other representations (some of the most evocative of which—the diaries of Emanuel Ringelblum and Anne Frank's *Diary of a Young Girl,* for example—are also "emanations," albeit literary ones). All this, however, applies to photography initiated in the Holocaust-past, with the figures or events embodied there themselves now past: gone, over. And so one might imagine—it *requires* imagining, since the conventions by themselves halt at this point—something that could reassert in the present, our present, *now,* the nonfigurative realism, the immediacy, of a presence that Barthes ascribes to photography in its relation to the past. Only such a means, it seems, could effect a passage between the Scylla of artistic fancy (does anyone now require images designed to produce a "moving experience" of the Holocaust?) and the Charybdis of didactic abstraction (exactly what is added at this point by hearing once again about the "unimaginable" nature of the Holocaust?), both these temptations threatening to turn the images of that subject into clichés.

It is precisely at this point that Shimon Attie's work seems to me to accomplish what much other Holocaust art fails to: it brings the terms of that past event into the present without diminishing or rationalizing either at the expense of the other. An instructive connection appears here, in both likeness and difference, between Attie's work and Claude Lanzmann's film *Shoah.* Lanzmann also sought to connect the past and the present by the artistic means of absence, so he viewed the Shoah not by revisiting or reconstructing its records (that is, by presenting images from the past) but by conveying the imprint of that past through voices speaking in the present: the voices of survivors, of perpetrators, of bystanders—through all of whom the past was then to be inferred. What this amounted to was an artistic enthymeme to which the viewer was then to supply the conclusion: the "veterans" of the Holocaust summoning now, by way of the marks it had left on them, the events they endured or (for the perpetrators) caused. In Attie's work, especially in his *Finstere Medine,* to which I principally refer, it is not only images taken from the past that confront the viewer, but their iteration in the present, staking a claim to the same spaces that they once had but that are now quite differently occupied. That is, the past is shown in the present.

Admittedly, the images that Attie projects of the past—the shops and shopkeepers, the residents, the passersby—constitute only a virtual present, but their imposition on actual space marks a more than virtual addition of the past to the actual present: the *addition,* now, rather than the subtraction that images of the past more typically impose. The main focus of images and interpretations of the Holocaust—in art and historiography, in its memorials as well as in its analysis—has been on palpable loss. Auschwitz has become a metonym not only for all six of the death camps, but for the ten thousand other concentration camps as well, for the "Final Solution" as a whole, and then for the act of genocide as such. It is important, however, to recognize another loss inflicted by these events, a loss which was by its nature less palpable but which in the end is not less actual or less a source of harm: this is the loss of what would have existed—lived, grown, worked, thrived—if the Holocaust had not occurred. Of course, there is no way of knowing the details of this existence, not even the numbers, let alone the identities, of those to whom it would have given life. But Attie's *Finstere Medine* gives body and definition, a human reality, to the shapes and spaces which what was then lost would have occupied, even if only by a virtual (but then not only virtual) image. This is the dialectical conclusion that emerges from his imposition of the photographic image of Jewish life in Berlin-past on life without Jews in Berlin-present.

I have been emphasizing the *Finstere Medine* rather than Attie's other projects mainly because that work's historical insistence and forcefulness—the limits it imposes on the imagination and thus the means of its sharp focus—seem to me more striking than do the later examples of his oeuvre cast in the same mold. To be sure, the later photographs also take on agency—not only making themselves available to the viewer but requiring him to engage them. But the faces projected at the Dresden railroad station (photographs of the Jewish deportees from that station) require more than they or their viewers can provide, and the subtext that remains to be supplied seems bound to diminish the point of the projection, if not to divert the viewers from it entirely. (This tactic—the assumption of a historical subtext in their ahistorical images—is a common feature of many strong Holocaust artists who, like Attie, require their audiences to supply the correlative of the "Final Solution." Consider only how impoverished an understanding would result without that subtext in the poetry of Paul Celan, in the novels of Aharon Appelfeld, even in the more nearly explicit paintings of Anselm Kiefer. It was Appelfeld who explained this tactic of indirection by an analogy: "One does not," he wrote, "look directly at the sun.")[5]

Earlier in the present discussion, I suggested that my description of Shimon Attie's work as "remarkably imaginative" was not entirely laudatory. What I meant by that qualification concerns the balance within the binary pairs whose conjunction Attie, like most Holocaust artists, constantly invokes: ethical judgment in relation to aesthetic appreciation, the status of the particular (or historical) event in relation to its universal or abstract implication. And the danger intrinsic to those polarities seems to me one that even in Attie's notable achievement impairs this work insofar as he often pushes further toward the second pole than his subject warrants and perhaps can bear.

For example: Attie himself reports that not all the slides from the Holocaust past that he projected onto buildings in the present were superimposed on their original sites; also that not all the slides of past scenes were photographs from the Scheunen Quarter or even from Berlin. In other words, he has conceded that if his viewers regard his photographic superimpositions as historically accurate, they will sometimes be mistaken; certain of the buildings, shops, pedestrians now seen could not have been seen where he projects them. But what difference does this make, we might well ask; after all, it is truly that past which is projected onto the present, if not in direct reflection on the present. Attie himself anticipates this question. Far from detracting from his project, he suggests, this historical conflation increases its effectiveness: Where he had to choose between being a good historian and being a good artist, he writes in his comments on the *Finstere Medine,* he "always chose the latter."[6]

But is the justification for that choice, or even for the distinction between history and art on the grounds he assumes, so obvious? Surely there might be loss, not gain, in the consciousness of artifice. Suppose, for example, that Primo Levi's account of his year in Auschwitz (*Survival in Auschwitz*) or of his lengthy journey back to Italy once the war was over (*The Reawakening*) turned out to be a composite of his own and other peoples' experiences, with some of the events "only" imagined; or that the accounts retold by the figures in Lanzmann's *Shoah* were in fact amalgams of various partial histories stitched together. Why is anyone troubled by the recent discovery that Binjamin Wilkomirski could not have experienced the events he relates in his much-praised "memoir," *Fragments*? The combination of art and history might be argued in these cases to have a stronger impact on an audience than if either one of that pair had been applied by itself, especially if history had been made to stand on its own. Well, perhaps—but certainly not if the audience had first been given to understand that the works involved were not such syntheses, and arguably not even if the audience were aware beforehand of the possibility. It might be objected that in the absence of information provided from external sources, there would be no way internally of distinguishing fact from fiction in Attie's work (as in much similar work). And if this is the case, the question would then go on, why should any external evidence that might be brought to bear make any difference when it is the text, after all, that is the thing? Well, again, perhaps—but also, unlikely. Merely knowing that the two alternatives are possible, like the possibility of forgery in paintings, makes a difference in the way one observes the works—especially those whose provenance seems to be beyond question. (It is, after all, the truly successful forgeries that have passed unquestioned.) The "reliable narrator" so important in certain fictional literary genres is arguably no less important in the memoir or autobiography; here, too, after all, the work's power draws fundamentally on the chemical aura of photography.

This issue of imagining arises in slightly different form in certain other statements by Attie as well. He has written that he does not consider himself a "Holocaust artist," and by this I understand him to refer mainly to the absence from his work of scenes depicting the manifold horrors of that event. On the account I have been giving, however, this absence, far from removing him from the association of Holocaust artists, places him in good standing among them. For Attie is far from alone in resisting a critical categorization based on the subject of his work. To be sure, he might also mean something else by this objection, and we have some indication of this when he elsewhere says that his work is not "about" the Holocaust, nor "about" the Nazis or the Jews in particular, but addresses man's inhumanity to man, the ways in which people commit acts of barbarism and cruelty against others. He moves in this direction more explicitly in his later work: for example, in the Denmark project—the series of underwater lights placed in Copenhagen's harbor. The sea rescue of the Danish Jews who were transported by their countrymen to Sweden in 1943, which is the manifest occasion of this work, turns out in his view to evoke also the plight of "present day boat-refugees." And so too in the Krakow project, in which he links the photographs of the prewar city to "post-Communist Poland's struggle . . . with both old and new forms of racism."[7] Attie proposes these "readings" of his work even though, in both instances, the photographs of Jews in the pre-Holocaust period stand at their center, impelling the project forward. Why, one asks, the constancy of that one source, if indeed it is suffering humanity that stands at the focus of its meaning?

Of course, irrespective of their particular subject, artists always face the question of how and where to circumscribe that subject, of which elements their work is to display and what implications it engenders. The cognate question for the viewer, how to determine what a particular text is "about," also recurs—since any work can be given alternate descriptions, set at different levels of generality as well as viewed from quite different perspectives. (Consider, for example, the Holocaust as viewed by a historian of Madagascar, that near-fictional area of relocation for the Jews as it was briefly considered by the Nazi hierarchy prior to the "Final Solution.") But to answer the question "What is the subject of *King Lear*?" by saying "a king named Lear" would be itself blind—as the alternative that reaches for that handy tool of literary appreciation, the "human condition," remains quite empty.

There should, it seems, be a way of mediating between the raw particular and the abstract universal that comes closer to the work in its significance—and as its specific subject exerts more pressure sometimes at one end of that spectrum, sometimes at the other. This is one way, it seems, that content may—must—act on form. And in the case of the Holocaust, that content, with its flagrant particularity (specifically, the Nazis and their allies attempting to destroy—also specifically—the Jews), is endangered, artistically as well as morally. Artistically *because* morally—by the push toward universalization. This is, I suggest, an important element of Adorno's warning about the barbarism of writing (one supposes also reading) poetry after Auschwitz that warrants continued attention; it points to the danger faced by any work, including Attie's, which thinks to use aspects of the Holocaust as an idiom or even a metaphor for other dark sides of human history or character (of which, of course, there are plentiful examples).

I realize that to introduce the content-form relation in this context suggests the claim that for some subjects or contents no artistic form may be adequate; that is, that art cannot (and therefore should not try to) represent it. Any such claim will undoubtedly be a red flag to the current widespread inclination to give art a virtual (that is, an actual) carte blanche: the benefit of clergy that the clergy themselves do not now often enjoy. Art in these postromantic terms has (or admits) no limits, either in content or form. But the still-persistent thesis of aesthetics that art involves a strong, arguably intrinsic relation between form and content entails that the balance between form and content is variable not only in respect to those elements within a single work but as such; that is, within the domain of art as a whole. The denial of this extension to the process of representation or to images as such would invite artistic and, depending on its ground, moral failing. The possibility that content may exceed any possible form has been cogently argued in accounts of the Sublime (as by Kant) which emphasize its links to the moral domain, with the Sublime in these terms evidence as well as expression of man's moral capacity and grandeur. Why, then, should this same possibility be ruled out for its inverse, the evil Sublime? These last comments are not directed against Shimon Attie's work as a whole or against the *Finstere Medine* in particular, which in itself bears comparison with the most acclaimed visual work by Holocaust artists. But they do clash with some of his work, as well as with what he says about it. He too might agree, however, that in the end an audience should trust the tale, not the teller—a principle which places a substantial burden on each of them, especially where the subject told of is the Holocaust.

Notes

1. See, e.g., Shimon Attie, *The Writing on the Wall: Projections in Berlin's Jewish Quarter* (Heidelberg: Braus, 1994) and *Sites Unseen* (Burlington, Vt.: Verve, 1998).

2. As in W. K. Wimsatt, Jr., *The Verbal Icon: Studies in the Meaning of Poetry* (Lexington: University of Kentucky Press, 1954), where Wimsatt and Monroe Beardsley carry on the battle of the (then) "New Criticism" against the "intentional" (i.e., historical, biographical) reading of literary texts.

3. Berel Lang, "Holocaust-Genres and the Turn to History," in *The Holocaust and the Text: Speaking the Unspeakable,* ed. Andrew Leak and George Paizis (London: Macmillan, 1999), 19.

4. Roland Barthes, *Camera Lucida: Reflections on Photography,* trans. Richard Howard (New York: Hill and Wang, 1981), 80.

5. In a private communication to me.

6. Attie, *The Writing on the Wall,* 11.

7. Attie, *Sites Unseen,* 28.

3 Rituals of Mourning and Mimesis

Arie A. Galles's Fourteen Stations | ANDREA LISS

Given the ruptures in understanding and the difficulties of memorializing the Shoah in post-Auschwitz culture and representation, the cruel paradox of Holocaust-related artwork is situated precisely in the demand that it both perform as a history lesson ("never forget") and provide sites for mourning. Indeed, the sheer horror of the events of the Shoah complicates their representation; the trauma they imprint on survivors and the post-Auschwitz generation compounds these difficulties. Yet the use of photography and artifacts as evidence of the events, the passage of events into memory, and the transference of images into the next generation's psyche are crucial bridges that translate the remnants of what took place. The most tense point in this fragile process of transmission occurs where contemporary rethinking of documentary, memorial, and artistic discourse is faced with the uneasy intersection of the demand for (often brutal) historical accuracy and calls for a more muted recollection of those who were violated. In this sense, traditional forms of remembrance that seek to disclose the events in all their horrible detail may seem to contradict representations that are sensitive to the danger of revictimizing the victims.[1] Indeed, the most theoretically challenging and pedagogically promising projects—including those designed not only by artists but by museum designers and educators—incorporate the difficult functions that photographs and artifacts are asked to fulfill as historical proof: to elicit empathy and to bear witness.[2] Artists who attempt to represent some semblance of the trauma of the Holocaust by incorporating documentary material in their work break open complex boundaries between aesthetics, the reception of difficult documents, and the challenge of their stagings in an exhibition context, thereby contributing to crucial thinking about interdisciplinary ways to create various modes of approach to the history and memory of the Shoah. These concerns are all the more germane in contemporary artistic negotiations where documents of atrocity are transformed into sources of mourning and memorials.

Arie A. Galles performs this double-edged act of historicizing and remembering the Shoah through the miming of none other than the Nazis' own lurid documentation: aerial reconnaissance photographs of the extermination camps. These images, some taken by the Luftwaffe and some by the Allied Air Force, were designed for the cruelest of coded camouflage. The Nazis photographed the killing fields to determine whether their clandestine massacres could be made invisible, in addition to adding to their perverse archive. And seemingly by chance, Allied planes photographed the extermination sites when they were part of an industrial installation or rail junction. Galles responds graphically rather than photographically to these mechanically reproduced images of deception. His ironic challenges are in the form of large charcoal and white conté crayon drawings that painstakingly heighten the hidden, horrific detail embedded in the photographs' chiaroscuro. Galles's *Fourteen Stations,* begun in 1993, is a large-scale installation that includes fifteen drawings mounted and numbered from right to left according to the Hebrew alphabet: Auschwitz-Birkenau, Babi Yar, Buchenwald, Belzec, Bergen-Belsen, Gross-Rosen, Dachau, Chelmno, Treblinka, Mauthausen, Maidanek, Sobibor, Ravensbrük, and Stutthof. Some of the "stations" capture the inception of the extermination planning process, such as the drawing of Babi Yar, the infamous ravine outside of Kiev that was the final stop for tens of thousands of Ukrainian Jews before they were shot. Galles's fifteenth drawing, *Khurbn,* gives a photographic record of Belzec taken by the Luftwaffe on May 26, 1940, before the camp was carved out of the forest. As Galles conceives the project, the full suite of drawings completes what he offers as a Kaddish, the Hebrew prayer for the dead.

Embedded in each drawing, under thick layers of charcoal, is a phrase from the Kaddish, the prayer being divided at the natural breaks in its recitation. When mounted together, the drawings in *Fourteen Stations* incorporate the complete yet obscured prayer. In the artist's veiled blessing on those who perished, I also hear echoes of voices radiating out from deep beneath the earth. This act of hushed observance suggests Galles's hesitancy about religious codification or a redefined sense of overt commemoration. More explicit are the *Gematria* poems written by Jerome Rothenberg in relation to each drawing, which are designed as an integral part of the installation.[3] Gematria is a mystical calculation of the numerical value of Hebrew words and their connection to other words. It forms part of a larger system through

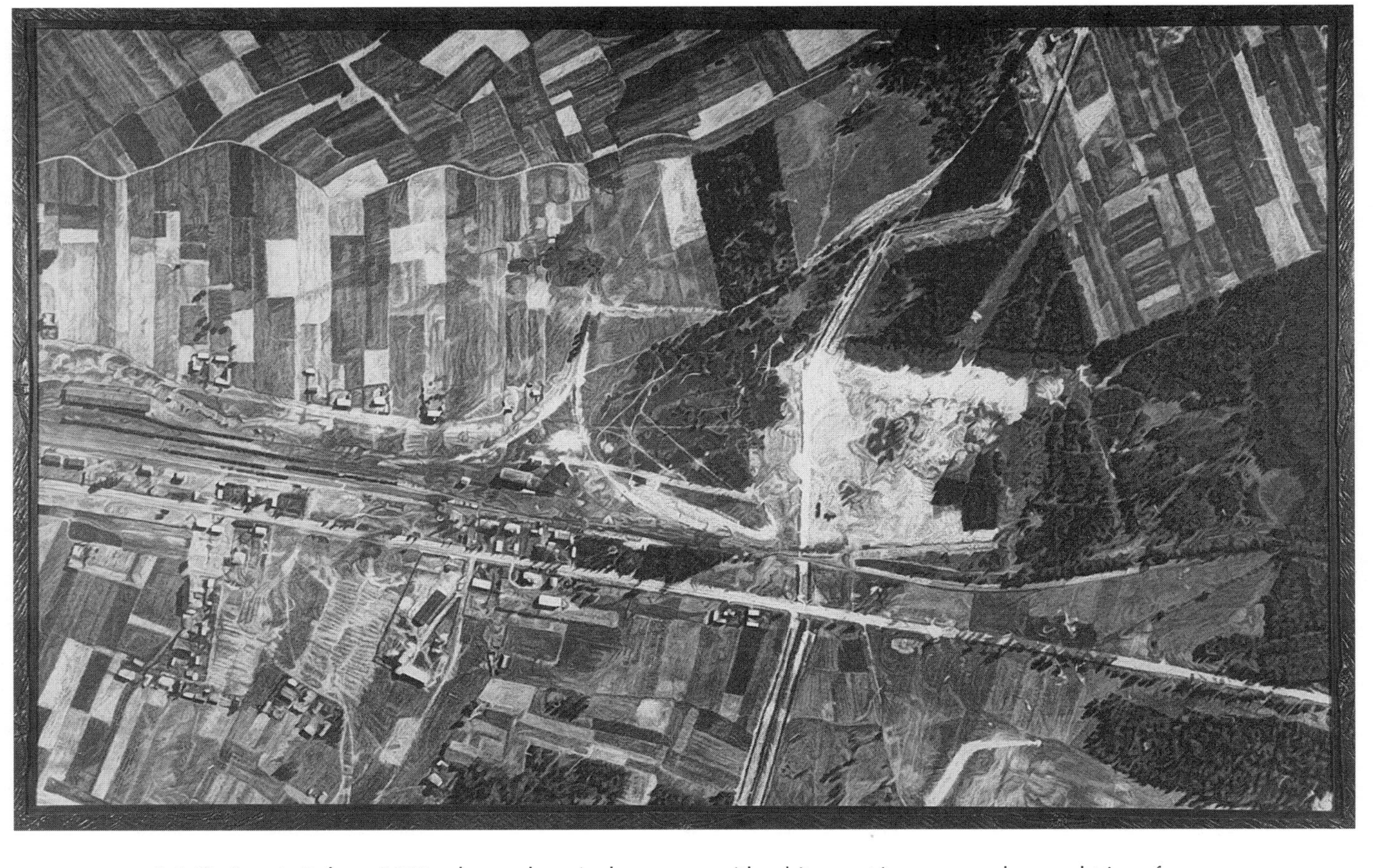

3.1 *Station 4: Belzec,* 1996, charcoal on Arches paper with white conté crayon and wrought iron frame, 47½" × 75". Courtesy Arie A. Galles. Photo by Tim Volk.

which the hidden and divine meanings of a biblical text can be discovered. Rothenberg applies gematria to the Hebrew and Yiddish spellings of the names of the camps, and takes a humanistic approach to the poems and the images. The juxtaposition of the poems and the drawings insinuates still other voices of terrible loss and longing, adding the poems' own sense of awe to the entire installation.

Imagine entering the octagonal installation under the influence of Galles's invocation of the Christian architectural tradition of centrally planned mausolea and martyria. Hanging murdered in Galles's sacred space is no single icon upon which multitudes can absolve their guilt. As the artist aptly puts it, "The people in the camps didn't die because of their sins, they died because of other people's sins."[4] The project's title, *Fourteen Stations,* makes ironic reference to Passion plays and Christ's Fourteen Stations of the Cross, confronting the smooth flow of antisemitism within Christianity, hitting it hard with the shock of these disorienting and disquieting ghost drawings of photographs. Galles also challenges those who insinuate that there has already been enough Holocaust memorializing:

> The crucifix is displayed in thousands of houses of worship, in sculpture and painting, craft and literature. Yet, after only fifty years, Jews should lay to rest the memory of millions of martyrs, and not disturb the world with the memory of their martyrdom, with the remembrance of the earthly hell that was the Holocaust.[5]

Through his unusual choice of imagery, Galles pierces even deeper into such misadvised suggestions that to focus on the horrors of the Holocaust is not only retrograde, but morbid. Morbidity suggests disease, an association that of course echoes the Nazis' insults. Thus for Galles to reveal the sites of planned exterminations as crimes rather than focusing on any individual image of a victim creates an immediate distance between the sheer bodily vulnerability of flesh and the presence of the artist. He strategically sets up this stance of seeming intactness as he defiantly enters the loaded realm of loss.

Galles was born in 1944 in Tashkent, in Uzbekistan in the Soviet Union. His family had been living in eastern Poland when the Nazis decreed that all remaining Jews would be shot. His parents fled, helped by Polish and Ukrainian families, and crossed the River San into Russia. Because they refused to accept Soviet citizenship, they were sent to Siberia by the NKVD (the precursor of the KGB), where Galles's grandparents and older brother and sister died of starvation in a work camp. The only remaining child, he returned with his parents to Poland when he was two. The family home had been destroyed and relatives massacred. His mother's sister and her entire family were murdered in the Belzec death camp.

"Under no condition can art express the Holocaust," Galles wisely cautions. "To withdraw art from confronting this horror, however, is to assign victory to its perpetrators."[6] Galles's sense of the limits of representation and his defiance of such restrictions deeply mirror the feelings of many other child survivors who grew up to be artists—they weren't meant to survive, let alone retaliate and create. Such multiple responses to their experiences are also intricately connected with the active shuttling back and forth of trauma, in which past and present interpolate surreally and simultaneously. For Galles, as for many other child survivors who returned to the land of the original massacres during their childhood, the trauma of the Holocaust in the present always commingles with the oftentimes unearthly quality of his everyday life in the past. Galles harbors early memories of being the only Jewish child in his school and attending religious classes with his Catholic classmates. He remembers visiting Swieta Gora [Holy Mountain] in Lubawka, Poland, with his parents and some of their Christian friends when he was five years old. The path up the mountain passes chapels containing life-sized polychrome sculptures representing the Fourteen Stations of the Cross. One chapel in particular still haunts him; it depicts Jesus being beaten, his hands touching his cheek. He still recalls, "Thickly carved crimson rivulets of blood ran down to his elbows. I ran out of the chapel screaming."[7] Galles further muses on the perversely layered priorities of horror:

> Although their tales evoked imagery of a distant monstrous land, the stories told by survivors of barbed wire crowned concentration camps were local history. The land on which such suffering took place was the flowered field upon which my friends and I ran and played.[8]

Galles's difficult choice to take on, draw from, and live with images of the Nazi death camps has, thus, at least two motivations: to convey the complex dislocation of the physical and psychic sites of his childhood and to substantiate the horrific landscapes of death, however unreal they seem, with the most factual of documentation. It is as if the utter shock of the extermination camp photographs stands in for the dislocated juxtaposition of horror and the eerie mundane that Galles and so many others experienced. Further, the sites themselves, as well as their photographic record, were intended to be ephemeral, yet were meticulously documented. For Galles's *Fourteen Stations* to become a Kaddish, a prayer for the dead, the artist had to do his own research to find the photographs and thus perform a doubled taking hold of what had been withheld: in personal terms, the concrete realization of what he as a child and his family had so radically undergone and, in historical terms, the acknowledgment of the calculation of the perpetrators and the nonchalance of the Allied forces. Both Allied and captured German photographs of concentration camps were kept hidden from the public in the United States National Archives for four decades, some of them declassified only in 1979 and still others only recently released. Reexamined by photographic interpreters, they clearly show evidence of gassing and cremation, undeniable proof of the mass murder that the camps perpetrated. The photographs also confirm how crucial rail lines were in the killing process—rail lines that were never blown up by the Allies to stop the massacres at the camps. Galles mined the public record, writing to the CIA under the Freedom of Information Act, and eventually was able to persuade the Cartographic Department at the National Archives to let him see copies of the aerial photographs he was seeking.[9] Galles's arduous research process was the first step in the transformation of the photographs from documents to documentary objects of intensified acknowledgment, commemoration, and contemplation.

These large-scale drawings do not merely reproduce the photographs. For each drawing, Galles selects one photograph of the site to work from, and compares it with current maps to see exactly where the site is located. He then blows up the area of the camp in his drawing to 47½ by 75 inches. Each drawing is built up with as many as eight layers of charcoal in different colors and textures. Deep, sensuous blacks and infinite shades of gray re-create the freight trains, pits, crematoria, fields, trees, and ashes first rendered through the diagrammatic and distanced black and white aerial photograph. The rich and almost overwhelmingly dense markings in the drawings reiterate the violence done to the landscape, as well as to the people forced to occupy these sites of devastation. Galles's lines, markings, cuttings, incisions, and demarcations are like the tearing and ripping apart of the earth and its perverse realignments that the aerial photographs convey. These emphatic marks also stand in for the artist's desire to recultivate, as it were, the fields of devastation: to enter them and to handle the soil, to caress it, as if to heal the irrevocable damage.

Galles spends four to six months working on each drawing. Given the sheer work involved, plus the disorienting parallax perspective of the aerial images compounded with what they picture, it is difficult to imagine the psychic stamina needed to complete a single drawing, let alone the entire project. Galles temporarily maintains his focus and his emotional wholeness by drawing the exacting details as conceptual entities of light, depth, and form; but then, as it must be, he is always stunned back into the realm of what they depict. Working on the image of Belzec, the site where his family perished, was especially hard. In the midst of drawing, he noticed a spot on the ground in the photograph that he realized was the last hundred yards his family had to run in terror before being gassed. Galles conducts, indeed, a strange performance of remembering through the seeming abstraction of drawing. As he puts it, "I codify with documentation what are only marks on paper produced by a piece of charcoal in my hand. I literally draw with ashes."[10] The artist's meditative yet guarded stance while drawing is akin to a trance. He seems oddly disengaged from the traces of bodies he hovers over while being completely immersed in them. This intense emotional engagement with the medium of drawing and the merging of this

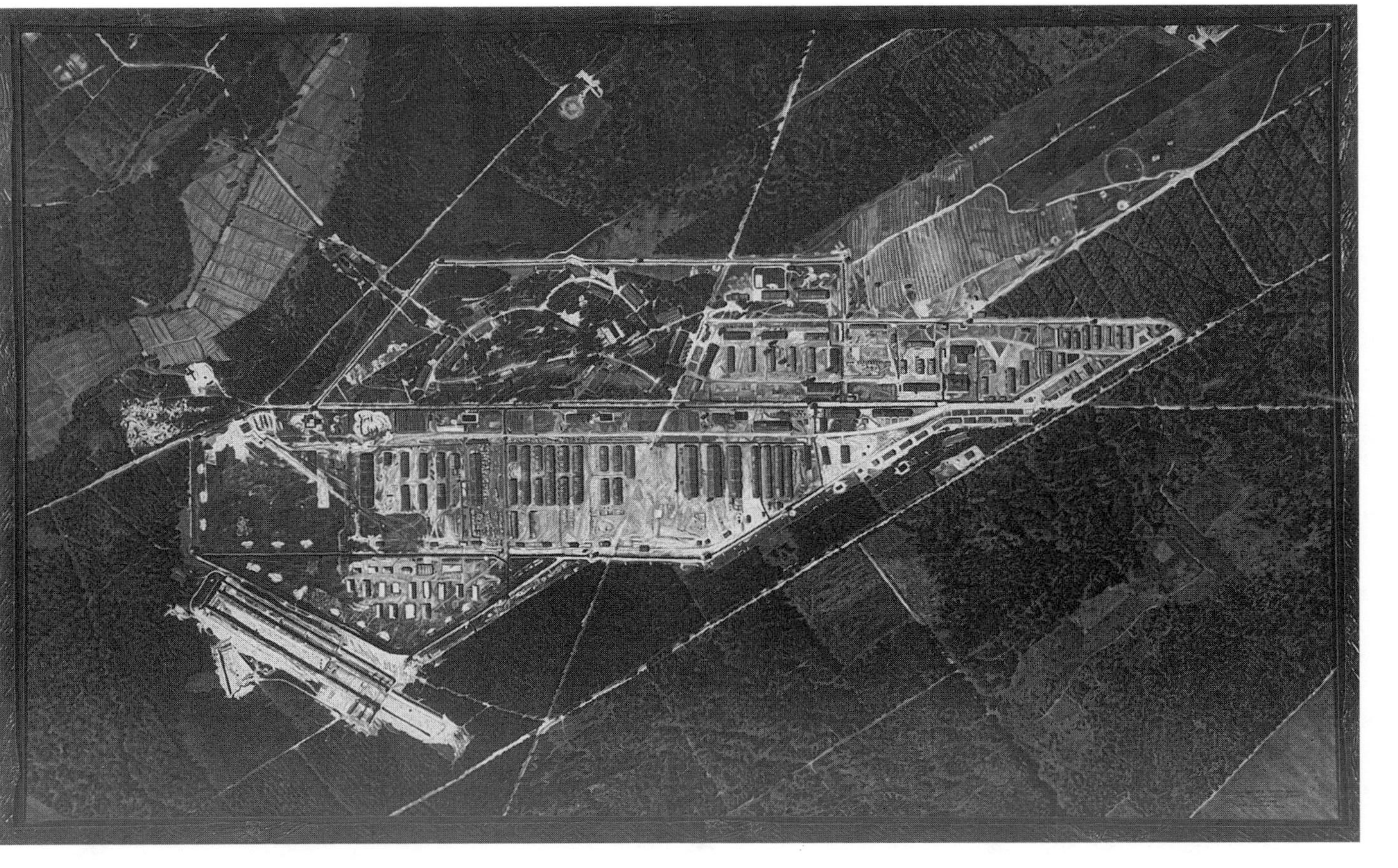

3.2 *Station 5: Bergen-Belsen*, 1994, charcoal on Arches paper with white conté crayon and wrought iron frame, 47½" × 75". Courtesy Arie A. Galles. Photo by Tim Volk.

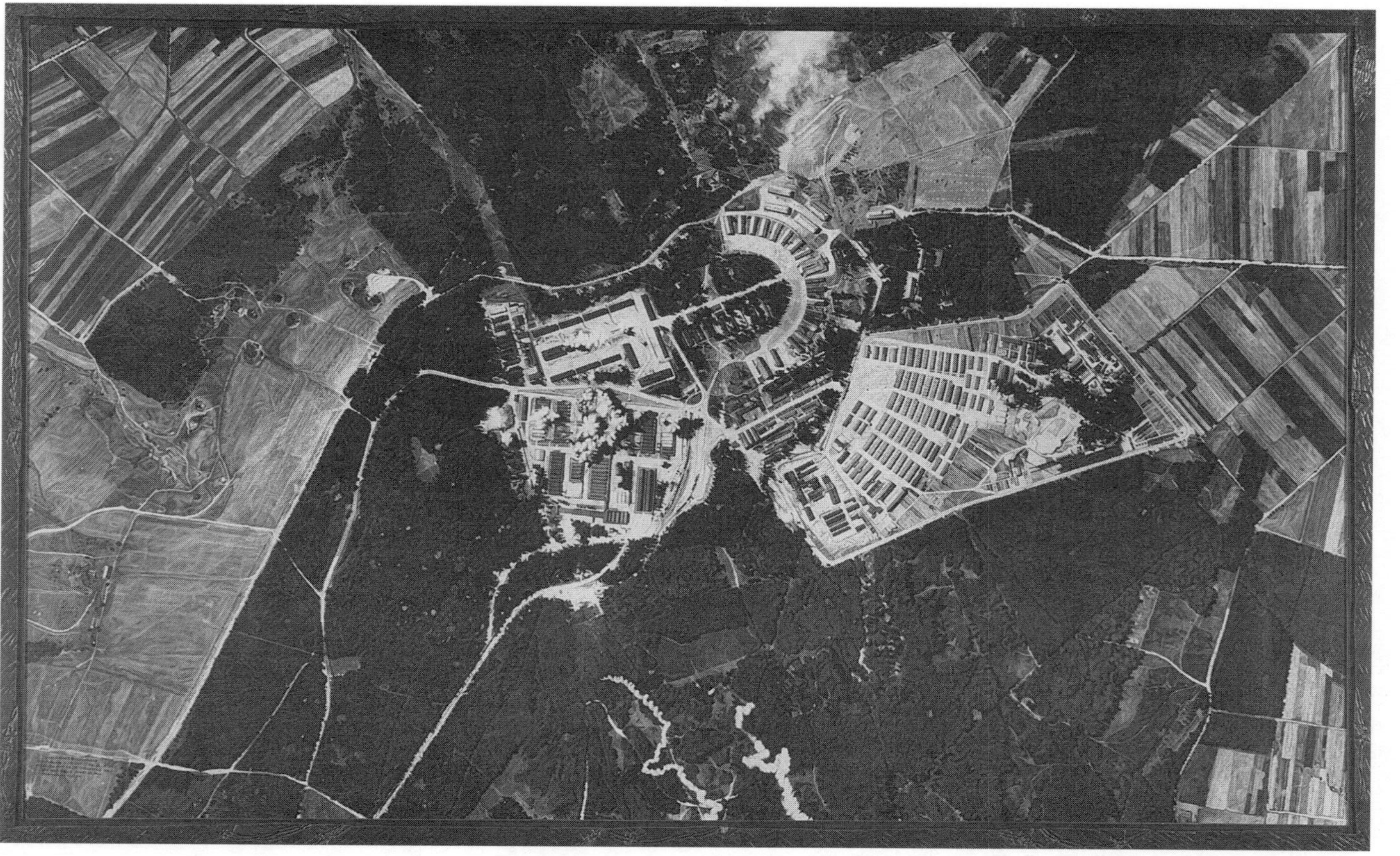

3.3 *Station 3: Buchenwald*, 1999, charcoal on Arches paper with white conté crayon and wrought iron frame, 47½" × 75". Courtesy Arie A. Galles. Photo by Tim Volk.

concentration with the object of the artist's observation are similar to a conceptual performance work. In a performance piece, the artist's process and personal responses to it are central to the work's significance and are made distinctly public. In *Fourteen Stations,* the concept of the piece is heavily indebted to its process, yet unlike in performance work, the self-referentiality of the artist is kept more private. The intense labor invested in the drawings speaks for the mourning process the artist has undergone.

How, then, does the viewer become a participant in the performance of witnessing, mourning, and memorializing that Galles re-creates for himself and in which the drawings are invested? The particular qualities of these remarkable drawings—their distanced softness, multiple layers of shading, and overall stillness—convey a hushed, commemorative sorrow without ever losing the eerie reality that they portray the exact location and layout of the Nazis' killing centers. Galles carefully and ironically uses strategies of drawing to bring the viewer into a receptive milieu for remembrance and engagement. I repeat what I wrote earlier about the drawings: they do more than merely reproduce the photographs. Galles uses repetition, mimesis, and obscuration in the many layers he uses to both support and buffer each drawing's difficult image. He first lays in the forms with a soft chamois towel, only to wipe them all out—or, rather, to grind the shapes into the paper, leaving a residue or ghost image. Then, using varying pressure on an eraser, he changes the forms into structures of light and dark. At this point, Galles likens the process to an unveiling. Next, he puts in the details using white conté crayon and charcoal, going over each layer again and again to build up darker darks and lighter lights. It is as if each dense layer provokes the distanced flatness of the original photographs, whose supposed clarity is masked by their own hyperdetail. The strategic use of repetition both to heighten details and to obfuscate serves as a reminder of what the aerial views actually pictured and what they hoped to obscure. Repetition in these drawings, in alternating layers of effacing and building up, thus becomes an emphatic representation of disbelief and documentation. Disbelief here means the deception the photographs conveyed as well as the difficulty of their ultimate reception. For example, we realize, as Galles did, that a white area becoming more distinct in the Auschwitz drawing is actually the representation of smoke coming out of a chimney. It is this difficulty that demands documentation.

Through the complex relationship between gentleness and irony in his approach to the imagery, Galles expertly targets the question of the status and transformation of the documentary artifact in the representation and display of Holocaust history and memory. As a documentary object, the artifact or photograph teaches and warns about the events. As a precious object, it also offers some form of restitution, some representation of justice, to those who experienced the inconceivable. Yet the duplicity of the object's status becomes ever

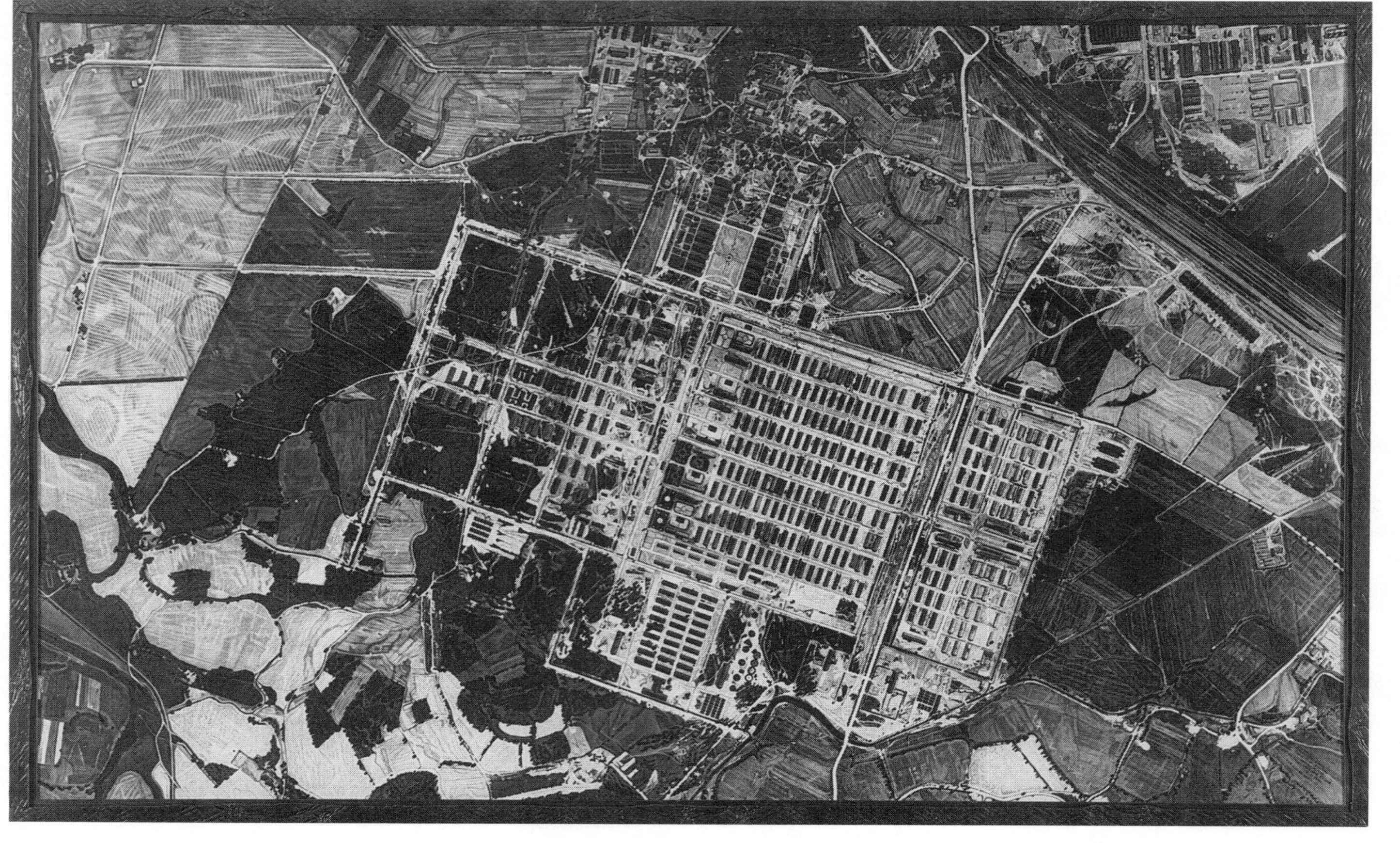

3.4 *Station 1: Auschwitz-Birkenau,* 1998, charcoal on Arches paper with white conté crayon and wrought iron frame, 47½" × 75". Courtesy Arie A. Galles. Photo by Tim Volk.

more pronounced when we consider in whose hands and minds it was first fashioned. In the case of those originating from or seized by the Nazis, the inevitable question is whether such objects should be considered precious or reviled. Of course, they are always one and the other, from the most personal objects (toothbrushes, shoes, family photographs) to the seemingly most objectified (camp uniforms, train cars, aerial photographs).[11] In these debates about the documentary object's duplicitous status, Galles tips the balance in favor of the precious, or the loved. He does this simply and brilliantly by ironically mirroring the Nazis' own documentary imagery. *Fourteen Stations* is a disquieting and respectful installation that presents the images of the camps as a testimony of atrocity without demeaning those who perished and those who survived, a strategy that allows the documentation to perform some of the work of mourning. As transfigurations of what they portray—sites of death—the drawings create spaces of mourning where there were no acknowledgments, where there were no blessings for the dead. They create incantation. They ask us to become joined, to touch, to caress. To caress, but to keep our distance.

In that we are overwhelmed and awed by the representation of the events, fear and empathy are themselves integral to a respectful remembrance, especially if such awe can be transformed from dread and terror into reverence and further dialogue. Galles translates the photographic documents, as crucial as they are, into objects of dispersed testimony and forms of contemporary empathy. Although there is more to respectful remembrance than the formation of empathy and the transposed engagement with another, an effective approach to historical trauma must always keep these desires in play against the limits of representation and the unknowability of "what happened." As a formidable documentary and an artistic and memorial restaging, *Fourteen Stations* acknowledges its desire to reveal, but not to reveal fully, creating multiple approaches through which the contemporary visitor can tentatively enter the transformed sites of trauma and perhaps experience relations of copresence and passing with those who are mourned.

Notes

1. For a study that considers these dilemmas of remembrance in relation to many twentieth-century extreme events, see Roger I. Simon, Sharon Rosenberg, and Claudia Eppert, eds., *Between Hope and Despair: Pedagogy and the Remembrance of Historical Trauma* (Lanham, Md.: Rowman and Littlefield, 2000), and especially my essay in that collection, "Artifactual Testimonies and the Stagings of Holocaust Memory."

2. See Andrea Liss, *Trespassing through Shadows: Memory, Photography, and the Holocaust* (Minneapolis: University of Minnesota Press, 1998).

3. Jerome Rothenberg is the author of more than fifty books of poetry, including *Poems for the Game of Silence, 1960–1970* (New York: Dial, 1971), *Poland/1931* (New York: New Directions, 1974), *Khurbn and Other Poems* (New York: New Directions, 1989), and *The Lorca Variations* (New York: New Directions, 1993). He has

also edited five assemblages of traditional and contemporary poetry, including *Technicians of the Sacred: A Range of Poetries from Africa, America, Asia, and Oceania* (Garden City, N.Y.: Doubleday, 1968), *Shaking the Pumpkin: Traditional Poetry of the Indian North Americas* (Garden City, N.Y.: Doubleday, 1972), and *A Big Jewish Book: Poems and Other Visions of the Jews from Tribal Times to Present* (Garden City, N.Y.: Anchor, 1978). His own poetry has been translated into French, Swedish, Flemish, Spanish, German, Dutch, Italian, Serbian, Polish, and Finnish. Rothenberg has received many awards, including the Guggenheim in 1974 and the PEN Oakland Josephine Miles Literary Award in 1994.

4. Quoted in Frank Fox, "Kaddish in Charcoal," *The World and I,* March 1998, 117, and at <http://fermi.phys.ualberta.ca/~amk/galles/fox.html>, accessed 20 December 2001.

5. Quoted in Matthew Baigell, *Jewish-American Artists and the Holocaust* (New Brunswick, N.J.: Rutgers University Press, 1997), 92.

6. Arie A. Galles, *Project Summary,* 1. Also see Galles, "Fourteen Stations"/"Hey Yud Dalet," at < http://fermi.phys.ualberta.ca/~amk/galles/galles.html>, accessed 20 December 2001.

7. Galles, *Project Summary,* 4. Also see Fox, "Kaddish in Charcoal."

8. Galles, *Project Summary,* 4. Also see Galles, "Fourteen Stations"/"Hey Yud Dalet."

9. Foremost among those who helped Galles with his research was Waclaw Godziemba-Maliszewski, head of the Society for Aero Historical Research and a pioneer in the interpretation of aerial photographs revealing the killing of twenty-seven thousand Polish officers by the Soviets in the Katyn Forest massacre. Frank Fox examines period aerial photographs of the site of this 1940 slaughter in his *God's Eye: Aerial Photography and the Katyn Forest Massacre* (West Chester, Penn.: West Chester University Press, 1999).

10. Galles, *Project Summary,* 7. Also see Galles, "Fourteen Stations"/"Hey Yud Dalet."

11. For a critical discussion on the complex status of artifacts in exhibition settings, please see chapter 4, "Artifactual Witnessing as (Im)Possible Evidence," in Liss, *Trespassing through Shadows.*

4 Trauma | DANIEL LIBESKIND

I think about trauma not only as an architect but also as someone who was born in the post-Holocaust world, with two parents who were themselves survivors of the Holocaust. The theme of culture and trauma, the void, and the experience of architecture can be talked about in conceptual terms as well as expressed in concrete reality. The theme involves a moment of awareness of that which really cannot be communicated in any explicit experience—a gap which exists among those who are survivors, which includes everyone born after those times—a gap which in time becomes obliterated and which generates in itself an even greater emptiness in the posthistorical world. Of course, in this state the difference between simulation and experience becomes very explicit: Experience of history is the relationship between what the void is and that absence which is not only relative but catastrophic and absolute.

If one really thinks about the change of the world that has come since 1945, one realizes that it is certainly not a matter of coincidence; the changes are due in large part to the fact that people were exterminated who would otherwise have formed a continuity with European and world culture. So I would say that the extermination of Jews, six million of them, and the many many others, millions of others, has led to quite a different vision of what history was and might yet be.

This experience was brought home to me in a very graphic and palpable form when I first came to Berlin some years ago. I went to the Weissensee cemetery. It is the largest Jewish cemetery in Berlin, and I walked through this incredible cemetery, which was still, with a kind of emptiness built into it. For those of you who have not been there, I will describe it to you. There are many huge marble tombstones which were erected by wealthy families for the future, to be engraved and inscribed as future generations passed away and new generations arose. As I walked through the cemetery (my wife and I were the only ones there; it was just after unification), I was struck by the fact that no members of these families could ever come back to see the emptiness of those slabs of marble. There would be no one to recognize that emptiness. The visitors who have come to see it are not part of these families; they are witnesses of another kind.

I have been thinking particularly about this because I am involved in a number of projects which challenge one's imagination of how to deal with the void, public space, culture, and trauma. Not the trauma of a singular catastrophe which can be overcome and healed, but a trauma which is structured both by the destruction of a community and by its real yet also virtual presence. This absence is structured in the city, in the topography of a country, and in the topography of Europe and the world. So I am very much interested in the cultural significance of the void—the void of public space, and the void of memory. What is the void's cultural presence today? What is its form and repression? What might it have been historically? How does it look? How does one encounter it or how does one not encounter it?

The need in architecture to respond to the questions of culture, of public space, of the void is very palpable, since in architecture the void is a space. It is a place of being and nonbeing. It is a place where one can hardly find traces of a relationship. And yet it has been recorded and presented in light, matter, and documents. One can attempt to have access to it through names and addresses, through a kind of haunting quality of spaces through which the passage of absence took place.

I recall vividly one of the Hasidic tales of the Holocaust, an interview with a survivor now living in Brooklyn. She was a prisoner in the concentration camp of Stutthof and felt she would never survive 1943–44. But one day, as she looked up into the sky, she noticed a white line, a perfect white line, and though she did not know why, she believed that thinking of that white line kept her alive. The interviewer, Yaffa Eliach, asked her what she thought the white line was, and she said she never really wondered, but in retrospect it might have been something as banal as the exhaust of an airplane or the traces of a cloud. In that place, in Stutthof in 1944, that singular vision had a significance which was surely obscure and enigmatic, and yet it transformed memory and communicated an experience.

There has been a lot of controversy recently—in Switzerland about the banking and gold issue, in Austria about the far right, and in Germany about the collaboration of major industries. For the first time, people are realizing that the next century may not be predictable: a further forgetting, a further distancing, a further abstraction. Globally, the enormous misproportion of that absence of a generation may appear and astound us with its implications. Think of the collapse of the Soviet empire, the emergence of the market economies of Poland, the Czech Republic, Hungary, the Baltic States, and the former Yugoslavia; think of what was involved in the rebuilding of Europe, the resources, the transferences of material possessions. Where did it all come from—from whose bank vaults? Certainly the search involves the issues of responsibility, the ethics of memory, the politics of space, and the rebuilding of sites and places which only yesterday were deemed immune to history.

In my view, the question of culture, public space, and the experience of architecture is part of a larger vision. I have read a number of texts which illuminate the problem of trauma from the psychoanalytical perspective, but I believe that when one actually enters the space of that trauma, the space of the city, the trauma cannot be interpreted simply. That is the difference between talking about the problem and being in it. In a literary context, one can interpret trauma, one can give it a connotation, one can cope with it in different linguistic settings. But no interpretation can eliminate the materiality, opacity, and thickness of the experience of walking, looking, touching, feeling where one is.

The projects on which I am working are explicitly related to public space, to memory, and to the concrete experience of architecture and the city. The Jewish Museum in Berlin, an urban space like Alexanderplatz or Tacheles, the museum of Osnabrück, the lands associated with the name "Sachsenhausen": all these projects are structured by a void and by trauma. The trauma, once again, is not understood in a psychoanalytical sense, but rather in a material sense. How does one pass on some truth about what it all really means? What does this history really mean? How does one communicate a unique encounter? In what context can that meaning emerge? How could those who are not interested in that meaning be involved in its construction? These are the ethical architectural issues with which I have been grappling.

One of the things that struck me when I entered the competition to redesign Alexanderplatz in Berlin was the resounding emptiness of the square. One has to match this emptiness with that other, subsequent emptiness, with the activity of Alexanderplatz seen in all of those photographs and documents prior to 1933. I analyzed ownership of the Jewish properties that had surrounded Alexanderplatz, those who lived there, Alfred Döblin's description of the working poor, and then the future vitality and potential of Berlin from this point.

Having done this, I asked myself, how did my results match up with the results of the Senate of Berlin? How did my experience of Alexanderplatz match up with the experience of the city administration? After all, it was they who directed this competition and determined the planning directives for the square. They provided tables of the number of square meters needed, the new office buildings to be built—a kind of rationality reappropriating a piece of land which I believed was not wholly amenable to pure manipulation.

The Berlin politicians pressed the architects to treat this site as a tabula rasa, an exercise in amnesia, a site without a past—as if Berlin were just any other city of the world to be developed. I felt that simply constructing many buildings and filling in the site did not necessarily diminish that emptiness. On the contrary, the filling of the emptiness might actually inflate it. The material idea of filling sites must be seen in a deeper sense in order to become a lifeline to the future and an embodiment of the past for those who were and are still a part of it.

I grew up in Lodz, a few hundred kilometers from Alexanderplatz. In fact, my uncle was a student in Berlin, and in our home we used to speak about Alexanderplatz; it was part of our minds' topography as we traversed that void of light and distance and culture. I decided to look at the hand of Alfred Döblin, a handprint which he made of his left hand in the 1920s, and in it I saw all the lines which describe Berlin as he saw it. I am not an occult architect, nor do I read palms, but one can see the lifelines of Berlin in that hand: the love lines, the lines of death, the lines of work. That left hand of Döblin's Alexanderplatz is, I believe, the real matrix that continues to hold out the open promise of that place. That hand, which might today still affect our lived experience of Alexanderplatz, is a figure that refers one across the emptiness of that public space.

In the ideological, scientistic, positivistic way of looking at the city, its context is what you see of its streets, its transformations, its history. So how does one view the void? What are the other possibilities? How does one view that which never has passed, the emptiness of a public space? Indeed, how does one view the void as the context of the city? History in Berlin has been traumatized into something that appears to be ahistorical, something that never took place in history because it was never part of history in the first place. The ahistorical dimension of the void has always puzzled me. Of course the void has a historical trajectory, a trajectory of fatality of western culture. At the same time there is something about the void that is, astonishingly, not coincidental with positivist history. That interests me very much as part of my work. The void embodies the literal annihilation of culture, the annihilation of the carriers of culture. Those people who read books were its carriers. Who remains who can still speak, remember, and see the white line in the sky?

One does not have to be either religious or nonreligious to see the importance of that extraordinary absence. The empty space, the empty history is to be rejoined—but how? How can the idea of planning cope with the rebuilding of the city and of the economy? No one is against rebuilding the city;

everyone wants to have a better city. Go on, get on with life, let's start living again. Let's move forward—but is it forward? Where are we heading? I think there is a different idea of planning, planning which is based not solely on the visible matrices, nor on the visible formal connections, or on communicative structures, but rather across those irreconcilable gaps which not even in the Derridean sense are traces.

And that is what I proposed: in order to deal with Alexanderplatz as a planner and as an architect, one would have to reopen a thoroughly other context allowing public space for the void: a context into which both those born and annihilated and also those shadowy figures who were never born, the traces of the unborn, could be incorporated. The visible is not the only context of the new planning; one also has to deal with the invisible, the annihilated couriers of culture, the true "spirit of Berlin."

Consider the six letters of "Berlin," which I have used and taken very seriously in my work in the city. What is in the name "Berlin"? What is in the name of that memory? My project for Alexanderplatz was based on those fugitive fault lines across which the city was devastated, but which nevertheless remain in my opinion the only lines on which the city can continue in the future. They are not necessarily coincident with rationality, with rational planning, with grids, with the power of building, with the city, because they depend on that which can be remembered and that which is remembered in the form of the immemorial. I speak now of the strategy of planning urban space and of the pragmatic devices with which a city such as Berlin can rebuild itself.

Berlin, by the way, is not the only city which lacks memory. I remember how shocked I was, as a child in Israel in the late 1950s (after we emigrated from Poland), that when we spoke Yiddish on the streets of Tel Aviv somebody would say, "Shhh! We are Israelis, this is a new place, this is not Poland. You are in another place now." I felt how difficult it was for us as immigrants to make another leap across a desert. The relationship of Berlin, Israel, New York, and other places—the radiation of events, of their "after-life," of trauma—cannot be manipulated with ease in any ideological setting.

With this in mind, I would like to refer to a project, another competition that I was fortunate enough to win and that is fully installed and open to the public now. It is a museum in the German city of Osnabrück, near the Dutch border. Osnabrück is an important Catholic city with deep historical roots. The museum is devoted to the works of a particular citizen of Osnabrück, Felix Nussbaum, a well-known and important painter of the early twentieth century. He had studied and painted in Berlin, received the Prix de Rome, and was a successful artist across Europe. But beginning in 1933 he lived another life. He was a fugitive in Germany and was chased across Europe by the Nazis. An optimist, he always thought he would win out. In his self-portraits he depicts himself as a survivor who will somehow tell the story. But

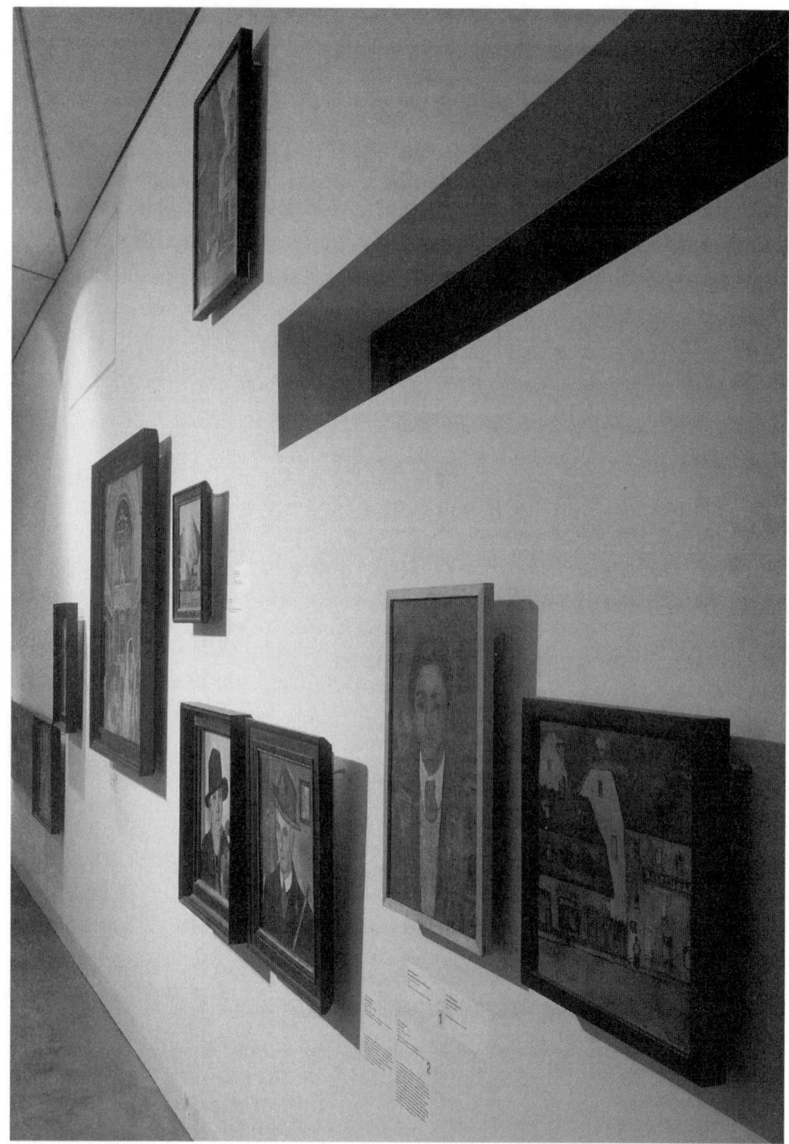

4.1 Daniel Libeskind, *Felix Nussbaum Haus*, Osnabrück, 1998. Courtesy Bitter Bredt Fotografie, Berlin.

unfortunately, tragically, he was deported on one of the last trains from Brussels to Auschwitz and exterminated.

Felix Nussbaum was almost completely eliminated from history. He is not even mentioned in the 1987 edition of the *Jewish Encyclopedia*. His life and works were only rediscovered in the past few years; only in the late 1980s and '90s was his oeuvre recognized as emblematic of all those who had been annihilated, together with the places of memory and the witnesses. The city of Osnabrück learned of his paintings, got them back, and made a commitment to build a museum to house them. The museum was to connect these paintings with the holdings of the other buildings on the site: the Kunsthistorisches Museum and the Schlikker'sche Villa, which house archaeological artifacts and folk art.

So Nussbaum is not only a painter but a creator of meaningful work. How to represent him? I represented him in a very simple way with three volumes. The first is a traditional wooden building which stands on the site in a special relationship to the old synagogue on Rolandstrasse, which was burned in 1938. I made a kind of traditional wooden building for about three hundred works painted in the 1920s and early '30s. That wooden space is violently cut by a dramatic second volume standing eleven meters high, fifty long, and only two wide (the minimum allowed by German regulations): the Nussbaum Gang. It is made of concrete and has no windows of any sort. And there I proposed to show the works that Nussbaum created in his flight through Europe. While a fugitive, he lived in tiny rooms and painted in very close quarters, sometimes a matter of inches. He could not stand back from the works to look at them. He painted in secret, in a kind of delirium of a historical notion of art. These paintings and drawings have only been viewed close up, never from some aesthetic distance. So I proposed to exhibit them in this narrow volume, and the city and the museum director accepted that these paintings should be seen in a different kind of public space.

One enters the wooden building, the Nussbaum Haus, which houses the prewar paintings, and then one passes through the narrow space of the concrete wall, the Nussbaum Gang, in order to get to what I have called the Nussbaum Brücke, a metal building, the third volume, built to hold the newly discovered paintings of Nussbaum, a collection which will slowly increase. During the last years of the war Nussbaum's signature was erased from most of his paintings, which were then resold as anonymous works.

The new museum is a gigantic empty wall, but as it moves from the past to the present and into its own future it is also a dense, sometimes claustrophobic, and sometimes traditional representation of culture and public space in Osnabrück. Again, I believe that it is important to reincorporate the experience of history and of the city into architecture, not only intellectually, but on all levels. Materiality collides with scale: the complete blankness of concrete collides with the articulateness of wood, passing through the tubular nature of steel—the matrix upon which the museum stands. The museum is designed as a topographical site in which one stands on irreconcilable pieces of land: one facing Hamburg, one piece facing Berlin, one facing Rome, one facing the concentration camps Nussbaum hoped to escape from, and then his journey back through the Benelux, through Amsterdam, to Belgium, and finally to Auschwitz.

I have tried to represent that destiny and make it available as an experience to people who fortunately never had to face and re-face their lives in the context that Nussbaum did. I tried not to be sentimental about Nussbaum. But one could look into those days and see a message like one in a bottle, coincidentally found somewhere. Who can possibly know what that message is and what can be passed on: what statement, which code? I thought that one should pass on everything in that message, including the darkness, the inarticulateness, the opacity, and that which cannot be analyzed.

The third project involves me in a difficult discussion of history and culture in Oranienburg, next to the concentration camps of Sachsenhausen. The lands that had belonged to the SS were to be urbanized. The brief called for building thousands of units of housing. I remembered my visits to Warsaw when I was growing up in Poland after the war. All traces of the ghetto had been obliterated by vast housing estates. I realized I could not build such housing here, and that I would be disqualified for not doing so. Nevertheless, I proposed an alternative. I understood that these sites in Brandenburg and elsewhere in eastern Germany were a major source of currency—land for development. So how is one to use such lands?

Sachsenhausen is not on some distant periphery in the wilderness of Brandenburg, but rather is in the center of Oranienburg. It is a black hole. A perfect triangle: at its apex, the ovens; at the bottom vertices, the commandant's villa and Himmler's administrative headquarters; along the base, the SS infrastructure of garages, housing, and so on; and in the center, the city of death. So this is not an innocent site. I was disqualified, as I had expected. However, I did receive an honorary prize for reminding people that this site had history.

Subsequently, the press began to discuss the fate of this eighty-hectare site, wondering why I had not put housing on it. The debate became, over the next four or five years, an interesting political process. My wife (who is also my partner), Mathias Reese (the project architect), and I have traveled regularly to Oranienburg and Potsdam to speak with officials, to address a variety of committees, the Bauausschuss (the committee for approving new buildings), the economic minister, the Gedenkstätte historians (the committee for dealing with memorials). Once in a while newspaper articles would appear, television programs would be aired. Slowly, over the years, the citizens of Oranienburg, the city officials, and the politicians of Brandenburg changed their minds. They prepared for a new type of building on this semi-profane land.

I had originally proposed to restore very little and to accelerate the ruin of the buildings in order to reveal the enormous infrastructural dimension of the relationship between Sachsenhausen, Oranienburg, and Berlin. Mr. Reese and I had numerous tough battles with those who wanted to restore everything in

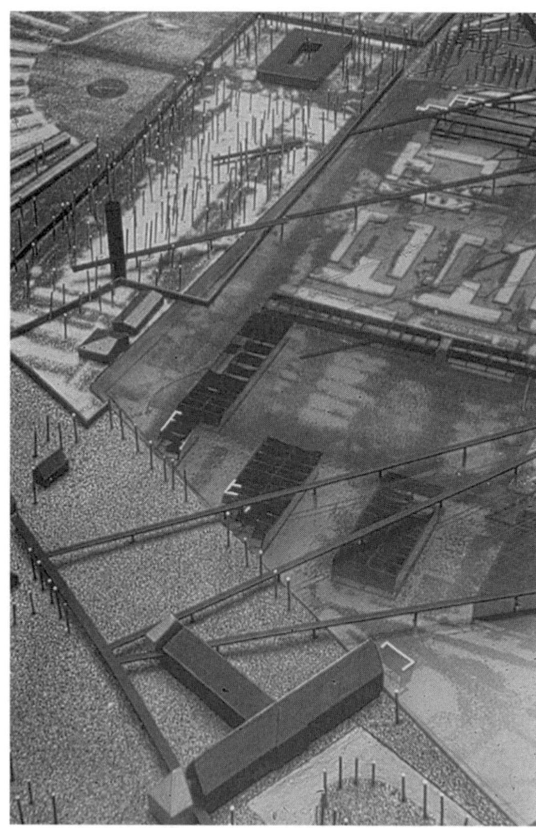

4.2 Daniel Libeskind, *Oranienburg Competition for Sachsenhausen*, 1993. Courtesy Steven Gerrard and Elizabeth Govan, Studio Libeskind.

the name of historical authenticity. Gradually, a meaningful approach was agreed upon.

Beyond the concentration camp itself and the SS camp, the lands had been filled with factories, waterworks, bridges, canals, locks, all built by slave labor. It was important to see and understand the topography in a new way. The current proposal calls for cutting the site in half and reordering it, turning one half into an archaeological park of ruined buildings, with canals and bridges. The other half will be regenerated by physically filling the polluted land with new earth, and by building within strict demarcations what I call the "Hope Incision," a configuration of buildings with specific uses: a youth hostel, public civic buildings, a university department, workshops for artisans and craftsmen, training sites for the underemployed and the unemployed. Currently, we enjoy the full support of the Gedenkstätte historians, the city, and the state government. The planning permission for the site is entering the final stages; we have nearly finished securing the necessary permits and investors are now being approached.

The project which brought me to Berlin and which inaugurated my architectural office and my career as an architect was originally called the Jewish Museum Department in the Berlin Museum. Over the next ten years the museum's name changed five times; it is now called the Jewish Museum Berlin, 2000 Years of German Jewish History, and is a fully autonomous cultural institution. The museum deals explicitly with the history of absence and the history of the void. When I first entered the competition to design it, I asked myself, how is one to design an integrated Berlin Museum and Jewish Museum? That was what the competition program called for. Under the aegis of the Aspen Institute, the program had been debated for almost a quarter of a century by historians, philosophers, Holocaust survivors, and political leaders. They had concluded that a museum of the history of Berlin must depict Jews as intrinsic and seminal.

How is one to show the specific history of Berlin? That, of course, was the challenge. I did one thing which was different from all 165 other entries in this competition. All the other architects designed what they called a "Jewish Department": a department with its own lock and key, its own doorway, its own four walls. I tried everything to avoid that. I tried to think of myself as a Berlin Jew, as an immigrant from Poland, as sitting in Alexanderplatz, working there, becoming part of the city. How would I do that? What would the strategy, the mental set, be? And how would I open this experience to all people? (On a personal note, while researching the competition, I found out that the first place to which Berlin Jews were deported was Lodz, the city in which I was born. I think that city must have signified for the Nazis the lowest type, the nadir, the counterpart of where the Berlin Jews thought they belonged, which was in elegant and cosmopolitan Berlin.)

I based the design of the museum on historical documents, both architectural and para-architectural ones: music, books, pictures, the eyes and the looks of people, photographs. I saw that Berlin was organized around a void and around a star that no longer shone. That star was assimilation, the total integration of Jews in Berlin. Walter Rathenau said in a famous speech in the late 1920s, "Now I feel that there is not an ounce of Jewish blood flowing through my veins." Those were among the last words he uttered before he was murdered by proto-Nazis. So I thought, what does it mean to be assimilated? What does it mean to be truly integrated into a culture? To feel that you have finally arrived?

Through the categories or dimensions of architectural thinking I drew the irrational star matrix that connected Germans, Berliners, and Jews across this absence of light. I "married" Rachel Varnhagen and Friedrich Schleyemacher: they lived and worked on opposite sides of a line which crosses Lindenstrasse 14, where the museum stands. Their addresses are linked, as are the addresses of Einstein, Mies van der Rohe, E. T. A. Hoffmann, Walter Benjamin, and

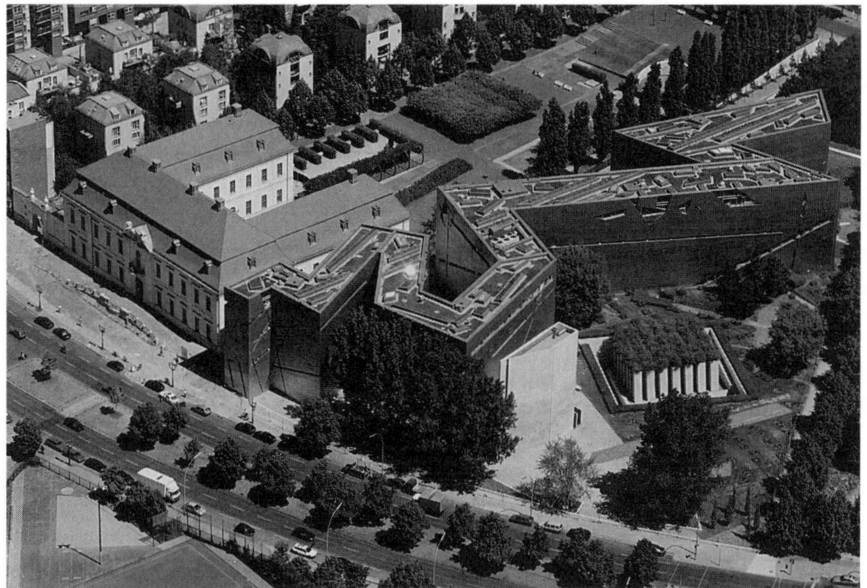

4.3 Daniel Libeskind, *Jewish Museum Berlin*, 2001. Courtesy Jewish Museum Berlin.

thousands of others—linked as one looks from one place to another, across housing projects, across historical events, across the empty sites of Berlin.

I took the complexity of this matrix as part of the light that comes into the museum, the light that cuts through the windows which are not regular windows, not just holes that bring light to the collection, but rather lights that fall from deep lines of intermarriage and lines of destiny which are irretrievable. Light and lines of retrospective annihilation reflected on the trauma of the after-death. All cultures have developed the notion of the after-death, of postmortem judgment. I thought a long time about what postmortem judgment meant. Who was it meant for? Where did it come from? What is the picture of that spiritual construct of postmortem justice? The irrationality of that matrix of light was the first dimension of this museum.

The second dimension was my quest to find out the names, births, and deaths of the Jews who lived in and around Berlin. I obtained from Bonn the two large volumes which contained the names of those who had been murdered. There were so many names, and they grew into thousands, hundreds of thousands, millions, if one went into Poland, Czechoslovakia, Hungary, and Russia, and everywhere else where Jews used to live. The haunting knowledge of these names was the second part of my research, which I incorporated into the numerical and geometric system of building this building.

The third and fourth dimensions of the project dealt with the incomplete: I wanted to make a building which was not simply a representation of culture or of art, but which was itself a mechanism by which visitors could interpret what had developed—by walking through it, by looking out of the windows, by opening the doors, and by traversing its space. And I did that in terms of two texts, one musical and the other literary.

The musical text was a text of Schönberg's, the text of his opera *Moses and Aaron.* He had written it next door to the Baroque building that had been renovated in the 1960s as the Berlin Museum, when he was a professor of music. I thought about what happened to Schönberg; *Moses and Aaron* was effectively the last thing he wrote. In the last act, the entire orchestra comes to play a single note. Even the survivors of Warsaw do not have that note anymore—that one note that comes to an end. Sixty instruments stop playing, and then the voice of Moses—not of Aaron but of Moses—speaks. That voice that speaks and that does not sing was distanced in the third act. I incorporated a certain geometry and spacing as the third act runs out of music. On the final pages of *Moses and Aaron* big Xs crisscross the page in a particular moment of revelation. I used this building to provide the completion of that last act because I believed it could not be completed musically, but rather with the making of a space where footsteps and the sound of echoes and silence followed. The fourth dimension was my interest in making the building respond to the apocalyptic tour of Berlin given by Walter Benjamin in his 1928 book *Einbahnstrasse* (*One-Way Street*). I positioned the sixty stations of the star with Benjamin's incredible text and I tried to make it a guidebook for the new citizens of Berlin, who would use the museum to find out about the past, present, and future of their city. I did not design a museum that treats the history of Berlin ethnographically, or that treats the history of the Jews of Berlin as an ethnography of the past. The history of the Jews is living, even in its absence, in its permanent potential, and it lives in its absent presence in the structure, in the collections of the city of Berlin, and in the space of the museum.

In the competition brief the architects were asked to ensure that the public enter the Baroque building first, before entering the new building. Visitors therefore enter on the ground floor and immediately see a form which is clearly not Baroque—the void of the entrance, which cuts into the Baroque building from the roof to below ground. Descending the staircase, they enter the history of Berlin, a history profoundly rooted in the foundations of Germans and Jews. There are three roads in this underground. The first road leads to the Garden of Exile and Emigration, a very special garden of forty-nine pillars, each one filled with earth. Forty-eight of them are filled with the earth of Berlin and stand for the formation of the state of Israel in 1948. The forty-ninth pillar is filled with the earth of Jerusalem and stands for the city of Berlin. The plane upon which the columns stand is tilted; although the columns are perpendicular to it, it itself is

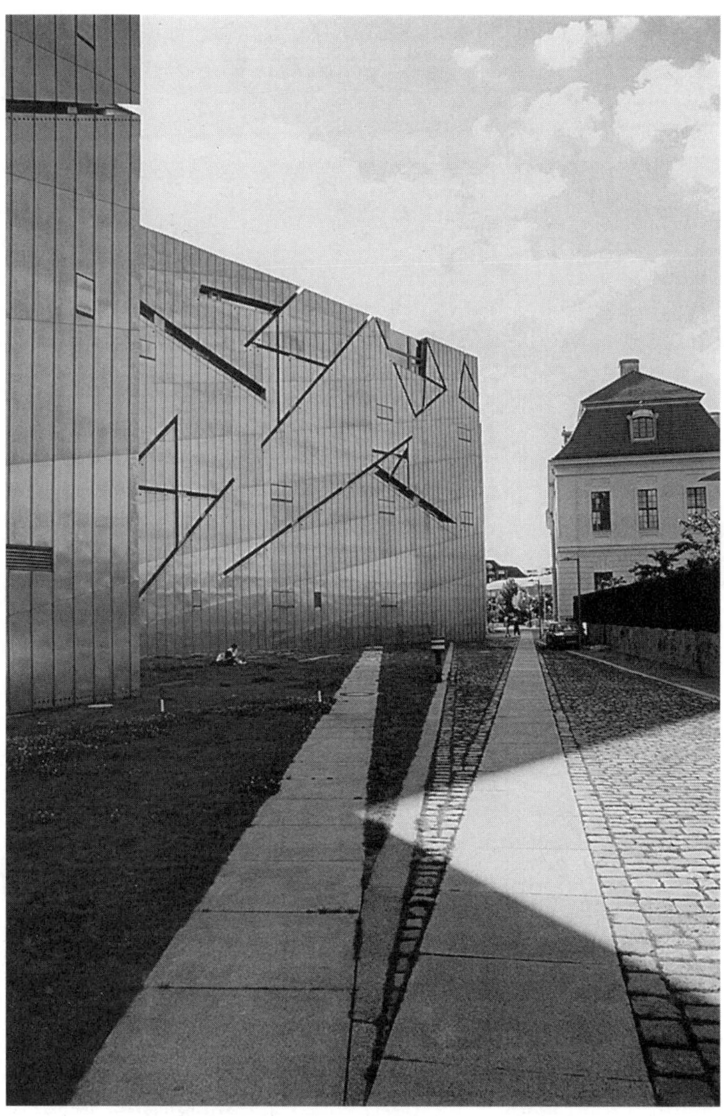

4.4 Daniel Libeskind, *Jewish Museum Berlin*, 2001.
Courtesy Jewish Museum Berlin.

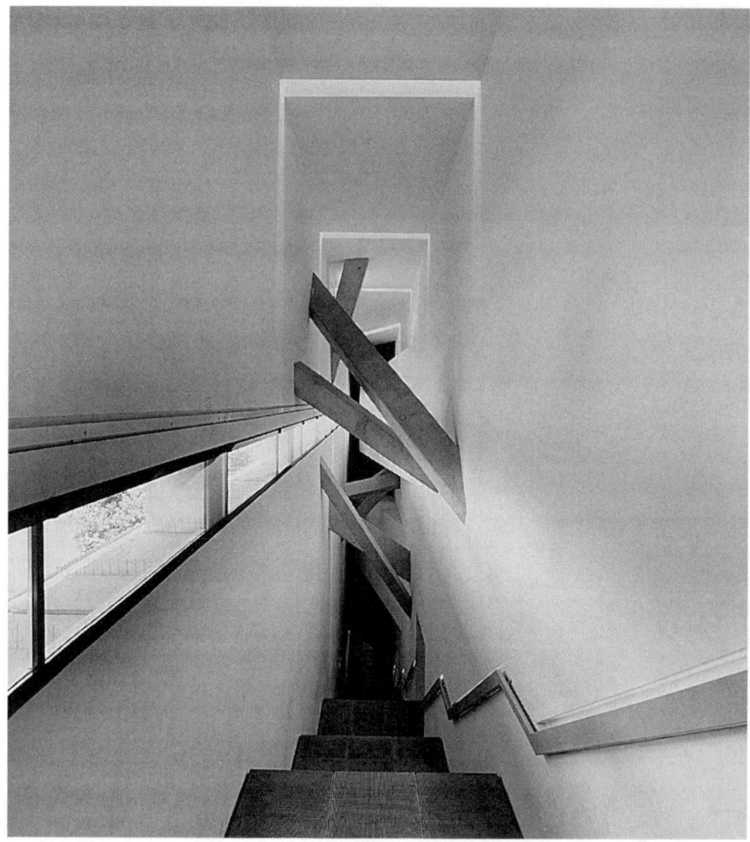

4.5 Daniel Libeskind, *Jewish Museum Berlin*, 2001.
Courtesy Jewish Museum Berlin.

not parallel to the ground, disorienting and even slightly nauseating visitors. The second road leads to the Stair of Continuity, which is the main stair leading up to the exhibition and gallery spaces on the first, second, and third floors. The third road leads to the dead end of the museum—the Holocaust Void, a concrete tower twenty-seven meters high, standing outside and completely separate from the museum. It is unheated. It is concrete inside and concrete outside. It has one vertical window, acutely angled, through which daylight is seen only as a reflected light. The road to the Holocaust Tower is the road to the end of the history of Berlin as we know it, and it is an empty space which is a physical reality, with tremendous acoustics, where one can hear all the sounds of the city, the traffic, children playing, and people walking by, but one is unable to get to them.

I have used the concept of the void not only theoretically but also spatially. The void is a space which cuts imposingly through the museum. It is 27 meters high, 4½ meters wide, and 150 meters long. It is not an atrium; it is not something you walk through; it is not something that can ever be seen in its entirety. It runs through all the collections and divides the building.

The void is divided into five separate parts. The first two voids, at the front of the building, are the deepest ones and can be entered from the underground Jewish religious collection. It is there that visitors first encounter the nothingness of the space of Berlin. These two voids are concrete on the inside, with a gray light falling down the shafts in a dramatic architectural structure. The two voids in the middle are completely impenetrable; no one can enter them. They can be seen from small vertical windows in the bridges, the bridges which literally and architecturally connect the museum gallery spaces. At the end of the museum lies the fifth and final void, which is entered through the temporary galleries. This final void is a dramatic space that refers most specifically to Schönberg.

The straight line of the void orients the visitor. It is concrete on the inside and graphite on the outside as it cuts through the exhibition walls. The bridges which cross the void are always symmetrical, with one doorway on the left and one on the right, and this design is repeated sixty times. Sixty stations, 120 doorways, in and out of the Einbahnstrasse. These doorways and bridges are not simply an architectural or aesthetic device. Rather I sought for a way to exhibit the works of Berliners.

How does one exhibit the work of Max Liebermann? One has to show his work as that of a well-known painter of Berlin, the president of the Prussian Academy of Art. But one also has to exhibit the work of Max Liebermann, the prominent Jewish citizen. So, I thought, on one side of the void visitors could see the work of Max Liebermann, the painter; then they would cross the void on one of the bridges, and on the other side they would see a letter from Max Liebermann's wife to the Gestapo in 1943, begging them not to deport her to Auschwitz. Of course, she did not manage to convince them, and committed suicide prior to her deportation. Or on one side of the void visitors would find Walter Benjamin, his writings about Berlin, his guidebooks, and on the other side they would see the nonexistent manuscript of the Messiah, the recreation of his suicide note. On one side, they could see Albert Einstein, the great Berliner, with his notes on relativity; on the other side the fifty top German scientists of Berlin condemning him to exile. So it is a kind of doubling of history. Walking through the museum is an architectural experience. There is a spacing of the void and the void bridges. There are the windows with their dramatic light, windows which form a facade representing a kind of topographical mapping of Berlin and the lost Berliners.

The visitor to this museum has to keep in mind that it is not easy to put continuity together across that which is forever gone. That is the meaning of my design for an integrated museum, a Jewish Museum. They are completely bound together, totally interpenetrated and integrated through the void, through that absence—for so much has been reduced to ash. The state of instability/stability, of disconnection/connection, of disorder/order will be understood intellectually and kinetically. I always remember the words of St. Augustine in *The City of God:* "Everyone is permanently leaving Babel, but some are leaving with their ankles and feet, and others are leaving it with their hearts and souls." I thought this was an incredible analysis—the complete spectrum—that white line mentioned by the survivor. The line of the impossible miracle. The unknown. As visitors traverse the museum, they will see that white line in the windows, the illumination of the void—the white line of hope along the visitor's route.

5 Memory, Counter-memory, and the End of the Monument | JAMES YOUNG

Among the hundreds of submissions to the 1995 competition for a German national "memorial to the murdered Jews of Europe," one seemed an especially uncanny embodiment of the impossible questions at the heart of Germany's memorial process. Artist Horst Hoheisel, already well known for his negative-form monument in Kassel, proposed a simple, if provocative, anti-solution to the memorial competition: blow up the Brandenburger Tor, grind its stone into dust, sprinkle the remains over its former site, and then cover the entire memorial area with granite plates. How better to remember a destroyed people than by a destroyed monument?

Rather than commemorating the destruction of a people with the construction of yet another edifice, Hoheisel would mark one destruction with another destruction. Rather than filling in the void left by a murdered people with a positive form, the artist would carve out an empty space in Berlin by which to recall a now absent people. Rather than concretizing and thereby displacing the memory of Europe's murdered Jews, the artist would open a place in the landscape to be filled with the memory of those who come to remember Europe's murdered Jews. A landmark celebrating Prussian might and crowned by a chariot-borne Quadriga, the Roman goddess of peace, would be demolished to make room for the memory of Jewish victims of German might and peacelessness. In fact, perhaps no single emblem better represents the conflicted, self-abnegating motives for memory in Germany today than the vanishing monument.

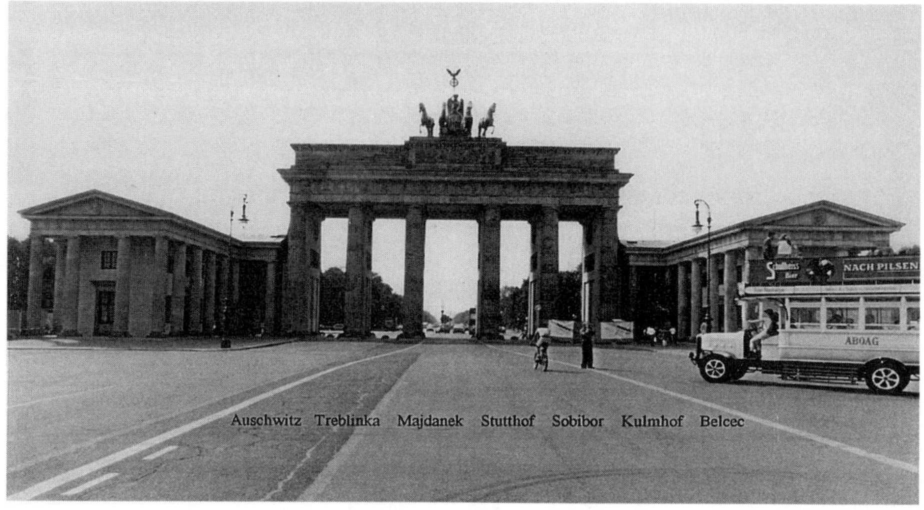

5.1 Horst Hoheisel, *Blow Up the Brandenburger Tor,* 1995.
Courtesy Horst Hoheisel.

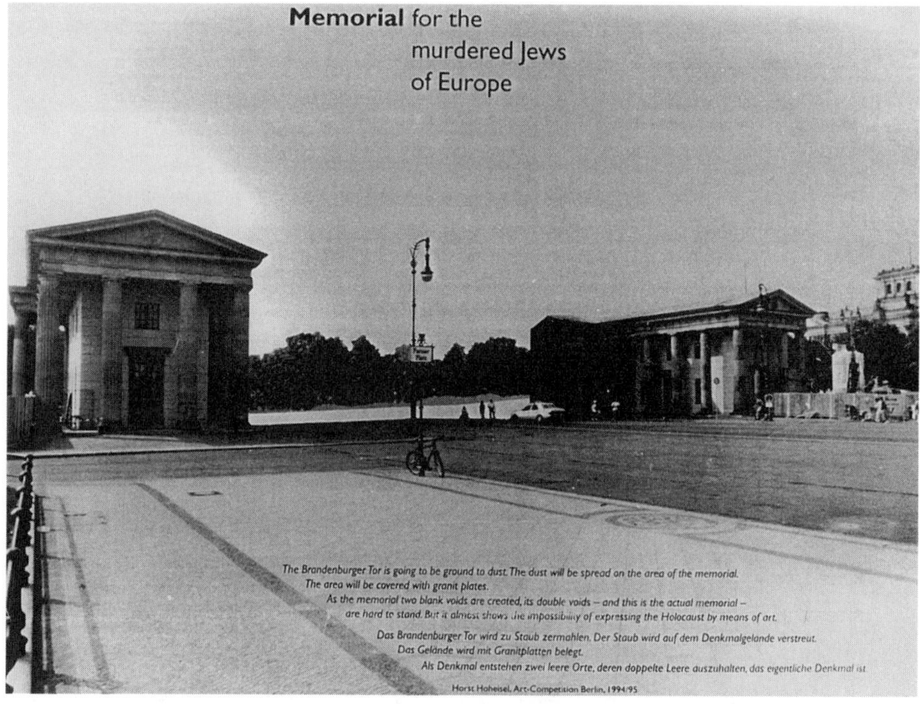

5.2 Horst Hoheisel, *Blow Up the Brandenburger Tor,* 1995.
Courtesy Horst Hoheisel.

Of course, such a memorial undoing would never be sanctioned by the German government, and this, too, was part of the artist's point. Hoheisel's proposal to destroy the Brandenburger Tor participated in the competition for a national Holocaust memorial, even as its radicalism precluded the possibility of its execution. At least part of its polemic, therefore, was directed against actually building any winning design, against ever finishing the monument at all. Here he seemed to suggest that the surest engagement with Holocaust memory in Germany may actually lie in its perpetual irresolution, that only an unfinished memorial process can guarantee the life of memory. For it may be the *finished* monument that completes memory itself, puts a cap on memory-work, and draws a bottom line underneath an era that must always haunt Germany. Better a thousand years of Holocaust memorial competitions in Germany than any single "final solution" to Germany's memorial problem.[1]

Like other cultural and aesthetic forms in Europe and America, the monument—in both idea and practice—has undergone a radical transformation over the course of the twentieth century. As an intersection of public art and political memory, the monument has necessarily reflected the aesthetic and political revolutions, as well as the wider crises of representation, following all of this century's major upheavals—including both the First and Second World Wars, the Vietnam War, and the rise and fall of communist regimes in the former Soviet Union and its Eastern European satellites. In every case, the monument reflects both its sociohistorical and its aesthetic context: artists working in eras of cubism, expressionism, socialist realism, earthworks, minimalism, or conceptual art remain answerable both to official history and to the needs of art. The result has been a metamorphosis of the monument from the heroic, self-aggrandizing figurative icons of the late nineteenth century, celebrating national ideals and triumphs, to the anti-heroic, often ironic and self-effacing conceptual installations marking the national ambivalence and uncertainty of late-twentieth-century postmodernism.

In fact, the monument as both institution and concept had already come under withering attack well before the turn of the century. "Away with the monuments!" Nietzsche declared in his blistering attack on a nineteenth-century German historicism that oppressed the living with stultified versions of the past, what Nietzsche called "monumental history."[2] To this cry, a chorus of artists and cultural historians have since added their voices. "The notion of a modern monument is veritably a contradiction in terms," Lewis Mumford wrote in the 1930s. "If it is a monument it is not modern, and if it is modern, it cannot be a monument."[3] Believing that modern architecture invites the perpetuation of life itself, encourages renewal and change, and scorns the illusion of permanence, Mumford wrote, "Stone gives a false sense of continuity, a deceptive assurance of life" (434). Indeed, Mumford went on to suggest that traditionally it seems to have been the least effectual of regimes that chose to compensate for their paucity of achievement in self-aggrandizing stone and mortar (434).

More recently, the late German historian Martin Broszat has suggested that, in their references to history, monuments may not remember events so much as bury them altogether beneath layers of national myths and explanations. As cultural reifications, in this view, monuments reduce or, in Broszat's words, "coarsen" historical understanding as much as they generate it.[4] In another vein, art historian Rosalind Krauss finds that the modernist period produces monuments unable to refer to anything beyond themselves as pure marker or base. After Krauss, critics have asked whether an abstract, self-referential monument can ever commemorate events outside of itself, or whether it only motions endlessly to its own gesture to the past, a commemoration of its essence as dislocated sign.[5]

Still others have argued that rather than preserving public memory, the monument displaces it altogether, supplanting a community's memory-work with its own material form. "The less memory is experienced from the inside," Pierre Nora warns, "the more it exists through its exterior scaffolding and outward signs."[6] In fact, Andreas Huyssen has even suggested that in a contemporary age of mass memory production and consumption, there seems to be an inverse proportion between the memorialization of the past and its contemplation and study.[7]

It is as if, once we assign monumental form to memory, we have to some degree divested ourselves of the obligation to remember. In the eyes of modern critics and artists, the traditional monument's essential stiffness and grandiose pretensions to permanence thus doom it to an archaic, premodern status. Even worse, by insisting that its meaning is as fixed as its place in the landscape, the monument seems oblivious to the essential mutability of all cultural artifacts, the ways the significance of all art evolves over time. In this way, monuments have long sought to provide a naturalizing locus for memory, in which a state's triumphs and martyrs, its ideals and founding myths, seem as naturally true as the landscape in which they stand. These are the monument's sustaining illusions, the principles of its seeming longevity and power. But in fact, as several generations of artists—modern and postmodern alike—have made scathingly clear, neither the monument nor its meaning is really everlasting. Both a monument and its significance are constructed in particular times and places, contingent on the political, historical, and aesthetic realities of the moment.

The early modernist ambivalence toward the monument hardened into outright hostility in the wake of the First World War. Both artists and some governments shared a general distaste for the ways the monument seemed formally to recapitulate the archaic values of a past world now discredited by the slaughter of the War. A new generation of cubists and expressionists, in particular, rejected traditional mimetic and heroic evocations of events, contending that any such remembrance would elevate and mythologize them. In their view, yet another classically proportioned Prometheus would have falsely glorified and thereby redeemed the horrible suffering they were called upon to mourn. The traditional aim of war monuments had been to valorize the suffering in such a way as to justify, even redeem, it historically. But for these artists, such monuments would have been tantamount to betraying not only their experience of the Great War, but also their new reasons for art's existence after the war: to challenge the world's realities, not affirm them.

As Albert Elsen has noted, modern and avant-garde sculptors between the wars in Europe were thus rarely invited to commemorate either the victories or the losses, the battles or the dead of World War I.[8] And if figurative statuary was demanded of them, then only anti-heroic figures would do, as exemplified in the pathetic heroes of Wilhelm Lehmbruck's *Fallen Man* and *Seated Youth* (1917). As true to the artists' inter-war vision as such work may have been, however, neither public nor state seemed ready to abide memorial edifices built on foundations of doubt instead of valor. The pathetic hero was thus condemned by emerging totalitarian regimes in Germany and Russia as defeatist for seeming to embody all that was worth forgetting—not remembering—in the war. Moreover, between the Nazi abhorrence of abstract art—or what it called *entartete Kunst* (decadent art)—and the officially mandated socialist realism of the Soviet Union, the traditional figurative monument even enjoyed something of a rebirth in totalitarian societies. Indeed, only the figurative statuary of officially sanctioned artists, such as Germany's Arno Breker, or styles like the Soviet Union's socialist realism could be trusted to embody the Nazi ideals of "the Aryan race" or the Communist Party's vision of a heroic proletariat. In its consort with two of this century's most egregiously totalitarian regimes, the monument's credibility as public art was thus eroded further still.

Nearly fifty years after the defeat of the Nazi regime, contemporary artists in Germany still have difficulty separating the monument there from its fascist past. German memory-artists are heirs to a double-edged postwar legacy: a deep distrust of monumental forms in light of their systematic exploitation by the Nazis and a profound desire to distinguish their generation from that of the killers through memory.[9] In their eyes, the didactic logic of monuments—their demagogical rigidity and certainty of history—continues to recall too closely traits associated with fascism itself. How else would totalitarian regimes commemorate themselves except through totalitarian art like the monument? Conversely, how better to celebrate the fall of totalitarian regimes than by celebrating the fall of their monuments? A monument against fascism, therefore, would have to be a monument against itself: against the traditionally didactic function of monuments, against their tendency to displace the past they would have us contemplate—and, finally, against the authoritarian propensity in monumental spaces that reduces viewers to passive spectators.

One of the most intriguing results of Germany's memorial conundrum has been the advent of what I would call its "counter-monuments": memorial spaces conceived to challenge the very premise of the monument. For a new generation of German artists, the possibility that memory of events so grave might be reduced to exhibitions of public craftsmanship or cheap pathos remains intolerable. They contemptuously reject the traditional forms of and reasons for public memorial art, those spaces that either console viewers or redeem such tragic events, or indulge in a facile kind of *Wiedergutmachung* or purport to mend the memory of a murdered people. Instead of searing memory into public consciousness, they fear, conventional memorials seal memory off from awareness altogether; instead of embodying memory, they find, memorials may only displace memory. These artists fear rightly that to the extent that we encourage monuments to do our memory-work for us, we become that much more forgetful. They believe, in effect, that the initial impulse to memorialize events like the Holocaust may actually spring from an opposite and equal desire to forget them.

In the pages that follow, I would like both to recall a couple of the counter-monuments I have already discussed at much greater length elsewhere and to add several more recent installations to the discussion. In this way, I hope to both refine and adumbrate the concept of counter-monuments in Germany, the ways they have begun to constitute something akin to a "national form" that pits itself squarely against recent attempts to build a national memorial to the "murdered Jews of Europe" in the center of the country's reunited capital, Berlin. As before, I find that the ongoing debate in Germany has been especially instructive in my own considerations of the monument's future in this decidedly anti-redemptory age.

HORST HOHEISEL'S NEGATIVE FORMS AND MEMORIAL *SPIELEREI*

Some ten years before Horst Hoheisel's proposal to blow up the Brandenburg Tor in Berlin, the city of Kassel had invited artists to consider ways to rescue one of its own destroyed monuments—the Aschrott Brunnen. Originally this had been a twelve-meter-high, neo-gothic pyramid fountain, surrounded by a reflecting pool set in the main town square, set in front of the city hall in 1908. It was designed by the city hall architect, Karl Roth, and funded by a Jewish entrepreneur from Kassel, Sigmund Aschrott. But as a gift from a Jew to the city, it was condemned by the Nazis as the "Jews' Fountain" and so demolished during the night of 8–9 April 1939 by local Nazis, its pieces carted away by city work crews over the next few days. Within weeks, all but the sandstone base

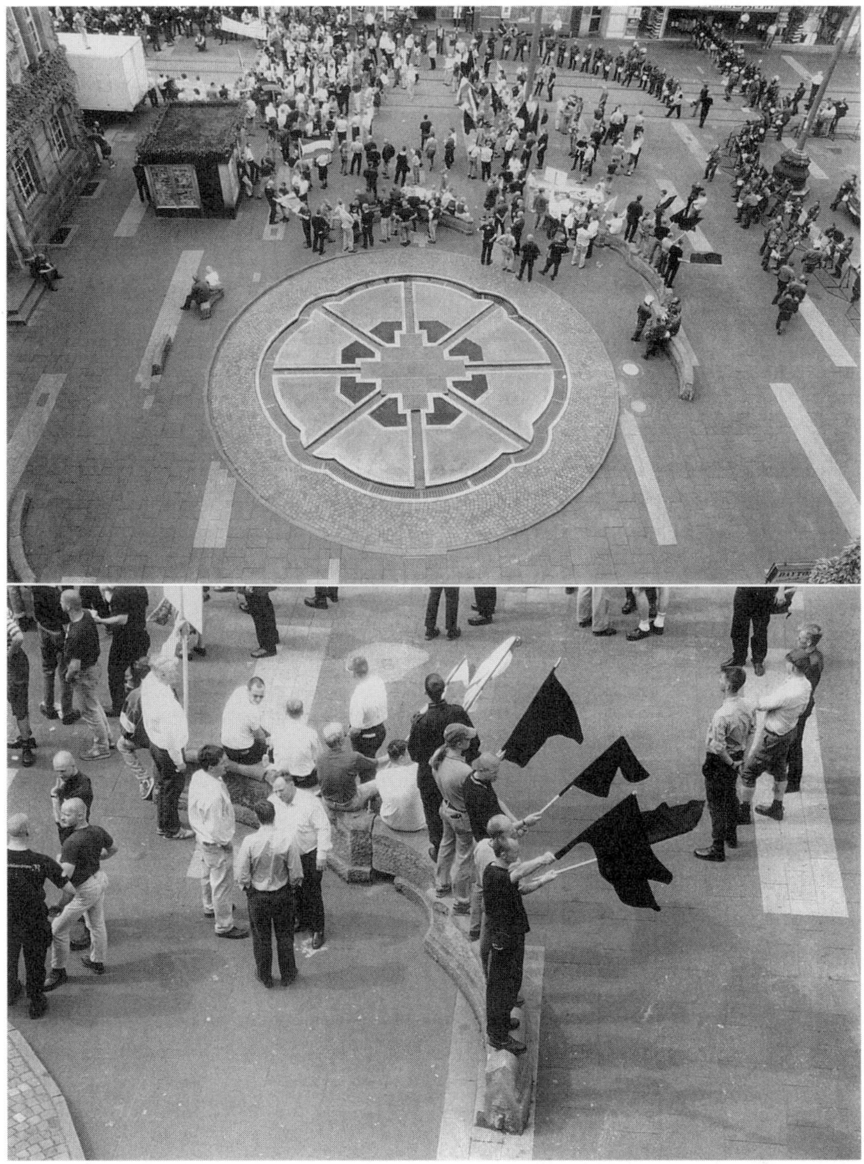

5.3 Horst Hoheisel, *Aschrott Brunnen Monument,* Kassel, 1987 (*above*) and neo-Nazis demonstrating on the monument, 1997 (*below*). Courtesy Horst Hoheisel.

had been cleared away, leaving only a great empty basin in the center of the square. Two years later, the first transport of 463 Kassel Jews departed from the Hauptbahnhof to Riga, followed in the next year by another 3,000, all murdered. In 1943, the city filled in the fountain's basin with soil and planted it over in flowers; local burghers then dubbed it "Aschrott's Grave."

During the growing prosperity of the 1960s, the town turned Aschrott's Grave back into a fountain, sans pyramid. But by then, only a few of the city's oldtimers could recall that its name had ever been Aschrott's anything. When asked what had happened to the original fountain, they replied that, to their best recollection, it had been destroyed by English bombers during the war. In response to this kind of fading memory, the Society for the Rescue of Historical Monuments proposed in 1984 that some form of the fountain and its history be restored—and that it recall all the founders of the city, especially Sigmund Aschrott.

In his proposal for "restoration," Horst Hoheisel decided that neither a preservation of the fountain's remnants nor its mere reconstruction would do. For Hoheisel, even the fragment was a decorative lie, suggesting itself as the remnant of a destruction no one knew very much about. Its pure reconstruction would have been no less offensive: not only would self-congratulatory overtones of *Wiedergutmachung* betray an irreparable violence, but the artist feared that a reconstructed fountain would only encourage the public to forget what had happened to the original. In the best tradition of the counter-monument, therefore, Hoheisel proposed a "negative-form" monument to mark what had once been the Aschrott Fountain in Kassel's City Hall Square.

On being awarded the project, Hoheisel described both the concept and the form underlying his negative-form monument:

> I have designed the new fountain as a mirror image of the old one, sunk beneath the old place in order to rescue the history of this place as a wound and as an open question, to penetrate the consciousness of the Kassel citizens so that such things never happen again. That's why I rebuilt the fountain sculpture as a hollow concrete form after the old plans and for a few weeks displayed it as a resurrected shape at City Hall Square before sinking it, mirror-like, twelve meters deep into the ground water.

The pyramid will be turned into a funnel into whose darkness water runs down. From the "architektonischen Spielerei," as city hall architect Karl Roth called his fountain, a hole emerges which, deep down in the water, creates an image reflecting back the entire shape of the fountain.[10]

How does one remember an absence? In this case, by reproducing it. Quite literally, the negative space of the absent monument will now constitute its phantom shape in the ground. The very absence of the monument will now be preserved in its precisely duplicated negative space. In this way, the monument's reconstruction remains as illusory as memory itself, a reflection on dark waters, a phantasmagoric play of light and image. Taken a step further,

Hoheisel's inverted pyramid might also combine with the remembered shape of its predecessor to form the two interlocking triangles of the Jewish star—present only in the memory of its absence.

In his conceptual formulations, Hoheisel invokes the play of other, darker associations, as well, linking the monument to both the town's Jewish past and a traditional anti-Semitic libel. "The tip of the sculpture points like a thorn down into the water," the artist writes. "Through this coming into contact with the groundwater, the history of the Aschrott Fountain continues not over but under the city." As an emblem of the Holocaust, the history of the Aschrott Fountain becomes the subterranean history of the city. In Hoheisel's figure, the groundwater of German history may well be poisoned—not by the Jews, but by the Germans themselves in their murder of the Jews. By sinking his inverted pyramid into the depths in this way, Hoheisel means to tap this very history. "From the depth of the place," he says, "I have attempted to bring the history of the Aschrott Fountain back up to the surface."

Of course, on a visit to City Hall Square in Kassel, none of this is immediately evident. During construction, before being lowered upside down into the ground, the starkly white negative-form sat upright in the square, a ghostly reminder of the original, now absent, monument. Where there had been an almost forgotten fountain, there is now a bronze tablet with the fountain's image and an inscription detailing what had been there and why it was lost. As we enter the square, we watch as water fills narrow canals at our feet before rushing into a great underground hollow, which grows louder and louder until we finally stand over the Aschrott Brunnen. Only the sound of gushing water suggests the depth of an otherwise invisible memorial, an inverted palimpsest that demands the visitor's reflection. Through an iron grate and thick glass windows we peer into the depths. "With the running water," Hoheisel suggests, "our thoughts can be drawn into the depths of history, and there perhaps we will encounter feelings of loss, of a disturbed place, of lost form."

In fact, as the only standing figures on this flat square, our thoughts rooted in the rushing fountain beneath our feet, we realize that we have become the memorial. "The sunken fountain is not the memorial at all," Hoheisel says. "It is only history turned into a pedestal, an invitation to passersby who stand upon it to search for the memorial in their own heads. For only there is the memorial to be found." Hoheisel has left nothing but the visitors themselves standing in remembrance, left to look inward for memory.

Neo-Nazi demonstrators protesting the Wehrmacht exhibition when it came to Kassel in June 1998 were granted permission by the mayor to hold their protest in the Aschrott Brunnen plaza, in front of Kassel's city hall. Here they stood atop the original fountain's foundation stones, which had been salvaged by Hoheisel to mark the perimeter of the original fountain. Skin-headed and tattooed, wearing black shirts and fatigues, the neo-Nazis waved black flags and taunted a crowd of counter-protestors who had assembled outside police barricades surrounding the neo-Nazis. In a press release, Hoheisel recounted a history of the site, beginning with the donation of the fountain to the city of Kassel by Sigmund Aschrott, through its demolition at the hands of the Nazis in April 1939, the memorial's dedication in 1987, and concluding with the neo-Nazis' demonstration there in June 1998. For Hoheisel, the neo-Nazis' "reclamation" of the site, their triumphal striding atop the ruins of the fountain that their forebears had destroyed in 1939, seemed to bear out his dark hope that this would become a negative center of gravity around which all memory—wanted and unwanted—would now congeal.

By this time, Hoheisel had initiated several other memorial projects, including another in Kassel. In 1991, he turned to the next generation with a more pedagogically inclined project. With permission from the local public schools, the artist visited the classrooms of Kassel with a book, a stone, and a piece of paper. The book was a copy of *Namen und Schicksale der Juden Kassels* [The names and fates of Kassel's Jews]. In his classroom visits, Hoheisel would tell students the story of Kassel's vanished Jewish community, how the Jews had once thrived there, lived in the very houses where these schoolchildren now lived, sat at these same classroom desks. He then asked all the children who knew any Jews to raise their hands. When no hand appeared, Hoheisel would read the story of one of Kassel's deported Jews from his memory book. At the end of his reading, Hoheisel invited each of the students to research the life of one of Kassel's deported Jews: where they had lived and how, who their families were, how old they were, what they had looked like. He asked them to visit formerly Jewish neighborhoods and get to know the German neighbors of Kassel's deported Jews.

After this, students were asked to write short narratives describing the lives and deaths of their subjects, wrap these narratives around cobblestones, and deposit them in one of the archival bins the artist had provided to every school. After several dozen such classroom visits, the bins had begun to overflow and new ones were furnished. In time, all of these bins were transported to Kassel's Hauptbahnhof, where they were stacked on the rail platform whence Kassel's Jews were deported. It is now a permanent installation, what the artist calls his *Denk-Stein Sammlung* [memorial stone archive].

This memorial cairn—a witness-pile of stones—marks both the site of deportation and the community's education about its murdered Jews, their absence now marked by the still evolving memorial. Combining narrative and stone in this way, the artist and students have thus adopted the most Jewish of memorial forms as their own, thereby enlarging their memorial lexicon to include that of the absent people they would now recall. After all, only they are now left to write the epitaph of the missing Jews, known and emblematized primarily by their absence, the void they have left behind.

Similarly, when invited by the director of the Buchenwald Museum, Volkhard Knigge, shortly after its post-reunification revisions to memorialize the first monument to liberation erected by the camp's former inmates in April 1945, Hoheisel proposed not a resurrection of the original monument but a "living" alternative. In collaboration with architect Andreas Knitz, the artist designed a concrete slab with the names of fifty-one national groups victimized here and engraved it with the initials K.L.B. (for *Konzentrationslager Buchenwald*), which had marked the prisoners' original wooden memorial obelisk. And as that obelisk had been constructed out of pieces of the barracks torn down by their former inmates—i.e., it had been enlivened by the prisoners' own hands—Hoheisel built into his memorial slab of concrete a radiant heating system to bring it to a constant 98.6 degrees Fahrenheit (37 degrees Celsius) that might suggest the body heat of those whose memory it would now enshrine. Visitors almost always kneel to touch the slab, something they would not do if it were cold stone, and are touched in turn by the human warmth embodied here. Dedicated in April 1995, on the fiftieth anniversary of the prisoners' own memorial (which lasted only two months), this warm memorial reminds visitors of the memory of actual victims that has preceded their own, subsequent memory of this time. In winter, with snow covering the rest of the ground, this slab is always clear, an all-season marker for the site of the prisoners' original attempt to commemorate the crimes against them.

CHRISTIAN BOLTANSKI, MICHA ULLMAN, RACHEL WHITEREAD

On a walk he was taking in Berlin's former Jewish Quarter, Christian Boltanski was drawn curiously to the occasional gaps and vacant lots between buildings. On inquiring, he found that the building at 15 and 16 Grosse Hamburgerstrasse had been destroyed by Allied bombing in 1945 and never rebuilt. In a project called *Missing House* that he mounted for the exhibition *Die Endlichkeit der Freiheit* in October 1990, the artist therefore set to work retracing the lives of all the people who had lived in this "missing house" between 1930 and 1945—both the Jewish Germans who had been deported and the non-Jewish Germans who had been given their home.[11]

He found family photographs and letters, children's drawings, ration tickets, and other fragments of these lives, photocopied them, and put them all together with maps of the neighborhood in archival boxes. At this point, he had nameplates hung on the white-plastered wall of the building next door to identify the now missing inhabitants, Jews and non-Jews—leaving the lot itself empty. His *Missing House* project thus became emblematic for Boltanski of the missing Jews who had once inhabited it; as its void invited him to fill it with memory, he hoped it would incite others to memory as well.

In two other installations, one realized and the other as yet only proposed, artists Micha Ullman and Rachel Whiteread have also turned to both bookish themes and negative spaces in order to represent the void left behind by the "people of the book." In order to commemorate the infamous Nazi book burning of 10 May 1933, the city of Berlin invited Micha Ullman, an Israeli-born conceptual and installation artist, to design a monument for Berlin's Bebelplatz. (See chapter 15, figure 15.5.) Today, the cobblestone expanse of the Bebelplatz is still empty of all forms except for the figures of people who stand there and peer down through a ground-level window into the ghostly-white, underground room of empty shelves Ullman has installed. A steel tablet set into the stones simply recalls that this was the site of some of the most notorious book burnings and quotes Heinrich Heine's famously prescient words, "Where books are burned, so one day will people be burned as well." But the shelves are still empty, unreplenished, and it is the absence of both people and books that is marked here in yet one more empty memorial pocket.

Indeed, the English sculptor Rachel Whiteread has proposed casting the very spaces between and around books as the memorial figure by which Austria's missing Jews would be recalled in Vienna's Judenplatz. In a 1996 competition initiated by Nazi-hunter Simon Wiesenthal, a distinguished jury of experts appointed by the city chose a brilliant, if abstract and controversial, design by the Turner Award–winning artist. Her winning proposal for Vienna's official Holocaust memorial—the positive cast of the space around books in an anonymous library, the interior turned inside out—thus extends her sculptural predilection for solidifying the spaces over, under, and around everyday objects, even as it makes the book itself her central memorial motif. (See chapter 15, figures 15.1, 15.2, 15.3, and 15.7.) But even here, it is not the book per se that constitutes her now displaced object of memory, but the literal space between the book and us. For, as others have already noted, Whiteread's work since 1988 has made brilliantly palpable the notion that materiality can also be an index of absence: whether it is the ghostly apparition of the filled-in space of a now-demolished row house in London (*House* launched Whiteread to international prominence), or the proposed cast of the empty space between the book-leaves and the wall in a full-size library, Whiteread makes the absence of an original object her work's defining preoccupation.[12] Like other artists of her generation, Rachel Whiteread is preoccupied less with the Holocaust's images of destruction and more with the terrible void this destruction left behind.

Given this thematic edge in all her work, it is not surprising that Whiteread was one of nine artists and architects initially invited to submit proposals for a Holocaust memorial in Vienna. Other invitees included the Russian installation artist Ilya Kabakov, the Israeli architect Zvi Hecker, and the American architect Peter Eisenman. As proposed, Whiteread's cast of a library turned inside out measures ten meters by seven, is almost four meters high, and resembles a solid white cube. Its outer surface would consist entirely of the roughly textured negative space next to the edges of book leaves. On the front wall facing onto the square there would be a double-wing door, also cast inside out and inaccessible. In its formalization of absence on the one hand and of books on the other, it found an enthusiastic reception among a jury looking for a design that "would combine dignity with reserve and spark an esthetic dialogue with the past in a place that is replete with history."[13] Despite the jury's unanimous decision to award Whiteread's design first place and to begin its realization immediately, the esthetic dialogue it very successfully sparked in this place so "replete with history" eventually paralyzed the entire memorial process.

For, like many such sites in Vienna, the Judenplatz was layered with the invisible memory of numerous anti-Semitic persecutions—a synagogue was torched here in a 1421 pogrom, and hundreds of Jews died in the autos-da-fé that followed. Though Whiteread's design had left room at the site for a window into the archaeological excavation of this buried past, the shopkeepers on the Judenplatz preferred that these digs into an ancient past also be left to stand for the more recent murder of Austrian Jews as well. And although their anti-Whiteread petition, with two thousand signatures, refers only to the lost parking and potential for lost revenue they fear this "giant colossus" will cause, they may also have feared the loss of their own Christian memory of this past. For to date, the sole memorial to this medieval massacre was to be found in a Catholic mural and inscription on a baroque facade overlooking the site of the lost synagogue. Alongside an image of Christ being baptized in the River Jordan, an inscription reads (in Latin): "The flame of hate arose in 1421, raged through the entire city, and punished the terrible crimes of the Hebrew dogs." In the end, the reintroduction into this square of a specifically Jewish narrative may have been just as undesirable for the local Viennese as the loss of parking places.

In fact, unlike Germany's near obsession with its Nazi past, Austria's relationship to its wartime past has remained decorously submerged, politely out of sight. Austria (with the tacit encouragement of its American and Soviet occupiers) practically founded itself on the self-serving myth that it was Hitler's first victim. That some 50 percent of the Nazi SS was composed of Austrians, or that Hitler himself was Austrian-born, was never denied. But these historical facts also never found a place in Austria's carefully constructed postwar persona. In a city that seemed to have little national reason for remembering the murder of its Jews, the entire memorial project was soon engulfed by aesthetic and political Sturm und Drang, and the vociferous arguments against the winning design brought the process to a grinding halt. Maligned and demoralized, Whiteread soon lost her stomach for the fight and resigned herself, she told me, to the likelihood that her memorial would never be built.

But then suddenly, in early 1998, the city of Vienna announced that a compromise had been found that would allow Whiteread's memorial to be built after all. By moving the great cube one meter within the plaza itself, the city found that it could make room for both the excavations of the 1421 pogrom and the new memorial to Vienna's more recently murdered Jews. Nonetheless, the debate in Austria has remained curiously displaced and sublimated. Lost in the discussion were the words one of the jurors—Robert Storr, a curator at New York's Museum of Modern Art—had used to describe what made Whiteread's work so appropriate in the first place. "Rather than a tomb or cenotaph," Storr wrote,

> Whiteread's work is the solid shape of an intangible absence—of a gap in a nation's identity, and a hollow at a city's heart. Using an aesthetic language that speaks simultaneously to tradition and to the future, Whiteread in this way respectfully symbolizes a world whose irrevocable disappearance can never be wholly grasped by those who did not experience it, but whose most lasting monuments are the books written by Austrian Jews before, during and in the aftermath of the catastrophe brought down on them.[14]

Rather than monumentalizing only the moment of destruction itself, Whiteread's design would recall that which made the "people of the book" a people: their shared relationship to the past through the book. For it was this shared relationship to a remembered past through the book that bound Jews together, and it was the book that provided the site for this relationship.

Though Whiteread is not Jewish, she has—in good Jewish fashion—cast not a human form but a sign of humanity, gesturing silently to the acts of reading, writing, and memory that had once constituted this people as a people. Now that Vienna has chosen to go ahead with Whiteread's allusive and rigorously intellectual design, both the city and its Jewish community should be congratulated: the Jewish community for the courage and audacity of its aesthetic convictions, and the city for finally bringing boldly to the surface its previously subterranean shame.

RENATA STIH AND FRIEDER SCHNOCK

As did the American artist Shimon Attie during his stay in Berlin, the Berlin artists Renata Stih and Frieder Schnock find their city essentially haunted by its own lying beauty, its most placid and charming neighborhoods seemingly oblivious of and indifferent to the all-too-orderly destruction of their Jewish communities during the war. Tree-lined and with its nineteenth-century buildings relatively unscathed by Allied bombs during the war, the Bayerische Viertel (Bavarian Quarter) of Berlin's Schoenberg district is particularly peaceful these days and off the tourist track. It was home to some sixteen thousand German Jews before the war, many of them professional and well-to-do, including at different times Albert Einstein and Hannah Arendt. But with nary a sign of the war's destruction in evidence, nothing in the neighborhood after the war pointed to the absence of its escaped, deported, and murdered Jewish denizens.

Haunted precisely by this absence of signs, and skeptical of the traditional memorial's tendency to gather what they thought should be pervasive memory into a single spot, Renata Stih and Frieder Schnock won a 1993 competition for a memorial to the neighborhood's murdered Jews with a proposal to mount eighty signposts on the corners, streets, and sidewalks in and around the Bayerische Platz. Each would include a simple image of an everyday object on one side and a short text on the other, excerpted from Germany's anti-Jewish laws of the 1930s and 1940s. On one side of such a sign, pedestrians would see a hand-drawn sidewalk hopscotch pattern, and on the other its accompanying text: "Arischen und nichtarischen Kindern wird das Spielen miteinander untersagt" [Aryan and non-Aryan children are not allowed to play together] (1938). Or a simple red park bench on a green lawn: "Juden durfen am Bayerischen Platz nur die gelb markierten Sitzbanke benutzen" [On the Bavarian Place, Jews may sit only on yellow park benches] (1939). Or a pair of swimming trunks: "Berliner Bademanstalten und Schwimmbader durfen von Juden nicht betreten werden" [Baths and swimming pools in Berlin are closed to Jews] (3 December 1938). A black and white rotary telephone dial: "Telefonanschlusse von Juden werden von der Post gekundigt" [Telephone lines to Jewish households will be cut off] (29 July 1940).[15]

With the approval of the Berlin Senate, which had sponsored the memorial competition, the artists put their signs up on lampposts throughout the quarter without announcement, provoking a flurry of complaints and calls to the police that neo-Nazis had invaded the neighborhood with anti-Semitic signs. Thus reassured that the public had taken notice, the artists pointed out that these same laws had been posted and announced no less publicly at the time—but had provoked no such response by Germans then. At least part of the artists' point was that the laws then were no less public than the memory of them now. Indeed, one sign with the image of a file even reminds local residents that "All files dealing with anti-Semitic activities [were] to be destroyed" (16 February 1945); and another image, of interlocking Olympic rings, recalls that "Anti-Semitic signs in Berlin [were] temporarily removed for the 1936 Olympic Games." That is, for the artists, even the absence of signs was an extension of the crime itself. Stih and Schnock recognize here that the Nazi persecution of the Jews was designed to be, after all, a self-consuming Holocaust, a self-effacing crime.

The only "signs" of Jewish life in this once-Jewish neighborhood are now the posted laws that paved the way for the Jews' deportation and murder. As part of the cityscape, these images and texts would "infiltrate the daily lives of Berliners," Stih has explained, no less than the publicly posted laws curtailed

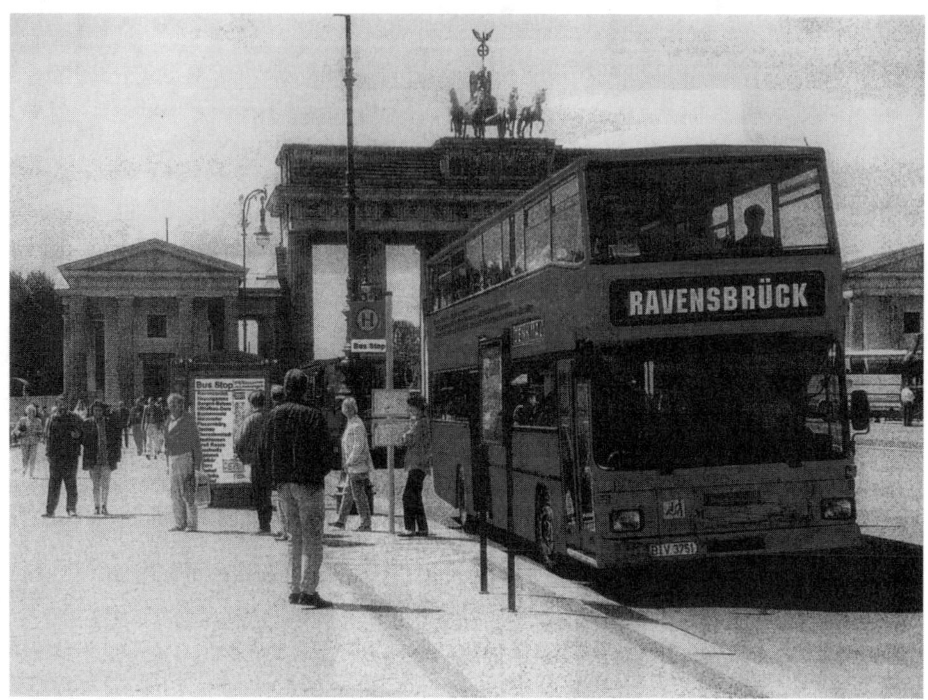

5.4 Renata Stih and Frieder Schnock, *Bus Stop—The Non-monument,* proposed for Berlin's *Memorial for the Murdered Jews of Europe,* 1995. Courtesy Renata Stih and Frieder Schnock.

the daily lives of Jews between 1933 and 1945. And by posting these signs separately, forcing pedestrians to happen upon them one or two at a time, the artists can show how the laws incrementally "removed Jews from the social realm," from the protection of law. These "places of remembrance" would remind local citizens that the murder of the neighborhood's Jews did not happen overnight, in a fell swoop, but over time—and with the tacit acknowledgment of their neighbors. Where past citizens once navigated their lives according to these laws, present citizens would now navigate their lives according to the memory of such laws.

In keeping with their vision of decentralized memory, of integrating memory of the Holocaust into the rhythms of everyday life, Stih and Schnock proposed an audacious "non-monument" to the 1995 international competition for Germany's national memorial to Europe's murdered Jews. Taking as their premise the essential impossibility and undesirability of a "final memorial" to commemorate the Nazis' "final solution" to the Jewish question, they submitted a design called *Bus Stop—The Non-monument.* Rather than filling the space of nearly twenty thousand square meters between the Brandenburger Tor and Potsdamer Platz in Berlin designated for the national memorial, they would keep it desolate as a reminder of the destruction brought upon Berlin by the Nazis, and turn it into an open-air bus terminal for coaches departing for and returning from regularly scheduled visits to several dozen concentration camps and other sites of destruction throughout Europe. "There is not one single bus stop in central Berlin from which you can take buses to the places listed in this schedule," the artists tell us in a forward to their project's precis.[16] Therefore, they call for a single place where visitors can board a bright red bus at a regularly scheduled hour for nonstop rides to visit both well-known sites such as Auschwitz, Treblinka, and Dachau and the lesser known massacre sites in the east, such as Vitebsk and Trawniki. A central steel and glass waiting hall flanking the 130-meter-long boarding platform would provide travelers with computer-generated histories and bibliographies of all the sites listed at the terminal, a kind of memorial travel office that would extol history and memory over the usual forgetfulness, the attempt at forced amnesia, that drives leisure vacations. Buses would leave hourly for sites within Berlin and daily for sites outside the city. Not so much a "central memorial" as a "centrifugal" memorial, *Bus Stop* would thus send visitors out in all directions into a European-wide matrix of memorial sites.

With twenty-eight buses making local Berlin runs every hour, and another sixty or so branching out daily for sites throughout Germany and Europe, this would also be, quite literally, a mobile memorial that would paint its entire matrix of routes with memory. By becoming such a part of everyday life in Berlin, these red buses emblazoned with destinations like Buchenwald and Sobibor will, the artists hope, remind everyone of the "thorough integration of the terror machinery [itself] into everyday life in Germany from 1933 to 1945" (6). At night the rows of parked and waiting buses, with their destinations illuminated, become a kind of "light-sculpture" that dissolves at the break of day into a moving mass to reflect what Bernd Nicolai has called "the busy banality of horror."[17]

Possibly the most popularly acclaimed of all entries in the 1995 competition, *Bus Stop* placed eleventh among the 528 submissions from around the world. Organizers at the time, intent on concentrating memory of Europe's murdered Jews into a single site in Berlin, felt that *Bus Stop* dispersed memory too far and wide, implicitly spreading the blame for the murder onto the regimes of conquered nations during the war. In response, the artists self-published a 128-page "Fahrplan," or time-table, of actual departure times of buses, trains, and planes in the public transportation sector for all the sites in their original memorial plan. Unlike the conventional time-table, however, it includes concise histories of the sites themselves, accompanying the hours of departure and return. The schedule to Lodz tells us both how to get there and how many Jews lived there before the war, how the ghetto there was established, when it was liquidated, how the deported Jews were murdered, and who did the killing. Similar histories accompany schedules to Lublin, Stutthof, Riga, Drancy, Babi Yar, and the other ninety or so destinations, including dozens in Germany alone.

Like other counter-memorials, *Bus Stop* would, in effect, return the burden of memory to visitors themselves by forcing them into an active role. Though the bus rides might recall the deportations themselves, these would be deportations not to actual history but to memory itself. Indeed, the ride to and from the sites of destruction would constitute the memory-act, thereby reminding visitors that memory can be a kind of transport through space in an ongoing present moment, as well as a transport through time itself. In this way, the memorial remains a process, not an answer, a place that provides time for memorial reflection, contemplation, and learning between departing and arriving.

For an American watching Germany's memorial culture come to terms with the Holocaust, the conceptual torment implied by the counter-monument holds immense appeal. As provocative and difficult as it may be, no other memorial form seems to embody both the German memorial dilemma and the limitations of the traditional monument so well. The most important "space of memory" for these artists has not been that in the ground or above it, but that space between the memorial and the viewers, between the viewers and their own memory: the place of the memorial in the viewer's mind, heart, and conscience. To this end, they have attempted to embody the ambiguity and difficulty of Holocaust memorialization in Germany in conceptual, sculptural, and architectural forms that would return the burden of memory to those who come looking for it. Rather than creating self-contained sites of memory, detached from our daily lives, these artists would force both visitors and local citizens to look within themselves for memory, at their actions and motives for memory within these spaces. In the cases of disappearing, invisible, and otherwise "counter" monuments, they have attempted to build into these spaces the capacity for changing memory, places where every new generation will find its own significance in this past.

In the end, the counter-monument reminds us that the best German memorial to the fascist era and its victims may not be a single memorial at all, but simply the never-to-be-resolved debate over which kind of memory to preserve, how to do it, in whose name, and to what end. That is, what are the consequences of such memory? How do Germans respond to current persecutions of foreigners in their midst in light of their memory of the Third Reich and its crimes? Instead of a fixed sculptural or architectural icon for Holocaust memory in Germany, the debate itself—perpetually unresolved amid ever-changing conditions—might now be enshrined.

The status of monuments in the twentieth century remains double-edged and is fraught with an essential tension: outside of those nations with totalitarian pasts, the public and governmental hunger for traditional, self-aggrandizing monuments is matched only by contemporary artists' skepticism about the monument. As a result, even as monuments continue to be commissioned and designed by governments and public agencies eager to assign singular meaning to complicated events and people, artists increasingly plant in them the seeds of self-doubt and impermanence. The state's need for monuments is acknowledged, even as the traditional forms and functions of monuments are increasingly challenged. Monuments at the end of the twentieth century are thus born resisting the very premises of their birth. As a result, the monument has increasingly become the site of contested and competing meanings, more likely the site of cultural conflict than of shared national values and ideals.

Notes

This essay is adapted from James E. Young, *At Memory's Edge: After-images of the Holocaust in Contemporary Art and Architecture* (New Haven, Conn.: Yale University Press, 2000). In it, I elaborate and expand on themes I first explored in "The Counter-monument: Memory against Itself in Germany Today," *Critical Inquiry* 18 (winter 1992): 267–296. Also see James E. Young, *The Texture of Memory: Holocaust Memorials and Meaning* (New Haven, Conn.: Yale University Press, 1993), 27–48.

1. For a record of this competition, see *Denkmal für die ermordeten Juden Europas: künstlerischer Wettbewerb: Kurzdokumentation* (Berlin: Senatsverwaltung für Bau- und Wohnungswesen, 1995). For a collection of essays arguing against building this monument, see *Der Wettbewerb für das "Denkmal für die ermordeten Juden Europas": Eine Streitschrift* (Berlin: Verlag der Kunst/Neue Gesellschaft für bildende Kunst, 1995).

On his proposal to blow up the Brandenburger Tor, see Horst Hoheisel, "Aschrott Brunnen—Denk-Stein-Sammlung—Brandenburger Tor—Buchenwald. Vier Erinnerungsversuche," in *Shoah—Formen der Erinnerung: Geschichte, Philosophie, Literatur, Kunst,* ed. Nicolas Berg, Jess Jochimsen, and Bernd Stiegler (Munich: Wilhelm Fink, 1996), 253–266.

2. Friedrich Nietzsche, *The Use and Abuse of History,* trans. Adrian Collins (New York: Macmillan, 1985), 14–17.

3. Lewis Mumford, *The Culture of Cities* (New York: Harcourt, Brace, 1938), 438.

4. Martin Broszat, "Plea for a Historicization of National Socialism," in *Reworking the Past: Hitler, the Holocaust, and the Historians' Debate,* ed. Peter Baldwin (Boston: Beacon, 1990), 129.

5. Rosalind E. Krauss, *The Originality of the Avant-Garde and Other Modernist Myths* (Cambridge, Mass.: MIT Press, 1988), 280.

6. Pierre Nora, "Between Memory and History: *Les Lieux de Mémoire,*" trans. Marc Rousebush, *Representations,* no. 26 (1989): 13. Reprinted from Pierre Nora, "Entre mémoire et histoire," *Les lieux de mémoire,* vol. 1, *La republique* (Paris: Gallimard, 1984), xxvi.

7. Andreas Huyssen, "Monument and Memory in a Postmodern Age," in *The Art of Memory: Holocaust Memorials in History,* ed. James E. Young (Munich: Prestel, 1994), 11. Also see Huyssen's elaboration of this essay in his *Twilight Memories: Marking Time in a Culture of Amnesia* (New York: Routledge, 1995), 249–260.

8. Albert E. Elsen, *Modern European Sculpture, 1918–1945: Unknown Beings and Other Realities* (New York: Braziller, 1979), 122–125.

9. For elaboration of this theme, see Matthias Winzen, "The Need for Public Representation and the Burden of the German Past," *Art Journal* 48 (winter 1989): 309–314.

10. From Horst Hoheisel, "Rathaus-Platz-Wunde," in *Aschrott Brunnen: Offene Wunde der Stadtgeschichte*. Subsequent quotations from Hoheisel on this memorial are drawn from this booklet.

11. See Andreas Fischer and Michael Glameier, eds., *The Missing House* (Berlin: Berliner Kunstlerprogram des DAAD für das Heimatmuseum Berlin-Mitte, 1990).

12. See Fiona Bradley, ed., *Rachel Whiteread: Shedding Life* (London: Tate Gallery Publishing, 1996), 8. Other essays in this exhibition catalogue for the retrospective of Rachel Whiteread's work at the Tate-Liverpool Gallery—by Stuart Morgan, Bartomeu Mari, Rosalind Krauss, and Michael Tarantino—also explore various aspects of the sculptor's gift for making absence present.

13. *Judenplatz Wien 1996: Wettbewerb, Mahnmal, und Gedenkstätte für die jüdischen Opfer des Naziregimes in Österreich, 1938–1945* (Vienna: Stadt Wien/Kunsthalle Wien, 1996), 94.

14. *Judenplatz Wien 1996,* 109.

15. See Renata Stih and F. Schnock, *Arbeitsbuch für ein Denkmal in Berlin: Orte des Erinnerns im Bayerischen Viertel—Ausgrenzung und Entrechtung, Vertreibung, Deportation, und Ermordung von Berlin Juden in den Jahren 1933 bis 1945* (Berlin: Gatza, 1993).

16. Renata Stih and Frieder Schnock, *Bus Stop Fahrplan* (Berlin: Neue Gesellschaft für bildende Kunst, 1995), 6.

17. Bernd Nicolai, "Bus Stop—The Non-monument: On the Impossibility of a final Memorial to the Murdered Jews of Europe," unpaginated brochure on the project published by Renata Stih and Frieder Schnock.

Part II

Personal Responses and Familial Legacies

6 Material Memory

Holocaust Testimony in Post-Holocaust Art

MARIANNE HIRSCH AND SUSAN RUBIN SULEIMAN

At the end of the first volume of Art Spiegelman's *Maus: A Survivor's Tale,* Vladek (the father) reaches the point in his narrative where he and his wife, Anja, are separated after arriving at Auschwitz. "This is where Mom's diaries will be especially useful," responds his son, Artie, who has been recording his father's testimony over a number of years. "They'll give me some idea of what she went through while you were apart." Vladek is evasive: "I can tell you. She went through the same what me: terrible." Not satisfied, Artie insists on searching for his mother's diaries: he has been asking his father to find them ever since he began his project, years after his mother committed suicide. Now, suddenly, Vladek remembers that he will never locate the diaries: "Those notebooks and other really nice things of mother one time I had a very bad day . . . and all of these things I destroyed. . . . These papers had too many memories. So I burned them." Artie's response ends the book: "Murderer."[1]

By burning the mother's notebooks and "other really nice things," Vladek has destroyed the material remains of his wife's life and therefore committed a kind of murder. Paradoxically, it was because the objects associated with Anja carried too many memories that Vladek burned them, as if he could burn them out of his own mind; and it was because they carried memories that Artie sought them. The mother's notebooks not only recorded her experiences in her own voice, the way Vladek's taped stories did, they also carried the material trace of her presence, her handwriting—literally, her traces. Like the other objects that had belonged to her (and that Vladek also burned), the notebooks were an index pointing to her physical existence. The term "index" comes from the American semiotician Charles Sanders Peirce, who defines three possible relations between a sign and what it stands for: the arbitrary relation that characterizes the symbol or linguistic sign; the relation of contiguity or cause and effect that defines the index; and the relation of resemblance, defining the icon.[2] Material traces like the mother's notebooks are indexical: the notebooks were "contiguous" to the mother while she lived, and can signify her ("stand in" for her) after her death. For Artie, they would have provided the mother's story to complement the father's; but they might also have functioned as a material connection to the mother's body. Whence Artie's accusation of murder.

As *Maus* makes stunningly clear, the post-Holocaust art of children of survivors both seeks and depends on material connections to the experience of the parents' generation. Despite the numerous distancing devices that shape Spiegelman's book—the graphic medium and commix form, the adaptation of the animal fable, the insistent emphasis on metanarrative commentary—there is an equally strong reliance on documentary connections to the real. Maps, precise descriptions of places and people, taped interviews (made available in edited form on the CD-ROM version), the rendering of the father's foreign accent, and above all the three photographs that jump out of the graphic visual field and suddenly provide concrete, indexical images of the mother, father, and dead brother all testify to the pull of such material connections. It's as though memory, and therefore the very possibility of narrative reconstruction and transmission, really were lodged in objects.

This connection appears to be as compelling for ordinary readers and viewers as it is for children of Holocaust survivors. It is not an accident that the experience so often cited by visitors to the U.S. Holocaust Memorial Museum as the most powerful is that of standing inside the railway car which had actually been used in the transports to the camps, or in front of the piles of shoes taken from victims. Post-Holocaust artists are necessarily confronted with the raw power of "the thing itself" as well as with the artistic imperative to transform, symbolize, and mediate. Many of their works are expressions of this double confrontation.

It would appear that the book, eminently lodged in the symbolic field of writing, would be most resistant to the incorporation of material objects. But the genre of the artist's book, in which the materiality of the object is an essential element, both emphasizes and offers the possibility of overcoming the limitations of the book form.[3] *Maus* is an outstanding example of the innovative potential of the post-Holocaust artist's book. However, as an artist's book it is unusual in its reproducibility: Spiegelman specifically sought to create a work that would have the widest possible accessibility and distribution. More in the tradition of the limited-edition work is Tatana Kellner's *Fifty Years of Silence,* based on the written testimonies of Kellner's parents, survivors of Auschwitz. Like Spiegelman's, Kellner's work arises out of a collaboration between survivor-parents—here both mother and father are included—and artist-child. It also poses, with shocking concreteness, the problematic relations that exist in both written testimony and visual figuration among material object, indexical trace, and symbolic expression.

THE APPROACH

The two of us come to *Fifty Years of Silence* from somewhat different vantage points, which tally significantly with the double nature and collaborative quality of this work. Susan Suleiman is a child survivor of the Holocaust. Born in 1939 in Budapest, she traces her earliest memories to the last year of the war in Hungary (1944–45), also the year of the Holocaust for Hungarian Jews. She and her parents survived with false identification papers. In her previous work, she has analyzed Holocaust memoirs by both child survivors and adult Hungarian survivors, and proposed the concept of "autobiographical reading" to account for the phenomenon of "reading another's story as if it were one's own."[4]

Marianne Hirsch, born in 1949 in Romania, is the daughter of Jews who survived the war under the Romanian pro-Nazi regime. Her work has focused on writing and artwork by those who have no direct memory of the Holocaust but whose lives are nevertheless intimately marked by stories they have not themselves experienced. She has proposed the concept of "postmemory" for this phenomenon of transmitted, borrowed or secondary, second-generation memory.[5] We thus read *Fifty Years of Silence* both as survivor memoirs and as the postmemorial construction of a child of survivors, offering a discourse to the second generation.

Fifty Years of Silence. Two books. They face each other mounted on lateral shelves in an exhibit at Boston's Photographic Resource Center in the spring of 1995. The exhibit, "Between Spectacle and Silence: The Holocaust in Contemporary Photography," includes art installations that evoke the memory of the Holocaust through different media: reconstructed objects in glass cases, layered photographic works, plaster installations, paintings, graphic texts. In a corner, Tatana Kellner's two books seem rather modest. As we walk through the exhibit together, trying to take in the whole before stopping to study individual works, our eyes come to rest, simultaneously, on the covers of Kellner's work. We do not yet know that these are books: all we take in, in a flash of recognition, are two pink arms protruding from two rectangular white surfaces. Cut off below the elbow, the arms and hands, fingers spread out, fill holes gouged into the center of what we now see are two white books whose texts unfold around the protrusions.

What makes the arms so arresting is not just the pink, too pink, molded shapes but the numbers displayed at the center of each forearm: B11226 on the right, 71125 on the left. As we walk up to the books and begin slowly to turn the pages, to scan the text and look at the pictures on the alternating translucent and opaque pages of each book, the stationary arms become all the more apparent; the tattoos, applied with seeming haste, at a slant, a bit wobbly, dominate the visual field. No doubt they evoke different associations in us, but for us as for most other viewers, they are marks of victimization and desubjectification. The number tattoo has become the predominant, perhaps even the unique, signifier of the Holocaust.[6]

"I have known since I was a child," we read on the first page, "that my parents were concentration camp survivors, since both of them had a number tattooed on their left arm. I used to spend a lot of time studying their tattoos, wondering what it must have been like. My mother never talked about her experiences. My father only talked about it when he was scolding us, especially about eating everything on our plates. Once when I was at his side on an after-dinner walk, he told a friend the stories of the medical experiments performed on him and the ten-day transport when people began devouring each other. I think he must have forgotten I was there. I didn't inquire any further for fear of hurting him."[7]

Fifty Years of Silence is the work of a child of survivors, born in postwar Prague. As Tatana Kellner goes on to say in the introductory page that appears in both books, she grew up in the city from where her parents had been deported and to which they returned after the camps. She and her brother and sister heard few stories and were left to wonder and speculate about their parents' wartime experiences. They grew up surrounded by anti-Semitism and suspicion, and they learned to dissimulate their Jewish identity: "The less we knew, the less we had to tell." Nevertheless, most of their parents' close friends were other camp survivors. Years later, after emigrating to the United States, after becoming an artist and having her first show, Kellner invited her parents to help her with a work that would be based on their reminiscences of the war. She wanted to tape their stories, but they preferred to write them for her in Czech and she undertook to translate their texts into English. "Except for questions I had in terms of accuracy, this is still not something we can talk about," she tells us when we ask her about her work in preparation for this essay.

The work—the two books that constitute *Fifty Years of Silence*—is the product of a collaboration between the parents, who read and critiqued each other's drafts, and the daughter who translated and edited them. Kellner constructed the templates (large format, with a hole in the middle) on which the parents handwrote their final Czech text. In the finished work, the parents' handwritten

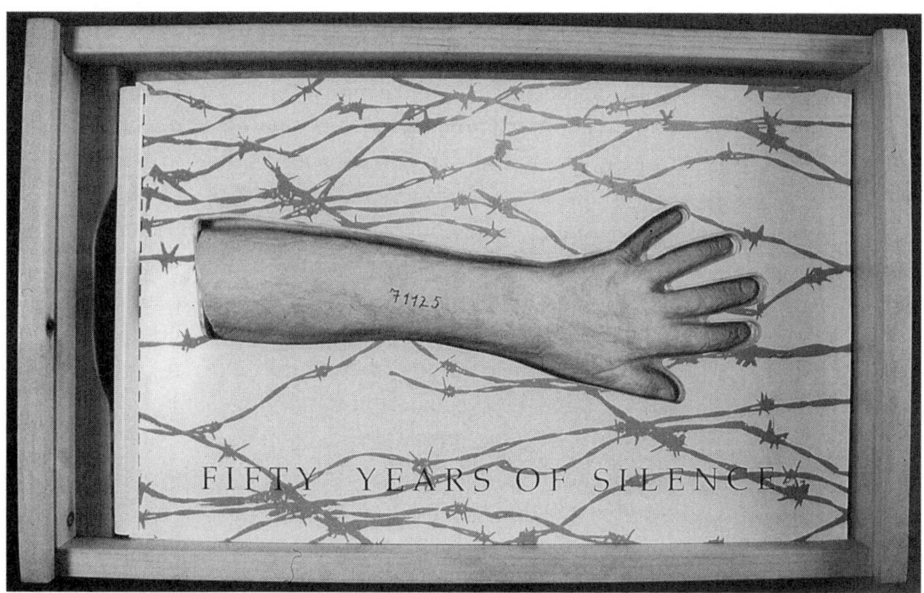

6.1 Cover, The Mother's Book. This and the other illustrations in this chapter are from Tatana Kellner, *71125: Fifty Years of Silence* and *B-11226: Fifty Years of Silence*, Rosendale Women's Studio Workshop, 1992, 1994. Used by permission of the artist.

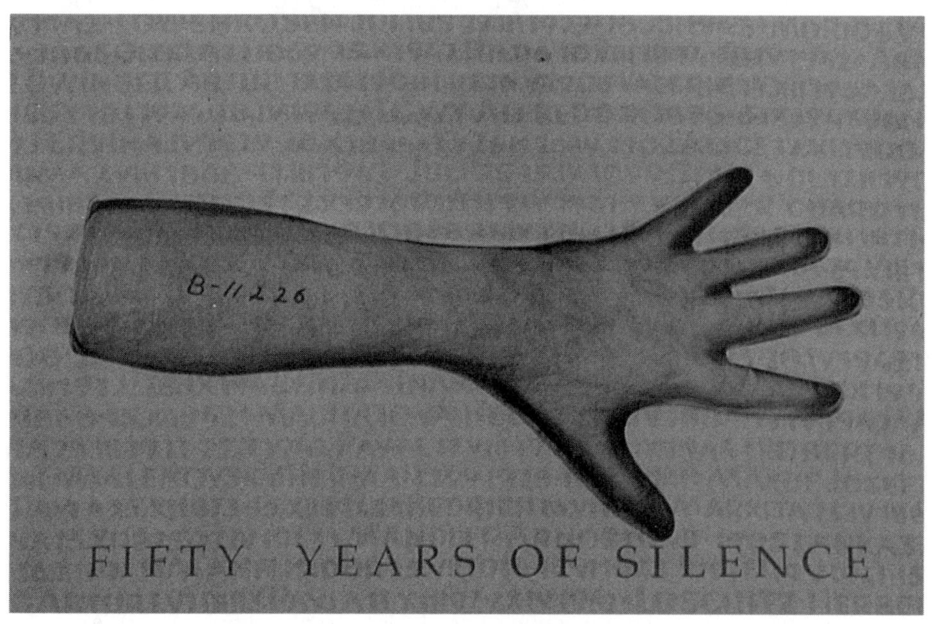

6.2 Cover, The Father's Book.

text, in blue ink on translucent pages, faces its typewritten translation (on opaque white pages) by the daughter. Superimposed on both versions are silkscreened photographs. Some were taken recently by Kellner on a trip to Prague and Auschwitz, and are mostly of roads, train stations, and what look like remains and memorial sites in the camp; others are family photographs spanning more than fifty years, from the parents' youth in Prague before the war to their old age in an American suburb. On some pages, the superimposed photographs are combined with long lists of names and what are evidently birth and death dates, taken from the memorial wall of Prague's Pinkasova synagogue. And of course, in the middle of each book there is the cast of the arm, whose making also required collaboration: the daughter had to ask her parents' permission to take casts and photograph the tattoos so as to be able to copy them exactly onto the pink hand-made paper surface. They wrote their stories around the empty hole left by the cast.

Although the process of producing this layered text was collaborative, both within and across generations, the books themselves remain separate, mounted on shelves next to each other but not touching. And the stories they tell are separate too. Eugene Kellner's narrative begins just before Christmas in 1942, when he and his family (including his first wife, who was pregnant at the time) were called for transport to the Theresienstadt concentration camp; it ends with his return to Prague in the spring of 1945, to find that only he and his mother had survived. Everyone else in his family, including his wife and infant son, had perished. His narrative makes no mention of what happened to him after 1945; his second wife, Eva, and their children, Tatana and her siblings, are not present in Eugene Kellner's text, though they appear in his book in many of the superimposed family photographs (chosen by Tatana, not by Eugene).

Similarly, Eva Kellner's narrative never mentions Eugene, her children, or her mother-in-law Olga. She begins her story with her birth and childhood ("I was born in a far away country in Central Europe. It was a different world.") and ends it in the summer of 1945 with her return to Prague, where she discovered that her immediate family had perished. An uncle took her in to "build a life as a free person not as *Häftling* [camp prisoner] 71225." She makes no mention of Eugene or her children, but as in Eugene's book, her artist-daughter has superimposed family photographs on her text.

The two books, then, are connected in the process of their production and through the images chosen by the artist who brings them into dialogue with each other. The reader/viewer can also unite them, serially if not simultaneously: we note that they are the same size, the same thickness, have the same kind of shiny white covers (but Eva's cover has black lines of barbed wire running down it, while Eugene's has black lines of printed names). And of course each one has its tattooed arm, similar to the other yet different.

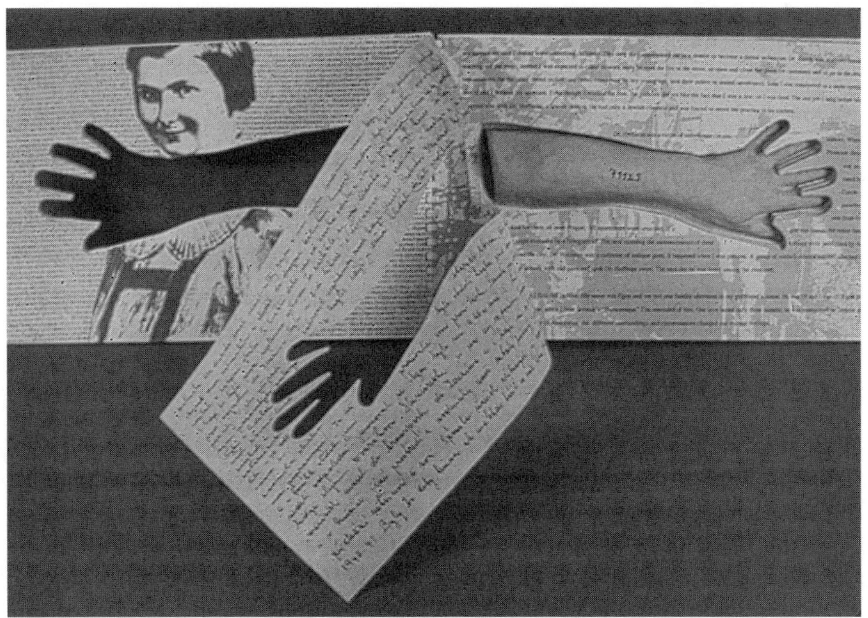

6.3 Layered pages, The Mother's Book.

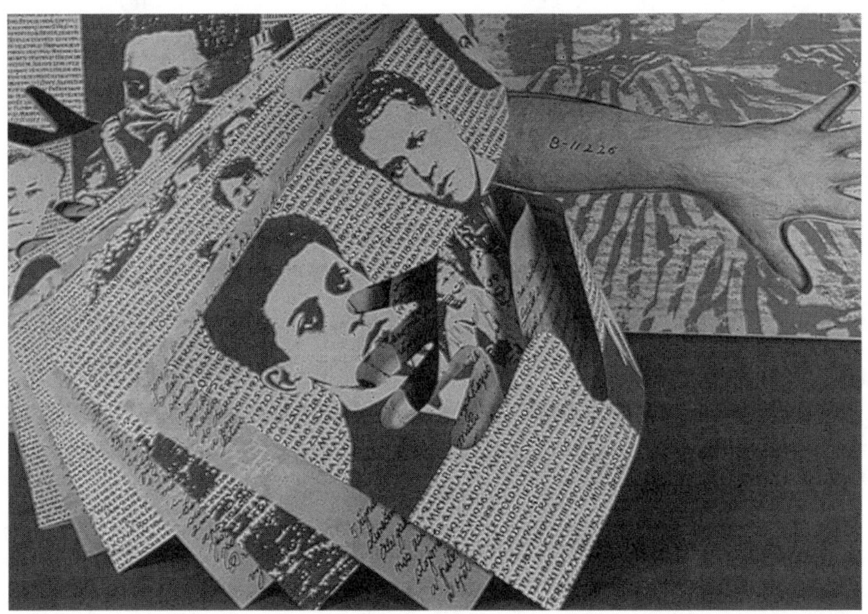

6.4 Layered pages, The Father's Book.

Tatana Kellner tells us that in order to underscore the visual parallelism, she took liberties with the arms and tattoos. While her mother's tattoo was on the outside of her forearm, her father's was on the inside; Kellner decided to place both numbers on the outside, thus maintaining the symmetry.

The play with similarity yet difference may be one way of effecting a "marriage" between the two books, which are maintained in their separateness but are also linked by identical aesthetic patterning and by the recurring superimposed photographs. The work of linking is accomplished by the daughter of these two survivors, who is literally the product of their union as well as the producer of their joined narratives.

The coexistence of opposites structures this work nowhere more obviously than in the tattooed arm at the center of each book. The arm is an ineluctable presence, almost unbearable to look at in its truncated "thereness"; but it also marks an absence, an empty space in the middle of each page. Similarly, the work consists of stories, layers and layers of them, but it is titled *Fifty Years of Silence.* It offers both a plethora of information, of voices, of "matter"—and a void.

The experience of reading/viewing the work emphasizes this contradictory structure: the written component presents a Czech text and its English translation, but for most viewers only the translation is intelligible. Nonetheless, we are invited to look at both of the facing pages, and we notice (by looking at the placing of proper names in the original and in the translation, for example) that the two sides don't quite match up: the stories take up unequal amounts of space on the page and the translation is often early or late, out of order with the original.

The superimposed pictures, too, are often hard to make out in the silkscreen wash, especially on the translucent pages: Is that a train station, or a scene in a camp barracks? Is that family photo prewar or postwar? Is the child Eva or Eugene, or one of their own children? Once in a while, words jump out of the photographs, arresting our reading of the underlying text: *"Halt," "Lebensgefahr."* Stop, life-threatening danger. Are these markers from now or then, addressed to camp prisoners, to the later viewer who took the photo (Kellner, on her 1990 trip to Prague and Auschwitz), or to today's reader?

The simultaneous, paradoxical coexistence of presence and absence, silence and voice, meaning and incomprehensibility, is a familiar trope of Holocaust literature. Kellner has found an original form for this trope. Her work suggests the silence with which she grew up, as well as her desire to know. With the arrest produced by the tattooed arm, it also suggests the difficult entry into this historical moment, the inevitable confusion and interferences that accompany any attempt today, in the United States, to "understand" what happened in Europe between 1939 and 1945. Even more significantly, Kellner has managed to elicit and to include her parents' stories, told in their own words and in their own handwriting, within and "next to" her own endeavor, both as autonomous narratives "outside" and as parts of a larger whole "inside."

THE PARENTS' NARRATIVES

In discussing how she got the idea for this work, Tatana Kellner told us, "These [her parents' narratives] were very run-of-the-mill stories; they had to be made more accessible, to draw the reader in." But what happens if, as an experiment, we read Eva's and Eugene's texts as independent memoirs? Does their "run-of-the-mill" quality fail to draw the reader in?

Quite the contrary: these memoirs are compelling and powerful, and like all Holocaust narratives by survivors who are not professional writers, they derive much of their power precisely from what could be called their "run-of-the-mill" quality. Spontaneously written and only very lightly edited, they resemble the video testimonies Geoffrey Hartman discusses as examples of "raw poetry."[8] What then do we think Tatana Kellner meant by "run-of-the-mill?" In one sense no Holocaust story is "run-of-the-mill" compared to the everyday lives we lead now, or to the prewar lives of their protagonists. But in another sense, one can call these stories "run-of-the-mill" because they are typical of what happened to those who survived the extermination camps: transport, arrival, shock, near-death, and one or more inexplicable strokes of luck—that's how it was for all those who have lived to tell their tale.

Eugene and Eva Kellner's tales are no exception: they are familiar, repetitive, and yet they draw us in. We read them at one sitting (we have procured the typescripts, reading them literally outside the completed work). Why? Because no amount of repetition can dull our fascination with the Event, the "thing itself" that Eva and Eugene lived through, the thing that is signified, emblematized, by their tattooed arms. In her essay "Representing Auschwitz," Sidra Ezrahi speaks of this fascination as the "absolutist" or "mythic" attitude toward Holocaust representation, on the part of both those who produce testimonies and those who receive them. For those who adopt this attitude (and at one time or other, everyone who has heard about the Holocaust has adopted it), the Event is primordial, every telling of it approaching the sacred.[9] One can never have "too much" of such telling, for every telling represents, and at times actually reenacts, the horror of that time and place in its timeless, eternal present. The fact that the Kellner testimonies are framed by the title *Fifty Years of Silence* emphasizes their mythic status: locked away, repressed, encrypted for half a century, they are, it seems to us, offered here especially so that we may read them, now. In fact, both Eva and Eugene Kellner shift often into the present tense when recounting their weeks and months in Auschwitz: the effect, as Ezrahi notes about similar testimonies, is to place their story sub specie aeternitatis (outside time, in eternity).

Can we analyze these mythic texts? Can we speak of a style, for example? How have these two people lived with their memories? What kind of people have they become? How might their texts help us understand both memory and survival?

Like most Holocaust testimonies, Eva's and Eugene's texts avoid describing emotion or affect. It is as if the more traumatic the events that are told, the less they allow an affective response on the part of the teller. Eva's tropes are ellipsis and irony: she reports her mother's death in Auschwitz almost in passing. Later she reports, matter-of-factly, that in the factory in Hamburg where she worked as a forced laborer in 1945 (transported there from Auschwitz), "sex was exchanged for bread; the SS men didn't seem to mind sleeping with Jewish women." The passive construction suggests, but does not tell, her own presence in these exchanges. In that same factory, she tells us, the prisoners had to wear coats with a bull's eye painted on the back, "all of this in order to find and shoot in the back prisoners in case of an escape." She adds the punch line parenthetically: "I wonder that no one in all this time has thought of using this as a fashion statement."

As for Eugene, he too takes pleasure in irony and understatement: "September evenings in Poland are freezing and standing naked outside, even for just one hour was not pleasant, to say the least." But his preferred discursive mode is starkly literal, avoiding tropes in favor of blunt, precise, brutal reporting. This accounts, perhaps, for his feeling, reported to us by Tatana, that his wife was "the better storyteller." His own storytelling, however, is powerful in its own way: "Because there was a shortage of Zyklon gas, children were thrown into pits, doused with gasoline and burned to death. This is how the life of my first son ended." A few months later, he and a wagonload of prisoners are left for ten days without food and water: "It was about the fourth night when I heard a terrible scream and discovered that some of the prisoners, led by their survival instinct began to kill the weaker prisoners, drinking blood and devouring their raw meat." This prose refuses to say things indirectly: it is stubbornly denotative and direct, like a punch in the face. One apparent exception is Eugene's metaphoric statement "The survival instinct made animals out of people." But upon reflection, one wonders whether the animal metaphor is not to be taken literally, a simple statement of fact. Eva's narrative also evokes animals, but with a characteristically ironic twist. About life in Auschwitz, she writes, "we are no longer human; any remnant of human dignity is beaten out of us. To compare us to animals is unjust to animals, who kill their prey out of hunger, not to torture."

Eva Kellner's refusal of metaphor, like Eugene's blunt, direct style, may seem to confirm the argument advanced by some Holocaust scholars, that survivor testimony provides the most direct and unmediated account of the Event itself.[10] In this sense too—the sense that they are historical documents and not artistic forms of expression—these testimonies might be called run-of-the-mill. However, this view assumes too clear a dichotomy between historical document, considered transparent and unmediated, and art, where mediation is necessarily recognized. If we read testimony differently, as many writers and scholars have begun to do, the text of memoir becomes as complex and in need of interpretation as any other. In his book *Beyond Despair,* Aharon Appelfeld suggests that testimonies are not revelations but repressions, an effort to externalize and thus veil the inner truth of the experience. As Ernst van Alphen remarks, "by 'the inner truth' Appelfeld does not mean the intimate inner psychological and emotional truth, nor some secret that is not told, but rather 'the survivor's sensation of non-identity, of a ghostly self damaged by years of suffering [that] slowly erased the feeling of humanity within.'"[11] As Charlotte Delbo wrote in the voice of one of her fellow deportees, "I died in Auschwitz but no one knows it."[12] Read in this light, Eva's and Eugene's testimonies do not break their fifty years of silence, but continue them: they are "run-of-the-mill" accounts, valuable testimonies even though, or perhaps because, they fail to get at the essence of the Holocaust.

THE DAUGHTER'S WORK

Many children of survivors echo Tatana Kellner's experience of living with a silent knowledge, an absent memory. For Tatana Kellner that absence had a signifier, her parents' tattooed arms and the story to which they metonymically and metaphorically refer: the arm is part of the story of the concentration camp, since the tattooing occurred there, and it also stands for the experience of the camp, both as bodily inscription and as trope. For Tatana, growing up, the arms may have seemed like screens which were at once masking the story and inviting a story to be projected onto them. She tells us that for her, visually, "it began with the arms" and she built the books around them.

The daughter's work is a response to the hunger for the Event figured by the tattoos; at the same time, it is a measure of how the second generation cannot have direct access to that event but must always work through mediations. By embedding the parents' testimonies into a richer, more challenging, if also perhaps more problematic, object, Kellner moves us from the mythic and absolutist attitude toward Holocaust representation to what Ezrahi calls the "dynamic or relativist position," which views Holocaust memory as a "construction of strategies for an ongoing renegotiation, . . . interpretive and narrative . . . of that historical reality."[13] This approach characterizes the work of the postmemorial artist, and links it to the self-reflexiveness of postmodern artistic production.

Indeed, *Fifty Years of Silence* is most productively read for the ways in which it comments both on the difficulties of remembrance and transmission and on the problematics of artistic representation, especially where Holocaust narratives are concerned. Kellner has found multiple ways of figuring this double commentary. We will discuss three figures in particular: encasing, layering, and juxtaposition.

The two books that make up *Fifty Years of Silence* are encased in plain pine boxes with sliding covers; each cover has two parallel vertical slats of wood that can be grasped to open the box. Into each cover is burned the number that will be repeated on the tattooed arm, corresponding to the parent whose story—and whose box—one is viewing. In order to handle the books, one must slide open the covers and lift the books out of their boxes. The figural resonances here evoke boxcars and the pine coffins of Jewish tradition: for many who died in them, the boxcars became coffins. But the figure of encasing has other implications as well. It refers to the viewer's relation to the work: in order to read the book, one has to disengage it from its protective cover—a troubling act, like opening a coffin to see what is inside. Encasing can also define the daughter's relation to her parents' narratives, figuring at once the daughter's desire to know and her resistance to, as Kellner puts it, "opening the book on their memories." Or, conversely, encasing can refer to the parents' memories themselves, which existed for fifty years "in a box" with no opening, in silence.

From a psychoanalytic perspective, Kellner's use of encasing can be related to the theoretical model of memory and transgenerational transmission proposed in Nicholas Abraham and Maria Torok's notions of the "phantom" and the "crypt." According to this model, a traumatic loss that was never properly worked through by the subject can be passed on to children and grandchildren without being consciously transmitted.[14] Entombed or encrypted by the subject, the unspeakable secret becomes a "phantom" that can haunt subsequent generations.

Borrowing Abraham and Torok's figure, one could say that Kellner's pine boxes are a concrete but also figurative crypt for her parents' traumatic experiences; the crypt is both a means of concealing and a means of preserving an unworked-through loss. Kellner creates the books of her parents' memories, but then places them in pine boxes as if to entomb them once again.

In a more specifically aesthetic perspective, the figure of encasing can refer to the framing activity of the artist. The boxes are then seen as frames that protect, enhance, and call attention to the aesthetic quality of the artwork. These two interpretive perspectives replay one of the ongoing tensions in this work, as in all artistic works that use the Holocaust as their primary subject: the tension between referentiality and aestheticism.

A similar multiplicity of meanings resides in the figures of layering and juxtaposition. Layering is most evident in the alternation of translucent and solid pages throughout the two books. The reading/viewing unit consists of two sheets: the translucent sheet on whose recto side are images of camps, train stations, and landscapes, and whose verso side inscribes the blue handwritten story in Czech; and the solid sheet whose recto side inscribes the typewritten translation of the testimony and whose verso side reproduces family photographs superimposed on the lists of names. On the right side of the open book, text and image emerge around the arm; on the left, text and image surround the die-cut hole in the shape of the arm. If one reads the Czech and English texts side by side (translucent on the left, solid on the right), each is legible, even though the translucent page also allows faint outlines of pictures to emerge from beneath. But it is when one looks at the recto of the translucent page that the layering becomes most evident and most evocative. The two texts and two sets of images are now superimposed on each other, creating the effect of a palimpsest. In some spots the English text is clearly legible beneath the Czech writing, while in others it is blocked out by the dark print of an image. The multiple projections and superimpositions, the hard-to-see and hard-to-read text and images give one the sense that something momentous is there, under the surface, although one cannot make it out.

Like encasing, the figure of layering also relates to Abraham and Torok's notion of the "phantom," since generational transmission can be thought of as a form of layering. Another psychoanalytic analogy might be Freud's famous image for memory and perception, "the mystic writing pad." The "magical" pad permanently saves inscriptions on a bottom wax layer, while the transparent top layers can be lifted and emptied of their inscriptions, either to make room for other, more recent ones or to protect the remembering subject from stimuli that may be too powerful, too exciting or enervating.[15] Aside from its analogy with memory, however, layering as Kellner uses it is a central aesthetic feature of the work. Each book consists of twenty "layered" units, and it is in the choice of images and their sequencing and alternation with text that Kellner's artistic labor is most apparent.

Finally, like encasing and layering, juxtaposition can be seen as a figure for the structure of traumatic memory as well as for the problematics of artistic representation. Students of traumatic memory have proposed a model of dissociation, based on the work of Pierre Janet, as an alternative to Freud's model of repression to represent the processing of trauma. The traumatic material is split off, intact, persisting on a parallel track to consciousness and the present, but still unavailable to narrative recall and assimilation.[16] Such splitting is in effect a kind of juxtaposition, since the traumatic experience exists, unintegrated, "next to" everyday living. In the book form, however, juxtaposition and layering imply each other: when the translucent page lies on top of the opaque one, the effect is one of layering; when the translucent page is turned, the Czech text and its translation are juxtaposed. Other juxtapositions include the placing of the books side by side, the regularly recurring alternation of solid arm and die-cut

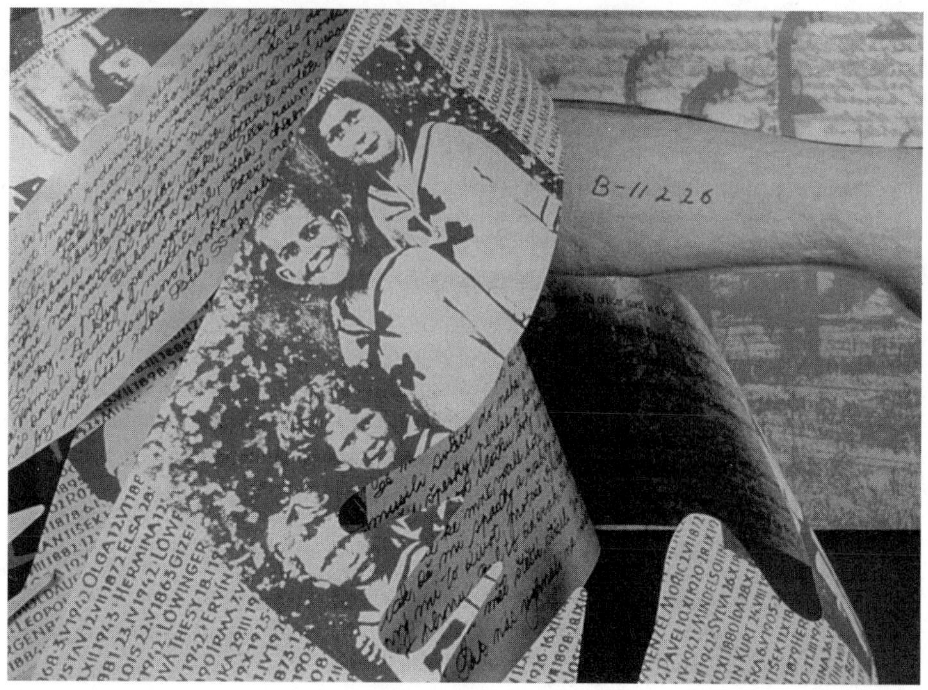

6.5 Image and text.

hole, and the parents' survivor perspectives juxtaposed with the daughter's postmemorial one. But this latter juxtaposition brings us back to the figure of encasing and to the problematic relationship between the parents' narratives and the daughter's artwork.

PASSING ON

The two perspectives, that of the artist and that of her parents, do not remain separate—Kellner embeds her parents' stories into her own text. In spite of the consent that her parents obviously gave her, one could ask: is she appropriating their stories for her own artistic purposes? Is her work too aestheticized? Is she framing their story in a mode too distant from their own idiom? These are questions with no easy or unequivocal answers—much depends on the viewer's assumptions, both ethical and aesthetic, concerning the nature and limits of Holocaust representation.

In our own view, Kellner's work both qualifies and focuses the status of her parents' testimonies. By embedding her parents' stories into her own artwork, Kellner includes them in a dialogue, casting herself as the active listener who enables their very emergence. In this sense, her introduction and translations, as well as the pages she produces, the books themselves, are her response to her parents' stories, the measure of her sympathetic act of listening. As an active listener, she becomes a second witness and herself a storyteller. The psychoanalyst Dori Laub writes about his work with Holocaust survivors that "there is a need for a tremendous libidinal investment in those interview situations: there is so much destruction recounted, so much death, so much loss, so much hopelessness, that there has to be an abundance of holding and of emotional investment in the encounter, to keep alive the witnessing narration."[17] In editing and translating her parents' texts, in going to Poland to visit the camp where her parents had been interned, and in constructing her book, Kellner has found a different listening mode, one she translates into an artistic strategy. She thus shifts her parents' testimonies from product to process, to a transactional, conversational encounter, made less absolute, more dynamic and multivalent through her intervention. Like Paul D. in Toni Morrison's *Beloved,* who says to Sethe that he would like to put his story next to hers, Tatana Kellner has placed her parents' stories of survival next to one another. Like the stories of Sethe and Paul D., Eva's and Eugene's are not stories "to pass on." But through the active listening of their daughter, and through the form she has found for her listening, they are passed on, nonetheless. It is true that they are also transformed in the process: there is no passing on without the mediation of a "passer."

After turning all the pages of *Fifty Years of Silence* one reaches the base on which each book rests: a sheet of pink hand-made paper holding the cast of the amputated tattooed arm, a sculpture signed and numbered by the artist. The numbers tattooed on the two arms are thus mirrored in the numbers indicating the edition of the artwork, signed by the artist's hand. Here ultimately is the unbridgeable distance between the experiences of the two generations: while the artist numbers her own work, separate from her body, the parents' arms were themselves numbered—not as works but as bodies deprived of human agency—by their Nazi victimizers. On the daughter's part, creative choice, the sign of artistic power; on the parents' part, a reminder of forcible dehumanization and powerlessness.

Eugene's text recounts the medical experiments that were performed on his hands in Auschwitz: "I had blood poisoning on both of my legs and frost-bite on both hands and feet. The experiments on my hands and feet started; they always healed one leg and one hand while infecting the other one. I don't know what they used but somehow both legs and hands, much to everyone's amazement, started to heal." This image of healing imposes itself, however tentatively, in relation to Tatana Kellner's work. *Fifty Years of Silence* may perform a work of healing for both the parents and the artist, and for the future generations who will read these books; but it also points, on its sculptural foundation, to the unbridgeable gap—the necessary failure—that exists between a horrific experience and its representation.

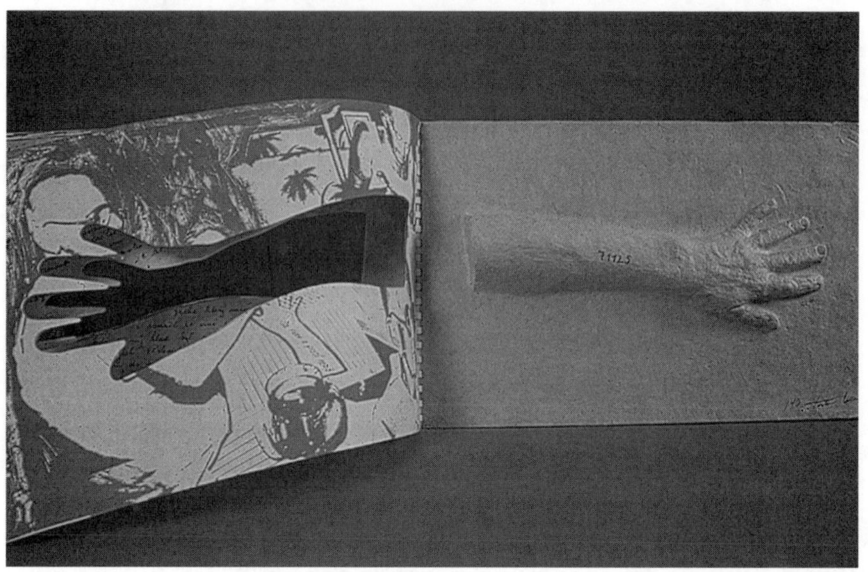

6.6 Last page and base, The Mother's Book.

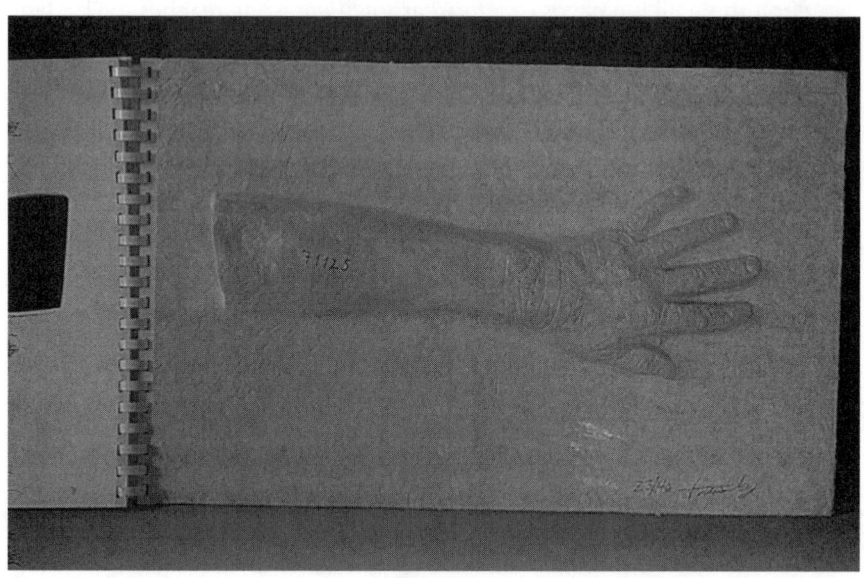

6.7 Base with artist's signature and numbering.

Notes

This is a slightly revised version of a chapter from *Shaping Losses: Cultural Memory and the Holocaust,* ed. Julia Epstein and Lori Lefkovitz. Copyright 2001 by the Board of Trustees of the University of Illinois. Used by permission of the University of Illinois Press. Earlier versions were presented at the Society for the Study of Narrative Literature Conference in Columbus, Ohio, in April 1996 and at the American Comparative Literature Association Annual Meeting in Puerto Vallarta, Mexico, in April 1997. We wish to thank Tatana Kellner for discussing her work with us and making it available for this essay, and Robert Seydel of the Photographic Resource Center in Boston for loaning us the two books.

1. Art Spiegelman, *Maus: A Survivor's Tale I: My Father Bleeds History* (New York: Pantheon, 1986), 58, 159.

2. Charles Sanders Peirce, *Collected Papers,* ed. Charles Hawthorne and Paul Weiss (Cambridge, Mass.: Harvard University Press, [1931] 1958).

3. For recent discussions of artists' books, see Johanna Drucker, *The Century of Artists' Books* (New York: Granary, 1995), and Joan Lyons, ed., *Artists' Books: A Critical Anthology and Source Book* (Rochester, N.Y.: Visual Studies Workshop Press, 1985). We are grateful to Karen Schiff for sharing her knowledge about this genre and discussing Kellner's work with us.

4. See Susan Rubin Suleiman, *Risking Who One Is: Encounters with Contemporary Art and Literature* (Cambridge, Mass.: Harvard University Press, 1994), and her edited volume *Exile and Creativity: Signposts, Travelers, Outsiders, Backward Glances* (Durham, N.C.: Duke University Press, 1998).

5. For an evolving definition of postmemory, see Marianne Hirsch, *Family Frames: Photography, Narrative, and Postmemory* (Cambridge, Mass.: Harvard University Press, 1997), especially chapters 1 and 6; Hirsch, "Projected Memory: Holocaust Photographs in Personal and Public Fantasy," in *Acts of Memory: Cultural Recall in the Present,* ed. Mieke Bal, Jonathan Crewe, and Leo Spitzer (Hanover, N.H.: University Press of New England, 1999), 2–23; and Hirsch, "Surviving Images: Holocaust Photographs and the Work of Postmemory," *Yale Journal of Criticism* 14, no. 1 (spring 2001): 5–38, and in *Visual Culture and the Holocaust,* ed. Barbie Zelizer (New Brunswick, N.J.: Rutgers University Press, 2001), 214–246. See also Andrea Liss's somewhat different use of the term "post-memories" in *Trespassing through Shadows: Memory, Photography, and the Holocaust* (Minneapolis: University of Minnesota Press, 1998).

6. In fact, number tattooing was practiced only in Auschwitz, not in any of the other concentration or death camps, but Auschwitz itself has become a kind of shorthand to signify "the concentration camp" or "the Holocaust." In recent discussions of Holocaust studies this shorthand has increasingly come to be seen as problematic because it reduces a complex, varied phenomenon to a single symbol, with a resulting simplification and erasure of differences. For a complete history of Auschwitz, see Debórah Dwork and Robert Jan van Pelt, *Auschwitz: 1270 to the Present* (New York: W. W. Norton, 1996), and Yisrael Gutman and Michael Berenbaum, eds., *Anatomy of the Auschwitz Death Camp* (Bloomington: Indiana University Press and the United States Holocaust Memorial Museum, 1994).

7. Tatana Kellner, *71125: Fifty Years of Silence* (Rosendale, N.Y.: Rosendale Women's Studio Workshop, 1992) and *B-11226: Fifty Years of Silence* (Rosendale, N.Y.: Rosendale Women's Studio Workshop, 1994).

8. Geoffrey H. Hartman, *The Longest Shadow: In the Aftermath of the Holocaust* (Bloomington: Indiana University Press, 1996), 153.

9. Sidra DeKoven Ezrahi, "Representing Auschwitz," *History and Memory* 7, no. 2 (fall/winter 1996): 121–154.

10. See, for example, Lawrence L. Langer, *Holocaust Testimonies: The Ruins of Memory* (New Haven, Conn.: Yale University Press, 1991).

11. Ernst van Alphen, *Caught by History: Holocaust Effects in Contemporary Art, Literature, and Theory* (Stanford, Calif.: Stanford University Press, 1997), 150.

12. Charlotte Delbo, *Auschwitz and After,* trans. Rosette C. Lamont (New Haven, Conn.: Yale University Press, 1995), 267.

13. Ezrahi, "Representing Auschwitz," 122.

14. Nicholas Abraham and Maria Torok, *The Shell and the Kernel: Renewals of Psychoanalysis,* vol. 1, ed. and trans. Nicholas T. Rand (Chicago: University of Chicago Press, 1994), chapters 4, 5, and 9.

15. Sigmund Freud, "A Note upon the 'Mystic Writing Pad,'" in *The Standard Edition of the Complete Psychological Works of Sigmund Freud,* translated under the general editorship of James Strachey in collaboration with Anna Freud, assisted by Alix Strachey and Alan Tyson, 24 vols. (London: Hogarth, 1953–74), 19 (1961): 227–232.

16. See Bessel A. van der Kolk and Onno van der Hart, "The Intrusive Past: The Flexibility of Memory and the Engraving of Trauma," in *Trauma: Explorations in Memory,* ed. Cathy Caruth (Baltimore: Johns Hopkins University Press, 1995), 158–182.

17. Dori Laub, "Bearing Witness or the Vicissitudes of Listening," in Shoshana Felman and Dori Laub, *Testimony: Crises of Witnessing in Literature, Psychoanalysis, and History* (New York: Routledge, 1992), 71.

7 Caught by Images

Visual Imprints in Holocaust Testimonies | ERNST VAN ALPHEN

What I saw with my wide-open eyes.

—Tadeusz Borowski, *This Way for the Gas, Ladies and Gentlemen*[1]

"Someday you be walking down the road and you hear something or see something going on. So clear. And you think it's you making it up. A thought picture. But no, it's when you bump into a rememory that belongs to somebody else."[2] Toni Morrison, in her novel *Beloved* (1987), writes about the importance and reality of what she calls "rememories," and what students of the Holocaust call, with a contradictory term, "traumatic memories." The key word here is "pictures." In an interview, Morrison insists on the visual quality of these images:

> What makes it fiction is the nature of the imaginative act: my reliance on the image—on the remains—in addition to recollection, to yield up a kind of truth. By "image," of course, I don't mean "symbol"; I simply mean "picture" and the feelings that accompany the picture.[3]

It is my conviction that current interest in specifically visual art related to the Holocaust finds in these statements by Morrison its raison d'être: both its explanation and its theoretical justification. Morrison is a writer, not a visual artist. Yet she insists on the founding, grounding function of specifically visual images in the "re-membering," the healing activity of memory that present-day culture, facing the disappearance of the eyewitness, is struggling to articulate and implement. Paradoxically, it is most clearly and convincingly through creative written texts, commonly called "fiction," that this visuality and its truthfulness can be assessed. This chapter, then, is about the "'picture' and the feelings that accompany the picture."

Joan B., one of the Holocaust survivors whose testimony was videotaped by the Fortunoff Video Archive for Holocaust Testimonies, recounts the following. She worked in the kitchen of a labor camp. When one of the inmates was about to give birth, the camp commandant gave the order to boil water. "Boil water. But the water wasn't to help with the act of giving birth. He drowned the newborn baby in the boiling water." The appalled interviewer asks, "Did you see that?" "Oh, yes, I did," the witness imperturbably replies. "Did you say anything?" the dialogue continues. "No I didn't." Later Joan B. offers the following comment: "I had a friend . . . who said that now when we are here, you have to look straight ahead as if we have [blinders] on like a race horse . . . and become selfish. I just lived, looked, but I didn't feel a thing."[4]

Although Joan B. has seen what has happened to the newborn baby, her act of looking seems to involve no more than the recording of a visual impression. One of the epistemological implications of seeing, namely apprehension, to discern mentally, to attain comprehension or grasp, seems to be lacking in her act of seeing. That which was visually distinguishable has been imprinted on her memory like an immutable photograph, but the traces of that visual imprint seem never to have been emotionally experienced, let alone worked through. She recounts an event which is no more than a visual recording. In her narration of it, the event seems not to have had any emotional or ethical dimensions.

Joan B.'s testimony is emblematic for the profound way the Holocaust has disrupted the conventional notions of seeing, of the visual domain, in Western culture. Since the Enlightenment the observation of the visual world has had a privileged epistemological status: it is a precondition and guarantee of knowledge and understanding. Being an eyewitness of something implies more or less automatic apprehension and comprehension of the observed situation or event.

This link between seeing and comprehension, however, has been radically disrupted in the experiences of Holocaust victims.[5] As I will argue, it is because of this disruption that "to see" and the description of visual imprints have such a central role in the testimonies of Holocaust survivors. But these eyewitnesses' testimonies of visual imprints concern events that cannot be processed in the same manner as those recounted in the eyewitness account in a police report. In Holocaust testimonies the visual functions more like the unmodified return of what happened, instead of as a mode of access to or penetration into what happened—instead of being the raw material to be processed into understanding. Even after all this time, that first step has still not been made. Yet the image is there; it refuses to budge.

Perhaps it is because of this strong, yet problematic, nature of vision in the face of a disaster of the magnitude of the Holocaust that so much intense debate concentrates today on visual art that represents it. Films such as *La vita è bella* and, before it, *Schindler's List* are criticized in terms of the "authenticity" of the representation, and blamed for lacking in that regard. These films are unfavorably compared to the classic *Shoah,* Claude Lanzmann's documentary film recording testimonies of survivors, comparable to those of Joan B. cited above. Lanzmann's witnesses *were there,* hence, their eyewitness accounts are authentic. They saw with their own eyes what happened, and the images are imprinted forever on their retinas. Begnini and Spielberg mocked this obsession with authentic vision by having the events represented by acting, the quintessential art of feigning, faking, cheating, and pretending. It is as if art itself is suspect in the face of the cultural need for authenticity.

Given how strongly vision has been bound up with truth and authenticity in the Western imaginary from the Renaissance on, it comes as no surprise that the question of historical truth in the face of a truth that is unbearable is played out so strongly today in the domain of visual art. Shakespeare's *Lucrece* is entirely structured around the opposition between vision as "true" and language as a fallen state of man, in which deception is the order of the day. But already, there, the opposition falls apart. And so it does today. An intense discussion is going on as eyewitnesses become rarer and fiction is one of the remaining options for keeping the memory of the events alive. Visual artists such as Christian Boltanski and Armando, to name two I have discussed elsewhere,[6] struggle to come up with strategies of representation that supplement the documentary mode that is no longer possible. And whereas the thrust of their work is obsessively singular in this attempt, the term "authenticity" does not apply to it at all. And insofar as their work is primarily visual, a case might be made for the separation of or distinction between the question of authenticity and vision per se.

But that distinction does not require giving up the primacy of vision. Instead, my thesis will be that it might be productive to distinguish vision from its most obvious vehicle, the eye. The issue is more complex than such media-essentialism as that privileging of the visual medium suggests. It is, in fact, twofold. First, vision does not automatically lead to "authentic" witnessing. For witnessing requires, in addition to seeing, accounting for what is seen, and the problem may be situated in that mediation or transmission. This problem of transmission occurs strongly in the face of traumatic experiences, and as I will argue, it is not resolved unless language intervenes. Second, vision does not necessarily lead to representation. There are other modes of communicating, or not-being-able-to-communicate, vision, in whatever medium. The artists I mentioned, among many others, are involved in searching for such alternative modes. In the context of a collection that centers the question of Holocaust representation on visual art, I propose to first probe the importance and modalities of vision itself in this context. That is to say, I will attempt to articulate what vision can mean, do, and achieve in the face of its most untenable confrontation, such as the one exemplified by Joan B.'s testimony. On the one hand, the visual imprint; on the other, the need to deal with it.

Tadeusz Borowski's *This Way for the Gas, Ladies and Gentlemen* acts out in an impressive way the dominant role of visual imprints in Holocaust "memories." I will take this book as a starting point to assess the place of visuality, seeing, and visual incapacitation in the commemoration of the Holocaust. The short stories included in this volume are inspired by Borowski's concentration camp experiences. But the background that informs them does not imply that they can be read like first-person testimonies in which the experiences of the narrator are central. Nor do they read that way. The first person in these stories identifies himself more like a reporter of a documentary: he recounts what happens around him. The order of the stories in the book is more or less chronological, although this order does not necessarily concern the chronological ordering of the life of the narrator. Rather, they are ordered according to the chronology of the generic event "the camp." Thus, the first story deals with arrivals in the camp, those which follow describe life in the camp, then we are told about the liberation. The last three stories, "The January Offensive," "A Visit," and "The World of Stone," recount life after having survived the Holocaust.

Given the inevitably retrospective nature of such accounts, the moment of narration in a Holocaust testimony is by definition situated after the liberation. That is why, in the case of *This Way for the Gas,* the last stories possess an essential relevance for the meaning of testimony as such. It is only in these stories that the narrated events are clearly distinguished from the narration of the events: the narration takes place after the liberation. In the stories set during life in the camp, in contrast, the often-used present tense, but also the typically narrative past tense, describe moments of narration that could, in a fictional mode, be contemporaneous with the events.

"A Visit" begins as if it tells about life from within the camp: "I was walking through the night, the fifth in line. An orange flame from the burning bodies flickered in the center of the purple sky" (174). The first-person narrator then discusses explicitly the impossibility of relating his feelings or self-experience. He presents himself as a kind of machine who could only record what he saw.

> In the soft darkness, I held my eyes open wide. And although the fever in my bleeding thigh was spreading throughout my entire body, becoming more and more painful with every step I took, I can remember nothing about that night except what I saw with my wide-open eyes. (174)

The leitmotiv of the visual act, of "what the first-person narrator saw," emphatically structures most of the following text, thus qualifying the nature of that act itself.

> In the days that followed I saw men weep while working with the pickaxe, the spade, in the trucks. I saw them carry heavy rails, sacks of cement, slabs of concrete; I saw them carefully level the earth, dig dirt out of ditches, build barracks, watch-towers and crematoria. I saw them consumed by eczema, phlegmon, typhoid fever, and I saw them dying of hunger. And I saw others who amassed fortunes in diamonds, watches and gold and buried them safely in the ground. . . . And I have seen women who carried heavy logs, pushed carts and wheelbarrows and built dams across ponds. . . . And I also saw a girl (who had once been mine) covered with running sores and with her head shaven. (175)

This narrative act of recounting what he has seen is first legitimized by the narrator as a kind of moral obligation to those who died in the Holocaust. This is a recurrent topos in many Holocaust testimonies. It is also presented as a last act of relating—recounting as a way of establishing a relationship—that the dying requested, in their desperate attempt to stay related. For "every one of the people who, because of eczema, phlegmon or typhoid fever, or simply because they were too emaciated, were taken to the gas chamber, begged the orderlies loading them into the crematorium trucks to remember what they saw. And to tell the truth about mankind to those who do not know it" (175). But gradually it becomes clear that the narrator does not tell what he has seen out of moral obligation. He simply cannot do anything else. It is still the only thing he sees, long after, although historically the Holocaust belongs to the past.

It is only at the end of the story that it becomes clear that the story is told from the position of having survived the Holocaust. "I sit in someone else's room, among books that are not mine, and, as I write about the sky, and the men and women I have seen, I am troubled by one persistent thought—that I have never been able to look also at myself" (176). This impossibility implies that the narrator is unable to pay attention to what happened to him in the camp, or to his life in the present, after the Holocaust, either. The two incapacities are, of course, causally linked, but that causality cannot be perceived by the subject caught in its web. He can only see again what he has seen. The substance of narration is the visual equivalent of a broken record. The record got stuck and the same images repeat themselves.

The images from the past are more vivid and intense then what he sees in the present. The impossibility of reintegrating himself in the present of post-Holocaust life is demonstrated in the last story, "The World of Stone":

> In contrast to years gone by, when I observed the world with wide-open, astonished eyes, and walked along every street alert, like a young man on a parapet, I can now push through the liveliest crowd with total indifference and rub against hot female bodies without the slightest emotion. (178)

> I climb unimpressed up the marble staircase, rescued from the fire and covered with a red carpet. . . . I pay no attention to the newly installed windows and the freshly painted walls of the restored building. I enter with a casual air the modest but cosy little rooms occupied by people of importance. (179)

The impossibility of the narrator's seeing the world around him after he survived the Holocaust forces us to reconsider the indication of time in the story "A Visit." At first sight time indications like "That night I saw" and "In the days that followed I saw" seem to refer to specific moments during life in the camp. But they now have become ambiguous. They can also refer to specific moments after the narrator survived the camp, moments in which he did not see anything other than these visual imprints from the past, more intense and immediate than the impressions in the present.

The distinctions made by the French psychiatrist Pierre Janet between habit memory, narrative memory, and traumatic memory can be helpful in further assessing the role of visual imprints in Holocaust testimonies.[7] Janet, working at the beginning of this century and influenced by the theories of Sigmund Freud, defines habit memory as the automatic integration of new information without much conscious attention to what is happening. Humans share with animals the capacity for this kind of automatic synthesis. Narrative memory, a uniquely human capacity, consists of mental constructs, which people use to make sense out of experience. Current and familiar experiences are automatically assimilated or integrated into existing mental structures. But some events resist integration:

> Frightening or novel experiences may not easily fit into existing cognitive schemes and either may be remembered with particular vividness or may totally resist integration.[8]

The memories of experiences which resist integration into existing meaning schemes are stored differently and are not available for retrieval under ordinary conditions. It is only for convenience's sake that Janet has called these unintegratable experiences "traumatic memory." In fact, trauma is fundamentally (and not gradually) different from memory, because "it becomes dissociated from conscious awareness and voluntary control" (160).

Trauma is failed experience, and this failure makes it impossible to voluntarily remember the event. This is why traumatic reenactments take the form of drama, not narrative. Drama just presents itself, or so it seems; narrative as a mode implies some sort of mastery by the narrator, or the focalisor. This is a fundamental difference that will be shown to define the role of vision in memories of the Holocaust. Because of their fundamentally dramatic nature, traumatic reenactments are dependent on the time frame of the "parts" scripted in the drama. In the words of Mieke Bal: "All the manipulations performed by a narrator, who can expand and reduce, summarize, highlight, underscore, or minimize elements of the story at will, are inaccessible to the 'actor' who is bound to enact a drama that, although at some point in the past it happened to her, is not hers to master."[9]

Although from a formal perspective Borowski's stories are narrative, not drama, the narration is overruled by the compulsive need to relate the traumatic reenactments of visual imprints. Or, to put it differently: Borowski's narration loses control over what the narrator has recorded in the past. The logical coherence produced by narration fades away and we get a random sequence of descriptions of visual imprints. Within his narration Borowski demonstrates and enacts trauma.

Janet's clinical distinction between narrative and traumatic memory ultimately concerns a difference in distance from the situation or event. A narrative memory is retrospective; it takes place after the event. A traumatic memory—or, better, reenactment—does not know that distance from the event. The person who experiences a traumatic reenactment is still inside the event, present at it. This explains why these traumatic reenactments impose themselves as visual imprints. The original traumatic event has not yet been transformed into a mediated, distanced account. It reimposes itself in its visual and sensory directness.

The writings of French Holocaust survivor Charlotte Delbo convey quite intensely this feeling that she is still inside the event which she relates.[10] She does not narrate in her stories "about" Auschwitz, but "from" it. It is, first of all, the visual directness of her narration which produces this effect. But from time to time she explicitly comments on the position from which she speaks. The words which she gives to her character Mado also account for her own writing:

> People believe memories grow vague, are erased by time, since nothing endures against the passage of time. That's the difference; time does not pass over me, over us. It doesn't undo it. I am not alive. I died in Auschwitz but no one knows it. (267)

"That's the difference": difference, as absolute as that between traumatic "memory" and narrative memory in Janet's theory, defines the importance and specific function of vision in Holocaust memories. Delbo tersely indicates that traumatic reenactments imply a different ordering of time. The traumatic event which happened in the past does not belong to a distanced past: it is still present in the present. In language, this would be the difference between the preterite or simple past, a narrative form that represents a punctual event that once happened and is now gone, and the imperfect, a form indicating an event whose effect continues in the present. In the rest of this essay I will show how this ordering of time caused and implied by trauma brings with it a reliving of the traumatic event as intensely sensory and especially visual.

Delbo was born in 1913 not far from Paris. During the war she joined a resistance group in Paris. Her husband, Georges Dudach, was also a member of that group. In March 1942 she and her husband were caught by the French police in their apartment, where they were producing anti-German leaflets. The police turned them over to the Gestapo. Her husband was executed in May. She herself was sent to Auschwitz in January 1943 in a convoy of 230 French women, most of whom were not Jewish (like Delbo) but were involved in underground activities. Until January 1944 she stayed in Auschwitz and in the camp Raisko, not far from Auschwitz. Then she was sent to Ravensbruck. Near the end of the war she was released to the Red Cross, who moved her to Sweden to recover from her malnutrition and ill health. Delbo has written many plays, essays, poems, and stories, all of them based on her camp experiences. Her most famous work, however, is the trilogy *Auschwitz et après* (translated into English as *Auschwitz and After*). She wrote the first part of this trilogy, *None of Us Will Return,* as early as 1946, but published it only in 1965. The second part, titled *Useless Knowledge* and also written immediately after the liberation, appeared in 1970, and the third part, *The Measure of Our Days,* was published shortly after that.

In her essays Delbo has made a distinction between "common memory" and "deep memory." This distinction is comparable to Janet's distinction between narrative memory and traumatic memory. Common memory is capable of situating Auschwitz within a chronological ordering. If a survivor is able to remember Auschwitz as integrated in a chronological ordering, it implies in fact that survival has been at the same time a redemption from the terrible events. Auschwitz is now at a distance: it belongs to the past. Deep memory, on the contrary, does not succeed in situating the events in the past, at a distance. Auschwitz still does not belong to the past and it will not do so in the experience of those survivors who remember in the mode of deep memory.

Delbo makes another distinction that acknowledges yet another crucial aspect of trauma: between "external memory" and "sense memory." External memory is articulated in the distancing act of narration. The person who has external memories knows that she or he remembers. When Delbo narrates "about" Auschwitz her words do not stem from deep memory, but from common, external memory. The emotional and physical memory of Auschwitz is, in contrast, only approached by means of sense (deep) memory. The memory is not narrated; rather, it makes itself felt. This kind of memory is symptomatic of Auschwitz: it is not a mediated account of it, but a leftover that makes its ongoing presence felt.

In her narrative texts Delbo manages again and again to let external memories of events in the past slip into sense memories which convey the events as taking place in the present. The text "Roll Call" in *None of Us Will Return* is a good example of such a categorical slippage. The text starts out as a description of a unique event belonging to the past: "SS in black capes have walked past. They made a count" (22). The narrated event seems to concern an event which is circumscribed in time: It is not an arbitrary roll call, but a specific one. The two short sentences are, however, followed by a third one: "We are waiting still." The past tense has been exchanged for the present tense; the progressive form of this third sentence is the linguistic marker of this exchange. The event which is punctual, hence delimited in time, has been transformed into an event which is durative, that is, which is ongoing in time and cannot be situated within a chronology.[11] After this sentence ten paragraphs follow, each consisting of a few (usually one) short sentences.

> We are waiting.
> For days, the next day.
> Since the day before, the following day.
> Since the middle of the night, today.
> We wait.
> Day is breaking.
> We await the day because one must wait for something.
> One does not live in expectation of death. One expects it.
> We have no expectations.
> We expect what happens. Night because it follows day. Day because it follows night. (22)

The transition from past tense to present tense and from punctual to durative event brings with it a transition in kinds of memory. The text that begins as a narration of a memory which can be situated in a chronological past slips into the narration of a situation which continues into the present.

This slippage into the present is accompanied by a change of the position of the narrating subject. The narrator of this eternal waiting is still "inside" the visual and sensorial experience of waiting which she describes. In the most physical way the sensorial experiences of this eternal waiting crawl upon the narrator and upon us, the readers. The memory of the infinity of waiting is not described "at a distance," but is brought about sensorially and visually.

A similar effect is elicited in the story "One Day," also in *None of Us Will Return.* It is again produced by a subtle use of grammatical tense. The title evokes the conventional beginning of a chronologically ordered account. First we read three long paragraphs in the past tense. In these paragraphs the efforts of a totally exhausted woman to remain on her feet, that is, to stay alive, are described in great detail.

> She was clinging to the other side of the rope, her hands and feet grasping the snow-covered embankment. Her whole body was taut, her jaws tight, her neck with its dislocated cartilage straining, as were her muscles—what was left of them on her bones.
>
> Yet she strained in vain—the exertion of one pulling on an imaginary rope. (24)

The woman's struggle is focalized externally, from a distance. After some paragraphs the description suddenly continues in the present tense: "She turns her head as if to measure the distance, looks upward. One can observe a growing bewilderment in her eyes, her hands, her convulsed face" (24). As unexpected as this change in grammatical tense, another change takes place: external focalization is exchanged for character-bound focalization. The thoughts of the woman are directly quoted.

> Why are all these women looking at me like this? Why are they here, lined up in close ranks, standing immobile? They look at me yet do not seem to see me. They cannot possibly see me, or they wouldn't stand there gaping. They'd help me climb up. Why don't you help me, you standing so close? Help me. Pull me up. Lean in my direction. Stretch out your hand. Oh, they don't make a move. (24–25)

After this quotation of the woman's thoughts, the narration falls back into the past tense and the third person for a paragraph, and after that, a first-person narrator takes the place of the external narrator. This time, however, the first person is not the struggling woman but one of the crowd of witnessing women. These onlookers are like Joan B., unable to relate what they see to themselves, hence unable to relate to the lone woman they are getting imprinted on their retina:

> All of us were there, several thousand of us, standing in the snow since morning—this is what we call night. Since morning starts at three A.M. Dawn illuminated the snow which, until then, was the night's sole light—the cold grew bitter. (25)

We read another page of the third-person narration of the dying woman. Then the first-person narrator/witness returns:

> I no longer look at her. I no longer wish to look. If only I could change my place in order not to see her. Not to see the dark holes of these eye sockets, these staring holes. What does she want to do? Reach the electrified barbed-wire fence? Why does she stare at us? Isn't she pointing at me? Imploring me? I turn away to look elsewhere. Elsewhere. (26)

Looking elsewhere first takes on a spatial meaning: she looks at another woman—a dancing female skeleton—in front of the gate of block 25. This object of the look is just a continuation of the sight of the dying woman, which she could not bear any longer. But then the "looking elsewhere" is transformed into a temporal displacement. The following sentence constitutes a paragraph in itself:

> Presently I am writing this story in a café—it is turning into a story. (26)

"Presently" (*maintenant*) marks a present, the moment at which the text is being narrated or written. The description of the woman's death struggle, however, also slips into the present: the past tense is again and again exchanged for the present tense. There seem to be two "presents," existing not after each other but next to each other.

The narrator's remark that her words are turning into a story seems to imply a negative judgment on her narration. When her words are forming a story the narrated events are situated at a distance, that is, in the past. Such a mode of narration does not do justice to her immediate and visual experience in the present of these events, which consists of nothing else but "witnessing."

The text which follows introduces an alternative mode of narration. With no indication of the changes, the narrative situation keeps transforming, even within one single paragraph. First-person narrators change in identity: the "I" who looks on and who witnesses transforms into an "I" who narrates a childhood experience; this "I" becomes the first person, who turns out be the dying woman.

> She no longer looks at us. She is huddling in the snow. His backbone arched, Flac is going to die—the first creature I ever saw die. Mama, Flac is at the garden gate, all hunched up. He's trembling. André says he's going to die.
>
> "I've got to get up on my feet to rise. I've got to walk. I've got to struggle still. Won't they help me? Why don't you help me all of you standing there with nothing to do."
>
> Mama, come quick, Flac is going to die.
>
> "I don't understand why they won't help me. They're dead, dead. They look alive because they're standing up, leaning one against the other. They're dead. As for me, I don't want to die." (27)

Voices and temporalities intermingle: it is almost impossible to distinguish them from one another, to become part of a single present. This seems to be the narrative alternative for the witnessing women who cannot bear to see what they are watching. Although they are not able to relate to her (they are not in a situation to do that), they absorb her into their self-experience. They become one.

When an SS man's dog finally kills the woman with a bite, a scream is heard:

> And we do not stir, stuck in some kind of viscous substance which keeps us from making the slightest gesture—as in a dream. The woman lets out a cry. A wrenched-out scream. A single scream tearing through the immobility of the plain. We do not know if the scream has been uttered by her or by us, whether it issued from her punctured throat, or from ours. I feel the dog's fangs in my throat. I scream. I howl. Not a sound comes out of me. The silence of a dream. (28–29)

The absolute distance which had until now defined the relation between the dying woman and the witnessing women has ultimately disappeared. The external memory in the past tense of a dying woman in the camp changes gradually into the sensorial experience of someone who is dying herself. The text we have read is, at the end, no longer the witnessing account of a specific event in the past. It has transformed into a direct experience in the flesh. When, in Auschwitz, the act of seeing has been fundamentally disrupted and, as a result, "to see" no longer implies relating to the object of the look—when seeing can still only mean witnessing—then a narrative solution is introduced to heal the insufferable condition of witnessing. Instead of seeing the other (focalizing her), the narrator becomes her by absorbing the woman's voice into hers.

The final paragraph of the story is a telling variation on the earlier reflection on the act of narrating this text. After a blank space the following sentence ends the story: "And now I am sitting in a café, writing this text" (29). This writing no longer consists of producing a testimony of what has happened in the past. In a painstaking process, Delbo's writing transforms before our eyes into a performance which gives voice to the object of her look: to the woman who died in the camp while she just looked on. The present in which this writing takes place emphatically does not situate the represented events in relation to it. It is not continuous with it; it is rather a second present next to the present in which the text is being written. Since the end of the woman's death struggle is systematically written in the present tense, this other or second "present" has to be explicitly marked in order not to merge with it: "And now I am sitting in a café, writing this text."

The title of the second part of Delbo's trilogy, *Useless Knowledge,* can be read as an outspoken statement to the effect that the visual and sensorial imprints left by life in the camps should not be confused with the substance of memory. The story "The Stream" is an especially good example of this distinction. The Holocaust is ineffable, specifically unnarratable because of the monotony of the days. There were barely any specific events. The text begins as follows:

> Strange, but I don't recall anything about that day. Nothing but the stream. Since all the days were the same, a monotony interrupted only by heavy penalties and roll calls, since the days were the same, we certainly had roll call, and, following roll call, work columns were formed, I must have been careful to stay in the same column as my group, and later, after a long wait, the column must have marched through the gate where the SS in the sentry box counted the ranks passing through. And after? Did the column go right or left? Right to the marshes, or left toward the demolition work, or the silos? How long did we walk? I have no idea. What work did we do? Neither do I recall that. (147)

While the narrator tries to recall a particular day—to represent it to her mind—she only remembers those things which recurred day after day. Nothing came to interrupt the repetition of the same.

The lack of markings in time can be sensed in the sentence that goes on and on. Just as the days were no longer separate units of time, Delbo's sentences espouse that sameness and continuity. Both are but a stream as formless as the stream in the marshes near which they were forced to dig. Now and then a slow-down is marked by a comma, but there is no full stop to mark the end of the sentence.

The narrator remembers only the stream. The memory of that stream has cast out all other impressions. But there are certain things which she can reconstitute: among them, how many women of her convoy were still alive on a particular day. The day of which she remembers only the stream must have been in early April, for it was sixty-seven days after their arrival in the camp. That day there were still seventy women of the group living. In the stream that is life in the camp the only marked, the only remarkable, fact is the presence of the other women with whom she was taken to Auschwitz.

But there is a second reason why life in the camp cannot be remembered in narratable moments. And, like the strong visuality we have seen at work so far, this reason belongs to the domain of the senses. The stench in the camp was unbearable. The constant stench of the crematorium, the stench of one's own body and that of others: so many smells numbed one's senses, so that none could be specifically smelled:

> What amazes me, now that I think of it, is that the air was light, clear, but that one didn't smell anything. It must have been quite far from the crematoria. Or perhaps the wind was blowing in the opposite direction on that day. At any rate, we no longer smelled the odor of the crematoria. Yes, and what also amazes me is that there wasn't the slightest smell of spring in the air. Yet there were buds, grass, water, and all this must have had a smell. No, no memory of any odor. It's true that I can't recall my own smell when I lifted my dress. Which proves that our nostrils were besmirched with our own stink and could no longer smell anything. (149–150)

After this testimony to the death of the sense of smell, the narrator describes in great detail the moment of that one day when the capo allowed her to wash in the stream. Yet the text ends with the sentence "It must have happened like this, but I have no memory of it. I only recall the stream." (153)

This contradiction does not mean that the narrator invented what happened that spring day. It means only that this day is part of her "external memory" of Auschwitz. Her deep or sense memory only sees, feels, smells the monotonous stream. It is this stream that defines life in Auschwitz and the only possible memory of it. Washing in the stream, that one event that stands out, is, in this sense, the one moment that she could wash herself of the stream.

The existence of two kinds of Holocaust literature confirms Janet's psychiatric distinction between narrative and traumatic memory, as it does Delbo's distinction between ordinary and deep memory and that between external and sense memory. These two kinds of literature maintain a distinctive, defining relationship with visual images as either imprints or "relatable" images—capable of entering into a relationship, as well as being narrated. Thus, we can conclude, visuality, the specific power of images, is definingly significant for the specific kind of memory that struggles to survive the Holocaust, remember it, and yet transform the visual fixation that assaults into a visual active remembrance that works through.

Images confirm, and further qualify, a distinction made in an important article by Sidra DeKoven Ezrahi.[12] Ezrahi distinguishes two different ways of representing the Holocaust, which reflect, in fact, two different aesthetics.

Though I wish to differentiate these two kinds of literature in terms of their relationship to vision, they share a common point of departure, which is at the same time their point of arrival: Auschwitz is the ultimate point of reference. It is a spot or event with which imaginative representations correspond or fail to do so. Both writer and reader are constantly positioned in relation to this epicenter, this point of no return. But Auschwitz, as epicenter of the earthquake that the Holocaust was in human history, is both a literal and a metaphoric notion. Auschwitz, writes Ezrahi, has become the metaphor of the earthquake that destroyed not only people and buildings, but also the "measure" through which destruction can be gauged (122).

This destruction of the ability to measure destruction results in Auschwitz's fundamental ambiguity as a historical site and event, as well as a symbol: forever caught in the ambiguity of its signifying force, Auschwitz can never be more than a symbol of what can no longer be symbolized. For we have lost the measure to decide of what Auschwitz is a symbol. In this sense, too, Auschwitz, and the Holocaust for which it synecdochically stands, cannot be represented. For the metaphorical principles of language have ceased to function. As a metaphor, /Auschwitz/ is overdetermined: "it" is so rich in meaning that nothing can be metaphorically compared to it. On the other hand, /Auschwitz/ is underdetermined as a metaphor, because it has no precise, measurable meaning. As an "empty" metaphor, it cannot illuminate new or unexpected aspects of human existence, as metaphors are called upon to do.

Ezrahi then proceeds to distinguish between two possible attitudes toward this paradoxical status of Auschwitz, as reference point of a metaphor that is both over- and underdetermined. One can adopt either a static or a dynamic attitude. The static or absolute attitude places the subject in front of a historical reality that is unbending and from which we can never be liberated. The dynamic attitude approaches the representation of the memory of Auschwitz as a construction made up of strategies deployed in order to come to terms with this historical reality, over and over again (122). This dynamic attitude implies, for example, that the unbudging reality of this past can sometimes be made livable by the deployment of certain conventions to represent the past. Such softening cannot be acceptable within the absolute attitude. For when a softening or even a curing emerges within the memory or representation of Auschwitz, the threatened relativization of the ultimate evil that happened there threatens Auschwitz's status as the ultimate point of reference of that evil.

It is here that Delbo's use of visuality can be of help. As in the case of Janet's distinction between narrative and traumatic memory, the issue is the distance that can be achieved from Auschwitz. The absolute attitude maintains that any distance is ethically unacceptable—indeed, cognitively impossible. Auschwitz is a historical reality which continues in the present; in grammatical terms, it is the agent of a progressive form. The dynamic attitude is continuous with narrative memory, whereas the absolute attitude appears to be the consequence of traumatic memory. Ezrahi alleges, precisely, Borowski's use of the present tense as an example. Borowski writes that "all of us walk around naked," implying that in post-Holocaust times we can only walk around naked. The ordering of temporality in his work is the temporality of trauma, in which the past is like a second present, continuously determining the present.

According to Ezrahi, Primo Levi writes about his experiences in Auschwitz from a totally different position. His writing fulfills a mission to testify to the events which he experienced in the past. He communicates something which is over and belongs to the past. Thanks to that, it can be narrated by means of conventional modes. This is why Levi can write in such a clear and accessible style. He does not have to struggle with a past which persists in the present in which he writes. For him Auschwitz is an event delimited in history.

It is important to emphasize that Ezrahi's claims about Borowski and Levi are not psychological conclusions about the feelings of these authors. Her conclusions concern the position in time from which they write in relation to the time they write about. They are conclusions about different kinds of narration. From this perspective she even goes as far as to make a distinction between Levi's suicide and those of Borowski and the poet Paul Celan. According to her, Levi's suicide was not "caused" by Auschwitz, because Auschwitz belonged for him to the past when he killed himself. It must have been something arbitrary which made him do it. The suicides of Borowski and Celan, however, were direct consequences of Auschwitz. Although they survived, they still lived "inside" the Holocaust after their survival. Until their suicides they remained "forever trapped within the electrified barbed wire" (125).

Ezrahi's analysis can help us characterize Delbo's writings as analyses of visuality as memory sense. Delbo's writings are exemplary for the aesthetic which Ezrahi has called "the static attitude towards the events." This attitude makes itself felt by extreme visuality and direct representation of the Holocaust past: it is so visual and direct that this past is experienced as present. Her character Mado's descriptions of her memories of the other inmates in the camp, in *The Measure of Our Days,* do not show any distance in time. She sees the other inmates and joins them.

> I'm not alive. I'm imprisoned in memories and repetitions. I sleep badly but insomnia does not weigh on me. At night I have the right not to be alive. I have the right not to pretend. I join the others then. I am among them, one of them. Like me they're dumb and destitute. I don't believe in life after death, I don't believe they exist in a beyond where I join them at night. No. I see them again in their agony, as they were before dying, as they remained with me. (261)

In this passage, Delbo emphatically distances herself from the idea that her visions are dreams or hallucinations of a life beyond. Her visions are her memories. They are just as visual as dreams are.

But here a tragic irony appears. Past and present change places. Whereas memories of the past appear to her as radically visual, her sensorial awareness of life after Auschwitz is veiled. There is something between the present and her access to it. She cannot really, clearly, see that present.

She describes her and her husband's different conditions of being in the present as two different kinds of sight.

> For him, I'm there, active, orderly, present. He's wrong. I'm lying to him. I'm not present. Had he been deported too it would have been easier, I think. He'd see the veil over the pupils of my eyes. Would we then have talked together like two sightless people, each possessing the inner knowledge of the other? (267)

Whereas her sight of the past is bright, her sight of the present is veiled. Life in the present is literally overshadowed by the persistence of the visual and sensorial directness of when the Holocaust events happened to her in the past. Thus the most crucial perversion the Holocaust wrought consists of blinding and sharpening sight, but in inverse proportion to what makes life livable. Past horror occupies the eye, blinding it to a present that can, therefore, not redeem, not erase, not facilitate forgetting.

In the tradition of western science and art, visuality has been the domain of both truth—in a positivist epistemology of observation—and imagination—as in visual art that "presents before our eyes" what is to be seen as meaning, beauty, or tragedy. This is paradoxical. The paradox is reinforced when we realize that a third domain invoked through thinking about vision is that of affect, both in sentimental and in, for example, pornographic terms. With Delbo's probing of a vision that does not see, as an image of a memory that cannot relate, a past vision whose present makes the present invisible, we understand the different possibilities of vision better. If we wish to understand the modalities of memorizing the Holocaust, as we must if we wish to prevent the past from recurring by its hallucinatory power over us, we must distinguish between different kinds of vision, different kinds of looking. It may be perverse, but then it may be, for that reason, only too appropriate, to invoke verbal memories written down by those who were there, to understand how it is that art, today, can work over, elaborate, work through, and keep in visual touch with a past that no image can represent.

Notes

1. Tadeusz Borowski, *This Way for the Gas, Ladies and Gentlemen,* selected and translated from the Polish by Barbara Vedder, with an introduction by Jan Kott (New York: Penguin, [1967] 1976), 174.

2. Toni Morrison, *Beloved* (New York: Alfred A. Knopf, 1987), 36.

3. Toni Morrison, "Site of Memory," in *Inventing the Truth: The Art and Craft of Memoir,* ed. William Zinsser (Boston: Houghton-Mifflin, 1987), 111–112.

4. Lawrence L. Langer, *Holocaust Testimonies: The Ruins of Memory* (New Haven, Conn.: Yale University Press, 1991), 123.

5. For an extensive analysis of why Holocaust experiences have disrupted the ability to remember, see Ernst van Alphen, *Caught by History: Holocaust Effects in Contemporary Art, Literature, and Theory* (Stanford, Calif.: Stanford University Press, 1997), especially chapter 2, "Testimonies and the Limits of Representation."

6. Alphen, *Caught by History.*

7. Mieke Bal, introduction to *Acts of Memory: Cultural Recall in the Present,* ed. Mieke Bal, Jonathan Crewe, and Leo Spitzer (Hanover, N.H.: University Press of New England, 1999), ix. For a discussion of Janet's ideas, see Bessel A. van der Kolk and Onno van der Hart, "The Intrusive Past: The Flexibility of Memory and the Engraving of Trauma," in *Trauma: Explorations in Memory,* ed. Cathy Caruth (Baltimore: Johns Hopkins University Press, 1995), 158–182.

8. Van der Kolk and van der Hart, "The Intrusive Past," 160.

9. Mike Bal, introduction to *Acts of Memory,* ix.

10. Charlotte Delbo, *Auschwitz et après* (Paris, Les Éditions de Minuit). This trilogy consists of *Aucun de nous reviendra* (1965), *Une connaissance inutile* (1970), and *Mesure de nos jours* (1971). The trilogy has been translated into English by Rosette C. Lamont as *Auschwitz and After,* with an introduction by Lawrence Langer (New Haven, Conn.: Yale University Press, 1995). Quotations in the text are from this edition.

11. For the distinction between punctual and durative events, see Mieke Bal, *Narratology: Introduction to the Theory of Narrative,* 2d ed. (Toronto: University of Toronto Press, 1997), 93.

12. Sidra DeKoven Ezrahi, "Representing Auschwitz," *History and Memory* 7, no. 2 (fall/winter 1996): 121–154.

8 Gays and the Holocaust

Two Documentaries | ROBIN WOOD

"Change everything. But how? Everywhere. Now."

—Jane Fonda in Godard's *Tout va bien*

Despite *Shoah,* the great length of which creates obvious impediments to frequent programming, the most widely known and celebrated documentary about the Holocaust is clearly *Nuit et brouillard,* written by Jean Cayrol, directed by Alain Resnais. This half-hour film always makes an indelible impression, part of its power (but also its limitation) being that it is less a straightforward documentary than a precisely designed and richly textured work of art, a "film-poem" that takes its place among a series of short films in which Resnais explored the themes that obsessed him during his early years of filmmaking: time, memory and forgetfulness, the legacy of the past and its relation to the present. Judged as a responsible account of the Holocaust the film leaves crucial issues unexplored. There is little analysis of how and why the Holocaust happened, remarkably small insight into fascism and its roots in western culture, and no very useful attempt to suggest how a recurrence of such forms of persecution might be prevented. The film, in fact, leaves the viewer with a sense of helplessness: such things have happened, they will happen again, the only safeguard is memory but memory is always fallible. Its final sequence, showing the prosecution of those involved in the "crimes against humanity," from commandant to executants, all of whom deny responsibility, culminates in the question "Who, then, is responsible?" It is the wrong question: What we should be asking is not Who? but What? (I should make it clear immediately that I take it as axiomatic that one's primary motive for writing about the Holocaust must be to help prevent future recurrences.)

Though neither of the documentaries under discussion here pretends to the status of Resnais's film as artwork, both (in different ways, from somewhat different viewpoints) offer more useful pointers toward an answer. I am prefacing the discussion with certain of my own reflections, without any pretensions to completeness. I offer them as possible stimuli to further debate, their very incompleteness underlined by their somewhat random nature: a series of probes that lay no claim to providing a fully coherent, let alone definitive, argument.

Imagining the Unimaginable

"Is there any cause in nature that makes these hard hearts?"

I am no more able to answer King Lear's question than was Shakespeare, but it evokes very precisely the great debate of our own age: Is there such a thing as "the human condition," "human nature," or are we socially constructed, hence changeable? We like today to believe the latter, discounting the former because it has been used consistently by conservatism as an excuse for not changing anything, and few today, surely, will want to reject the arguments for our changeability that have developed out of the highly sophisticated (and generally convincing) theories of ideology elaborated since the '60s. However, a doubt still lingers: Can theories of social construction account for everything?—can they account for the Holocaust? Are human beings naturally cruel? Is there some ineradicable streak of savagery, barbarism, malignancy in the human race inherited from our primeval, even prehuman, ancestors, and latent within us, waiting for circumstances favorable to its eruption? My point is that, whatever doubts remain, it has become impossible to shrug our shoulders and say, "Well, it's part of the human condition": If we are to an appreciable degree socially constructed, then we can change a great deal and no longer have a pretext for laziness. Perhaps we can even, with the tools and weapons now at our disposal, forestall another Holocaust, creating a culture within which such barely imaginable enormities could no longer happen. The undertaking is daunting: It requires a thorough and radical restructuring not only of our social system but of ourselves, of the ways in which we organize our lives, of our ways of thinking and feeling. But only when we have completed this task will we be able to answer Lear's question.

This will, eventually, be an article about the persecution of gays under the Nazis, but it cannot be only about that or it will have failed to address the real issues. I begin by defining a context: the context which made the Holocaust possible, but also what remains—not in Nazi Germany but within our own so-called democratic world—the context within which another holocaust, given certain not altogether unlikely sociopolitical developments, could happen.

The Personal Is Political: Myself as Nazi and Victim

I have many things in my life that I am ashamed of, and one of the worst is also one of the earliest in memory. When I was about seven years old I dug up some worms in the garden one day and laid them out, writhing, on a glass frame in the brilliant sunlight. I had intended to leave them only for a few minutes, but something distracted me and I forgot about them. When I remembered, they were shriveled up, completely dry, dead. I was horrified at what I had done, and remain so today. The question is, Why did I do it in the first place? I think because I felt entirely disempowered. I was the last child of five, the next twelve years older; on some less-than-conscious level I must have realized that I was an "accident." No one treated me cruelly. My mother made up for not wanting me by spoiling me; my father thought I was a "sissy" and was always trying to toughen me up with violent tickling games, which made me feel completely powerless and invariably ended in my tears, but were not intentionally cruel; my older siblings largely ignored me but were not unkind. It was around that time that I had had my first erection (the first I was aware of), a response to a (male) character in a film I saw, and it puzzled and troubled me. Curious as this may seem today, I had not, at that late age, been informed about what are known as "the facts of life" (as though they were the only ones), though I had certainly been made aware that my so-called private parts were somehow ugly, dirty, and shameful, and that there was some mysterious secret concerning them that I must never find out (I was twelve when I finally made the shocking discovery). So perhaps the worms were Freudian symbols. They were, in any case, small living creatures over which I had complete power, power of life and death, power of pleasure and agony. I am glad only of the shame I experienced later; I know I enjoyed the actual deed, with a sadistic pleasure. The roots of fascism are there, at the heart of family life; the nuclear family is itself structured upon degrees of power and disempowerment, and most forms of neurosis that are not directly linked to economic disempowerment have their roots in the family structure. This seems the moment to salute and recommend—to anyone who hasn't already read it—Alice Miller's brilliant essay "Hitler's Childhood"—with the proviso that Miller (entrenched in psychoanalytical theory but rejecting most of Freud) cannot go far enough.[1] She is amazing on the systemic abuse of children within families, but appears quite unable to question the family as an institution: the outcome of her analyses ultimately amounts to little more than that parents should be more decent and beating abolished, which leaves intact the patriarchal structures and prevents any suggestion of alternative forms of social organization and childrearing, leaving untouched the crucial question as to whether biological parents (with their own agenda, not necessarily related to the child's good, and generally obsessed with reproducing him or her in their image, with their own beliefs and preferences, thereby inhibiting any possible progress beyond) should have such definitive control over their children's upbringing.

When I was ten, during World War II, in an all-boys' school in England, I found myself at the worms' end of the spectrum. A group of older boys, having discovered that I was physically weak, hopeless at and uninterested in sports, with a bad stammer and weird interests such as Hollywood musicals and romantic pop songs, tormented me repeatedly and mercilessly, partly physically but more mentally, with taunts, never stopping until I was reduced to lying on the ground with my hands over my ears and screaming hysterically (the play areas were unsupervised, and the worst crime one could commit was "sneaking"). Once, during that period, I found another group of boys teasing the school's sole mentally handicapped boy, the oldest in the school, sent there presumably because his parents had some fantasy about his becoming "normal" in that environment. They were imitating his speech difficulties and his erratic hand and shoulder movements. I joined in, the victim seizing his opportunity to become the Nazi. Fortunately, this took place indoors and the headmaster found us. The other boys were driven off with an angry rebuke but I was taken into his study and made to sit down. He reminded me gently of my stammer, and asked how I would feel if other boys teased me. I remember it as my moment of deepest shame—worse than discovering the dehydrated worms, because here someone else knew about my crime.

Four years later the war ended and I saw the concentration camp films on a newsreel. I find myself unable adequately to describe the effect they had on me: words like "horror," "shock," "repugnance" do not convey for me the profundity and intensity of the disturbance I experienced and which continued with me for many years. Although my stammer was always at its worst on the telephone, I used (secretly—I was afraid of being called a coward) to call up cinemas when there was a film I wanted to see and struggle to ask what was in the newsreel. I already adored Hitchcock's movies, and at the age of fourteen was fascinated by the idea of psychoanalysis, and I went with some of my family to see *Spellbound,* an experience I had longed for above everything. In the foyer was a poster announcing the newsreel: pictures of the victims of the Hiroshima atomic bomb. I still wonder how I got through the next few minutes. I couldn't confess how terrified I was to my adult siblings; they would notice if I closed my eyes; I couldn't pretend to be suddenly ill. We were late, and the newsreel was over. But I couldn't enjoy the film. My heart was still pounding violently and I kept imagining what the pictures in the newsreel would have been like.

Was I so upset because I saw myself as one of the victims of these twin enormities committed by members of the human race, or because I knew I might myself have been among those who committed them?

Godard, Bergman, and the Holocaust

Neither Jean-Luc Godard nor Ingmar Bergman made a film directly about the Holocaust, but each made one very distinguished film which, on the filmmaker's own testimony, relates to it obliquely. Godard, defending *Les carabiniers* to a generally hostile press, remarked that the film that needs to be made about the Holocaust is a film about the guards, not the victims; Bergman, when he made *Skammen* [The Shame], commented that he had been wondering how he would have acquitted himself under concentration camp conditions. The two films are as different as possible from one another, with Bergman, as usual, seeing everything in personal terms, Godard, equally characteristically, in political, but they have two things in common: both (insofar as they can be read as relating to the Holocaust) are indeed about the guards rather than the victims; and in both cases the appalling behavior of the leading male characters is connected to (significantly different) forms of disempowerment. Bergman's protagonist is a sensitive musician, a violinist formally with the Stockholm Philharmonic, stranded and isolated by a civil war which he neither understands nor participates in; the film charts his transformation, through a series of incidents over which he has no control, from a weak, somewhat spoiled, but in no sense evil human being to a strong and totally ruthless and conscienceless killer. Godard's soldiers enlist because they are promised the spoils of war; they are the lowest of the low in the capitalist economy, living in a wasteland, ignorant, uneducated, essentially innocent, not even aware of their own socially conditioned brute stupidity. As soldiers they loot, execute, commit atrocities, without the slightest qualm. They return from the war unchanged, with the promised spoils in the form of a veritable mountain of postcards encompassing all the wonders of civilization, and are promptly executed for having participated on the losing side.

It is significant that these two great filmmakers, who expressed a desire to refer (at least) to the Holocaust in their work, did so obliquely: few would relate either of the above films to the concentration camps without the hints of their directors. Implicitly, they recognize the impossibility of imagining the unimaginable. Lesser figures in fictional cinema have been less prudent. Robert M. Young's *Triumph of the Spirit* is at least an honorable attempt, sparing its audience little (which is probably why it gets shown so seldom), but it seems to me marred by its (understandable) desire to find something upbeat or uplifting to salvage, a dubious enterprise in this context. The same might be said of *Schindler's List,* though I cannot escape the sense (here and in *Saving Private Ryan*) of something essentially self-serving in Spielberg's work. "Self-serving," however, is too mild a word for the critically acclaimed, Oscar-honored, *La vita è bella:* "self-congratulatory" would be nearer the mark. To use the Holocaust as a pretext for a massive ego-trip is to me quite unpardonable.

Power and Impotence

There is a scene in Howard Hawks's masterpiece *Rio Bravo* in which Dude (Dean Martin), as sheriff's deputy, refuses to admit the local quasi-fascist land baron, Nathan Burdett (John Russell), and his henchmen to the town unless they surrender their guns first. Burdett tells Dude, who has been for some years notorious as the town drunk, ready to retrieve coins from spittoons for the sake of alcohol, "Every man should have a taste of power before he dies." The moment crystallizes two types of power: Burdett's, the power of money, the power of numbers, the power of weaponry, the power of ruthlessness in pursuing his selfish aims; and Dude's, which is at this point in the film power over himself, as victor in his personal battle for self-respect, supported by the knowledge that he is taking a stand for fundamental human decency.

The only legitimate form of power has nothing to do with possessions, position, wealth, or physical strength; it has everything to do with self-respect, which presupposes a considerable degree of self-understanding and which cannot be bought with money. I have not so far been talking about fascism per se but about the frighteningly fertile soil within which fascism can germinate, take root, and flourish: soil to which every aspect of our current sociopolitical organization contributes. Fascism—the rule of power, by force if necessary—is a political movement that develops out of advanced capitalism. Within the capitalist system, money is power, poverty is disempowerment, and as capitalism advances (arguably toward the destruction of life on our planet, through the devastation of the natural environment) the gulf between the powerful and the disempowered widens, and the acquisition and hoarding of wealth becomes an essentially meaningless but increasingly obsessive end in itself. Corporations flourish and grow; governments and the media depend upon them for their strength and continuance. Money, through the media it buys, corrupts multitudes into electing the very people who may destroy them. It is difficult to think of any common form of human relationship today that is not contaminated (to a greater or lesser degree) by money-values. And self-respect, the one legitimate form of power, evaporates and is not even missed (except perhaps in bad dreams and psychosomatic illness). The possibility of another fascism, even another Holocaust, is very much with us. Within the present organization the most we can do is try, by whatever "democratic" means remain, to build safeguards—which will become increasingly inadequate as capitalism "advances" further. The larger question is whether the continuance of the present organization is now inevitable. It is not a matter of changing a system; it is a matter of changing ourselves with it.

Capitalism is, almost by definition, built upon structures of power and disempowerment, and those structures are not mere abstractions, are not passive or merely there. They breed. Where any acceptable form of political organization would encourage cooperation, capitalism breeds competition, one-upmanship, dog-eat-dog struggle. We have multimillionaires and we have the homeless. For some obscure reason the former believe they have a right to their wealth and their power, even if they don't know what to do with it; meanwhile, every winter, the latter die in our midst of frostbite and malnutrition. Everyone within our culture experiences either power or powerlessness or both, the latter containing within it, as a logical consequence, the desire for the former.

At present, in Canada, a new political party, the Alliance party, is forming, and gaining a huge popular following. It represents the extreme Right and has vast amounts of money backing it (in the form of "business"—has anyone wondered why a common childhood euphemism for shitting is "doing one's business"?). As I write, the Alliance have just chosen their leader, a highly charismatic and articulate pedagogue who has already made clear his antagonism to abortion rights and gay rights and his commitment to capital punishment (though he says he won't act on these beliefs unless "the people" want him to—with, of course, the implication that if "the people," sufficiently mystified and intimidated, can be persuaded that they want him to, he will do so promptly, merely obeying their wishes—any results will not be his fault). He may well become Canada's next prime minister. Does this ring a certain bell? Our new prospective prime minister[2] is also a fervent Evangelical, and throughout history religious extremism has always provided the most potent rationale for persecution. In fact, only one major factor is lacking for a new fascist takeover: extreme economic crisis, as background and pretext for the promise of new strength, power, and glory. The current grotesque (and steadily increasing) division between rich and poor, however, might become a partial substitute: a potential vast increase of economic power could easily (and entirely hypocritically) be proffered as a means of improving the lot of everyone.

Sexuality and Power

We know now that homosexuality is not unnatural; neither is it a "choice" or even a "preference." No one "chooses" his or her sexual orientation—though one could speak of someone who is fully bisexual "choosing" to have sex with either a man or a woman, or having a "preference" for one or the other. Sexuality evolved drastically when creatures began to walk upright, its primary aim and function undergoing fundamental change. It is no longer possible to talk of procreation as its primary function: The number of times human beings have sex strictly in order to produce babies is now enormously exceeded by the times they have sex simply for the sake of the experience. Anyone who practices birth control in any form (including simple withdrawal) implicitly acknowledges this. The primary function of human sexuality today is mutual pleasure and communication, and from the moment that is accepted the gender of the partner becomes irrelevant. With the growing acceptance of homosexual practice, it seems plausible to argue that the ultimate destiny of human sexuality may be bisexuality, or the freely flowing movement of sexuality without fixed aim.

One cannot understand or explain the resistance to—and, in the extreme, the condemnation and persecution of—homosexuality without first examining sexuality's power structures. Women are "passive," men are "active"—that has always been the legend. It ignores, of course, the activity of women and the passivity of men, and has always been the basis for the supposition that the man is "naturally" the dominant sex, not just in the simple matter of intercourse but as the "breadwinner," the "man of the house," the lord of the manor, and the master of the universe. But the time when women (supposedly horrified by the "dirtiness" of sex, as proclaimed by men, who went ahead and did it anyway) were taught to "lie back and think of England" is long past, as one can see from typical scenes of intercourse in practically any contemporary Hollywood movie. Recognition of this has, unfortunately, not made much headway beyond the sex act, despite the enormous strides of 1960s–70s feminism. Men have, on the whole, found that they can derive a lot of pleasure from women who take the sexual initiative in the bedroom (it can save them a lot of hard work, and they can still believe if they wish that it is all being done for their pleasure rather than their partner's), but they have proved more reluctant to allow initiative in the boardroom. Women have been allowed to join the masculinist club. The membership fee is the prompt sacrifice of all their finest qualities as women, all those traditionally "feminine" qualities that men are not supposed to share (if they reveal them, they are "sissies"), together with any inconvenient lingerings of a feminist conscience. They can then become almost-men: their membership will never be quite complete. Their allotted role is analogous to that of collaborators during World War II, shameful and ignominious. Meanwhile, their fellow women are still being raped and battered and murdered daily at home and gang-raped and slaughtered in those wars we read about in our newspapers. Everyone seems to agree nowadays that rape is all about power rather than sexual pleasure, and housewives are typically battered because they have questioned their husbands' authority. Fascism, at least as much as charity, begins at home. And the children, arguably the most disempowered of all, without even the right to call the cops if they are struck, grow up among fascism's roots.[3]

GAYS AND THE HOLOCAUST

The Necessary Scapegoats

Political fascism grows out of the fertile soil I have tried to describe when certain favorable political and economic circumstances develop. I have already suggested that those favorable circumstances are at least embryonically present today, and if we don't want another Holocaust but are reluctant to transform the basis of our culture, we shall have to be ready to defend with extreme vigor the always precarious and vulnerable safeguards of the quasi-democracy (government of the people by the rich and powerful, for the rich and powerful) that exist: notably, the rights of women and the rights of minority groups, racial or otherwise.

Fascism dazzles the unwary and ignorant (along with its immediate beneficiaries) with signifiers of power, national dignity and prosperity, and the "triumph of the will": those who go under deserve their fate, either because they protest or simply because they are weak (in wealth, in numbers, in positions of power). Fascism celebrates "possession of the phallus" (the "Hitler salute" surely dramatizes an erection). And the dazzlement, the glamour of fascism requires scapegoats, those who don't possess it. Political dissidents can be readily suppressed: they are the opponents of "progress." But their persecution and punishment cannot be too openly publicized without the grounds for their dissidence becoming dangerously apparent: it is easier and more convenient simply to brand them as perverse "freaks," send them to prison, and have them disappear, soon forgotten. The best scapegoats are minority groups, and the more unpopular the better. Join the powerful and you automatically become empowered, but to express that power you require a victim: it's the story of the worms or the schoolyard bullies magnified into a political movement. If I do not analyze here the reasons why Hitler and his Nazi party chose the Jews as primary scapegoat, it is purely because I am sure the task is being done better and more thoroughly elsewhere in this volume. My own task is to explain why gays (essentially gay men—few lesbians were sent to the camps) became the secondary scapegoat (and we must not forget the other minorities, notably the Roma, who were also Hitler's victims).

The very furtiveness of gay life made gays an easy target; it also partly explains why the number of the Holocaust's gay victims is small in relation to its Jewish victims. Homosexuals conducted their personal lives, necessarily, in secret; their sexual orientation was not inscribed within their passports. Very simply, they were less easy to track down. They had also been taught (as I was) to be deeply ashamed of what they were, of the very basis of their being. Many must have accepted their victimization as well deserved (as I probably would have, in that country at that time, given the circumstances of my own upbringing, the guilt and self-loathing I was taught to experience for just thinking certain thoughts). And they were very, very unpopular. After Jews, they were the perfect scapegoats, with the enormous weight of popular (and essentially heterosexual male, thus rooted at the very base of fascism) disgust supporting their persecution.

Suppose the current movement to the right across both the U.S. and Canada culminates in a fascist takeover, and those in power feel the need for a new

Holocaust. Such a takeover does not appear imminently possible, but while corporate capitalism continues to flourish and expand, while "the people" are kept in their current state of mystification by the capitalist media, and in the total absence of an effective Left, it need not be that far away—think how swiftly it happened in Germany, and how unprepared were the victims, forever telling themselves that "these things don't happen to us." Who will be the necessary victims? Not the Jews again: the Nazi Holocaust is still too present, its realities too terrible, its horrors too familiar. The most obvious primary target is the blacks, already associated in the popular imagination with crime and slums, extremely vulnerable in their generally underprivileged position—already our police can gun down unarmed blacks and emerge more or less unscathed. But gays will be next, their current positive image in the media swiftly reversed, their at most marginal connection to traditional "family values" skillfully played upon by the Right, their sexual freedom perceived (quite rightly) as a serious threat to the heterosexual monogamy that is in any case today more an empty formula than a reality (it became logically unnecessary with the acceptance of birth control). With the media locked into the capitalist organization and easily taken over by the wrong Right government, the demonization of blacks and gays will be a simple matter. "Sexual perversion" will be a useful term: there will be no need to brand gays criminals, they can simply be seen once again as "sick" and sent off to "rehabilitation centers" (they won't be called camps) to be "cured." When the cure is shown not to work, they will disappear. And today, thanks to their new exposure in the media and the great gains they have made, and with their commitment to "gay pride" and "coming out," gays are far more visible than they were in Hitler's Germany. There is even a new law in Canada making it obligatory for gay and lesbian partners to list themselves as "same-sex couples" in the forthcoming census—welcomed, quite rightly, as a great advance in legal recognition, but also, for a hypothetical fascist government, as convenient as a stamp on a passport. How many among the heterosexual population will be ready to stand up for them, to resist the anti-gay propaganda, to risk their own reputations and positions in society? How many whites will come out for blacks? The honorable ones, of course. For the rest (those, at least, with some glimmering of a conscience), there will be the usual excuses: our wives, our families, our children, our positions. We are not black, after all. . . . We are not gay. . . . It isn't really our concern. . . .

The Long Silence

Stuart Marshall's *Desire* (the earlier of the two documentaries I will discuss) ends with a lengthy sequence showing the various memorials to Holocaust victims in capital cities. The last, significantly in Amsterdam, is the only one that commemorates gays. Everywhere else, silence. Does anyone want to argue that this is solely because there were vastly fewer gay victims than Jewish—in other words that a mere ten to fifteen thousand human individuals (the current official estimate) don't matter? The general public can be excused for this silence on grounds of ignorance: as they were never told, they couldn't know. But all our officials and spokespersons knew. When Alain Resnais and Jean Cayrol made *Nuit et brouillard,* by far the most famous of Holocaust documentaries, they must certainly have known. They mention other groups, other triangular badges worn by political prisoners and the Roma, but for them the pink triangle did not exist or was an embarrassment. It is only quite recently that the persecution of gays has received wide attention, one important turning point being the play *Bent.* Today, at last, Holocaust museums are beginning to include memorials to gays alongside those to the Jewish victims, though even this has not occurred without opposition from religious fundamentalists. Silence can be construed as implicit condonation: homosexuals got what they deserved.

The silence (or occasional opposition) of fundamentalists (both Jewish and Christian) has its religious sanctions. Their beliefs commit them to a literal reading of the Old Testament, and they are presumably obligated to condone the persecution of homosexuals. After all, their God (arguably the most monstrous character in the whole of narrative fiction) not only condemns homosexuality (in Leviticus) but personally conducted His own gay Holocaust (witness the myth of Sodom and Gomorrah, detailing the wiping out of an entire population because they were practicing an allegedly "unnatural" sexuality). I imagine that today, with the spread of more enlightened attitudes among the public at large, even the most rigorous and fanatical must experience some qualms. But that is the sort of unresolvable quandary commonly faced by those who continue to believe in ancient superstitions inscribed in texts produced thousands of years ago within cultural situations totally different from our own. Do these remarks offend the religious? Perhaps, before they complain, they will bear in mind how deeply their religion offends me. Isn't it time we all agreed to what is obvious: that we do not and cannot know how life began or what its destiny is, and should all join in acknowledging that unknowability, not in worship but in openness of spirit? Isn't the world, and our lives within it, astonishing enough without our needing, in our obsession with power, to invent some monstrous patriarchal figure as its inventor? Whatever divides is evil; whatever unifies is good—provided the unification forbids exceptions and welcomes diversity.

THE FILMS

Paragraph 175

Paragraph 175 (1999) is the work of Rob Epstein and Jeffrey Friedman, already noted for their previous film about gay history, *The Celluloid Closet* (1995), which dealt with the representation of gays in (mainly Hollywood) movies. A film about the entertainment industry, and aimed at audiences interested in Hollywood movies, the earlier work was (one might argue) weakened by its desire to be itself entertaining: witty, perceptive, meticulously researched (while owing a great deal to the late Vito Russo's book of the same name), it seems afraid to make too many demands on its audience. *Paragraph 175* has this advantage: you can't make an "entertainment" film about the Holocaust—because of not only the difference in subject matter, but also the difference in anticipated spectatorship; it is consequently the more rigorous work. As I write, it has not been shown publicly; I am indebted to Epstein and Friedman's generosity for their loan of an advance video. A more conventional documentary than *Nuit et brouillard,* it makes a less indelible impression, not only because it has no pretensions to Resnais's auteurist artistry but because it refuses all opportunities to appall us with the more horrific images available from concentration camp footage. Its aim is frankly educational and informational, and it wants us to grasp and reflect upon what we are shown and told rather than be emotionally overwhelmed. It seems to me deeply moving and troubling, but this is due to the lucid and highly intelligent presentation of the content rather than to any equivalent of Resnais's and Cayrol's undeniably potent visual and verbal poetry. It is, quite simply, more useful than *Nuit et brouillard,* and its usefulness is by no means restricted to its central preoccupation with the persecution of gays: In its historical research it is one of the most enlightening films I have seen about the Holocaust as a necessary consequence of Nazism, not as some kind of inexplicable aberration but as a logical growth out of history.

The film takes its title from an article in the German penal code, dating from 1871 and still intact in West Germany as late as 1969 (East Germany repealed it one year earlier); it took almost a hundred years and a Holocaust to rectify this inhuman and totally irrational affront to personal freedom. "Paragraph 175: An unnatural sex act committed between persons of the male sex or by humans with animals is punishable by imprisonment; the loss of civil rights may also be imposed." (One might add, parenthetically, that nothing speaks more eloquently of the accepted view of gay men than the casual juxtaposition of sex between consenting adults with the opportunistic and obviously abusive use of animals.)

This formed the legal basis of the Nazi persecution. At the film's end, the commentary (beautifully delivered by Rupert Everett) tells us that "[a]fter the war, all those persecuted by the Nazis under Paragraph 175 were classified as criminals. At century's end, not one has received legal recognition as a victim of the Nazi regime." The naked fact says more about the continuing vulnerability of gays in our culture than any amount of protest, as does the fact that Heinz Dormer, the most visibly devastated of the film's interviewees, was "repeatedly re-arrested under Paragraph 175 in the '50s and '60s. He tried and failed to receive reparations."

Epstein and Friedman owe much of their information to the research of the young historian Klaus Müller, who also participates in the interviews. He tells us at the outset, "I grew up in Germany, and I never, ever heard about the persecution of homosexuals." It was Müller's research that led to the inclusion of gays in the U.S. Holocaust Museum. The film, though Everett's narration, gives facts and figures: "A hundred thousand men, most of them from German-Christian families, were arrested. An estimated ten to fifteen thousand were sent to concentration camps. Today, fewer than ten of these men are known to be alive." The film skillfully intercuts a sketched history of gays in Germany from the '20s to the aftermath of World War II with the testimonies of some of the "fewer than ten" surviving internees and one woman who escaped to England (with the help of a woman "who looked like Marlene Dietrich"!), included for her insights into the parallel (though unlegislated and nonlethal) persecution of lesbians. (She is also Jewish, however, and tells us that, had she not escaped, she would have ended up in Auschwitz, where her entire family perished.) The history and the interviews consistently reinforce and illuminate each other, the latter often very poignantly personalizing the former. It might be added here that the film quite transcends what many might assume to be its mandate and its limitation: a "mere" protest by "others of the same persuasion" against the persecution of a single minority group. In fact, it seems to me obligatory viewing for anyone interested in the realities of Nazism and the Holocaust. But people who feel and think in those terms carry within themselves the germs of fascism, and in any case will have skipped this essay . . .

What was Nazism really about? And why was it so terrifyingly successful? The German people at large may well not have grasped the realities of what was happening to certain of their fellow humans, but the majority seem to have been solidly behind Hitler in principle, quite carried away by and caught up in the enthusiasm, the charisma, the Power of the Symbolic Phallus, in which they were promised a share, and were content to remain in what we may now regard as culpable ignorance. One episode (in Nazi history, in the Epstein/Friedman film) is especially resonant here: the sequence showing the closing of Magnus Hirschfeld's Institute of Sexual Science, followed by the burning of its entire library, followed by the burning of books in huge bonfires throughout Germany—books by "Jews, intellectuals, leftists, and other so-called degenerates." Very shortly after this, "[o]n July 14th, 1933, six months after coming to power, the Nazi party [became] the only legal party." Here we have, summed up, the enormous attraction of simplicity: We really don't have to do anything. We don't have to think (the problem with "intellectuals," as '50s America discovered with its "UnAmerican Activities Committee," which began with Communism and ended up with "anyone who thinks"), we don't have to change anything (the problem with "leftists," ditto), and we don't have to accept (or coexist with?) anyone we perceive as different from ourselves (Jews; gays; in America also blacks and other ethnic groups, which have never yet "melted" in that country's "pot"). It's the simple solution to life's bewildering complexities, it solves so many of our nagging little problems and discomforts at a blow: first you establish a norm, then you make it absolute. What it amounts to is the final elimination of "Otherness" in all its possible forms.

The refusal to accept Otherness pervades western culture—has always pervaded it, and continues to do so despite all the work done on it by those troublesome "intellectuals" (no wonder the Nazis burnt their books). Only small, marginalized, and therefore vulnerable groups (such as the hippies in the '60s) have dealt with it positively and effectively, but, identifying themselves as "Other" to mainstream culture, they have been unable to withstand its massive powers of assimilation. My own country, Canada, calls itself a "multicultural society," and it is indeed a damn sight nearer to being one than, for example, Britain or the United States, yet it still has a frighteningly long way to go, and its progress toward multiculturalism is being steadily undermined by the general shift to the right. Until we can accept Otherness, the threat of a new fascism will remain. Gay men, of course (along with, according to "Paragraph 175," anyone found to be fucking cows, chickens, or aardvarks), were in a special category of the unacceptable. The official account of the unacceptability is attributed to Himmler: "Seven to eight percent of men in Germany are homosexual. . . . Our nation will fall to pieces because of that plague. . . . Those who practice homosexuality deprive Germany of the children they owe her." So the birthrate in Germany drops by 7 to 8 per cent: at least seven in every hundred future Hitler Youths never materialize. But isn't this rationale undermined by the Nazis' failure to persecute lesbians (beyond breaking up their culture and driving them underground)? The official word was that lesbians can be reclaimed: such foolish women are just "going through a phase"; they can be easily cured. First (minor) point: western psychiatric (so-called) science still believed as late as 1970 that gay men could be "cured" too: as a bewildered and suicidal gay man with a wife and three children, I was offered and I refused (twice) "aversion therapy" (i.e., look at photos of naked men, get an erection, get an electric shock), which was going to "cure" me of one of my defining characteristics as a human being. Second (major) point: The Nazi animus (absolutely logical) against gay men was that they complicate things so much and raise difficult questions—anathema to the cult of the simple solution. Nazism was very clear about gender issues: Men are men, women are women, and never the twain shall meet except in God-and-Hitler-sanctified copulation to produce more Nazis. The man has the Phallus, the woman does not (though compliant women can be used, in suitably subservient positions, in concentration camps, like secretaries or "personal assistants" in business offices under capitalism). The men display their phallic power every time they raise their arms in the Hitler salute; the men are (in theory at least) Aryans, of the Master Race and proud of it, blond, handsome, physically strong, totally committed to their duties; they recognize sex as the means to reproduce their replicas, or girls who can in their turn produce . . . etc. (Isn't it somewhat ironic that this Aryan/Wagnerian physical stereotype, promulgated by Hitler and his henchmen so insistently, is by no means reproduced in Hitler himself or in any of the prominent Nazi leaders?) Gay men (and lesbians, of course) break down the gender barriers, throw the whole simplistic notion of sexuality and gender into the chaos that it actually is, and which we should sensibly, intelligently, and humanely accept and learn how to cope with.

It is the interviews that give *Paragraph 175* its depth and its directness. They are extraordinary in themselves, these testimonies from now-aged men who themselves endured and survived the camps, but the intensity of their effect is strengthened by their contrast with the objective historical analysis within they are placed. There is the confused nightmarish vision of Heinz Dormer, the most visibly shattered, with his constantly trembling left hand, his frail voice rising in near hysteria (the "singing forest," men hanging on hooks from high poles, howling and screaming—"Inexplicable. Beyond human comprehension. And much remains untold"). Whether memory or part-hallucination, his vision carries the force of remembered suffering so appalling as to seem surreal. And there is the rage of Pierre Seel, the man from Alsace who had sworn until the interview "never to shake hands with another German": "I wasn't even eighteen. Arrested, tortured, beaten. Without any defense, without a trial . . . I don't even mention being sodomized, being raped" . . . his friend Jo killed, then eaten by German shepherd dogs. Or Gad Beck's memory of the arrest of his young Jewish lover Manfred, whom he almost saved by borrowing a Hitler Youth uniform and getting him out of the police station. But Manfred went back: his whole family had been arrested with him, he was the only strong one and couldn't abandon them. He was never seen again, though his beauty and goodness are still visibly and movingly present in a photograph. Epstein and Friedman succeed brilliantly in balancing analysis with emotional impact, the two coloring each other without ever canceling each other out.

Desire

Superficially, Stuart Marshall's *Desire* (1989) may look like the same kind of film: Like *Paragraph 175* it relies for its information on "talking-head" interviews, increasingly in its second half, alternating these with historical footage; the shot of Magnus Hirschfeld by a balcony window is common to both films, and *Desire* also treats the burning of Hirschfeld's library and the closing of his Institute of Sexual Science as the film's (and the Holocaust's) pivotal moment (Hirschfeld was both Jewish and gay). Yet despite such overlaps *Desire* is a very different film, in certain respects a different kind of film. Subtitled *Sexuality in Germany, 1910–1945,* it has a narrower focus, a less detailed analysis of the Nazis' rise to power, yet one takes away from it the sense of a film of greater breadth and certainly of more conscious artistry. The Epstein/Friedman film is probably more useful for its clear and effective dissemination of important information, and it is to be hoped it will find a far wider public than Marshall's (which seems scarcely to have been shown, though it is available on video in specialty stores with an interest in nonmainstream material). But *Desire,* while respecting the documentary format, also transcends it, offering a deeper and more complex emotional experience.

The difference may be pinpointed in the films' very different uses of classical music. *Paragraph 175* uses it as a simple, unobtrusive accompaniment, and without much imagination: the slow movement of Sibelius's Fifth Symphony has no particular resonance in this context (a hundred other pieces would have done as well), and the Adagietto from Mahler's Fifth Symphony seems something of a cliché, an automatic response: the film's attitude seems to be, well, after all, it will be familiar to many from *Death in Venice,* and it's already associated in people's minds with gay material. One may reasonably, however, question the appropriateness of the association, Visconti's film being in effect a monumental act of gay self-oppression. But in fact the music counts for so little that this is neither here nor there. Marshall, on the other hand, presents his music, not as accompaniment, but in its own right and very pointedly: the music of the greatest Jewish composer (Mahler again, but here a relatively little-known song) and the greatest (reputedly) gay composer, Schubert. (The jury is still out as to whether Schubert was gay, bisexual, or heterosexual, the second option currently appearing the most likely.) Their music becomes an integral part of the film's meaning, emotionally as well as intellectually.

The use of the slow movement of Schubert's C-major string quintet, among the most remarkable, mysterious, and disturbing pieces in the whole of western music, composed when he knew he was dying of syphilis (the nineteenth-century equivalent of AIDS, of which Stuart Marshall was dying when he made his film), is especially resonant: The music becomes an elegy for the sufferings of gays throughout the ages. The film's closing sequence, the montage of Holocaust monuments mentioned above, is made almost unbearably moving by its juxtaposition with Mahler's "Ich bin der Welt abhanden gekommen" [I have lost touch with the world]: the film is lifted to a plane of universal tragedy, the camera rising, as the song closes, away from the monument, over the surrounding trees and buildings, to the sky, as the last note dies and we are left with silence and the emptiness of infinite space. There is nothing comparable in *Paragraph 175,* where it would in any case be inappropriate. It must also be admitted that the effect of this almost six-minute sequence depends at least partly on the spectator's recognition of and response to the Mahler song: in terms of "dissemination of information" it could even be considered counter-productive. Music is only one means by which deep emotion is expressed in and aroused by Marshall's film, which seems to grow in stature with every viewing. Epstein and Friedman are admirable documentarians; Marshall was an artist. One is not necessarily more valuable than the other (though I am aware that my own bias is showing through!); we need both, urgently, in a period when the "art of film" seems increasingly to be merged with the technology of "special effects," which represent neither. *Desire* shows evidence of an extreme sensitivity to the interrelations of the different aspects of cinema, the rhythms of camera movement, editing, and sound. Marshall's death after the film was completed can be taken as our loss of a potentially great filmmaker.

"They always referred to Nature, but they never meant sex or sexuality with it" says Marion de Ras, a historian, in *Desire*. For its first half hour, *Desire* does not explicitly suggest that it is a film about the Holocaust; Hitler and the Nazis are not referred to until around the film's midpoint. Its opening section is a detailed and fascinating account of the "nature" movement in pre–World War I Germany, at once the high point and the decadence of German Romanticism. Nature was worshipped, but it was an idealized, highly selective Nature, far removed from "Nature red in tooth and claw," and equally removed from the natural proclivities of human sexuality. Young people went off to camps in the countryside to cultivate their bodies and cleanse their spirits, rejecting modernization, industrialization, technology. The nudist movement flourished at the same time, and young men and women were encouraged to admire their own and others' bodies, but not in any sexual way. The camps seem to have been strictly segregated along gender lines: photographs show even young boys and girls in separate groups. Male was male, female female, and never the twain should meet, except later in holy matrimony, for the propagation of children and the continuance of the family system. Both male and female were associated insistently with water (cleanliness of mind and body), but surviving photographs reveal an interesting distinction: girls by still water (placid lakes), boys by running water (streams, waterfalls): the active male, the passive female. The irony of all this is of course that the patterns of organization greatly encouraged precisely what was forbidden: homosexual and lesbian desire. Most interesting is perhaps the fact that while all this was going on not one but several distinct gay liberation movements were originating and growing, among them Magnus Hirschfeld's, based on theories of innateness and demands for equality.

Then came the First World War, the collapse of the German economy, and the great period of what the Nazis were later to categorize as "degeneracy": the extraordinary blossoming of a gay and lesbian subculture in the cities, especially in Berlin. One must not mistake this for any realistic form of gay liberation: Its outward signifiers are easily read as "decadent," the guilty pleasures of a still criminal minority, the decadence representing a defiance of all the traditional norms that easily lent itself to being read as "immorality." Despite Hirschfeld's efforts to have it repealed, Paragraph 175 was still there in the penal code, ready to be reactivated at the "appropriate" historical moment.

Everything was in place for the rise of the Nazi party: Economic catastrophe and the pervasive sense of defeat and powerlessness; the necessary scapegoats on whom the ills could somehow be blamed; the ideological ideal of purity (as usual at the expense of all sense of complexity and contradiction)—all that "nature," all that "health," all that cleansing water—easily translatable into notions of racial purity and the need for racial purification; the ideal of strict gender difference, perfect men, perfect women, as if coming from different planets; and a whole "decadent" subculture of "immorality" to embody everything that "we" repudiated. It was all there for Hitler and the Nazis to orchestrate, with the simple promise of empowerment, cleanliness, and glory: the Master Race, strong, blond, physically and morally healthy and pure, with all its seductive simplicities, with all its denial of human complexity, diversity, and "otherness."

Strong, blond, and Aryan as some might be, gays and lesbians were treated in the camps as the lowest of the low. Gay men were not sent to gas chambers: they were not an identifiable race that could be exterminated. Instead they served two functions: they were used as workers in the most menial chores, and they were used for "scientific" experiments (often involving castration), in attempts to find "cures." And they were the ultimate outcasts, generally ostracized and treated with contempt by the other prisoners. Many, no doubt, were in a sense complicit in their fate: they had grown up in a culture where they were officially regarded as "sick," "perverted," "immoral," "evil," and must (for all the exhilarations of a flourishing gay culture) have internalized such attitudes. Only a very small proportion of those interned survived; many died or were murdered relatively early. As for lesbians, although they were not explicitly criminalized under Paragraph 175, many were arrested as "asocials" (a very common label, which could be applied to almost anyone) and used in the camps as prostitutes for the guards. They too were treated with scorn by their fellow victims, who, while totally disempowered, must have experienced a certain shameful sense of not being the worst.

TOWARD A FULLY HUMAN FUTURE

A great deal more could be said about both of these remarkable and salutary films; I very much hope that no reader will take away from this essay the feeling that they have been adequately "covered" and that consequently there is no reason to see them. Both seem to me essential viewing for anyone concerned about the Holocaust past and possible Holocausts future. But, reading through what I have written, I feel I have unwittingly set myself a challenge of which I was certainly not aware when I began and which I feel little confidence in being able to meet. What follows is an attempt (drawing together what I have taken from the films and from my own experiences of life in western capitalist civilization) to offer some kind of recipe for the prevention of future Holocausts. The ingredients will be both radical and controversial; they will be furiously rejected by many. But I have to say that to me they seem the merest common sense. In fact, they amount to no more than a spelling out of the line from Godard's *Tout va bien* quoted at the beginning of the essay: "Change everything." More specifically, all the power structures on which our culture is built must be dismantled.

First, then, the great progressive movements that developed in the late '60s, gathered such impetus in the '70s, and appear at present to have reached a temporary stasis—the women's movement, gay liberation, anti-racism—must be revived and reinforced. They made significant progress (now partly recuperated into the existing system), but it is not enough. Their basic aims must be rethought and further radicalized, the issues they raised probed deeper. Above all, they must establish links, recognizing the common goal ("Change everything") that underlies their differences. The diversities of race, gender, sexuality must be fully recognized, accepted, welcomed. Progress can be made not only by the connecting of movements but at the level of the individual: every positive relationship—friendship, love, marriage—between two people of different races or sexual orientations is a blow against potential fascism. Acceptance and understanding must replace the tendency to incorporate, to turn the Other into a replica of the Self.

Our whole notion of family must be rethought and drastically revised. Essentially this would entail weakening the generally artificial bonds of biological parentage. Our culture's power structures begin within the traditional family structure. Society seems to have moved some way from the traditional patriarchal model (father as breadwinner and "boss," mother as housewife, a.k.a. domestic servant), but the shift has created its own problems. With both parents going out to work, the business of parental childrearing develops intolerable strains and anxieties from which, ultimately, everyone suffers. We are always being told that children need love; it seems to me they need respect even more: to be listened to, to have their individual voices heard and honored. How much attention can be given their problems, their desires, their thinking, by a father and mother already exhausted by their jobs and preoccupied with their own problems? In any case we should begin asking ourselves whether the biological parents are really the ones best equipped to raise children. How many mothers and fathers can honestly say that they don't want power over their offspring, don't want to mold them into some kind of replica of themselves, can permit them the freedom to go beyond them into new places, forge new kinds of relationships, discover new values? And why should children be made to feel that it is their duty to love their parents? Perhaps their parents are unlovable, in which case the obligation to love them can only engender the most psychologically damaging guilt feelings. We need to look again at the possibilities of communal living and sharing, to begin to question our notion of "home" as some kind of closed-in space that shuts out the world and its multiplicities. Children need an environment within which they can choose their major relationships. I suspect that, given the freedom, a great many would not choose their own parents.

In this connection, as I began (almost) with childhood memories, perhaps I may be permitted one more, this time a very early one indeed: I cannot have been more than four years old, but it made an impression on me that remains as vivid as ever today, although it was only with the rise of radical feminism in the '60s that I understood its full significance. I used, with my parents, to visit my grandmother in the country, staying weekends. She seemed to me incredibly old: as my mother must then have been about fifty and was the youngest of her children, I suppose she was in her eighties, and she died soon after. I was allowed to visit her in the mornings in her bed, as she ate her breakfast from a tray, and those were among the happiest moments of my childhood. I adored that old woman, her gentleness, the softness and the scent of her wrinkled skin, which I loved to touch, the spontaneous tenderness she offered me (perhaps because she had to deal with me only once a year). On the morning I remember, I reached over to hug her and rub my face against hers, and I murmured, quite spontaneously, "I love you best in all the world." Immediately I sensed her stiffen; she detached my arms from her neck and pushed me gently away. "You must never say that," she told me. "You must love your father best, and then your mother. And then you can love me." She had been, of course, brought up in the mid-Victorian period; such an exchange would be unlikely to happen today, in so many words. But are we yet entirely free of the kind of thinking behind it? I couldn't love my father; he was unapproachable, and our only contact that I recall was the violent and aggressive tickling. The only practical consequence of her admonition was to make me feel terribly guilty, without in the least knowing why I should feel it. This sweet old woman was oppressing and essentially betraying three people at a blow: me, my mother (her own daughter), and herself—for I am sure she didn't like my father any more than I did. Things have changed. But doesn't this still ring a bell, however faintly, in our own experiences of families? The Bible tells us, "Honor thy father and thy mother." But what if they are not honorable?

Our notions of sexual organization are also rooted in power structures, in the notion of "ownership." The enormous ideological weight of monogamy has been greatly lessened since the challenge to the previously unquestioned rightness of patriarchy (the father's line must be preserved, therefore the woman's "fidelity" must be guaranteed, if necessary with a real or metaphorical chastity belt to which the husband keeps the key) and the spread of methods of birth control. Shouldn't we begin to ask ourselves whether it really matters if the children are biologically our own? Don't all children need and deserve respect and love? It shouldn't matter whose they are in the biological sense, and they shouldn't belong to anyone: children are not possessions. Neither have we the right to assert the power of possession over our partners or to limit their freedom in any way.

It is within this context that the wider acceptance of homosexuality and lesbianism becomes of general significance, not only to gays and lesbians. Freed of the paraphernalia of the traditional family, gays are in the best position to lead the way toward a new, freer, more generous and accepting organization of sexuality. Those of the Right frequently raise the objection that, if homosexuality is allowed to spread, there will be fewer children. The fatuousness of this strikes me as staggering, and not merely because there is nothing to prevent gays and lesbians from procreating and raising children if they want to. One of various current and very serious threats to the future of life on our planet is overpopulation. This is common knowledge: it's impossible that even the densest and most insulated of right-wingers have not heard the news. True, overpopulation is a greater problem in the so-called "underdeveloped" countries. But if the populations of the "advanced" western countries decreased, they would be able to accept far more immigrants and develop the ideal of the multicultural society, with its erosion of racial barriers. Common sense must tell us that, within the existing state of things, the fewer children who are born the better.

Following these trains of thought, however, we have eventually to face what is at present the supreme obstacle. Unless the socioeconomic/political base changes, the superstructures cannot change (though within the existing system they can be modified). The ultimate obstacle is capitalism itself, especially in its terrifying current form of globalization (greeted all over the west as its ultimate and irreversible victory). While capitalism lasts, the power structures that support it and which it in turn supports will last with it; any modifications will be those that capitalism feels it can safely permit. The most depressing feature of North American culture today is not merely the steadily consolidating power of the embryonically fascist Right, but the corresponding absence of an effective Left. It has become easy today to feel that it is all too late, that (as Medea cries out at the end of Pasolini's splendid movie) "Nothing is possible any more." Such despair is a trap that at all costs must be avoided, even if one can produce little to oppose it but the tired old cliché "While there's life, there's hope." There is life: it continues within the progressive movements, no longer strenuous and self-assertive, but by no means obliterated. We have, ultimately, to rethink the socialist alternatives: to return to Marx, Engels, Trotsky not as disciples but as rigorous critics, sorting out what can be salvaged, what must be jettisoned or changed, what safeguards are necessary to prevent a recurrence of that alternative form of fascism, Stalinism. And any movement resulting from this has to be popular: to impose a true socialism would be a contradiction in terms. I do not at this moment in time see any evidence of even the first stirrings of such a movement. Probably, before anything concrete materializes, the culture (and the planet) will have to deteriorate much further, beyond the point where people can be kept in their current state of mystification and be fobbed off with empty promises of capitalist "success," possessions, vacuous entertainments. By then it may be too late. The Soviet Union certainly made its major contribution to global warming, the greenhouse effect, the destruction of the environment, but its day is passed and it can no longer be held up as a scapegoat. The burden now rests squarely on the shoulders of capitalism. The ultimate question may not be "Do we care if there's another Holocaust?" but "Do we want life on the planet to continue?" If the answer to either or both of these questions is Yes, then my arguments seem to me to make complete and incontrovertible sense.

I have often found myself categorized (dismissively, of course) as a "utopianist." But I don't necessarily believe in the possibility of a human utopia: To return to my beginning, it remains possible that there are indeed "causes in Nature" that "make these hard hearts." What I have tried to say is that there are far more causes to be found in Culture, and Culture can be changed. And wouldn't any changes in Culture gradually affect the evolution of Nature—of what, at least, we call "human nature"? Nothing in the world is entirely static; even the Egyptian empire crumbled eventually. Think how much our culture has changed (not entirely for the worse) in the past fifty years. Even if a utopia can never be achieved, isn't it a good idea to have a goal toward which to progress? Isn't it time for the human race to take charge, instead of just allowing itself to be carried along on the shifting tides of ideology?

So, dismiss all this as inane utopianism (or worse) if it suits you. To me, it represents an attempt to inject a modicum of common sense into a culture that increasingly strikes me as deeply pathological. And at the very least, if my recipe ever reached general acceptance, a future Holocaust would become not only impossible but literally unthinkable.

Notes

1. In Alice Miller, *For Your Own Good: Hidden Cruelty in Child-Rearing and the Roots of Violence,* trans. Hildegarde and Hunter Hannum, 3d ed. (New York: Noonday, 1990).

2. We were, in the event, spared this, and the "highly charismatic and articulate pedagogue" is now, even to his former supporters, mercifully a lost cause. But my general point remains unaffected by a single debacle.

3. Why is "fuck" commonly used as a swearword—and not merely a swearword but *the* swearword, the worst, used when you cannot think of anything else? Why do people (usually men, but nowadays one hears women say it too) regard "Fuck you" as the worst thing they can say in anger or indignation? Men have always "fucked" women; it is only very recently (since the radical feminist movement?) that women have been said to fuck men, and it doesn't mean quite the same thing: Its male meaning implies "possession of the phallus," in both literal and symbolic terms. If the term were used solely to characterize the subject as taking the dominant position in sexual activity, it would be harmless, but it isn't. "Fuck you," as a swear term, can mean many things, but basically it means "I think you are contemptible." The person who is fucked is contemptible: does no one ever pause to think about the implications of this usage? It implies, with absolute clarity, that women—the people who traditionally get fucked—are contemptible. So how are these "fuckers" supposed to feel when they realize that men sometimes get fucked? Clearly such men are contemptible too, and not at all the kind of men "we" want to be. So "Fuck them—bash them, beat them, kill them, so that we can distance ourselves from them: we are not like them, like women; we do not get fucked. We do the fucking." And it's true—the symbolic potency of the phallus is significantly weakened in sexual intercourse when both partners have one. This is not to say that gay relationships are somehow miraculously freed from the power structures that pervasively characterize our culture. One might, however, adapt one of Freud's celebrated utterances and say that in gay male sex "sometimes a penis is just a penis." And, for all the gains in gay rights over the past decade, for all the apparent acceptance of gays in the media, the prejudice is still there, underneath, awaiting the backlash. Until women have real equality, gays will remain an endangered species.

Hitler wanted a Germany free, not merely of homosexuals, but of homosexuality. This desire was just one of his many absurdities, which would be funny if they hadn't led to such appalling results, and while gays remain (though today less overtly) objects of contempt, women will too. If a new fascism arises, both will suffer.

The difference will be that you can't put women in concentration camps for being women. You can, however (Hitler could, and many men and a few terrorized women today would agree with the justice of his policies) put gays into them.

9 War Stories

Witnessing in Retrospect | MARIANNE HIRSCH AND LEO SPITZER

The head of the Vilna Gestapo told us: "There are ninety thousand people lying here, and absolutely no trace must be left of them."

—Motke Zaïdl, *Shoah,* Claude Lanzmann[1]

A peaceful landscape. . . . An ordinary field with flights of crows, harvests, grass fires. . . . An ordinary road where cars and peasants and lovers pass. . . . An ordinary village of vacationers—with a marketplace and a steeple—can lead all too easily to a concentration camp. . . . Struthof, Oranienburg, Auschwitz, Neuengamme, Belsen, Ravensbruck and Dachau were names like any others on maps and in guidebooks. . . . The blood has dried, the tongues are silent. The blocks are visited only by a camera. Weeds have grown where the prisoners used to walk. The wires are no longer alive. No footstep is heard but our own.

—*Night and Fog,* Alain Resnais and Jean Cayrol[2]

More and better than the word . . . [photographs] recapture the impressions which the camps, well or badly preserved, more or less transformed into grand sites and sanctuaries, make on the visitor; an impression that is strangely deeper and more unsettling for those who have never been there than for us few survivors.

—"Revisiting the Camps," Primo Levi[3]

How does the memory of genocide survive for future generations when both political interest and the passage of time itself conspire to erase its traces from the landscapes of the present? The three epigraphs we have chosen for this essay reflect on this question in texts that employ a familiar trope in the memorialization of war and historical trauma: the return to the place of perpetration in order to reveal the effects of time on memory and forgetting. They show not only how much has already, in one or several decades after the end of the Second World War, been covered over, forgotten, but also how ordinary fields and peaceful landscapes might have looked before they became concentration camps. Thus Resnais's *Night and Fog* is intent on exposing viewers to what is left once "the blood has dried" and "the weeds have grown up again," assuring us, at the same time, that we cannot truly see that past—that no description can provide the right impression, and that "it is impossible to capture what remains" in images and words. It is this contrast that the film wants to underscore, by insisting both on change and erasure ("weeds have grown where the prisoners used to walk") and on sameness and continuity ("an ordinary road where cars and peasants and lovers pass"). Black and white archival images bring the past back to the in-color present in *Night and Fog,* overshadowing and displacing that present with their stark power. In his afterword to a photo exhibition, "Revisiting the Camps," Primo Levi also extols the power of photography to evoke past realities for future generations. But the statement made by Motke Zaïdl in *Shoah* underscores how hard the Nazis worked to erase the memory from the landscape and how difficult it is to restore visibility and reality to crimes that have been deliberately submerged and thus forgotten.

We use this transaction between memory and forgetting, reflected in these epigraphs, to introduce a recent work with similar preoccupations: Mikael Levin's 1997 exhibition and book *War Story.* In 1944–45 the American writer and journalist Meyer Levin traveled through Europe with the French photographer Eric Schwab to seek out and document the devastation of Jewish life by the Nazis, and to witness the liberation of the camps. Fifty years later, in 1995, Meyer's son Mikael, a photographer, retraced his father's journey "to photograph in the places where my father and Eric experienced the war."[4] His book assembles Schwab's original images, his own later ones, his father's 1950 memoir *In Search,* and some of the dispatches sent home by Meyer Levin in the closing months of World War II. *War Story* is a record of a triple collaboration, between writer and photographer, son and father, photographer and photographer. Unlike the works of Lanzmann, Resnais, and Levi, however, who lived through the times and were directly touched by events that their works depict and address, Mikael Levin's *War Story* is an illustration of a particular kind of secondary witnessing. It is a son's postmemory of traumatic scenes and events that preceded his birth but which, nonetheless, shaped the consciousness of the second generation, to which he belongs.

The term "postmemory" describes the relationship of children of survivors or witnesses of cultural or collective trauma to the experiences of their parents—experiences that were transmitted to them only as stories and images, but that were so powerful, so monumental, as to constitute memories in their own right. Through its secondary, or second-generation, memory quality—its basis in displacement, its belatedness—the term is meant to convey its temporal and qualitative difference from memories of contemporaries. Postmemory is a powerful form of memory precisely because its connection to its object or source is mediated not through recollection but through projection, investment, and creation. It describes the relationship of the second generation to the first—their curiosity and desire, as well as their ambivalences about wanting to own this knowledge.[5]

Second-generation artists like Mikael Levin have begun to forge an aesthetic that reflects the subjectivity of those "born after." But Levin is also one of a smaller number of such artists who engage in direct dialogue with members of the survivor generation, and his *War Story,* like Art Spiegelman's *Maus,* Tatana Kellner's *Fifty Years of Silence,* and Jeffrey Wolin's *Written in Memory,* is thus an example of the type of collaborative text that juxtaposes the voices and perspectives of both generations.[6] But what is the nature of this intergenerational collaboration? Characteristically, the younger artist, even one who, like Mikael Levin, reveals little about himself, retains ultimate editorial power, shaping the final text, but only through complex negotiation with the survivor's primacy as the direct witness to the events of the past. Levin is eager to grant that primacy:

> I see my approach as very different from that of the many "re-photographic" projects that are around. I try to make this clear in never actually exactly rephotographing the scene. If taken in the same spot, my photo is always at least slightly dislocated. So these are not mirror-images. In showing Eric's photos next to mine, it was not so much a comparison of then and now, but rather a desire to make the point that I knew my experience was totally different from theirs, that what I was seeing was so totally different that I couldn't possibly claim to be having some sort of parallel experience, and that I knew I could not possibly comprehend what they had actually experienced.[7]

In the genre of intergenerational memoirs, however, Levin's text occupied a special place, since Meyer Levin and Eric Schwab were themselves already secondary witnesses—latecomers to the events they documented.

Mikael Levin does not tell us very much about the reasons behind his own search in his *War Story.* His introductory note to the book, explaining his insertion of his father's autobiographical and journalistic writings and his own and Eric Schwab's role as photographers, is exceedingly brief and elliptical:

> "Europe: the Witnesses" is the second part of my father's autobiography *In Search.* It covers the years 1944–45, during which my father, as a war correspondent,

> made a journey through Europe seeking out the remnants of the Jewish communities. My photographs follow the chronology of that journey. I have also inserted some of the original material—cable dispatches, newspaper clippings—written by him at that time. The photographs from 1945 were taken by Eric Schwab, my father's jeep-mate, during the course of their journey.[8]

By failing to explain his motivations, and by inserting himself into the narrative in only the most minimal way, as a pair of eyes or a camera, Mikael Levin appears to take his story of transmission out of the realm of the personal and familial, inviting a more broadly public generational and political reading. We can suppose that, like Resnais, Lanzmann, and the photographers in Levi's exhibition before him, he is "in search" of what, at the sites of so much devastation, can still today, over fifty years later, be detected through the camera lens.

Meyer Levin, of course, was himself not a direct victim of the Holocaust but a journalist from the U.S. who had gone to Europe in 1943 "to report on the war, the fate of European Jews, and on Jewish and non-Jewish soldiers of the American army and their fight for the defeat of Nazi Germany."[9] Journeying through a devastated Europe, he was an eyewitness to the liberation of concentration camps and the discovery of mass graves, and his contemporary reportage to the Overseas News Agency reveals a powerful identification with the war's Jewish victims, his contained anger, and what seems like an increasingly passionate desire to transmit what he had seen. His memoir *In Search,* however, which constitutes the primary narrative of *War Story,* was written after the war, in the late 1940s, and was not published until 1950. As such, it was already a revision of his contemporary journalistic dispatches—a recollection reconstructed from the vantage of a new present.

In retracing his father's journey, Mikael Levin thus repeats his father's double act of witnessing, in retrospect. He tries to see what his father saw, to see as if through his father's eyes, but also to be a witness to his father's witnessing. In doing so, he exposes the layered nature of his father's story—the tension between experience, remembrance, and narrative reconstruction. Republishing Meyer Levin's memoir alongside his own photographs, Mikael Levin stages an intergenerational conversation about war, memory, and the difficulty of transmission. In an article on two photographs of former concentration camps and their relationship to the landscape tradition, Ulrich Baer stresses that "the younger Levin's task consists not only in capturing his father's sense of shock but also in conveying the distance that separates us from it."[10] As Baer sees it, Mikael's challenge is to show not only what his father saw, but also what he didn't see—the void, absence, nothingness, and incomprehension he encountered in his search.

The contrapuntal images in *War Story* expose and make visible the hidden presence of an unmastered historical past. They work to counteract not just the effects of time, but also more deliberate efforts to erase the traces or to submerge the Holocaust within a broader historical narrative of World War II, and to "move beyond it."[11] As a photographer, Levin explores the power of photographic images to carry memory for the second generation, to provide a medium through which traces of an impenetrable past can survive and be mobilized in the service of secondary, postmemorial witnessing.

It is our argument that, like *Shoah* and *Night and Fog,* Levin's work is successful when it accentuates the oppositions between continuity and difference, memory and forgetting, recall and repression. He brings the past into the present and manages to do so in a way that does not congeal or contain it. He shows the dangers of its commodification without necessarily participating in it. At the same time, Mikael Levin's work also brings to the foreground the frustrations and failures of transmission that characterize the aesthetics of postmemory.

Mikael Levin's visual layering of past and present, as well as his juxtaposition of words and images, is worth exploring in detail. *War Story* is composed of five different visual and narrative levels: (1) Meyer Levin's dispatches, sent back from Europe to several different news services, printed in narrow columns at the edges of some of the book's pages; (2) in larger type, the narrative centerpiece of the book, Meyer Levin's memoir *In Search,* detailing chronologically his trip through Europe in 1944–45; (3) also on the margins in small type, and only appearing occasionally, a few notes by Mikael Levin identifying some of the images and texts; (4) a set of photographic images taken by Eric Schwab in 1944–45, labeled by Mikael Levin, and reproduced throughout the text, in small size; (5) another set of photographs, most of them unlabeled, taken by Mikael Levin in 1995, occasionally at the same sites depicted in the Schwab photos. These larger images usually fill an entire page.

The book's first two pages (14–15) introduce us to this narrative complexity. On the left side is an image taken outside of Paris of a stop for bus 143, named "Drancy: Square de la Libération." An elderly woman is seated, waiting for the bus; behind her is an ad for Ikea. The right page initiates Meyer's Levin's autobiographical narrative with the assertion "From the beginning I realized I would never be able to write the story of the Jews in Europe." At the bottom right of the same page is Mikael's note explaining the layout of his text. The next page continues the narrative of Meyer Levin's arrival in Paris, his meeting with surviving Jews, and his realization that "[t]hrough Drancy, a prison barrack on the outskirts of Paris, the Jews of France had passed toward Auschwitz." On the facing page, an image of a modern town square with, at its center, the signpost "Conservatoire Historique de Drancy." That "prison barrack" has obviously become a modern town, as Mikael's note on the following page explains: "After the war, the deportation center was converted

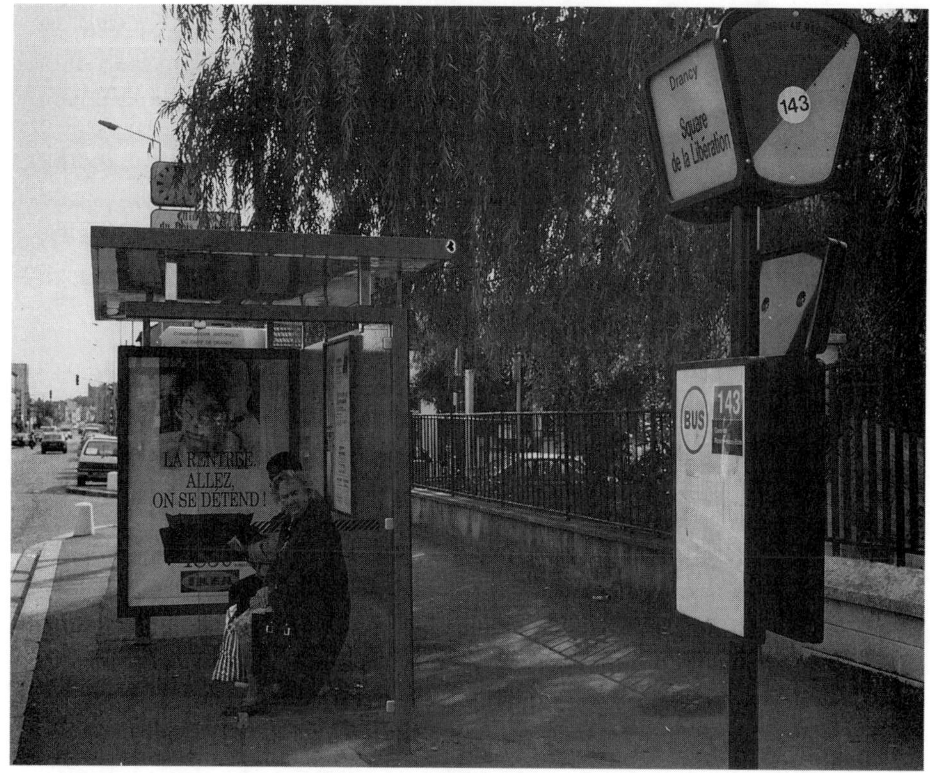

9.1 Mikael Levin, *Untitled* (from War Story–Drancy, 1995). Courtesy Mikael Levin.

into low income housing. Today those buildings are mostly inhabited by North African immigrants." The site of the camp and the monument that marks it can be visited but the camp itself is no longer there. All that remains is the name of a bus stop, a monument recently erected. The traffic signs in the picture can be read symbolically: there are arrows pointing as well as signs barring entrance, crosswalks, and no-parking signs. For the contemporary visitor who wants to remember Drancy, those ambiguous signposts are not enough. Meyer Levin's eyewitness account and Mikael's notes contain the hope that a fuller picture might emerge, but even Meyer himself arrived too late to witness the deportations. His narrative, belated, is already a hearsay account and the photographs taken by his son can be only shadows of shadows.

The first few pages of *War Story* indicate that Meyer Levin had begun his trip in the company not of Eric Schwab but of Morley Cassidy, an Irish-American journalist with whom he shared a jeep. In this first part, the book's photographs consist entirely of images taken by Mikael—reflections of his effort to reconstruct his father's journey in the present. Mikael's images of towns, woods, fields, and roads, of soccer fields and pharmacies, are meant to be visual complements in the present to Meyer's moving recollections of, for example, the Battle of the Bulge and other late battles of the war, or of his stop in a Belgian town which became the site of a massacre by retreating German troops a few days later. The pictures we see are like the images of present sites in *Shoah* or *Night and Fog;* the deeper story they tell is invisible to the eye.

The texture of Mikael Levin's narrative changes about one-third of the way through, however, when Meyer Levin and Eric Schwab become jeep-mates and Mikael's pictures begin to parallel not only Meyer's story but also Schwab's photos. Some of the pictures of modern-day towns already include a palimpsestic image of a past demolished by the war. This is true of Dueren, for example (95, 96, 97), where drawings of the old town cover the walls of two modern buildings, reminders of the Allied bombings in 1945 described by Meyer in his dispatch to the Overseas News Agency. Here the past is painted onto the present, inscribed on the town's modern buildings. But a few pages later (100), we see two of Schwab's photographs of the rubble and tanks in front of the Cologne cathedral and, on the facing page, the same shot taken by Mikael of the cathedral entrance, now full of carefree tourists and visitors. In the present image of a restored cathedral square the past is entirely concealed, invisible: the reader must make the connection, engage in the dialogue offered by the postmemorial artist.

These two types of juxtaposition each have their own poignancy. On the one hand, Mikael Levin searches out the inscriptions of the war's history in the landscapes of present-day Europe. His 1995 picture of the Judengasse in Frankfurt, for example, is one of the most complex in the book (120, 21). Here nondescript modern buildings stand next to older ones; walls are covered with graffiti and posters. The street is virtually deserted; only one passerby is visible. The Jewish inhabitants of Frankfurt's Judengasse have certainly been chased away or murdered, and no memorial marks this history. In fact, one of the torn posters on the wall next to the street sign "Judengasse" deplores this absence and demands public memorialization: "We demand memorial plaques for the Jewish children murdered by the Nazis, and for the Sinti and Roma who were murdered." And below: "Nazis are murdering again today." Adjacent to it is another poster, celebrating one hundred years of photography and depicting the face of a man whose eyes have been replaced by a camera. Can photography respond to the demand for remembrance and reparation, Levin seems to ask? Can his project restore the lost images of the Judengasse? And can it provide an adequate account of responsibility, as the torn poster demands?

Mikael's depiction of Buchenwald begins to do just that. Meyer Levin's narrative and analysis in his memoir are interrupted by two long double-column reports to the Overseas News Agency, detailing his encounter with inmates and

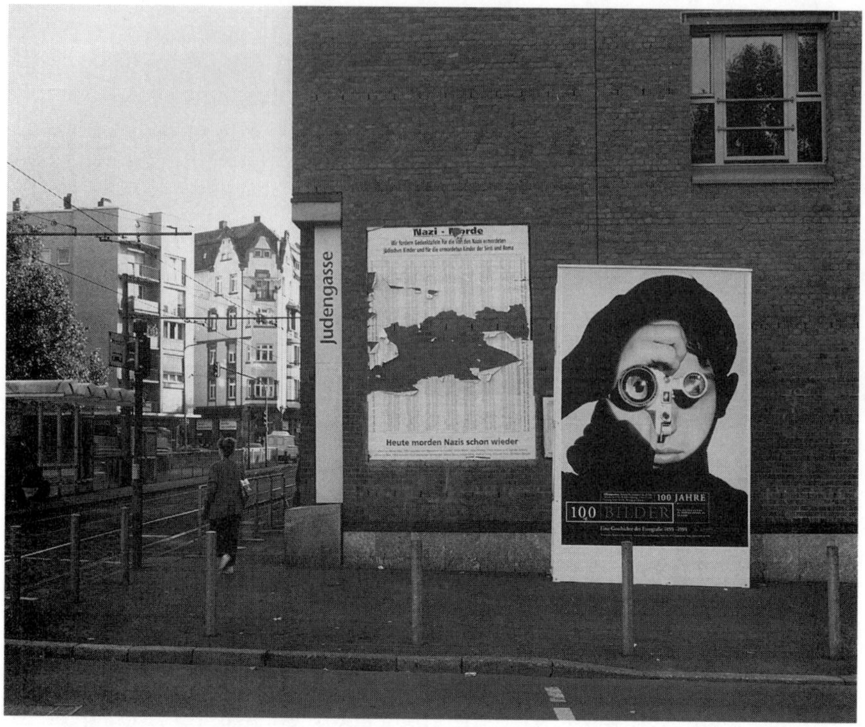

9.2 Mikael Levin, *Untitled* (from War Story–Frankfurt-am-Main, 1995). Courtesy Mikael Levin.

his description of torture instruments and evidence of "scientific experiments" he found in the camp. Visually, the narrative begins with a large image of a paved road bordered by forests, labeled "Road to Buchenwald—Blutstrasse (the road of blood)" (142). The next two pages are punctured by small reproductions of Schwab's images, one labeled in Schwab's hand "Deportees of Barracks 61"—a famous image of emaciated men gazing out of their bunks, with one naked skeletal figure in the foreground; the other, an image of a man holding something that looks like a sling standing in front of a pile of objects, labeled by Schwab "Torture instruments." So far Mikael's opaque present-day images and Schwab's all-too-telling past ones are kept separate. But, on the next two pages (146, 147), a small and a large picture of the same doorway are juxtaposed. Schwab's is taken from closer range; it reveals emaciated corpses piled on top of one another in the dark doorway. In Mikael's image, the dark interior is empty. The traces are gone; they survive only in the visual juxtapositions of *War Story.* The open doorway is a trope of the threshold that the postmemorial generation ultimately finds so impossible to cross: we know

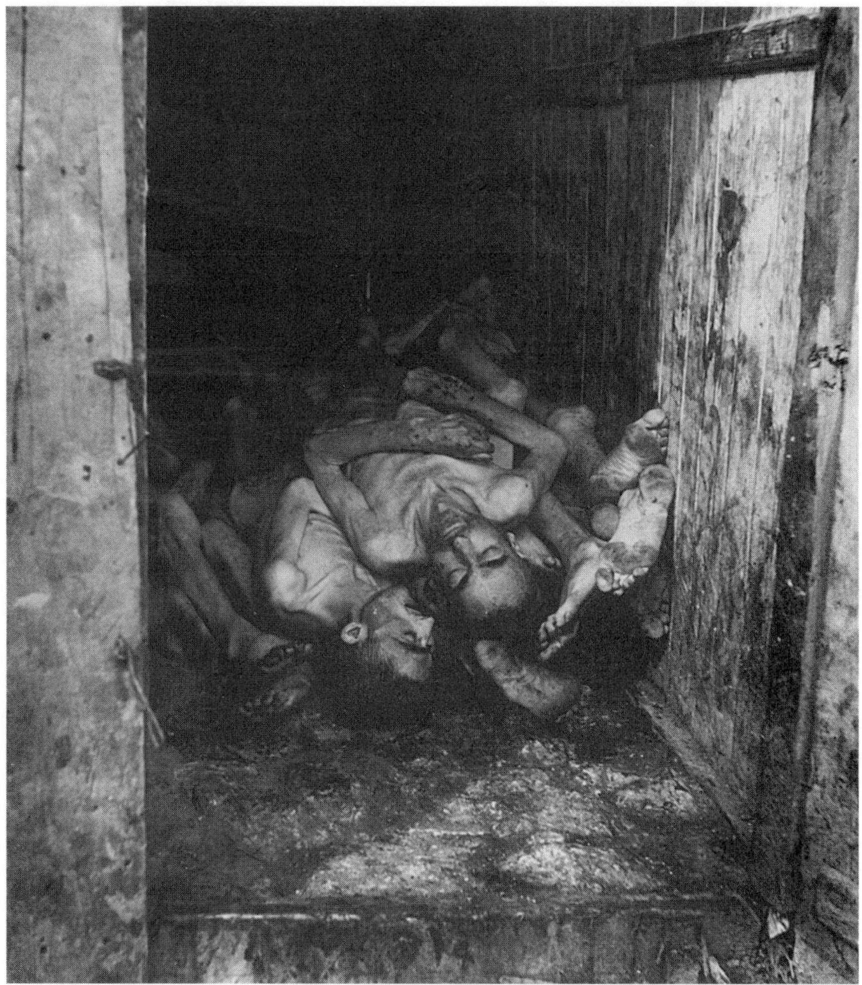

9.3 Eric Schwab, *Buchenwald*, 1945. Courtesy Mikael Levin.

that those corpses were/are there, but for us, as Mikael Levin's 1995 image shows, the doorway is dark and empty.

The same encounter occurs in the 1995 image of an empty railway track in Seeshaupt, which remains unreadable until it is juxtaposed to the 1945 picture of the same spot in which Schwab captured the bottom of a train car and a corpse in prison uniform lying beside the track (162, 163). Equally opaque is the image of a heavily wooded garden with a closed iron gate taken in 1995 Dachau (171). The closed gate is itself an emblem of the impenetrability of these images. But on the facing page (170), taken from a greater distance, is a

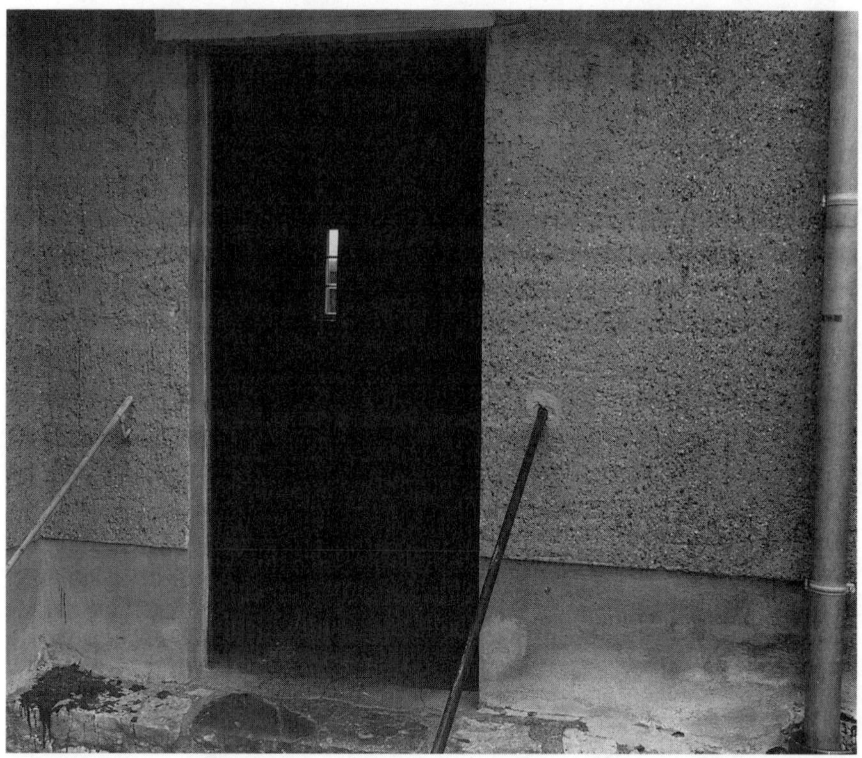

9.4 Mikael Levin, *Untitled* (from War Story–Buchenwald, 1995). Courtesy Mikael Levin.

picture of the same garden with some of the same trees, albeit younger, in the background, and the same gate. Only here two prisoners in striped uniforms are piling naked corpses on top of one another into a flatbed truck. Behind the truck, barely visible, is the head of an American GI, wearing a helmet, supervising the work.

Mikael Levin's juxtapositions attempt to restore visibility to a history that has been lost in this European landscape. *War Story* places images and narrative accounts into dialogue and relies on its readers to receive and continue that dialogue. Mikael Levin never describes his own journey through Europe for this project. But one particular image in *War Story* gives us perhaps the most resonant sense of his own participation in the process of receiving and further transmitting the history he encounters. "I found a farmer who recognized the place where Eric Schwab had taken the photo fifty years earlier," he writes adjacent to his father's description of the American liberation of the Austrian countryside (208). Schwab's small photo shows a tank and several American GIs in a beautiful springtime landscape. On the facing page, a man's

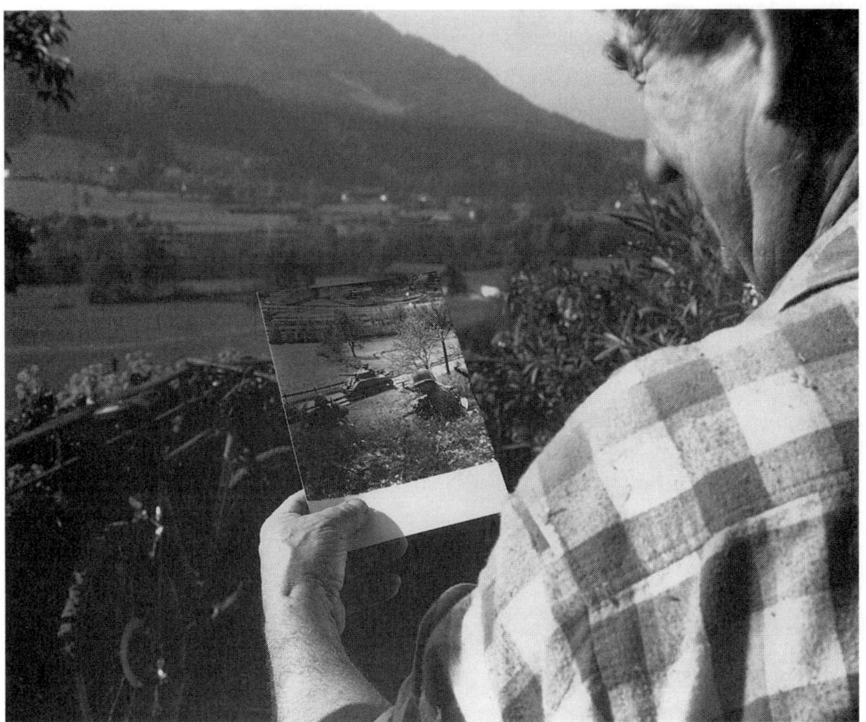

9.5 Mikael Levin, *Untitled* (from War Story–Itter, 1995). Courtesy Mikael Levin.

hand holds Schwab's picture in a scene that is identical to the one depicted. The man's bicycle stands by the fence where the tank once stood. The old photograph is contained within the new image, opening in it a door to the past. But that opening is also the result of the transgenerational conversation between the photographer and the farmer, a conversation recorded in the image and inviting the viewer perhaps to catch a glimpse through the tear he makes in the layers of memory and time. Bringing Schwab's picture back to the site and to one of its inhabitants, Mikael reanimates the Austrian landscape with a story that until now has been invisible, if not forgotten.

Mikael Levin's project is part of a larger memorial effort. Some memorials at concentration camp sites, for example, include old photographs that prompt remembrance and reconnect the past with the present. But these efforts at reconnection carry with them certain dangers as well, as one particular image in *War Story* suggests. One 1945 concentration camp photograph by Schwab shows the emaciated head of a man gazing out of his bunk, his torso naked, his chin resting on the wooden planks, his eyes staring into space (183). On

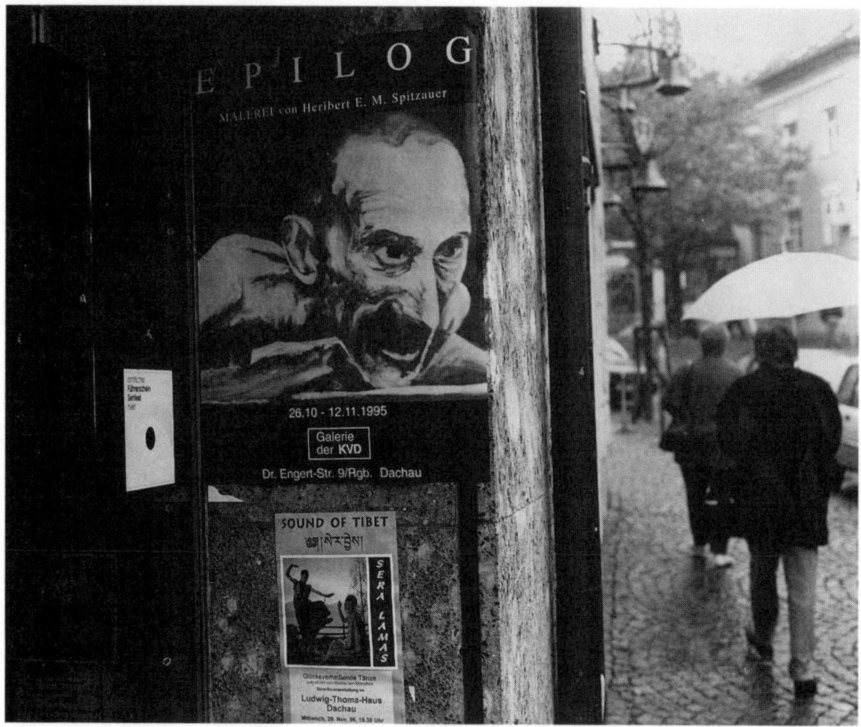

9.6 Mikael Levin, *Untitled* (from War Story–Dachau, 1995). Courtesy Mikael Levin.

the facing page, Mikael Levin has reproduced a street scene from present-day Dachau. Pedestrians with umbrellas are walking past a doorway on which two posters are hanging. The lower one advertises a concert, "Sound of Tibet"; the upper one a painting exhibition tellingly titled "Epilog," by the artist Heribert Spitzauer. The poster for the exhibit is of a painting of an uncannily similar face, a painted version of a survivor photograph.[12] With this poster in the town of Dachau, Mikael Levin has yet again found the inscription of the past in the present, but now in the form of a commodity. A photographic image served as model for a painter whose painting in a gallery in Dachau is advertised on a poster that has become the subject of Levin's photograph—reproduced in his own exhibition and book. An image of a survivor has circulated in multiple sites, part of numerous exchanges and conversations that continue and perpetuate memory and postmemory. At the same time, duplicated in poster form, removed from their context and site, these images risk being reified in the realm of commerce. If recontextualized past images mobilize memory, what happens when they are commodified, repeated, overused? This could indeed be an "Epilogue," a closing of memory rather than an opening, reinforcing Lanzmann's fear of using archival images in his own memorial work. What is more, the street scene in Dachau, grainy and blurred in Mikael Levin's photograph, echoes the famous painting of rainy-day Paris by Gustave Caillebotte, testifying to the inevitable, if troubling, aestheticization fundamental to the medium of photography.[13]

Two conceptions of time motivate the memory and postmemory of World War II and of the Holocaust. One is progressive, forward-moving. It has to do with the working-through of the past, the movement toward a future. That working-through, whatever its quality, must entail forgetting. The other involves a durational view of time, a repeated confrontation with the past, the effort to undo erasure and forgetting by reopening past wounds. The layered structure of the works of artists like Lanzmann, Resnais, and Levin reinforces the workings of durational time, helping to counteract forgetting. At the same time, these works do include elements that are forward-moving—at least in their acknowledgment that they can evoke or suggest past experience, but that they cannot mimetically reproduce it. That acknowledgment of distance can in itself be seen as an attempt to work through.

We cannot help but wonder, however, about the kind of intervention a work like Mikael Levin's can ultimately make in the face of the willful erasures of history and the involuntary erasures of time. Photographs have figured prominently in the artistic representations of the postmemorial generation because they offer a material indexical medium through which one might literally recall—and thus make present—a lost past. Yet their two-dimensionality and flatness, their limiting frames, continue to signal their remove from both past and present—their effective unreality. Even as they seem to open doors to the past, they bar access to it, signaling both the lure and the frustration of visual remembrance. It is thus tempting to see the 1945 pictures as full of memory and historical meaning and the 1995 ones as empty, opaque, and unreadable. But Schwab's own images already highlight photography's retrospective and evanescent quality, its entwinement in death and loss. Susan Sontag has asserted that "all photographs are memento mori."[14] As Schwab snaps the shutter in 1945, Europe is already moving toward the Cold War, toward German reconstruction, and toward the *Historisierung* of a criminal past. The bodies are being buried, the rubble is being cleaned up.

Try as he may, Mikael Levin's artistic efforts cannot counteract the process of loss and transformation or restore visibility to a history lost in the landscape. What he does accomplish is to make visible a layer beneath which a loss is buried. His work, in this sense, is not an act of restoration but an act of mourning, a stone marking a visit to a gravesite. If anything, it makes us conscious of a forgetting that was always already there—a forgetting that is indeed already inscribed in Eric Schwab's jolting visual record.

In this light, *War Story* might fruitfully be read in relation to the photographic project *The Writing on the Wall: Projections in Berlin's Jewish Quarter,* by the American photographer Shimon Attie.[15] Like Mikael Levin, Attie exploits photography's capacity to evoke absence as well as presence, loss as well as forgetting. Visiting Berlin in 1991, Attie began to ask, "Where are all the missing people? What has become of the Jewish culture and community which had once been at home here?" (9). A concerted search led Attie to the discovery of a number of historical photographs of Berlin's Scheunenviertel, its Jewish quarter, during the 1920s and '30s. Making slides of them and using several powerful projectors, he projected these old images onto the precise locations where they were originally taken, thus "rebuilding" the ruined world on the very location of its ruin. By rephotographing the projections, Attie created layered images which have become moveable memorials that viewers can invest with their nostalgic and elegiac needs. In his *Writing on the Wall,* the site of destruction has been reconnected to the site of commemoration.

Attie's works have a dual status: they are both what he has called "events on location" and still images reproduced in a museum installation and in book form. As events or performances, his projections made powerful interventions in the present landscape of Berlin: "I wanted the projections to serve as insertions into the visual field of the present. The projections would be on view for one or two evenings, visible to neighborhood residents, street traffic and passersby" (9). Attie describes the course of the year in which he worked on his projections and the change in the reactions of the local inhabitants, as well as his conversations with them. The photographer was welcomed by some and cruelly harassed by others; he had water poured on him and his equipment, he was screamed at and threatened. "I would not feel safe doing such a project today," he comments.

Attie's fear and hesitation indicate how very present this past can still be in the European landscape, and how sensitive and powerful its recall can become. Artists like Mikael Levin and Shimon Attie can recall it in the confrontations they stage as they bring their cameras to the sites of retrospective witnessing. But when their layered projections enter the medium of the museum and the book, inviting the participation of temporally and geographically more distant viewers, can this power and danger still be mobilized? How wide is the circle of postmemory, how far into the future can the process of retrospective witnessing reach?

Shimon Attie has carefully explained the desires that have motivated his search. In contrast, Mikael Levin's silence becomes all the more curious. While Attie came to Europe as an American Jew of the second generation in search of a lost Jewish world, Mikael went to follow his father's search for the remnants of Jewish life. In this sense, Mikael staged a different kind of return altogether: the return of a son to his father's past. His reticence to reveal much about himself or his own search—the scarcity of his own textual commentary in his *War Story* project—has the effect of highlighting and making us focus more exclusively on his father's narrative. Mikael's publication of *War Story* in 1995 may thus have been motivated in part by his desire to foreground his father's quest for a Jewish identity in the rubble of a destroyed Jewry, as an implicit explanation for Meyer's subsequent "obsession" about his "censored" script of *The Diary of Anne Frank* and the frustrations that led to his severe and long-lasting depression. After all, one critical biographical account of Meyer Levin and the contested story of the Anne Frank play had just been published, and a second one was about to appear.[16] But, most certainly, Mikael the photographer, reconnecting to his father textually and through the photos of Eric Schwab, also seems determined to bring his father's voice and sensibility into present currency. Read in this way, Mikael Levin's project becomes a reencounter between son and father—a personal act of mourning and remembrance.

Notes

1. Claude Lanzmann, *Shoah: An Oral History of the Holocaust: The Complete Text of the Film* (New York: Pantheon, 1985), 13.

2. Jean Cayrol, "*Night and Fog* (*Nuit et Brouillard*)/The script for Alain Resnais' film," in *Film: Book 2: Films of Peace and War,* ed. Robert Hughes (New York: Grove, 1962), 234–235.

3. Primo Levi, "Revisiting the Camps," in *Holocaust Memorials: The Art of Memory in History,* ed. James Young (New York: Prestel, 1994), 185.

4. Mikael Levin, personal communication, 20 September 2001.

5. For an evolving discussion of postmemory, see Marianne Hirsch, *Family Frames: Photography, Narrative, and Postmemory* (Cambridge, Mass.: Harvard University Press, 1997), esp. chapters 1 and 6; Hirsch, "Projected Memory: Holocaust Photographs in Personal and Public Fantasy," in *Acts of Memory: Cultural Recall in the Present,* ed. Mieke Bal, Jonathan Crewe, and Leo Spitzer (Hanover, N.H.: University Press of New England, 1998), 2–23; Hirsch, "Surviving Images: Holocaust Photographs and the Work of Postmemory," *Yale Journal of Criticism* 14, no. 1 (spring 2001): 5–38, and in *Visual Culture and the Holocaust,* ed. Barbie Zelizer (New Brunswick, N.J.: Rutgers University Press, 2001), 214–246; Hirsch, "Marked by Memory: Feminist Reflections on Trauma and Transmission," in *Extremities,* ed. Nancy K. Miller and Jason Tougaw (Urbana: Illinois University Press, forthcoming [2002]); Hirsch, "Nazi Photographs in Post-Holocaust Art: Gender as an Idiom of Memorialization," in *Phototextualities,* ed. Andrea Noble and Alex Hughes (Albuquerque: University of New Mexico Press, forthcoming [2002]); and Omer Bartov, Atina Grossman, and Molly Noble, eds., *Crimes of War: Guilt and Denial* (New York: The New Press, forthcoming [2002]). See also Andrea Liss's somewhat different use of the term "post-memories" in *Trespassing through Shadows: Memory, Photography, and the Holocaust* (Minneapolis: University of Minnesota Press, 1998).

6. Art Spiegelman, *Maus: A Survivor's Tale I: My Father Bleeds History* (New York: Pantheon, 1986) and *Maus: A Survivor's Tale II: And Here My Troubles Began* (New York: Pantheon, 1991); Tatana Kellner, *71125: Fifty Years of Silence* (Rosendale,

N.Y.: Rosendale Women's Studio Workshop, 1992) and *B-11226: Fifty Years of Silence* (Rosendale, N.Y.: Rosendale Women's Studio Workshop, 1994); Jeffrey A. Wolin, *Written in Memory: Portraits of the Holocaust* (San Francisco: Chronicle, 1997).

7. Mikael Levin, personal communication, 20 September 2001.

8. Mikael Levin, *War Story* (Munich: Gina Kehayoff, 1997), 5.

9. Hanno Loewy, "Retracing a Journey through Europe," introductory essay in Levin, *War Story*, 5.

10. Ulrich Baer, "To Give Memory a Place: Holocaust Photography and the Landscape Tradition," *Representations* 69 (winter 2000): 47.

11. See Ulrich Baer's suggestive discussion of the place of trees in Levin's images: "[His] photographs show the trees as part of the Nazis' design and record this deceptive air of normalcy, without succumbing to it, as evidence of the scope of the destruction. . . . The trees are themselves evidence of the Nazis' effort to conceal the traces of their deed" (Baer, "To Give Memory a Place," 51).

12. Initially we believed that the image on the poster was a painted version of Schwab's photograph. But Mikael Levin informed us that Schwab's images were thought to be lost until he discovered them in the Agence France-Press archives. The image on the poster could have been taken from Margaret Bourke-White's often reproduced photo of Buchenwald survivors. In fact, Schwab's 1945 photo "Deportees of Barracks 61" (144) uncannily resembles that famous image.

13. Gustave Caillebotte, *Rue de Paris, temps de pluie* (1877), The Art Institute of Chicago.

14. Susan Sontag, *On Photography* (New York: Anchor, 1977), 15.

15. Shimon Attie, *The Writing on the Wall: Projections in Berlin's Jewish Quarter* (Heidelberg: Braus, 1994).

16. For accounts of the suppression of Meyer Levin's "more Jewish" script for the stage version of *The Diary of Anne Frank* and its effects on Levin's later life and career, see Lawrence Graver, *An Obsession with Anne Frank: Meyer Levin and the Diary* (Berkeley and Los Angeles: University of California Press, 1995), and Ralph Melnick, *The Stolen Legacy of Anne Frank: Meyer Levin, Lillian Hellman, and the Staging of the Diary* (New Haven, Conn.: Yale University Press, 1997).

Part 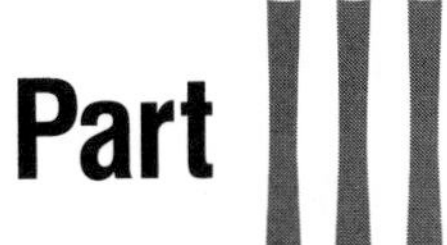

Memento Mori: Atrocity and Aesthetics

10 The Iconic and the Allusive

The Case for Beauty in Post-Holocaust Art | JANET WOLFF

> For a self-willed man in a room with windows overlooking a concentration camp to paint a compote is not serious; his sin is one of negligence. The real crime would be in painting the concentration camp as if it were a compote—in the same spirit of research and experimentation.
>
> —Jean-Paul Sartre[1]

> I also wanted to make a *beautiful* painting. . . . I wanted the ultimate beauty of the painting to surpass the subject matter. I wanted to use a rainbow with a Holocaust.
>
> —Audrey Flack[2]

> [B]eauty, far from contributing to social injustice . . . , or even remaining neutral to injustice as an innocent bystander, actually assists us in the work of addressing injustice.
>
> —Elaine Scarry[3]

The Jewish Museum in New York mounted a dual exhibition in January 1997—Morris Louis's *Charred Journal* series of 1951 and Rico Lebrun's *The Holocaust Paintings* of 1955–59. Their juxtaposition, at the time, confirmed for me a long-standing preference for abstract or allusive art (and a strong dislike of too-literal figurative work) where representation of the Holocaust is concerned. Lebrun's paintings and drawings, with titles like *Buchenwald Pit* and *Study for Dachau Chamber,* employ imagery from concentration camp photographs in semi-abstract compositions from which emaciated limbs and broken bodies stand out with horrific clarity. The works are made on a monumental scale, which, in a display of a dozen such images, overdetermines the assault on the viewer.[4] Louis's works, in contrast, are highly abstract. They require knowledge and work on the part of the viewer—even their title gives nothing away. It is known, however, that "charred journals" refers to the Nazi book burnings.[5] The works are small, and are either acrylic on canvas or ink and pencil on paper. The six paintings consist of white lines and scribbles on a dark ground, whose visible brushstrokes suggest charred wood or paper. Although the works are almost entirely nonfigurative, the white shapes occasionally form recognizable signs and symbols—Hebrew letters, numbers, a Star of David.[6] Reference to the Holocaust is indirect and allusive, rather than direct and confrontational. The exhibition curators suggest similarities in the two projects.

> Both Louis and Lebrun demonstrated an understanding that strict realism could not convey the enormity of the Nazi atrocities. Beyond the aesthetic and philosophical decision to use abstraction, these artists also relied on black and white. Both strategies—abstraction combined with a limited palette—were common distancing mechanisms for artists who struggled to depict events they had not witnessed firsthand.[7]

The reviewer for the *New York Times,* however, clearly perceived the radical difference between the two artists:

> Louis, at least, approached his theme obliquely, as if aware that to say anything at all is to say too little and too much. This was not the route taken, however, by . . . Rico Lebrun. . . . Visions from which we should avert our eyes are pumped up to Michelangelesque scale; a clamorous painterly virtuosity all but overwhelms images that should be greeted by visual silence . . . [Lebrun's] impassioned modernist vocabulary might have been effective in the cause of a different political art, an art of activism and advocacy, say, like the revolution-inspiring murals of Diego Rivera. But applied to the Holocaust, stylistic passion becomes theatricality and theatricality is an affront.[8]

The obvious value judgment in the comparison ("at least," "should be greeted," "an affront") accords with my own prejudices in this regard. It allows me, for instance, to confirm my absolute distaste for the Holocaust imagery of George Segal and Jerome Witkin—in the one case, for the presumption that the literal depiction of bodies (here in three-dimensional form) could be adequate to its subject, and in the other for the collusion, to no redeeming effect, with the pornography of violence.[9] What I hope to do in this essay is explore this prejudice, and try to ascertain whether the privileging of the allusive over the figurative and the iconic is more than a personal preference. It is a complicated

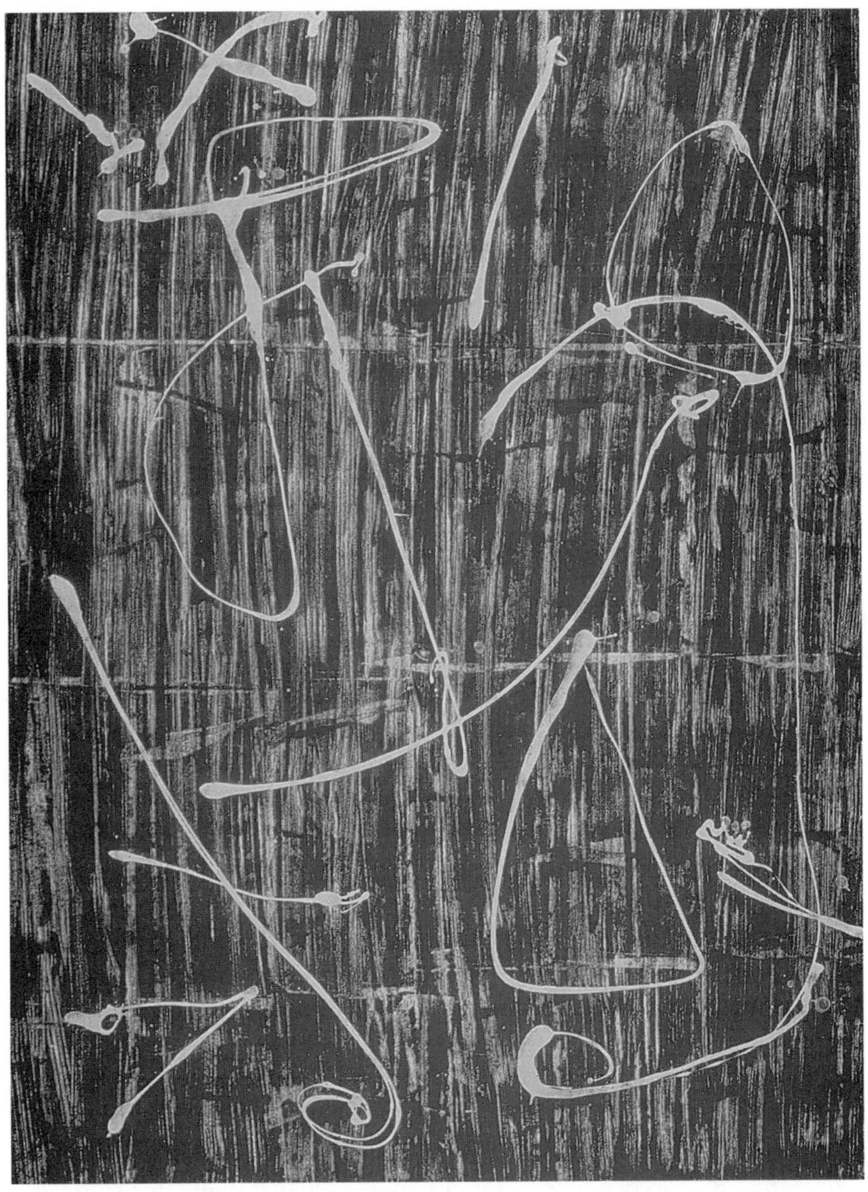

10.1 Morris Louis, *Charred Journal: Firewritten V*, 1951, acrylic on canvas (34" × 26"). Copyright The Jewish Museum of New York / Art Resource, N.Y. Used by permission.

question, and one in which questions of moral judgment ("should this be shown?") overlap with questions of aesthetic judgment ("is this a good work of art?") and of political efficacy ("does this document the events, or teach/engage/mobilize the viewer, adequately?"). Central to much of the debate has been the issue of beauty, and the persistent—and well-founded—fear of the aestheticization of the Holocaust. In making the case for an aesthetics of allusion and uncertainty, I will also suggest both the possibility of beauty and its value in post-Holocaust work. The question of beauty in the politics of representation is not, of course, implied by the preference for allusive, indirect imagery—in that sense, I will be addressing two separate issues here. But the literature on appropriate representation for art of the Holocaust is pervaded by debates on the pros and cons of beauty and aesthetic pleasure (as access and consolation on the one hand, and as apolitical aestheticization on the other). Toward the end of this essay, then, I will turn to this second, related question. I take the view, which I will elaborate there, that the beautiful in post-Holocaust art, far from operating as inappropriate redemption or depoliticization, can serve the important role of engaging the viewer in a sympathetic, but by no means passive, reflection on its theme.

Objections to the iconic and the figurative in art of the Holocaust have been based on various grounds, and I want to begin by distancing myself from some of those arguments. In the first place, I do not take the view that the Holocaust is somehow "unrepresentable" (a belief usually aligned with the argument that the Holocaust is "unique," as well as "outside history").[10] This is not, of course, a denial of the absolute horror of the events encompassed by the term, the extreme sadism and inhumanity of the individual and collective acts, and the unprecedented scale (and rationalization) of the genocide. Even here, I have to admit, I was inclined to use adjectives like "inconceivable" and "unimaginable." But the fact is that we *can* conceive of and imagine these events, not least because of the representations we have inherited from witnesses, in verbal, written, and visual form. The Holocaust is exceptional in its extremity and its scale. It is not unique, in the sense that there have been other historical events with which it shares some characteristics (systematic murder on the basis of ethnicity, for example), though it is unique in the sense that any event is unique—historically and geographically specific, larger or smaller than similar events, affecting this population rather than that, and so on. Even Claude Lanzmann, who does want to insist on a certain "uniqueness" of the Holocaust, refuses any implication that this means it is outside history.

> To say that the Holocaust is unique and incommensurable does not imply that it is an aberration that eludes all intellectual or conceptual comprehension,

> which falls outside history and is denied the dignity of being a historical event. On the contrary, we consider the Holocaust to be a completely historical event, the legitimate, albeit monstrous, product of the entire history of the Western world.[11]

In other words, the responsibility to understand and explain the Holocaust cannot be shirked on the grounds that it is somehow beyond comprehension. In the same way, neither is it beyond representation; the question is what kind of representation is appropriate for its portrayal.[12]

Criticisms of realist art have focused on the ethics of the portrayal (and hence re-presentation and reproduction) of violence and atrocity. The various objections are to the risk of attracting the viewer to the pornography of violence; to the gratuitous nature of such representation, with its consequent repetition of the assault without justification; to the inevitable alienation of the viewer (what Inga Clendinnen calls "the Gorgon effect"[13]), which preempts the educative or empathic intent of the work; and to the particular violations of the taboo on certain subjects (especially, it seems, the portrayal of the gas chambers themselves). Andrea Liss, in her careful study of the place of documentary photography in Holocaust memory, refuses to reproduce in her book photos from the Nazi archives, which, she believes, "cast the shadows that haunt and warn second and third post-Auschwitz generations not to revictimize the victims."[14] Clendinnen reports that she has stapled together certain pages in a book about the Holocaust, on the grounds that the horror depicted is fiction rather than documentary, and hence gratuitous.[15] Saul Friedlander and others have warned against the re-creation of the appeal of violence and fascism, in facilitating the circulation of the imagery of sadistic practice; in particular, such critics have strongly opposed the reuse of documentary photographs (for example, of concentration camp victims) in artworks, rendering them available for a second-level violation by the voyeuristic gaze.[16] For Liss and others, in any case, certain kinds of imagery (documentary or otherwise) are totally out of bounds. A number of people have commented on the fact that in Steven Spielberg's Holocaust film, *Schindler's List,* there is a shocking—almost unwatchable—scene in which viewers are led to believe they are about to see women and children asphyxiated in a gas chamber. In fact, after a long moment of unbearable suspense, the showerheads emit water, not gas. But the point, for some, is that an ultimate taboo has nevertheless been violated. Yosefa Loshitzky offers the following critique:

> [Spielberg was the first mainstream Hollywood Jewish filmmaker to break the] taboo of explicitly imagining the Holocaust and the gas chamber as its ultimate sacred center and horrifying metaphor. In essence, Spielberg violated the ancient Jewish biblical prohibition against creating images as it had been unconsciously resurrected in the moral taboo on representing the Holocaust. This violation culminated in what Terrence Rafferty describes as Spielberg's camera

> taking us "even further, straight into the heart of darkness: we follow the women who wound up at Auschwitz-Birkenau into the showers. . . . It is the most terrifying sequence ever filmed." . . . The camera's penetration into the gas chamber was perceived by some as a violation of the Holy of Holies. . . . Within this economy of scopophilic desire, *Schindler's List* provided an audience hungry for a spectacle of atrocity with the illusion of being there.[17]

In fact, there are precedents for the visual portrayal of the gas chambers—for example, Lea Grundig's 1943–44 drawing, *Treblianca,* and Zinovii Tolkatchev's 1944 *Gassing* (though perhaps it is not accidental that such images have never been in wide circulation).[18] Other examples of the perceived transgression of the acceptable limits of representation include Robert Morris's employment of photographs of the piled bodies of concentration camp victims in his Holocaust paintings of the mid-1980s,[19] and Nancy Spero's reproduction of a documentary photograph of the hanging of Masha Bruskina in a 1993 installation, and her inclusion of a photograph, found on a member of the Gestapo, of another woman, naked, bound, and about to be hanged, in her work *Ballad of Marie Sanders, the Jew's Whore* in the same year.[20] In these cases, though, the offense (for those who construe it thus) is the actuality, rather than the realism. The equally graphic representations of bodies in the work of Witkin and Segal are fictions, and hence (for some) more acceptable than the recirculation of images of actual victims. (This is a reversal of Clendinnan's argument that there is less excuse for fictional horror than for documentary depiction.[21])

My own objection to the realistic representation of the Holocaust does not distinguish between documentary and fictional accounts, or even between "acceptable" and taboo subjects. Nor is it based on the important point (made some time ago by Sartre, and repeated more recently by certain artists and critics) that a too-graphic, confrontational imagery will only have the effect of turning the viewer away, though I think that these issues of tactical aesthetic choices are important with regard to the artistic intention to engage and inform the viewer.[22] Rather, I want to suggest that the iconic, realist work—that is, the work that presents a literal, illusionistic representation—performs a premature movement of closure, enticing the viewer to accept the belief that he or she has now seen the object (the event, the moment, the Holocaust itself). This seduction is partly the product of the persistent myth of the transparency of realist modes of representation and of documentary practice, which forecloses for most viewers (who, after all, are not trained in critical visual literacy) the recognition that this is in the end only a story—selective, partial, provisional, and highly mediated. It is also the result of the particular invitation of much realism (in whatever medium) to a passive reception, the work of narrativizing and making sense having been undertaken already by the producer. It is this combination of false coherence or closure and refusal of dialogue between work and viewer that leads me to defend my preference for the non-iconic—not (again) because of the unique or ineffable nature of the Holocaust, but because any art which addresses the world (to record and testify, to express shock and empathy, or to warn against repetition of events) must, I would argue, engage its audience in an active form of viewing.[23] It is for this reason that I want to consider the possibilities for nonrealist art, or rather for an art of indirection, while also addressing the limits, in turn, of abstraction, and I will turn to this in a moment. First, though, I want to review the case that has been made in defense of realist and figurative art of the Holocaust.

Scholars of Holocaust art have pointed out that the tendency among witness-artists—for example, those incarcerated in the Terezín concentration camp—was to produce more or less realist documentary works.[24] The foremost imperative was to record and provide testimony. In addition, for those who were subject to the trauma of the ghettos and the camps the prevailing response was loss of affect—a psychological state which translated into the dispassionate mode of documentary realism. According to Amishai-Maisels, a "heightened realism" was the predominant style of artists in the camps, though in retrospect, after the end of the war, some of those same artists allowed themselves both the possibility of feelings and the artistic license to portray their anger, horror, fear, and outrage in less neutral—often expressionistic—ways. Among other examples, she discusses Boris Taslitzky's work while he was imprisoned in Buchenwald and later, after liberation.[25] A painting from 1950, commemorating the death in Auschwitz of a French Resistance leader, abandons the naturalism of his wartime drawings in favor of an expressionism of exaggerated gestures, elongated bodies, and agonized expressions.[26] The argument for a responsible documentary art is also made by some—artists as well as critics—in relation to contemporary practice, on the grounds that the duty to record extends beyond the witnesses themselves to the secondary observers. In many cases, "documentary" is equated with realist and figurative art. For others, the indexical is at least as vivid and effective as the iconic—for example, the exhibition of shoes, or hair, or possessions of the victims, common in Holocaust memorial museums. Gerda Meyer-Bernstein, whose work includes a 1989 installation consisting of a pile of six hundred suitcases with names, birthdates, and prisoners' tattooed registration numbers printed on them, explains the imperative "to document the Holocaust . . . to confront people bluntly, forcing them to deal with their feelings and attitudes about the Holocaust."[27] Lawrence Langer's argument is that only "literalism" in Holocaust representation is acceptable, in order that the "specific inhuman content" of the Holocaust be clearly perceived. Otherwise we risk "preempting" the Holocaust by rendering it paradigmatic or exemplary in order to point out moral lessons or retrieve moments of redemption. Our responsibility, according to Langer, is to confront the details of particular tortures and killings and not to avoid incorporating their representation in literature, film, and art.[28]

I will come back to the question of whether it is only realist art that can portray the Holocaust responsibly (and the related question of what kind of realism can best do so). Here I would simply point out that nothing follows about particular visual style from either the imperative to document or the commitment to confront and portray the worst atrocities. That is, the question of whether illusionistic realism, "heightened realism," expressionism, semi-abstraction, or even abstraction can meet these demands has to be addressed. And this is both a matter of the relationship of representation to reality (in the light of the critique of the view that realism is somehow "transparent" and unmediated) and a matter of viewers and their interpretations. But there are two other points to be made in defense of realism, and they must be borne in mind in reviewing competing aesthetic strategies in art of the Holocaust. First, as Ken Johnson has pointed out in relation to the art displayed in the Holocaust Museum in Washington, D.C., the problem with total abstraction is that it may not convey any particular meaning to the viewer, at least without additional information. So, in the abstract works by the four artists included in the Museum (Ellsworth Kelly, Sol LeWitt, Richard Serra, and Joel Shapiro), the task of memorializing the Holocaust is bypassed. Those who selected the work were concerned to avoid the kind of representational work which risked trivializing the Holocaust, but as a result they chose paintings that, "by their representational and expressive reticence, seem bent on renouncing the very opportunities built into the memorializing enterprise."[29] For that reason, some of those inclined to favor abstraction (perhaps because of a reluctance to attempt to represent directly something so far beyond normal experience, or because of a fear of rendering it mundane) have returned to figurative work, which does not have to rely on extraneous clues or information to direct viewers to its import.[30] A different, but related, problem with abstract art, and in fact with any avant-garde representational practice, is its reliance on the assumption of competent viewers—that is, an audience of those with the cultural capital necessary to know how to look at modernist work. It seems likely that a study of the social basis of aesthetic preference with regard to post-Holocaust art would confirm Pierre Bourdieu's findings that class and education correlate with more "advanced" taste in the aesthetic realm. Discussing this question in relation to strategic choices made about Holocaust memorials, James Young stresses the needs of a "lay public" and the probable preference among the general public for figurative work (something like the *Warsaw Ghetto Monument,* with its heroic figures, rather than, say, Sol LeWitt's totally abstract *Black Form* of 1989, in Hamburg-Altona).[31] This reminder that in legislating for "appropriate" Holocaust representation we need to remain sensitive to diverse structures of viewing—what Young calls the "social aesthetic of Holocaust memorials"—is important, though it is also relevant to bear in mind whether the work in question is "public art" (like a memorial, or the art in the Holocaust Museum) or "gallery/museum art," whose constituency is already self-selected. It is worth remembering, too, that the debate about the Vietnam Memorial in Washington, D.C., and the decision to supplement Maya Lin's granite slab with a figurative group (by sculptor Frederick Hart) were not the product of popular dismay at the more abstract work, but rather a response to the objections of a small group of veterans who felt the need for a more heroic monument. It is Maya Lin's memorial which, from its dedication in 1982, has proved by far the more compelling, evocative, and consoling to a broad population.[32] I think we must conclude that, while the critic is obliged to pay attention to the potential elitism of dismissing the popular aesthetic, just as problematic is the presumption that certain aesthetic forms are beyond the grasp of an uneducated populace.

The case I want to make is for what I am calling (following Friedlander) an art of "allusive realism" in Holocaust representation. In Friedlander's words, "literary and artistic works which give a feeling of relative 'adequacy' in bringing the reader and viewer to insights about the Shoah" have as a common denominator "the exclusion of straight, documentary realism, but the use of some *allusive or distanced realism.*"[33] This idea of a nonmimetic, nonabstract form of representation can be found in the work of other writers on the art and literature of the Holocaust, though not always based on the same rationale—for instance, in the concepts of "Holocaust effects" (Ernst van Alphen), "translucent mimesis" (Andrea Liss), "aesthetic uncertainty" (Bryan Cheyette), and the strategy of "indirection" (Inga Clendinnen, John Czaplicka).[34] Although for some this imperative stems from the perceived unrepresentability of the Holocaust (a notion with which, as I have indicated, I disagree[35]), in general the preference for indirect and allusive aesthetic strategies is based on a resistance to a too-facile account with claims to both coherence and closure. Cheyette puts it like this:

> When you read much fiction and poetry there is very little sense of the limitations inherent in representing this history. There is a sense that the history of [the] Holocaust can be contained, can be turned into material which writers themselves formalize. But it is this very idea that the material can be contained, can be redeemed by metaphors, by language or literary form that I worry about. . . . [T]he most lasting literary responses include a painful sense of what can and cannot be said; at their best, these works challenge as well as utilize a poetic language which assumes that everything can be turned into a metaphor. They utilize and also undermine the language of realism which assumes everything can be turned into a reliable documentary form.[36]

In the field of visual representation, a similar case has been made for artists whose representation of the Holocaust is equally indirect. For example, Anselm Kiefer's *Margarethe* and *Shulamith* paintings, based on Paul Celan's Holocaust poem *Death fugue,* evoke their theme obliquely, through reference to the poem, the named biblical Jewish figure, and the imagery itself (a menorah in the background of a vaulted brick chamber in *Shulamith,* straw standing for the "strawblond" hair of the Aryan woman in *Margarethe*).[37] Two works—separated by thirty years—seem to me to be among the most successful, and compelling, examples of post-Holocaust art. The first is R. B. Kitaj's *If Not, Not* of 1975–76, a dense and complex work whose meaning is far from obvious. Indeed, according to Kitaj himself the painting is about many different things.[38] The clearest reference to the Holocaust is the Auschwitz gatehouse standing at the top left of the image. The "strewn and abandoned things and people" throughout the canvas can also be interpreted as the after-effects of some catastrophe. For those familiar with Kitaj's work and writings, the figure of a man with a hearing aid in the bottom left corner of the painting is recognizable as "Joe Singer," his recurrent image of the archetypical Jewish scholar-male. Finally, Kitaj's own "Preface," written on the occasion of his 1994 retrospective exhibition at the Tate Gallery, London, gives further clues to the reading of the image, and the overdetermination of its meaning, with its references to T. S. Eliot's *The Waste Land,* Conrad's *Heart of Darkness,* Giorgione's *Tempest,* and the Holocaust, as well as the links perceived, and intended, between these. One might object that the complexity of this work gets in the way of its ability to serve as post-Holocaust art, and there have certainly been those who have voiced strong opposition to Kitaj's tendency to rely on literary references and on words themselves (in his prefaces).[39] My own view is that, on the contrary, this very complexity and the refusal of any attempt at simple and direct representation of the events of the Holocaust engenders that "adequacy" sought by Friedlander.

The second work which achieves this effect is Ben Shahn's 1944 painting *The Red Stairway.* A first reading of the image might suggest a couple of links to the Second World War, if not specifically to the Holocaust: the one-legged (war-wounded?) man climbing the stairway; the desolation of the landscape; and, of course, the date of the work itself. Commentators on Shahn's work have pointed out that his references to the Holocaust, and to broader issues of Jewish identity, tended to be hidden within other themes—the war in general, the situation of the oppressed in peacetime.[40] *The Red Stairway,* like other works of that period, refers "to the devastation of European Jewry, as well as more overtly to universal suffering during the war."[41] The ability to "read" beyond the universalistic condemnation of war is dependent on knowing something of Shahn's practice, then, which—more than is the case with the Kitaj painting—renders the work potentially obscure as a Holocaust painting. But

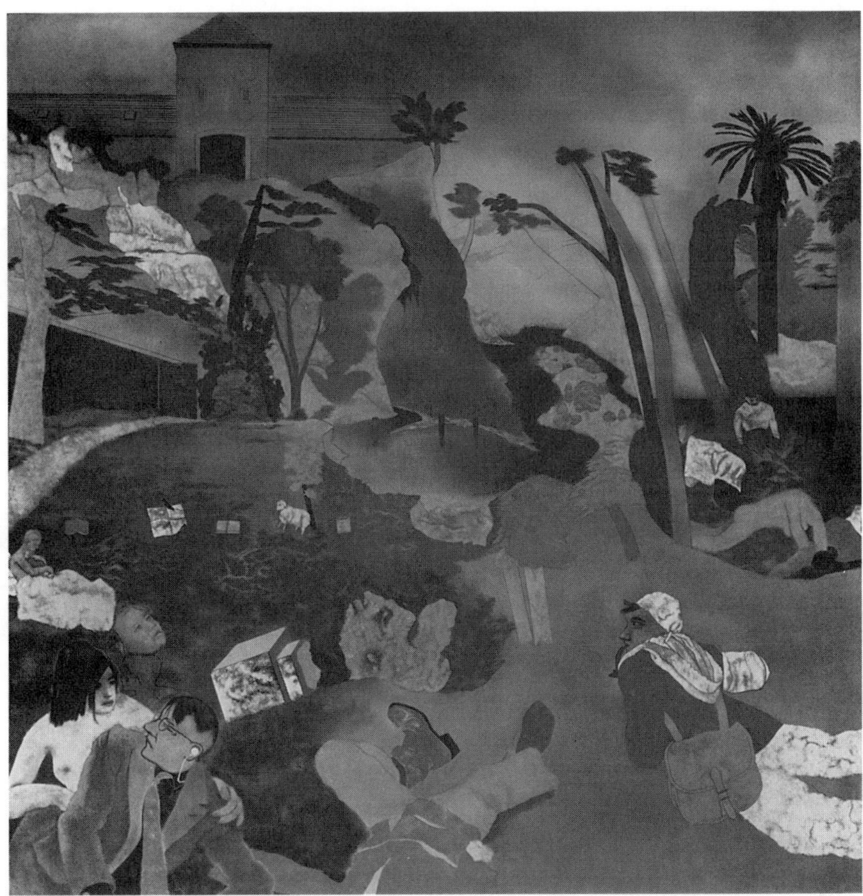

10.2 R. B. Kitaj, *If Not, Not,* 1975–76, oil on canvas (60" × 60").
Courtesy National Galleries of Scotland.

such difficulty is easily countered or remedied by the wall text, the catalogue, and the context of display. (For example, the inclusion of the work in the 1998 Shahn retrospective at the Jewish Museum in New York is likely to have prompted a different, more "Jewish," interpretation than its more usual display at the Saint Louis Art Museum.)

I want to stress here the dual aspect of this "aesthetics of uncertainty," this recourse to an "allusive realism." The drive to indirection and complexity is both a response to the recognition of the inadequacy of art to comprehend (in both senses) the Holocaust and, at the same time, an insistence on the dialogic participation of the viewer, whose active engagement is thereby guaranteed. This positioning of the viewer, as one involved in a "retrospective contemplativeness"[42] which necessitates the work of reconstruction, is founded on both a

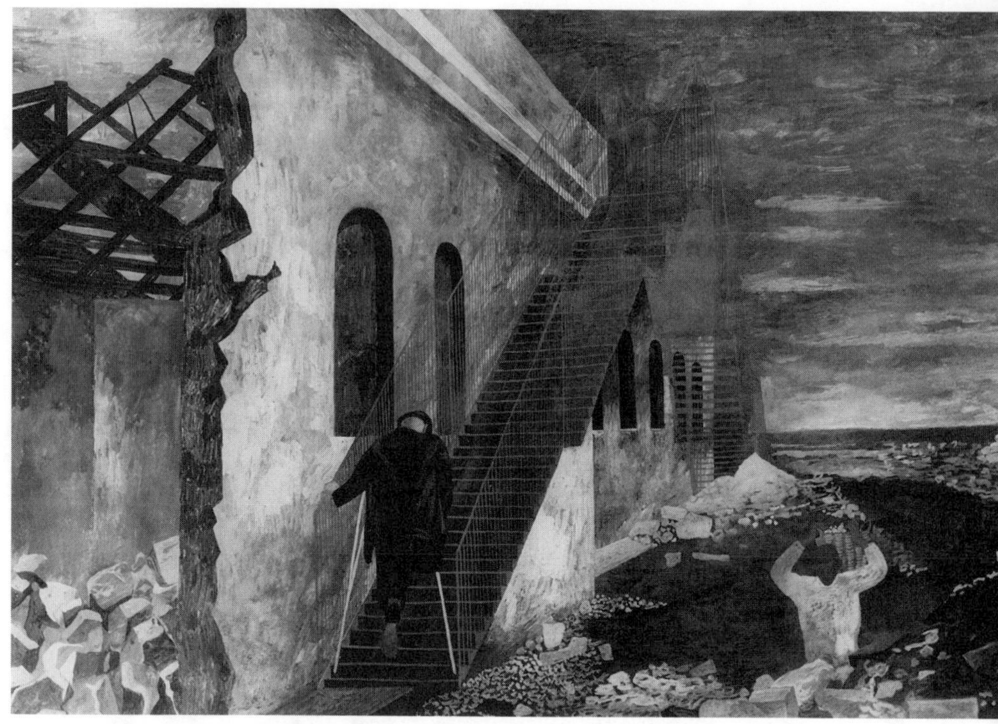

10.3 Ben Shahn, *The Red Stairway*, 1944, tempura on masonite (16" × 23$^{15}/_{16}$"). Courtesy The Saint Louis Art Museum.

moral and an aesthetic imperative. Here I find George Steiner's concept of "tactical difficulty" useful in exploring the logic of a certain kind of representation. Although in this context Steiner, discussing European and American poetry, is not concerned either with the Holocaust or with visual imagery, his explanation of the author's choice of "difficulty" fits well the requirements of "adequacy" of post-Holocaust art.

> [T]here is . . . an entire poetic of tactical difficulty. It is the poet's aim to charge with supreme intensity and genuineness of feeling a body of language, to "make new" his text in the most durable sense of illuminative, penetrative insight. But the language at his disposal is, by definition, general, common in use. Its similes are stock, its metaphors worn down to cliché. How can this soiled organon serve the most individual and innovative of needs? . . . The authentic poet *cannot* make do with the infinitely shop-worn inventory of speech, with the necessarily devalued or counterfeit currency of the every-day. He must literally create new worlds and syntactic modes. . . . If the reader would follow the poet into the *terra incognita* of revelation, he must learn the language. . . . The underlying maneuver is one of *rallentando.* We are not meant to understand

easily and quickly. Immediate purchase is denied us. The text yields its force and singularity of being only gradually. In certain fascinating cases, our understanding, however strenuously won, is to remain provisional. There is to be an undecidability at the heart, at what Coleridge called the inner *penetralium* of the poem.[43]

Of course, the case could be made that any art strives to achieve this effect—that this is what differentiates it from kitsch.[44] In the case of art of the Holocaust, the aesthetic imperative is compounded by a moral imperative which insists just as strongly on the denial of "immediate purchase."[45] Whether the object of the work, from the point of view of the artist, is to document, to memorialize, or to register a personal response, the tactical difficulty of allusive imagery is most likely to engage the viewer in the necessary dialogue and reflection. As I have suggested, abstraction, by definition devoid of mechanisms of allusion and reference, can only operate as an adequate Holocaust art when it is aided by text or context. Literal realism has the double disadvantage of alienating the viewer (when it employs too-graphic images) and of engendering a passive, unreflective response. Returning to the Louis and Lebrun exhibitions at the Jewish Museum, we can reconsider their relative strategies and merits. Louis's *Charred Journals,* though risking the evacuation of meaning in their almost total abstraction, nevertheless implicate the viewer in retrospection on Nazism and the Holocaust by their minimal use of figures and letters, their visual evocation of the burnt page and titular reference to the burning of books, and, of course, their contextual display on this occasion, alongside Lebrun's *Holocaust Paintings* and supported by wall texts and an exhibition brochure. Within such a framework, the works succeed as art of the Holocaust—elegiac, thoughtful, and thought-provoking representations which respect the viewer's intelligence and ability to work with the given image. The Lebrun paintings fail, on the other hand, because their confrontational visual strategy, operating by shock, is more likely to distance their audience and, at the same time, foreclose dialogue and reflection in its insistence on a singularity of meaning and judgment. The works are not realist in general, but their employment of vividly realist elements (bodies, limbs) exemplifies, I would argue, the distortions and failure of iconic imagery in post-Holocaust art.

Often combined with the objection to a facile aesthetic is a resistance to beauty in the art of the Holocaust. The fear is that visual pleasure negates horror, by aestheticizing violence and atrocity, by proposing redemption in the face of outrage, or by providing consolation in the encounter with beauty. Shoshana Felman records Paul Celan's rejection of his own classic Holocaust poem, *Death fugue,* in favor of a "less melodious, more disrupted and disruptively elliptical verse" which (in his own words) "distrusts the beautiful."[46]

Sartre's comment about painting the concentration camp as if it were a compote (quoted at the beginning of this essay) is founded on the same concern. But he goes on in the same essay, in a discussion of art about war and violence and of the work of the nonfigurative artist Robert Lapoujade, to approve the beauty in his paintings.[47] His strongest objection is to the literal depiction of violence and of mutilated corpses, and he insists on the artist's responsibility to creativity and beauty. His own solution, in the case of the art of violence, is to favor nonfigurative art, which can display beauty without aestheticizing its subject matter. I believe that the case can be made for beauty in nonabstract Holocaust art as well, and I want to conclude by returning to my three opening quotations, and to their condensed argument (implicit in the order in which I have cited them) in favor of beauty even—or perhaps especially—in the context of post-Holocaust art.

In proposing this, I am in some ways operating in concert with the much-remarked "return to beauty" at the end of the twentieth century, and the delayed reaction to the logic of the "anti-aesthetic."[48] But it is important to recognize the diverse motivations behind this anti-anti-aesthetic move, which in some cases is merely a new version of the long-standing conservative resistance to political art and to postmodern art practice.[49] More interesting is the reconsideration of the politics of representation by those who "got the point" of the anti-aesthetic, and of the postmodern critique of representation and the institutions of cultural practice. From the 1970s to the 1990s, a certain orthodoxy developed on the need to eschew visual pleasure and to follow the Brechtian example of estrangement and disruption—a point of view famously expressed in the area of film studies by Laura Mulvey's pronouncement in 1975 that beauty must be destroyed.[50] The objective of critical theory in general (feminism, poststructuralism, museology, postcolonial theory) has been to deconstruct the canon by demonstrating the contingencies of its creation and maintenance through a variety of discourses, institutions, and power relations. The corollary, for many, has often appeared to be the need to suspect the seductions of the aesthetic. Bourdieu's sociological revision of Kant's aesthetic appears to leave little room for an innocent enjoyment of the encounter with the object, which is irredeemably contaminated by its social and political coordinates.[51] The curator of a 1999 exhibition, *Regarding Beauty,* comments on "the extraordinarily strained relationship between art and beauty at century's end."[52] The exhibition itself, though, at the Hirschhorn Museum in Washington, D.C., in late 1999, participates in the reevaluation of beauty in the postcritical period. It has become increasingly clear to many artists and critics that the production and enjoyment of visual pleasure need not signify an abandonment of politics and critique.[53] Kathleen Marie Higgins has made this case well:

> Beauty seems at odds with political activism because it is not a directly practical response to the world. It inspires contemplation, not storm and fury. But politically motivated artists, I submit, have much to gain from beauty. Beauty encourages a perspective from which our ordinary priorities are up for grabs. . . . In the first place, contemplation of beauty provides the receptive condition in which we can recognize our own moral insights. Beauty creates a space for spiritual openness.[54]

The distinction made by Walter Benjamin, in a study of two poems by Hölderlin, between beauty as consolation and beauty as a mark of presence, which has been clarified and developed by Howard Caygill, suggests the possibility of the latter in a nonconsolatory post-Holocaust art.[55] In the second poem, "beauty is no longer called upon to console in the face of death" since "in the second version beauty flows from the overcoming of danger."[56] The contrast is between a beauty allied with life against death (that is, as consolation before the threat of death) and a beauty "in which death is incorporated into life, and in which beauty is not a consolation for the threat of death, but a mark of its presence in life."[57] What this might mean in the field of visual art remains to be explored, of course. My suggestion is that such a distinction allows us to acknowledge the "aestheticizing" risks of a facile, consolatory, beauty while choosing an aesthetic—adequate to its grave and challenging subject—that not only permits the complex beauty of "presence," but urges us to promote the beautiful in the art of the Holocaust.

I conclude, then, with two examples of such work. Throughout, I have expressed a preference for a certain type of post-Holocaust art—allusive and indirect, realist but not literal, perhaps semi-abstract while avoiding total abstraction. In all cases (Louis, Kitaj, Shahn) I have opted for work which also gives visual pleasure, and which manifests its own particular beauty. The two examples of the work of contemporary artists—one a British painter living in Berlin, the other a Canadian sculptor currently living in the United States—illustrate for me the possibilities of complexity, seriousness, and beauty in art of the Holocaust. Sally Heywood's *The Burning* of 1993 is, first of all, a ravishing, multicolored oil painting. Semi-abstract, it nevertheless highlights the dome of a building in the top center of the image.[58] That the building is a synagogue we know both from Heywood's related works (*The Reconstruction of the Synagogue* [1991], for example) and from an artist's statement.[59] The allusion to Kristallnacht and to the situation of the Jews in Berlin is clear, though the viewer has to do the work of interpretation. Drawn in by the visual appeal of the work—its gorgeous color and its complex composition, at the same time frenetic and arresting—the viewer takes up the invitation to grasp its meaning. This beauty, of course, cannot be consolatory, given the subject matter of the work and the aggressive visibility of the act of destruction. But it creates exactly that "space," suggested by Higgins, which enables engagement with its topic,

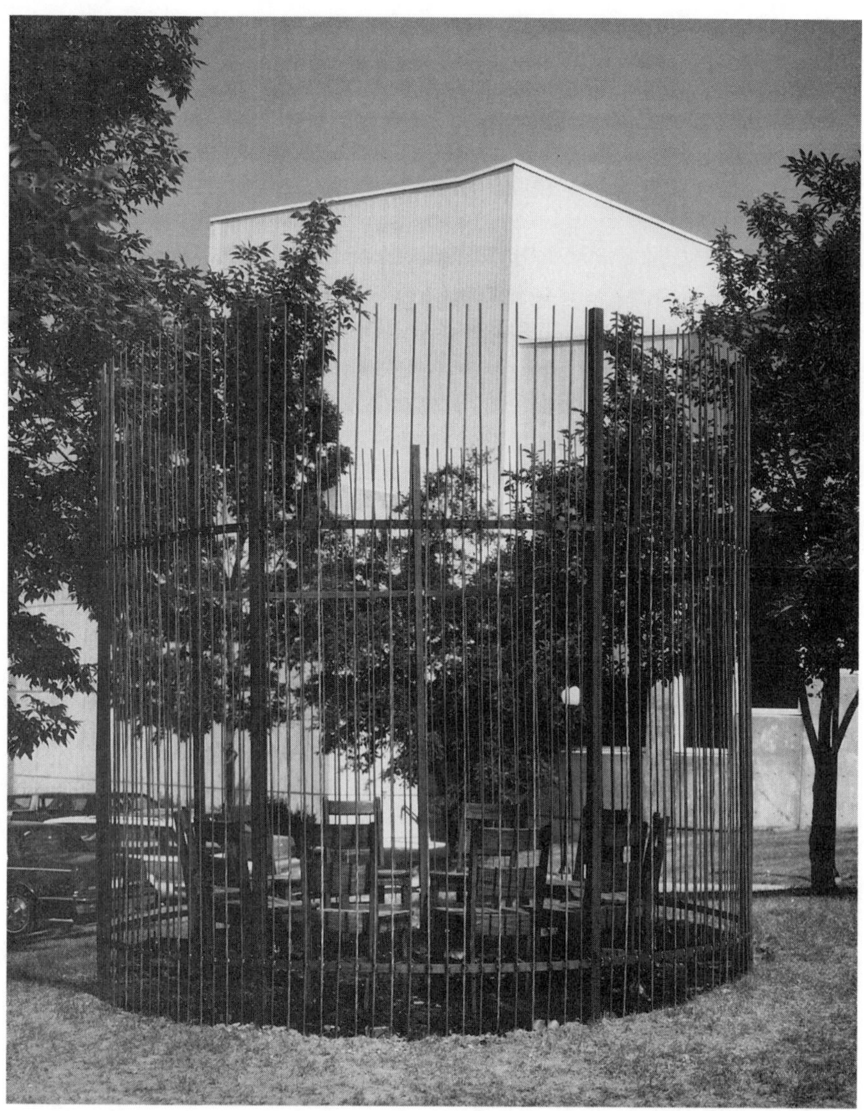

10.4 Cyril Reade, *Minyan*, 1995, steel, oak chairs, burnt timbers (10' high × 10' diameter). Courtesy Cyril Reade. Photo by Michael Mitchell.

and in doing so, it offers a representation which employs visual pleasure in the context of a serious response to the events of the Holocaust. The same is true of Cyril Reade's 1995 installation, *Minyan*. This work, situated on the grounds of the Bathurst Jewish Centre in Toronto, Canada, consists of ten oak chairs, arranged in a circle and placed on scraps of charred timber inside a tall circular fence of steel posts. The chairs were intended to weather and erode through all the seasons of the year.[60] A minyan is the quorum of ten men required in Jewish law for any public worship. The work as a whole thus operates a complex set of meanings and connotations: Jewish tradition; absence and loss (the empty chairs); community, exclusion, and imprisonment (the three aspects of the surrounding fence); ritual and destruction (positive and negative references to burning). The invocation of the Holocaust and its effects on the lives of Jews—individual Jews and Jewish culture as a whole—is inescapable, yet at the same time both indirect and irreducible to any simple formula. Like Heywood's painting, the installation begins its appeal to the viewer through the beauty of its construction—its materials, its ineluctable and measured erosion and decay, its elegance of composition (the height of the fence bestowing gravity and signifying the overwhelming extent of external constraint, while at the same time allowing the autonomy and dignity of the minyan), and, not least, its attractive outdoor setting, with its own seasons of growth and death. The work has an elegiac quality which is again by no means consolatory—for there is no way out of the circle, and no respite from the effects of the weather. The effect, then, is the employment of beauty in a complex and allusive work of art of the Holocaust.

Notes

1. Jean-Paul Sartre, "The Unprivileged Painter: Lapoujade," in *Essays in Aesthetics* (London: Peter Owen, 1963), 74.

2. Audrey Flack, *On Painting* (New York: Harry N. Abrams, 1981), 78, 81. Quoted by Ziva Amishai-Maisels, *Depiction and Interpretation: The Influence of the Holocaust on the Visual Arts* (New York: Pergamon, 1993), 17.

3. Elaine Scarry, *On Beauty and Being Just* (Princeton, N.J.: Princeton University Press, 1999), 62.

4. The largest, charcoal on canvas, is 98" x 80", and most of the twelve works shown are in the range of 75" x 86".

5. The Jewish Museum brochure, *Morris Louis: The Charred Journal Series, 1951, and Rico Lebrun: The Holocaust Paintings, 1997* (New York: The Jewish Museum, 1997), states that Louis told this to the organizers of a 1953 exhibition of his work.

6. Holland Cotter, "The Holocaust through Visions Abstract and Figurative," *The New York Times,* 17 January 1997, C27.

7. Mira Goldfarb Berkowitz and Susan Chevlowe, *Morris Louis: The Charred Journal Series, 1951, and Rico Lebrun: The Holocaust Paintings, 1997.*

8. Cotter, "Holocaust," C27.

9. In deciding which works to illustrate for this article, [illegible] the total number of images in the book, [illegible]

include reproductions of those works which, for me, were such an "affront." Throughout, however, I refer the reader to places where they can see examples of this work. The Segal sculpture, *The Holocaust* (1984), is represented most prominently on the front cover of the Jewish Museum's catalogue *The Art of Memory: Holocaust Memorials in History,* edited by James Young (New York: Prestel, 1994). Jerome Witkin's *The Butcher's Helper: Buchenwald, 1941–1945* (1991) is reproduced (in black and white) in Matthew Baigell, *Jewish-American Artists and the Holocaust* (New Brunswick, N.J.: Rutgers University Press, 1997), as figure 26. Several of the Lebrun works mentioned are reproduced in Amishai-Maisels, *Depiction and Interpretation.*

10. Here I agree with others who resist this mystification of—and hence the refusal to analyze—the Holocaust. See, for example, Philip Lopate's brilliant and provocative essay "Resistance to the Holocaust," in *Testimony: Contemporary Writers Make the Holocaust Personal,* ed. David Rosenberg (New York: Random House, 1989), 285–308; and Inga Clendinnen, *Reading the Holocaust* (New York: Cambridge University Press, 1999), in which she argues strongly against the idea that the Holocaust is unique and outside history.

11. Claude Lanzmann, "From the Holocaust to the Holocaust," *Telos,* no. 42 (winter 1979–80): 137–138.

12. A related argument, associated in particular with Saul Friedlander, proposes that in the case of the Holocaust, a reality so extreme could not be contained within the limits of realist language. But, as James Young has pointed out, it is clear that realism (visual as well as literary) is no more a natural language than modernist representational practices (James Young, *Writing and Rewriting the Holocaust: Narrative and the Consequences of Interpretation* [Bloomington: Indiana University Press, 1988], 16–18). One could say, then, that the debunking of realism's claim to transparency and mimesis at the same time cancels its imperative to "tell the truth."

13. Clendinnen, *Reading the Holocaust,* 4.

14. Andrea Liss, *Trespassing through Shadows: Memory, Photography, and the Holocaust* (Minneapolis: University of Minnesota Press, 1998), 3.

15. Clendinnen, *Reading the Holocaust,* 172. The book in question is Nabokov's *Bend Sinister,* which Clendinnen discusses as an indirect account of the Holocaust. The stapled pages deal with the murder of an eight-year-old child.

16. See, for example, Saul Friedlander, *Reflections of Nazism: An Essay on Kitsch and Death* (Bloomington: Indiana University Press, 1993).

17. Yosefa Loshitzky, "Holocaust Others: Spielberg's *Schindler's List* versus Lanzmann's *Shoah,*" in *Spielberg's Holocaust: Critical Perspectives on* Schindler's List, ed. Yosefa Loshitzky (Bloomington: Indiana University Press, 1997), 110–111. In the same volume, this scene is also discussed by Miriam Hansen and by Sara R. Horowitz.

18. Both are reproduced in Amishai-Maisels, *Depiction and Interpretation.*

19. Reproduced in Amishai-Maisels, *Depiction and Interpretation.*

20. The first is reproduced in Baigell, *Jewish-American Artists,* figure 38; both are reproduced and discussed in Jon Bird, Jo Anna Isaak, and Sylvère Lotringer, *Nancy Spero* (New York: Phaidon, 1996).

21. A different defense of fiction has been made in a review of Ian MacMillan's novel about the Treblinka uprising, *Village of a Million Spirits.* The reviewer writes, "Eloquently, MacMillan shows that the truth we can absolutely, factually know about the Holocaust is not the whole story. It is the experience only of those who saw and remembered and came back to tell us. But to understand completely, we must go beyond all this to the rest of the story, to the truth and the experience of the millions

who died. The only way to get at that truth is to imagine it. And the only way to imagine it is through art" (Zofia Smardz, "Hell with the Lid Off," *New York Times Book Review,* 21 November 1999).

22. Sartre puts it like this: "Attempts to depict acts of violence, mutilated corpses and living bodies racked, tortured and burned have been sterile. By falling back upon visual conventions, artists have shown us a moving side of reality and have conditioned us to react as we normally would—with horror, anger, and especially with the silent flood of sympathy that makes every man experience the wounds of other men as so many holes in his own flesh. This unbearable spectacle puts the spectator to flight. A painting may evidence ingenious composition, correct proportions and harmony, but everything is wasted if the spectator flees and fails to return" (Sartre, "The Unprivileged Painter," 73).

23. These arguments are to some extent those of writers in defense of modernism—for example, Colin MacCabe's famous critique of classic realist cinema and its denial of contradiction, or its predecessors in Brecht's and Adorno's arguments for the political importance of a modernist art practice (in theater and music) which refuses passive—"affirmative"—reception. See Colin MacCabe, "Realism and the Cinema: Notes on Some Brechtian Theses," *Screen* 15, no. 2 (summer 1974): 7–27 and note 45 below.

24. See Janet Blatter and Sybil Milton, "Art from the Whirlwind," in *Art of the Holocaust* (New York: Routledge, 1981); James E. Young, "Memory and Countermemory: Towards a Social Aesthetic of Holocaust Memorials," in *After Auschwitz: Responses to the Holocaust in Contemporary Art,* ed. Monica Bohm-Duchen (Sunderland: Northern Centre for Contemporary Art; London: Lund Humphries, 1995), 78–102; *Seeing through "Paradise": Artists and the Terezín Concentration Camp* (Boston: Massachusetts College of Art, 1991).

25. Amishai-Maisels, *Depiction and Interpretation,* 6–10.

26. The painting is *The Death of Danielle Casanova at Buchenwald,* 1950 (in the Musée de l'histoire vivant, Montreuil-sur-seine); it is reproduced as black and white plate 11 in Amishai-Maisels's book.

27. Cited by Baigell, *Jewish-American Artists,* 52. The work in question, *Block 11,* could be described as an icon of an index, since the suitcases are not the actual ones used and abandoned by Holocaust victims.

28. Lawrence L. Langer, "Pre-empting the Holocaust," *The Atlantic Monthly,* November 1998, 105–115. See also his book *Preempting the Holocaust* (New Haven, Conn.: Yale University Press, 1998).

29. Ken Johnson, "Art and Memory," *Art in America* 81, no. 11 (November 1993), 95.

30. For example, see Amishai-Maisels's discussion of the work of former camp inmate Zoran Music and refugee artist Corrado Cagli (*Depiction and Interpretation,* 272–279).

31. Young, in Bohm-Duchen, *After Auschwitz.* Both works are reproduced in his essay.

32. Jan C. Scruggs and Joel L. Swerdlow, *To Heal a Nation: The Vietnam Veterans Memorial* (New York: Harper and Row, 1985), esp. 80–107; John Bodnar, *Remaking America: Public Memory, Commemoration, and Patriotism in the Twentieth Century* (Princeton, N.J.: Princeton University Press, 1992), prologue (though Scruggs and Swerdlow do quote Ross Perot's comment about Lin's monument that "It's something for New York intellectuals," 68).

33. Saul Friedlander, ed., *Probing the Limits of Representation: Nazism and the "Final Solution"* (Cambridge, Mass.: Harvard University Press, 1992), 17.

34. Ernst van Alphen, *Caught by History: Holocaust Effects in Contemporary Art, Literature, and Theory* (Stanford, Calif.: Stanford University Press, 1997); Liss, *Trespassing through Shadows,* 120; Bryan Cheyette, "The Uncertain Certainty of *Schindler's List,*" in Loshitzky, *Spielberg's Holocaust,* 226–238; Clendinnen, *Reading the Holocaust,* 165; John Czaplicka, "History, Aesthetics, and Contemporary Commemorative Practice in Berlin," *New German Critique,* no. 65 (spring–summer 1995): 155–187. A related, but somewhat different, argument is made by Laub and Podell for an "indirect and dialogic" art of the Holocaust, which they characterize as "the art of trauma": Dori Laub and Daniel Podell, "Art and Trauma," *International Journal of Psycho-Analysis* 76, no. 5 (1995): 991–1005.

35. As Friedlander says, "The extermination of the Jews of Europe is as accessible to both representation and interpretation as any other historical event" (Friedlander, *Probing the Limits,* 2).

36. Martin Amis, Bryan Cheyette, Lucy Ellman, and Joseph Skibell, "Writing the Unwritable: A Debate on Holocaust Fiction," *The Jewish Quarterly,* no. 170 (summer 1998): 14. A similar reasoning leads Michael Rothberg to the conclusion that only a postmodern, not a modernist, aesthetic is appropriate to the Holocaust: "After Adorno: Culture in the Wake of Catastrophe," *New German Critique,* no. 72 (fall 1997): 45–81.

37. See Lisa Saltzman, "To Figure, or Not to Figure: The Iconoclastic Proscription and Its Theoretical Legacy," in *Jewish Identity in Modern Art History,* ed. Catherine M. Soussloff (Berkeley and Los Angeles: University of California Press, 1999), 67–84, and Saltzman, *Anselm Kiefer and Art after Auschwitz* (New York: Cambridge University Press, 1999). *Shulamith* is reproduced in both texts, *Margarethe* in the book on Kiefer. For a more critical account of Kiefer's Holocaust paintings, see Jed Perl, "A Dissent on Kiefer," *The New Criterion* 7, no. 4 (December 1988): 14–20. For the view that conceptual (postmodern) visual art best achieves this strategy of indirection, see Martha McWilliams, "Order out of Chaos: 'Burnt Whole': Contemporary Artists Reflect on the Holocaust," *The New Art Examiner* 22, no. 2 (April 1995): 12–17.

38. R. B. Kitaj, preface to *If Not, Not,* in *R. B. Kitaj: A Retrospective,* ed. Richard Morphet (London: Tate Gallery, 1994), 120.

39. See my essay "The Impolite Boarder: 'Diasporist Art' and Its Critical Response," in *Critical Kitaj: Essays on the Work of R. B. Kitaj,* ed. James Aulich and John Lynch (Manchester: Manchester University Press, 2000), 29–43.

40. See Ziva Amishai-Maisels, "Ben Shahn and the Problem of Jewish Identity," *Jewish Art* 12/13 (1986–88): 304–319; also Amishai-Maisels, *Depiction and Interpretation,* 310–313.

41. Susan Chevlowe, "A Bull in a China Shop: An Introduction to Ben Shahn," in *Common Man, Mythic Vision: The Paintings of Ben Shahn,* ed. Susan Chevlowe (New York and Princeton, N.J.: The Jewish Museum and Princeton University Press, 1998), 16.

42. John Czaplicka takes over Aby Warburg's phrase here, in connection with his own arguments about appropriate Holocaust memorialization: "History, Aesthetics, and Contemporary Commemorative Practice," 158.

43. George Steiner, "On Difficulty," in *On Difficulty and Other Essays* (New York: Oxford University Press, 1978), 34–35.

44. Here I am not following Greenberg's famous distinction (Clement Greenberg, "Avant-garde and Kitsch," *Partisan Review* 6, no. 5 [1939]: 34–49). In other words, "art" (as opposed to "kitsch") does not differentiate between "high" art and popular culture, or even between commercial and noncommercial art. It is a matter of originality, and of challenge to the audience or viewer. In this sense, both high art and popular culture can be categorized as kitsch in some cases.

45. This is something like the Brechtian argument about the role of the "alienation-effect" in theater, or Adorno's favoring of the "difficult" music of Schoenberg over that of Stravinsky, and over popular music—the stress on the "negative" role of modernist art, which works to engage a critical consciousness on the part of its recipient. See Bertolt Brecht, *The Messingkauf Dialogues* (London: Eyre Methuen, 1965); Theodor W. Adorno, "Arnold Schoenberg, 1874–1951," in *Prisms,* trans. Samuel and Shierry Weber (London: Neville Spearman, 1967), 147–172; Frankfurt Institute for Social Research, *Aspects of Sociology,* trans. John Viertel (London: Heinemann, 1973), 111–112; Adorno, "Perennial Fashion—Jazz," in *Prisms,* 119–132. See also Herbert Marcuse, "The Affirmative Character of Culture," in *Negations: Essays in Critical Theory* (London: Allen Lane, 1968), 88–133.

46. Shoshana Felman, "Education and Crisis, or the Vicissitudes of Teaching," in *Testimony: Crises of Witnessing in Literature, Psychoanalysis, and History,* ed. Shoshana Felman and Dori Laub (New York: Routledge, 1992), 35. Jed Perl's critique of Kiefer's work, mentioned earlier, is partly based on its aestheticizing tendencies, its texture which "seduces more than it illuminates" (Perl, "A Dissent on Kiefer," 15).

47. "His triptych is beautiful without reserve—and can be beautiful without remorse. Beauty is not hidden in nonfigurative painting. It shows through. The painting exhibits nothing. It lets horror seep down but only if it is beautiful—that is, organized in the most complex and fertile manner" (Sartre, "The Unprivileged Painter," 88).

48. An influential text in this move was Dave Hickey's book *The Invisible Dragon: Four Essays on Beauty* (Los Angeles: Artissues, 1993). Among many contributors to the debate—though not necessarily in dialogue with one another, and not all concerned primarily with contemporary art practice—are the following: Arthur C. Danto, "Whatever Happened to Beauty?" *The Nation,* 30 March 1992; "Aesthetics and the Body Politic," *Art Journal* 56, no. 1 (spring 1997); "B Is for Beauty," *New Art Examiner* 21, no. 8 (April 1994); Richard Bolton, "Beauty Redefined: From Ideal Form to Experiential Meaning," *New Art Examiner* 21, no. 3 (November 1993): 27–31; "Symposium: Beauty Matters," *The Journal of Aesthetics and Art Criticism* 57, no. 1 (winter 1999); Francette Pacteau, *The Symptom of Beauty* (Cambridge, Mass.: Harvard University Press, 1994); Scarry, *On Beauty;* Hilary Robinson, "Beauty, the Universal, the Divine: Irigaray's Re-valuings," in *Women Artists and Modernism,* ed. Katy Deepwell (Manchester: Manchester University Press, 1998), 159–174; Hal Foster, *Compulsive Beauty* (Cambridge, Mass.: MIT Press, 1993); Ken Johnson, "A Post-retinal Documenta," *Art in America* 85, no. 10 (October 1997): 81–88; Neal Benezra and Olga M. Viso, *Regarding Beauty: A View of the Late Twentieth Century* (Washington, D.C.: Hirschhorn Museum and Sculpture Garden, Smithsonian Institution, 1999). The classic collection of essays on the anti-aesthetic is Hal Foster, ed., *The Anti-aesthetic: Essays on Postmodern Culture* (Seattle: Bay, 1983).

49. For example, many of the essays, and the introduction, in Bill Beckley's edited volume *Uncontrollable Beauty: Toward a New Aesthetic* (New York: Allworth, 1998). See also Martha Bayles, *Hole in Our Soul: The Loss of Beauty and Meaning in American Popular Music* (New York: Free Press, 1994).

50. "It is said that analyzing pleasure, or beauty, destroys it. That is the intention of this essay" (Laura Mulvey, "Visual Pleasure and Narrative Cinema" [1975], in *Art after Modernism: Rethinking Representation,* ed. Brian Wallis [New York and Boston: The New Museum of Contemporary Art and David R. Godine, 1984], 363).

51. Pierre Bourdieu, *Distinction: A Social Critique of the Judgment of Taste,* trans. Richard Nice (Cambridge, Mass.: Harvard University Press, 1984).

52. Neal Benezra, "The Misadventures of Beauty," in Benezra and Viso, *Regarding Beauty,* 19.

53. Elaine Scarry has made the more radical claim that beauty has a positive function in addressing injustice, on the grounds that "beautiful things give rise to the notion of distribution, to a lifesaving reciprocity, to fairness not just in the sense of loveliness of aspect but in the sense of 'a symmetry of everyone's relation to one another'" (*On Beauty,* 95). I don't find this particular argument persuasive, though I do endorse her conclusion, quoted at the beginning of this essay.

54. Kathleen Marie Higgins, "Whatever Happened to Beauty? A Response to Danto," *The Journal of Aesthetics and Art Criticism* 54, no. 3 (summer 1996): 283.

55. Walter Benjamin, "Two Poems by Friedrich Hölderlin: 'The Poet's Courage' and 'Timidity,'" in *Selected Writings,* vol. 1, *1913–1926* (Cambridge, Mass.: Harvard University Press, 1996), 18–36; Howard Caygill, *Walter Benjamin: The Colour of Experience* (New York: Routledge, 1998), chapter 2, esp. 38–52.

56. Caygill, *Walter Benjamin,* 39.

57. Ibid., 49.

58. Unfortunately, this work can really only be appreciated in full color. Because the illustrations in this book are only in black and white, I will have to refer readers to the color reproduction of Heywood's *The Burning* as figure 59 in Bohm-Duchen, *After Auschwitz.*

59. Bohm-Duchen, *After Auschwitz,* 149–150. Both works are illustrated in this catalogue, and were included, together with a related drawing by Heywood, in the exhibition, first shown in London in 1995.

60. On its initial installation, in June 1995, there was also a related indoor part of *Minyan,* in two galleries in the Koffler Gallery at the Bathurst Jewish Centre. See the catalogue, *Cyril Reade: Minyan* (North York and Toronto: Koffler Gallery, 1995). At the time of writing, the outdoor installation is still in place.

11 Burnt Books and Absent Meaning

Morris Louis's Charred Journal: Firewritten *Series and the Holocaust* | MARK GODFREY

Morris Louis, born Maurice Bernstein in 1912 to immigrant Jews living in Baltimore, is today best known for the paintings he produced in the last ten years of his life. During that time, cramped into a room at the back of his Maryland house at a deliberate distance from New York, Louis made hundreds of canvases in three main series: the *Veils,* the *Unfurleds,* the *Pillars.* The paintings were introduced primarily through the Modernist criticism of Clement Greenberg and Michael Fried, who argued that it was the task of painting to explore those elements which distinguished it from other arts. Greenberg and Fried discussed how Modernist paintings acknowledged the flatness of the stretched canvas, how spectators enjoyed an optical encounter as they viewed the painting, how optical space depended on paint handling, on color, shape, and scale. Narrative, ethnic identity, historical reference, and memory were not—at least explicitly—of concern.[1] Louis's late work could be deployed as the very demonstration of their theory.

In his monograph on Louis, for instance, Michael Fried described the optical effects of Louis's *Unfurled* series, in which diagonal streams of paint crossed the bottom corners of the painting, leaving between them a vast space of untouched canvas. These rivulets overcame the traditional function of the drawn line: they did not mark the perimeters of shapes, but seemed "*all* perimeter."[2] It was their positioning against the central expanse of blank canvas

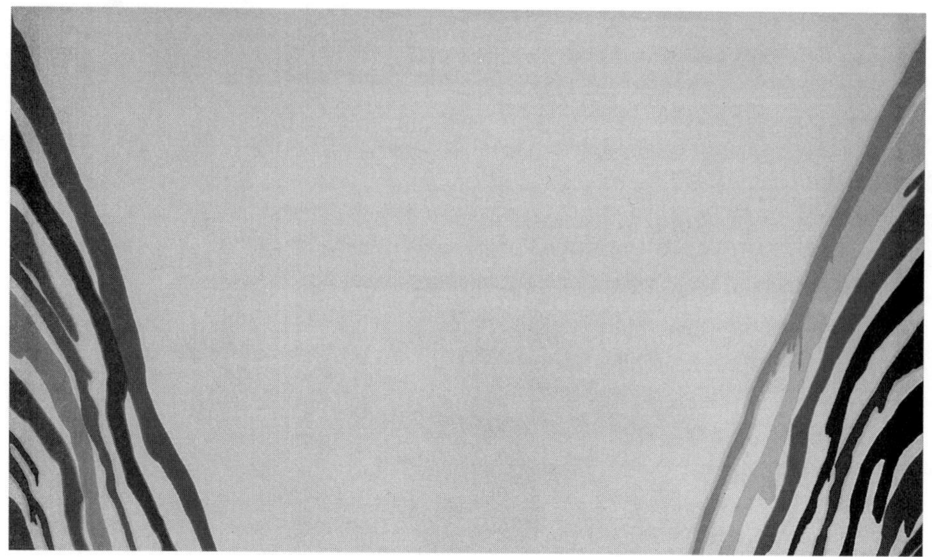

11.1 Morris Louis, *Alpha-Phi,* 1960–61. Courtesy Tate Enterprises Ltd.

which gave these lines a special significance. Fried quoted Greenberg's comment that "[t]he first mark on a surface destroys its virtual flatness" (32). For Fried, these lines seemed to play out the *"firstness of marking"* (33): these paintings were about what happens when a mark is made on the surface—the mark announces itself as figure, against the ground behind. Since this ground was so expansive, the untouched canvas at the center of the *Unfurleds* seemed like an "infinite abyss": "One's experience of the *Unfurleds* can be vertiginous" (33).

Fried used the metaphor of an empty page to describe the canvas: the *Unfurleds* had an "original blankness (the blankness, one feels, of an enormous *page*)" (32). The works were "wholly abstract embodiments or correlatives of . . . the will or impulse to draw, to make one's mark, to take possession, in characteristic ways, of a plane surface" (35). The idea of the page (as opposed to canvas) would seem to invoke the mark on it as a mark of writing; as a Modernist, Fried, though he tempted this invocation, thought of the first mark on the "page" as a visual mark, the mark that initiated a figure/ground relationship, that created optical space. The impulse to "take possession" of the page could thus only be considered as the impulse to mark it with visual content, a kind of content which does not exist prior to the marking. However, if the implications of the canvas as page were followed in the most obvious manner, the first mark on it would then be considered a written (not drawn) mark. Then, rather than initiating visual content, these first marks would initiate content associated with writing. The first mark would signify the impulse to make meaning, to represent.

For Fried, Louis's career truly began with a breakthrough moment in 1953 when he realized the formal possibilities of staining the canvas with thinned acrylic paint. Fried all but ignored the series Louis had made in 1951—the *Charred Journal: Firewritten* paintings. The notions of the "page" and of "writing," kept separate in Fried's account, are jointly written into their titles. Yet the only way that Fried could write about these paintings was through the idea of the visual mark—through drawing, not writing—and, consequently, his account addresses the significance of their form, not their other possible meanings. They were clearly "influenced" by Jackson Pollock, but "Pollock remains exactly that, an influence" (13). They did not announce, as the later work would, Louis's extension of Pollock's experiment with drawing, and thus remained "of minor importance." It is to these works that I want to turn.[3]

The *Charred Journal: Firewritten* series comprises seven small canvases (approximately 35" high and 30" wide), each differentiated by a number or letter. Alongside the enveloping expanses of the *Unfurleds,* these paintings might seem frail and insubstantial. Their surfaces, however, reveal a complexity that requires sustained description. While a spectator might see the canvases as flat surfaces, description must prize the surface apart, working an inverse archaeology from the bottom layer of paint upward, and thereby reconstructing the various techniques Louis practiced, from first to last.

The first stratum of paint is a colored under-layer. Louis would later work directly on raw duck, but in 1951 he primed his canvases. A light monochrome coat would here have sufficed to seal the holes in the weave, but what is seen—particularly from close up—is a range of tones. These vary between paintings: in *Charred Journal: Firewritten II,* they are yellowy brown; in *IV,* salmon pink. In *Charred Journal: Firewritten B* they are a light sky-blue. All of these pigments are pale and subtle, and appear to the viewer where the next layer of paint, a black, fails to cover the surface.

Once the under-layer was dry, Louis applied black acrylic. It seems to have been laid down variously with a knife or a brush, and rather than covering the entire surface, the brush marks leave gaps through which the colored under-layer is seen. These gaps are both between strokes and between bristles, suggesting that the brush either was not loaded with paint or was somewhat dry when it touched, and moved down, the canvas. The strokes are always vertical, so that the black resembles the carbon trace a candle marks on a wall. They leave the surface looking dirty rather than covered, patchy and charred.

The next stage of the process was the construction of grid lines. These become increasingly visible as one moves back from the painting. The grid lines lie over the black layer in three paintings: *IV, B,* and *C.* Here, the grids have been made by pouring a dark black in thin lines across and down the surface. The lines stretch to all four edges of the canvas, dividing the surface into unequal rectangles. They are deliberately wavy, their thickness never

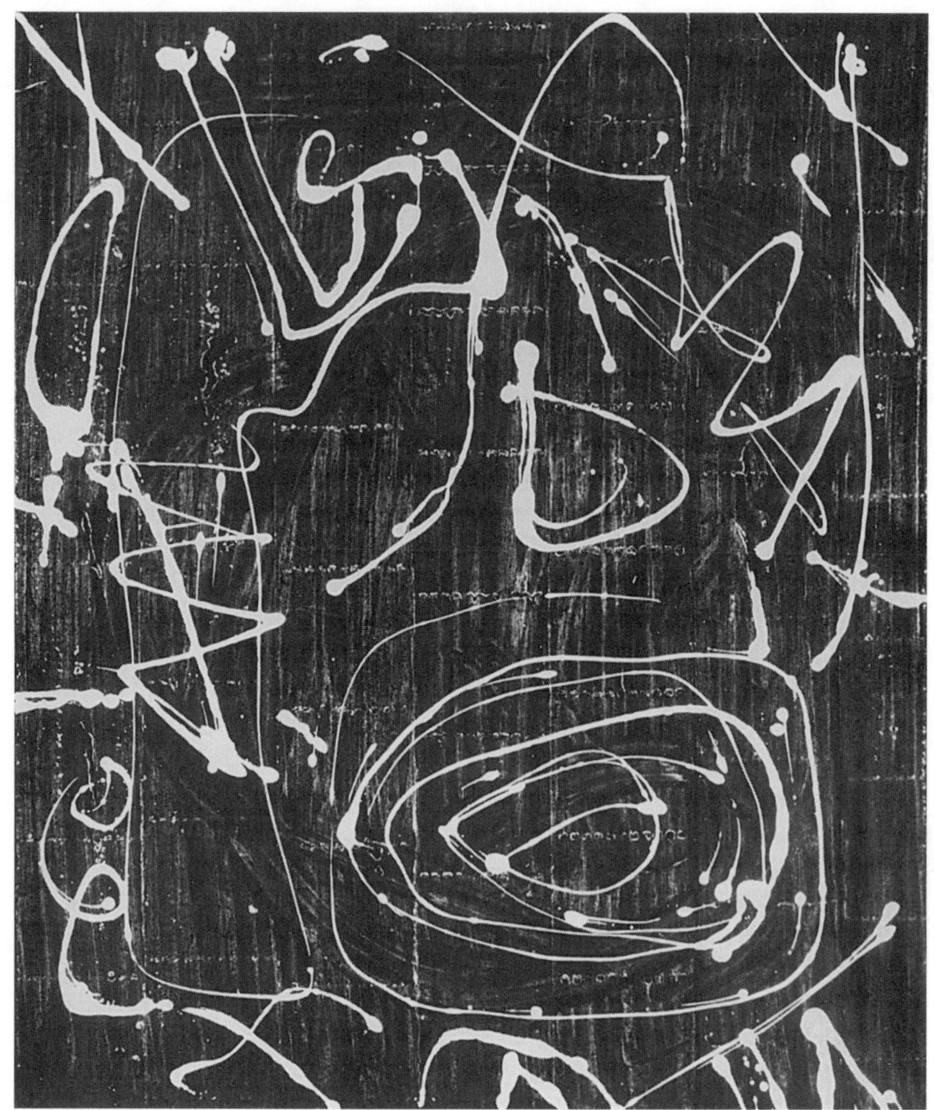

11.2 Morris Louis, *Charred Journal: Firewritten II*, 1951, acrylic on canvas (35" × 30"). Courtesy Louisiana Museum of Modern Art, Humlebaek, Denmark.

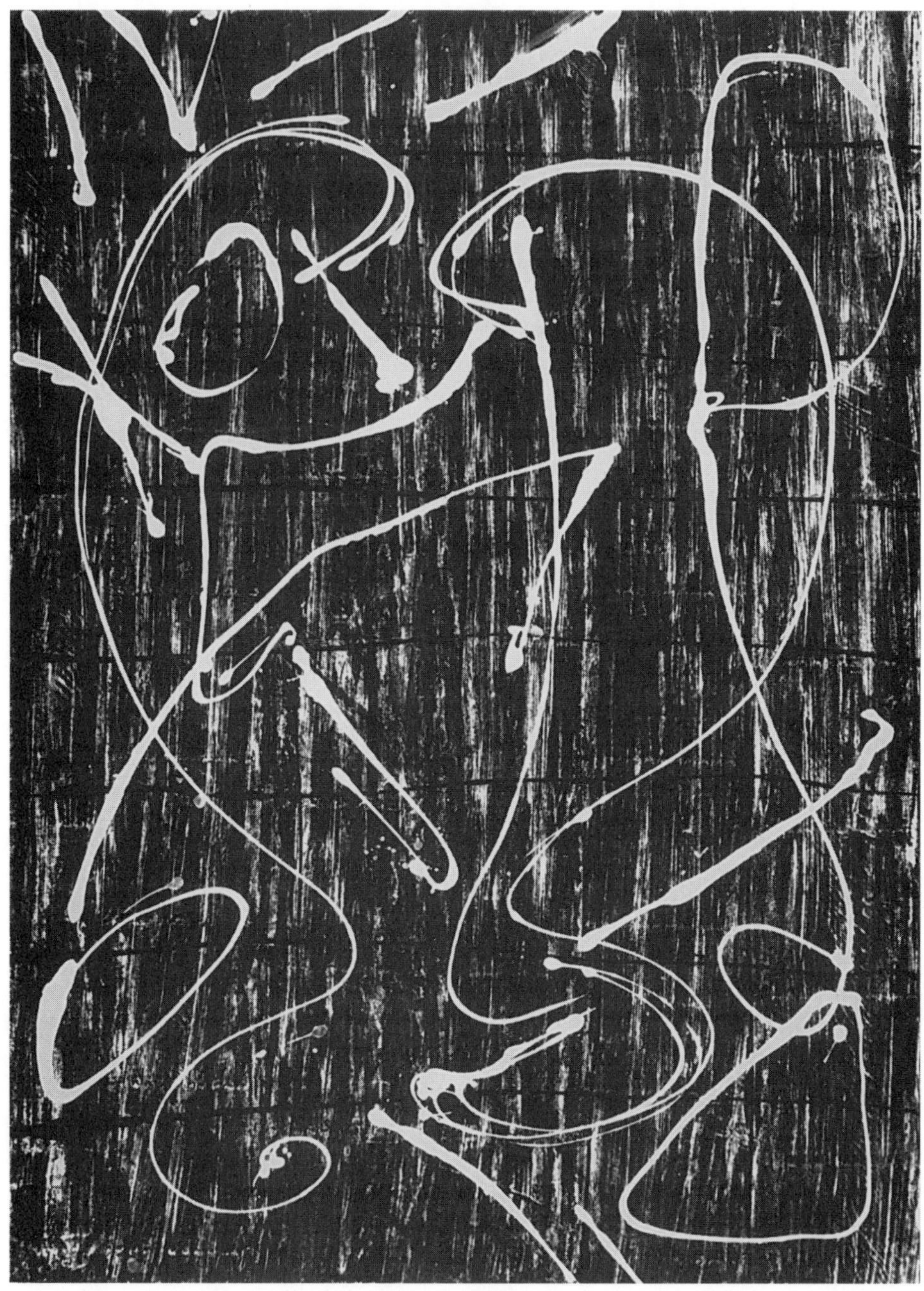

11.3 Morris Louis, *Charred Journal: Firewritten IV*, 1951, acrylic on canvas (35¼" × 30"). Courtesy Louisiana Museum of Modern Art, Humlebaek, Denmark.

constant. In *B,* some verticals are allowed to split before rejoining. In the other four paintings, the grid has been marked quite differently. Here, patches of the under-layer of paint stretch across or up the surface. These grids have been made by the removal, rather than the addition, of paint, and the lines' colors are the yellowy and salmon hues described before. Leon Berkowitz, who ran the Washington Workshop Center for the Arts, where these paintings were first exhibited, described the extraordinary procedure Louis employed. After "pressing lengths of toilet paper into the wet paint of the background," he said, he removed the paper and with it, the black paint.[4] If this gives a sense of Louis's experimentation, the painstaking nature of the procedure is exposed when we notice that in these four paintings the horizontals are not straight, but broken up between the verticals. Short lengths of paper must have been pressed individually between the vertical lines, carefully removed, and then placed again between the next two verticals, still along a horizontal, but at a slightly higher or lower level.

The top layer of paint is the white acrylic swerving around the surfaces. Once the black was dry, and the grids complete, the canvases would have been lifted from their easels and placed on the floor. Bending low down over the canvas, Louis then must have poured white paint, using an instrument that enabled him to control the flow without overprecision: the white lines differ in their width, suggesting that paint flowed at different speeds as he moved the pouring instrument over the surface. We know that Louis must have been close to the paintings when he poured the white paint: we rarely see splash marks at the beginning of a strand, a necessary consequence of pouring from a distance.

In each painting, rather than being concentrated in the center or toward one edge, the white lines cover the surface. But though there are several lines across each painting, they do not dominate or crowd the surface as much as traverse it with regular density. The number of individual pourings differs between paintings: in *V* and *C,* Louis poured around ten different trails of white paint across the surface; in *I* and *II,* there are at least double the number of individual pourings. Compared, however, to a Pollock painting such as *Number 26A, 1948: Black and White* (1948), there is in all the *Charred Journal: Firewritten* paintings a sparsity of poured lines. Whereas Pollock blotted out most of the underlying canvas, the black ground of these paintings is never eclipsed. The sparsity of lines also means that each line can be distinguished separately, read as a character would be. Each painting contains a variety of long lines and short lines, angular jolts and graceful curves. There are collections of lines which seem to resemble recognizable configurations—the number three (*I*), a zigzag (*II*), a triangle within a triangle (*I*), a spiral (*II*), a cross (*V, A*)—and collections that look like a chaotic mess. There are moments when a line is followed by another, bending with it as it copies its contours (*IV*), and

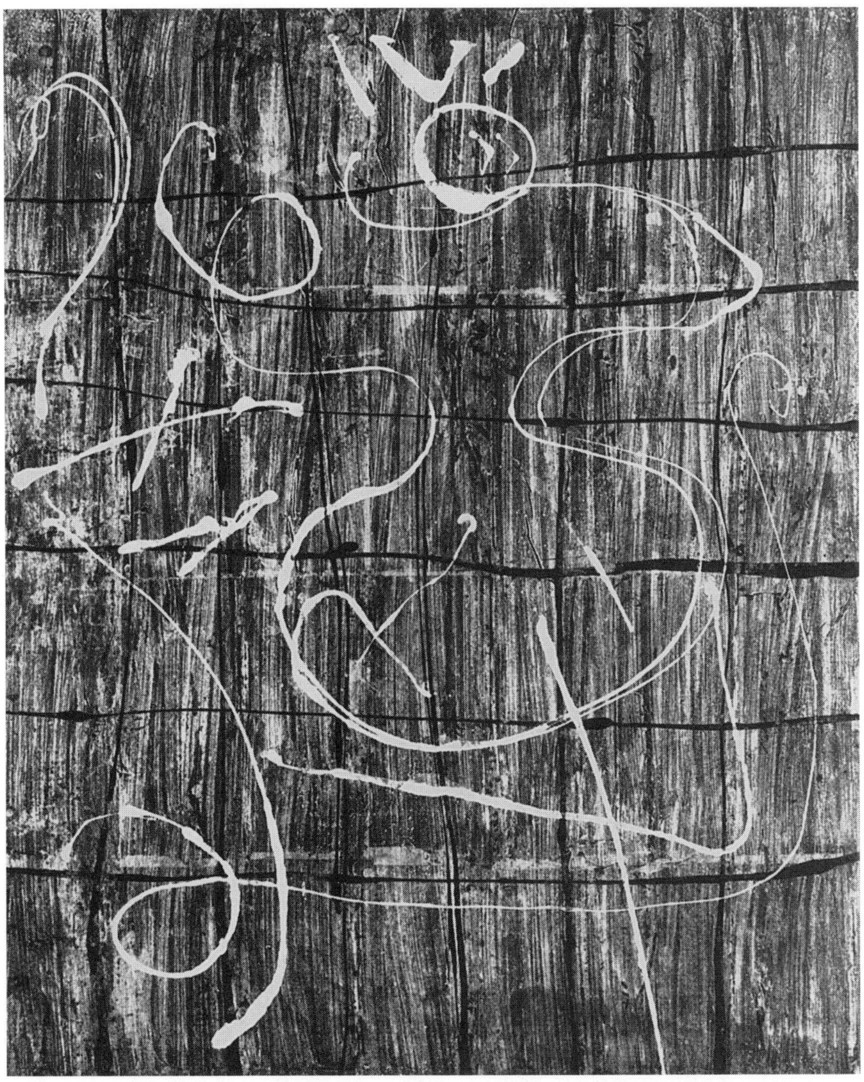

11.4 Morris Louis, *Charred Journal: Firewritten B*, 1951, acrylic on canvas (36⅛" × 30"). Courtesy Louisiana Museum of Modern Art, Humlebaek, Denmark.

moments when white lines—for instance, the two longest in *Firewritten IV*—seem to mirror each other across an invisible line of symmetry. A final feature of the white lines is revealed from very close to the surface. The white paint, though slightly raised from the surface, has a rather weak consistency, and is somewhat transparent. The black beneath it is always visible.

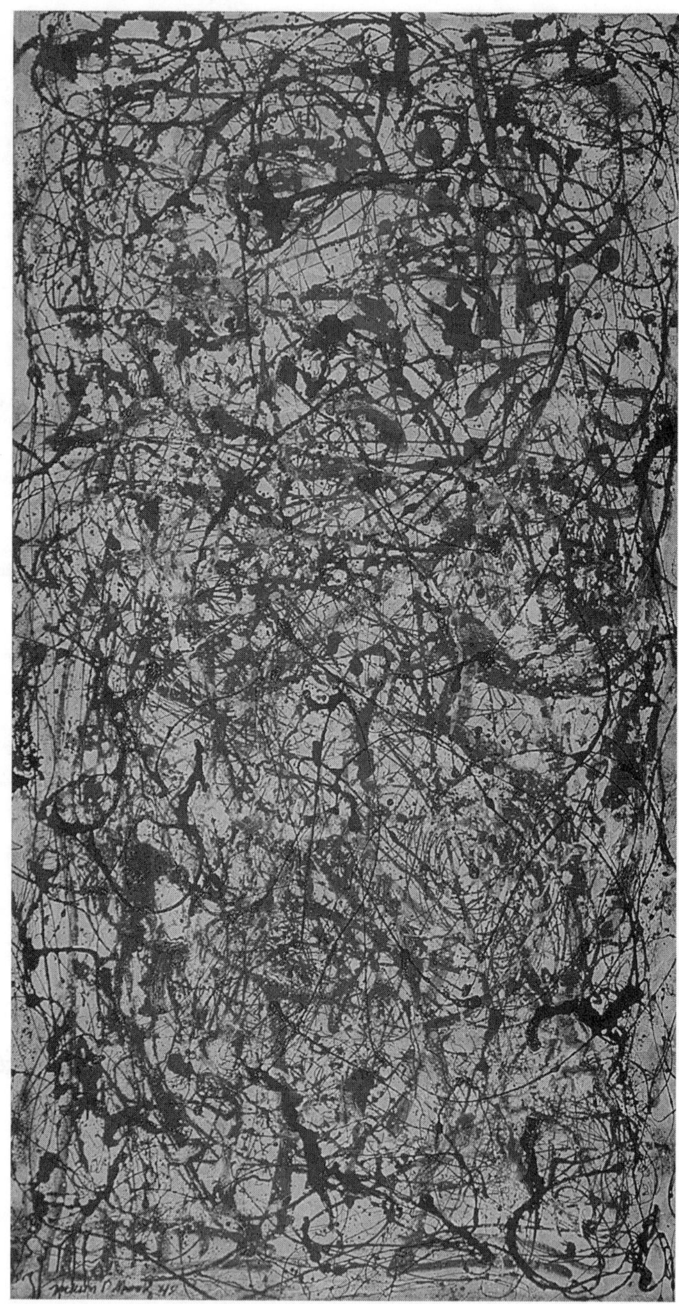

11.5 Jackson Pollock, *Number 26A, 1948: Black and White*, 1948, Centre Pompidou. Pollock-Krasner Foundation/ARS (New York)/SODRAC (Montreal) 2001 / Art Resource, N.Y.

This kind of description allows us to grasp the deliberation behind the making of these paintings. In building an impression of the layer-by-layer construction of the surface, such description exchanges the instantaneous visual encounter of a painting for a sense of slowness. It enables the imagination to picture moments of time past: the movements of the painter around his studio, his concentrated choices of paints and implements, the laborious actions of bending down and picking up. But will this detailed attention to process and surface tell us much more? Will it tell us about a different time past in addition to the history of the construction of the paintings—about the history of other events, or about the time of memory? Will it even tell us about the history and the memory of the Holocaust?

One of the reasons why we might expect these surfaces to relate to the Holocaust derives from details gleaned from exhibition history. The *Charred Journal: Firewritten* paintings were the first works in Louis's first solo exhibition, and at the opening of this show, press visitors received a small text whose author—Berkowitz again—recorded artistic influences and praised formal innovations. The *Washington Post* review of the exhibition, however, states that the *Charred Journal: Firewritten* series was "based, according to the artist, on the book burnings of the Nazis."[5] Louis must have found time at the opening to speak to his reviewers, to supply information not found in the pamphlet and only (as we shall explore) suggested by the paintings' titles. Perhaps there was anxiety that the "subject" of the paintings would be missed; perhaps Louis had wanted the information to be included in the pamphlet and was making up for its absence. Whatever the circumstances, the information he gave requires us to insert into our image of Louis in his studio an ongoing sense of purpose during the construction of the *Charred Journal: Firewritten* series: a desire for the paintings to have historical meaning, and not just appearance.

The need to talk about the book burnings indicates that Louis did not fully trust the paintings to reveal any connections to these fires, but, even if the relationship of object to history required such intervention, we can still ask how the surfaces, as I have described them, might relate to the Holocaust without such intervention. This enquiry must proceed by adding to descriptions of process and surface the figure of the spectator, asking what thoughts the encounter with the series might trigger. But who is the spectator we imagine? An ideal spectator? Myself as spectator? A historical spectator? Today, an encounter with the paintings is conditioned by hindsight about the history of Modernist art, by theories of interpretation and spectatorship that have developed since the 1950s, and, not least, by the institutional circumstances in which the objects are found. (The paintings are divided today between the Jewish Museum in New York and the Louisiana Museum in Denmark, which received them from Louis's widow in recognition of Danish support for Jews during the Holocaust.) The historical spectators—and it is necessary to retain a notion of the plurality and diversity of possible historical spectators—were conditioned by other circumstances. In describing the encounter, it will be important to differentiate an ideal spectator position, alive to all the myriad readings of the paintings, and the different positions of different historical spectators.

We can start, though, with an imagined historical spectator to gain a sense of such a spectator's expectations of abstract painting in 1953. This spectator would have seen the *Charred Journal: Firewritten* paintings in a small artist-run institution some twenty minutes' walk from the Mall called the Washington Workshop Center of the Arts. Though the institution's primary function was to offer courses such as "Ceramics for Beginners," "Understanding Music," and Louis's own "Oil Painting," it was also the venue for cutting-edge art in Washington, D.C. Familiar with the Workshop program and with recent advanced painting, a historical spectator might have expected many things of abstract art. Knowing the work of Jackson Pollock, he or she might have desired a surface to deliver what Clement Greenberg had described as "a sumptuous variety of design and incident."[6] Eagerly awaiting Willem De Kooning's debut Washington exhibition—it opened at the Workshop a month after Louis's closed—such a spectator might have looked forward to a "an uncrowded canvas" with "heavy somatic shapes"—again, Greenberg's words (229). But in 1953, his Modernism was not yet entrenched enough for viewers to expect of abstraction *only* surface, and indeed even Greenberg attested to this. Reviewing an exhibition by Adolph Gottlieb, another abstract painter, he had attended to "the 'symbols' [he] puts into his canvases." Though these had "no explicit meaning," they called up, in the spectator, "racial memories, archetypes, archaic but constant responses" (188). A painting might contain symbols that conjured "racial" memories, then, but these were never specific. A work might even relate to recent history. Recalling paintings such as *The Escape Ladder* from his *Constellations* series, works made under the shadow of Spanish fascism, Joan Miro had spoken of his use of a ladder-like grid in a *Partisan Review* interview of 1949 as a form that meant "escape," though he stumbled over his terms, calling the form within three sentences "nostalgic," "plastic," "symbolic," and "poetic."[7] We know, and perhaps the historical spectator knew, that Louis, who in the 1930s had participated in the pro-Republican movement, had recently used Miro's metaphorical form. A painting called *The Ladder* of 1949 shows such a one stretched across its surface. But if this brief context reveals that the symbol still had some currency within abstraction, and that a spectator might have anticipated some vague symbolic referent, the idea that an abstract painting could refer to a specific historical moment, a particular event such as the book burnings, would have been, and indeed remains, extremely problematic.

But perhaps a painting with an explicit symbol might. In 1951, Louis had also painted *Untitled (Jewish Star),* and it is the only painting of that year other than the *Charred Journal: Firewritten* paintings that he allowed to survive. Though he had exhibited it at the Workshop in a group exhibition some months before his solo show, this painting was—importantly—never part of the *Charred Journal: Firewritten* series. Yet, unlike all the rest of Louis's oeuvre, it is constructed in exactly the same way as the *Charred Journal: Firewritten* paintings, except for the presence of strokes of orange and yellow paint above the black acrylic as well as below it. The painting's significant difference, though, is that its white lines form the well-known configuration of two interlocking triangles. "Racial memories" were certainly conjured here, but, unlike Gottlieb's symbols, it was specifically Jewish memory that was in play. The presentation of the Star of David might very well have enabled a spectator to recall the history of the Holocaust, through the recollection of Nazi laws decreeing that Jews wear the yellow star. Indeed, writing in *Commentary* in 1949, Gershom Scholem had investigated "The Curious History of the Six-Pointed Star." He stressed its nonreligious history and recognized that its contemporary meaning grew from its having been the "badge of shame for millions of our people."[8] Scholem's text went on to posit that the star might now begin to suggest light as well as death, that it could be used as a symbol of cultural optimism as well as a memorial, and perhaps this is true of the star here, surrounded as it is by a halo of yellow and orange. But if this painting—like Jasper Johns's *Star* of 1954, itself commissioned by a Jewish friend who had fled Nazi persecution—points both backward to a traumatic history and forward to a tentative but much desired sense of optimism and unashamed pride, and while doing so suggests the multiple potentials of the symbol rather than its redundancy, these readings seem of little help when we return to the starless surface of the *Charred Journal: Firewritten* paintings.

What is the significance of the absence of the star in the *Charred Journal: Firewritten* paintings? Maurice Blanchot, to whose text *The Writing of Disaster* I will return, and who was aware of its etymology, related "disaster" to the "night delivered of stars," to "the void of the sky."[9] Were we to take this insight into account to help us interpret the relationship of starless paintings to the disaster of the Holocaust, we would have to acknowledge that this kind of intertextual reading was hardly possible for historical spectators, even if they had seen *Untitled (Jewish Star)* previously. But keeping with an ideal spectator, we can posit different possibilities for the absence of the star. Perhaps the star had posed a problem by being too Jewish a symbol. This is not to suggest that the public declaration of ethnic identity was difficult for Louis: his widow stresses he never shied away from Jewishness.[10] The problem might have been that, in allowing its spectator to recall Nazi persecution, the star excluded the memory of other, non-Jewish victims, who might be admitted to the memorializing possibilities of the *Charred Journal: Firewritten* paintings. Or perhaps the absence of the star might reveal a hesitancy to employ the symbol per se,

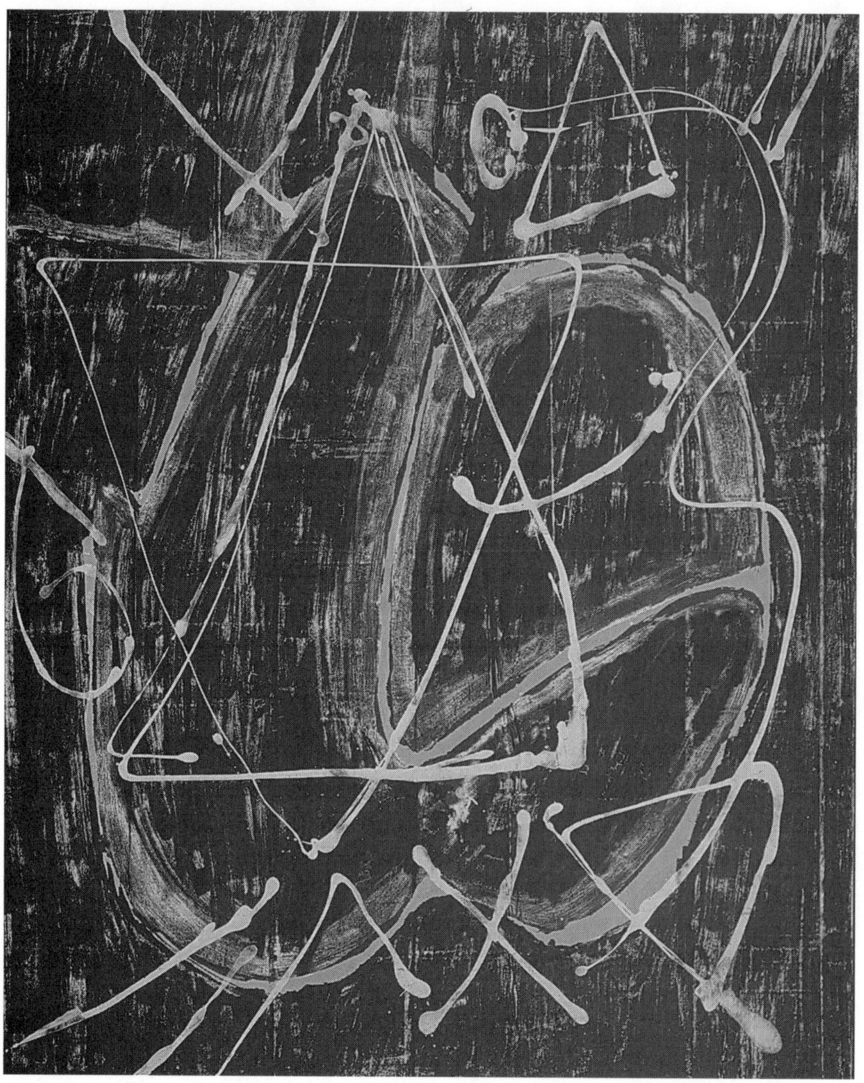

11.6 Morris Louis, *Untitled (Jewish Star)*, 1951, magna on canvas (34" × 28½"). Copyright The Jewish Museum of New York / Art Resource, N.Y.

a hesitancy we might even detect on the surface of *Untitled (Jewish Star)*, which, it should be stated, presents its star only tentatively, in juxtaposition with indecipherable collections of white lines. The roots of this hesitancy are divided. Totalitarian reliance on the organizing power of the symbol might have made any use of symbols problematic after the Holocaust; just as, for some survivors, the German language was forever tarnished, so too symbolic

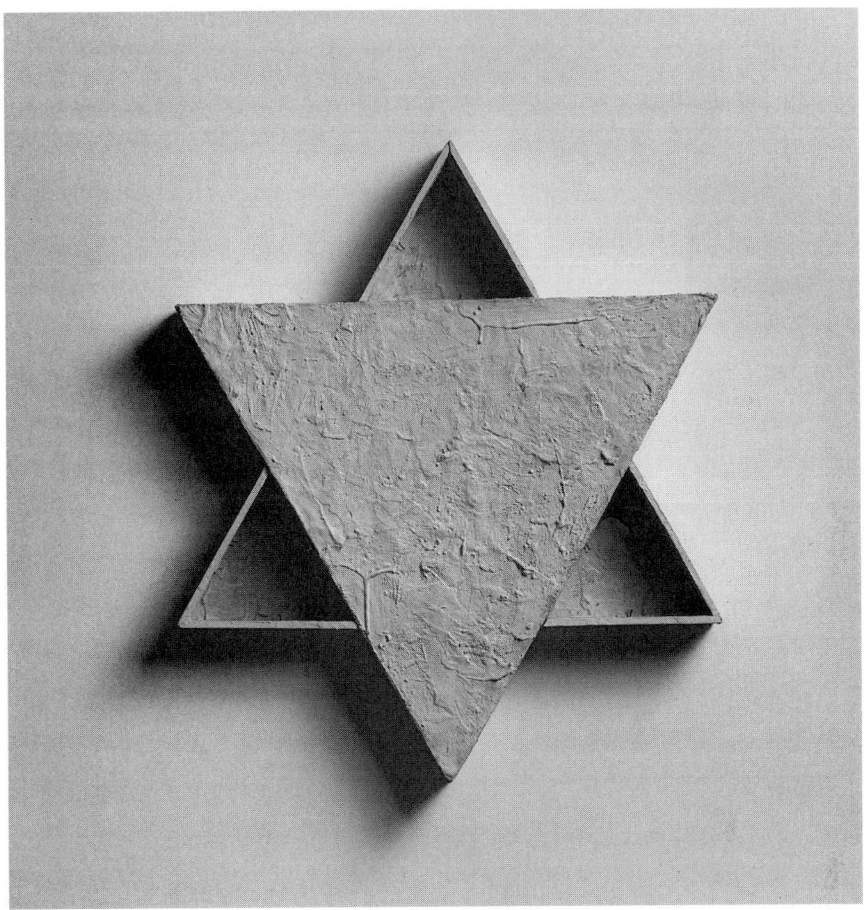

11.7 Jasper Johns, *Star*, 1954, oil, beeswax, and house paint on newspaper, canvas, and wood with tinted glass, nails, and fabric tape (22½" × 19½"). Courtesy The Menil Collection, Houston.

language was problematized. Or from the perspective of art practice, perhaps any use of a symbol on a surface was increasingly difficult. Though, as we have seen, Johns could paint a star as a commission the year after the exhibition of the *Charred Journal: Firewritten* paintings, this was only months before his *Flag* (1954–55) strategically emptied out the symbol, posing its abstraction as a counter to its obvious "meaning." So the Magen David in *Untitled (Jewish Star)* might signal the swan song of the symbol that would be absent from advanced painting from then on.

These are possibilities, but I want to suggest that the absence of the star creates, for historical and ideal spectators, the presence of a space of indeterminacy. The *Charred Journal: Firewritten* paintings might relate to the Holocaust through their very refusal of the direct symbol, through the possibilities created by the spectator's inability to establish a straightforward connection of surface—through symbol—to history. This is an argument I will come back to, but before exploring this space of indeterminacy, I want to describe how interpretative possibilities might have been built up during the encounter with the *Charred Journal: Firewritten* paintings.

The most obvious interpretative possibility would seem to derive from the predominance of black paint on the surface. Confronted by blackness, we might imagine that the historical spectator of the *Charred Journal: Firewritten* paintings, recognizing the color of mourning, was caused to consider an object of mourning. The context for such painting was, after all, the memory of the well-publicized strategies of Picasso's *Guernica,* whose "shock lies in the very fact that color is totally absent. The black, gray, and white treatment of a particular theme serves to give it great force."[11] These last words are Louis's, and I do not want to suggest that blackness had no resonance as a signifier of mourning. But this argument ignores the colors present on the surface, and, as importantly, it ignores the fact that, at this precise time, black and white painting, rather than indicating gloom, was the mode par excellence of advanced artistic practice. In 1948, writing on Willem De Kooning, Arshille Gorky, Adolph Gottlieb, and Jackson Pollock, Greenberg had commented that "[b]y excluding the full range of color, and concentrating on black and white and their derivatives, the most ambitious members of this generation hope to solve . . . the problems [of painting] involved."[12] In 1950, there had been an exhibition at the Samuel Kootz Gallery, *Black or White: Paintings by European and American Artists,* which included Hans Hofmann, William Baziotes, Mark Tobey, and Bradley Walker Tomlin, and for which Robert Motherwell wrote the catalogue essay.[13]

But if the simple significance of blackness as a mourning color is in doubt, a different associative possibility of black paint is essential to a consideration of the encounter with the *Charred Journal: Firewritten* paintings. It is through the series's title that the black paint gains its importance: the title provokes the associative interpretations that the series offers for its viewers. The words "Charred Journal" tempt the spectator to connect the canvases' blackened surfaces to the idea of a burnt page, and consequently to link the delicate under-layer colors with that which was burned. This metaphor might actually be grounded in resemblance, for, unlike the very different black surfaces made by the various painters I have just mentioned, the look of a burnt page here is courted: Jackson Pollock's, Clifford Still's, Franz Kline's, or Robert Motherwell's blacks might appear reflective, textured, intense, or dull . . . but never so much like charred paper. Through the connection of surface to the burnt page, a link is established (a link which, as I will argue, is always necessarily frail) to the Nazi book burnings, and the spectator, both historical and ideal, is provoked to ruminate on this event.

But of course, neither today nor in 1953 would the book burnings be recalled as a *unitary* event. The significance of the book burnings was that they would be remembered at once as a specific moment in the history of Nazi persecution—a night of bonfires in May 1933 outside Berlin University, reported with minimal attention in Washington and rather more focus in New York—and, at the same time, as an incident with much wider significance. It was not just in the 1950s that they held symbolic significance: as soon as they occurred, their symbolism was recognized. On 11 May 1933, the editor of the *New York Times* wrote that "[t]hey certainly symbolize something! Such an exhibition of the new national spirit, silly and shameful as it seems, bespeaks a mass-movement plainly touched with insanity."[14] In 1953, with twenty years of historical hindsight, the significance of the book burnings would have been felt to be far, far greater.

Two overlapping spheres of interest must be examined to probe what the memory of the book burnings might have suggested for a spectator in 1953. The first sphere is that of the secular Jewish intellectual, and the second, that of the leftist, anti-Stalinist American. The overlap of these cultures is broad, so much so that the pages of *Commentary* and *Partisan Review,* their main vehicles of discourse, blur together when we notice the continual reappearance of the same writers. Though I want to position Louis, and the majority of his viewers, within the overlap, I need—for a while—to unfix the spheres.

For the secular Jewish intellectual, the memory of the book burnings contributed to an ongoing cultural anxiety. Under what Blanchot has termed "the surveillance of the disaster,"[15] writers were busy interrogating the fuller implications of the cultural exclusion evidenced most concretely in May 1933. Immediately after the book burnings, Nazi legislation had prevented Jews from publishing in German and from using the Gothic typescript. Such laws were premised on notions that just as Jewish blood infected the Aryan body, so Jewish use infected the language. In 1953, it was increasingly evident how widespread these premises were. Sartre's *Anti-Semite and Jew,* widely discussed after its American publication in 1948, recalled those who "declared a Jew forever incapable of understanding a line of Racine."[16] If Sartre's text highlighted the pervasiveness of cultural anti-Semitism, it was also part of the problem, as his schema left no space for authentic secular Jewish culture. Commentators such as Harold Rosenberg, whose responding article "Does the Jew Exist?"[17] attempted to find such space, had barely recovered from Sartre's text when, later in 1949, they were forced to negotiate a local offence. The Bollingen Poetry award for that year was awarded to Ezra Pound, and in the wake of the award, *Commentary* published a symposium titled "The Jewish Writer and the English Tradition." Intellectuals who had once sidelined reservations about anti-Semitism now met it head on. Clement Greenberg's brother Martin expressed the situation of the culturally excluded Jew most forcefully, writing, "To use a language and not to own it, to live with a literature and not to possess it—this is only to say that I am a Jew."[18] Alfred Kazin, meanwhile, questioned whether to burn Pound's book, and concluded, "No, no: there have been too many books banned and burned already. We have been too long on the *index expurgatorius* to make one of our own."[19]

The book burnings of 1933 were invoked in 1949, then, only to be discarded as an impossibility, a reaction to a threat suited to barbaric regimes, and never to Jews. And with the invocation and refusal of a book burning in America, we come to the second sphere of history, for books *were* burned in the United States at this time: not by enraged New York Jews, but by good clean American librarians. Under the politics of McCarthyism, a politics, it should be remembered, that was centered not twenty minutes from Louis's studio, librarians were known to destroy books whose presence might bring suspicion of un-American affiliations. A 1959 study on censorship records a librarian telling the researcher "in a self-pitying way . . . Did you ever try to burn a book. It's very difficult."[20] Did Louis know of such events? His wife was a school principal, and perhaps encountered pressures to censor reading lists. However, in an interview she indicated that though each day brought more news of old friends now hounded by the House UnAmerican Activities Committee, she had never known of actual book burnings in early 1950s Washington,[21] and indeed, instances were extremely rare. But if contemporary book burnings were unknown to Louis and his spectators, I still want to suggest, through the terms the Chicago-based Jewish philosopher Louis Strauss used in 1952, that the idea of Nazi book burnings was invoked to share, through "private communication" with "trustworthy and intelligent readers,"[22] a critique of McCarthyism. And Louis was not the only artist on the left to use the strategies Strauss had articulated in *Persecution and the Art of Writing.* Indeed, the very metaphor of book burnings had currency beyond his paintings. Ray Bradbury's novel *Fahrenheit 451* of 1950 described a dystopia in which firemen hunt libraries to burn. Though the veil of Bradbury's story was somewhat more transparent, for those reading between the lines it was, like the *Charred Journal: Firewritten* paintings, an indictment of the present.

I am arguing, then, that, provoked to recall the book burnings, historical spectators might have been reminded of the cultural anxieties facing contemporary Jewish intellectuals, and of the more tangible threats bearing on those whose sympathies lay on the left. For some spectators, as for Louis, both these burdens were felt at once. One of the only historical spectators who recorded memories of the paintings was the acrylic paint maker Leonard Bocour, and his response seems to locate the series' significance exactly within the overlap of these concerns. Remembering that Louis's "whole gang was very, very left," he goes on to state that Louis "did a whole series of paintings called the *Charred Journals.* And I have one of them. . . . It was all black and white really. And, as I say, he was aware of the world he lived in and he was certainly anti-Nazi."[23]

Like the surface of the paintings (and unlike Bocour's description), the experience of the encounter was never so black and white. But before I turn from the black paint to the white, I want to take a moment to posit another dimension of the rhetoric of the *Charred Journal: Firewritten* paintings. They might prompt memories of the human disaster at the same time as thoughts of a cultural and political one, since the burning of the books acts as a metaphor for the burning of bodies. Through the ancient naming of Jews as "the people of the book," through the resonance of Heine's prophecy "Where they burn books, they will burn people," through the knowledge that, traditionally, Jewish artists could only be scribes, the hand-made Jewish book is bound up with the body, and though these phrases plunder Jewish history, all the destroyed bodies of the Holocaust—Jewish and non-Jewish—seem tentatively addressed through the idea of the book burning.[24]

In introducing fragments of Jewish sources, I must emphasize how difficult it is to ascertain the extent to which familiarity with these texts on the part of historical spectators can be assumed, despite evidence that does suggest a postwar growth of interest in Jewish myth amongst American Jews. It is with such material that I will continue as I investigate how the white lines on the surface might relate to the readings I have described so far, and I use this material with the knowledge that Louis supplemented *his* sketchy awareness of Jewish history with research on the origin of Jewish writing when working in 1934 on *The History of the Written Word,* a Public Works of Art Project mural for a Baltimore school library. Once more, I turn to the 1951 title to describe how it conditioned the encounter with the surface. If the word "Charred" addressed the blackness of the surfaces, then "Firewritten" seems to address the white lines. But what is firewriting? Surely fire destroys writing, rather than creating it?

In early Midrashim (rabbinic collections of biblical exegesis), and Kabbalistic commentaries on them, the origin of the Torah is discussed again and again.[25] The Torah is not formulated as a historical narrative, as the five books describing the story of the time from the creation to the arrival in Canaan, nor is it a literal object—an actual white parchment inscribed with letters of black ink. However, both these formulations are in play in a wider notion of the original Torah. According to some mystical texts, at its origin (long before the events it describes), the Torah consisted of both the words of the Torah and all the interpretations of them. Some origin myths concern the ways through which the written Torah (the books) and the oral Torah (the future interpretations) became distinct, and it is here that the notion of firewriting becomes significant, for the written Torah was thought to burn before God in letters of white fire on the black fire of the oral Torah, letters which were not, at first, recognizable.

Various Kabbalistic texts describe different versions of these myths, some associating the oral Torah with white fire, the written one with black. What is important is not a precise point of Kabbalistic scholarship, but rather the notion that firewriting is associated—even through a lay understanding—with the creation of the book, rather than with its destruction. Indeed, white fire is the original form of writing in the original book, the medium of writing. It is also important to note that the myths themselves are clearly extremely visual, describing the origin of the book through the distinction of figure and ground that occurs when white fire is seen against black, but also when black ink stands out against white parchment. Turning back to Louis's paintings, the myths seem first to inform the way we could now think about the mark as a figure against a ground. The myths provide an alternative origin for the conception of the "first mark" that has little to do with Greenbergian flatness. More importantly, through the myths, the white lines become suggestive of the renaissance of writing. The Jewish book, as well as being destroyed by flames, was born in flames.

If the memory of this legend encourages for the spectator the development of a precarious optimism, looking back at the discourse of post-Holocaust Jewish intellectuals, we can see that the desire for optimism was desperate, and continually expressed. In his 1945 editorial for the first issue of *Commentary,* Elliot Cohen hoped that the new journal would be a crucible for a Jewish renaissance, and described the establishment of the periodical as an "act of faith," the lighting of "our candle" in "the midst of this turbulence and these whirlwinds."[26] If this metaphor shows another way in which fire—here a candle of faith—suggests optimism rather than destruction, unlike the word "Firewritten," Cohen's is a general, even Catholic, metaphor and not a Jewish one. In relation to the *Charred Journal: Firewritten* series, the yearning for some kind of Jewish optimism is evidenced as much by the regenerative suggestions of the particular myths in play as by the very fact, despite the damage done to Jewish culture, of their continued use. The white lines can be considered through other myths. If the word "Firewritten" establishes a connection between the white lines and a Kabbalistic notion of white fire, the arrangement of the lines might recall a Hasidic text which imagines that before creation, the Torah "formed a heap of letters," an "incoherent jumble"[27] that arranged itself into words as the events it described took place. Through another suggestion of the origin of the book, rather than its destruction, again there is an idea of rebirth. A third myth is better known to secular Jews. When Moses destroyed God's tablets on seeing the Golden Calf, the letters that God had written flew away, since they were indestructible. Describing the paintings, Louis's wife said he had tried to "capture the effect of letters and symbols rising like ashes from the surface of a burned page."[28] Perhaps, as this memory of Louis's intention intimates, the paintings suggest that, like God's letters, the writing burned by Nazi fires would not be destroyed, but would fly away unharmed. Or conversely, to sidestep the problematic question of Louis's intention while retaining the suggestion of the Moses myth, the letters that flew away at Sinai might reappear after the book burnings across the blackened pages of Jewish history, perhaps to form a new Torah.

For a spectator familiar with these myths, interpretative possibilities abound, and well they might, for the spectator's encounter takes part in a tradition of Jewish hermeneutics. After all, the great Biblical commentator Rashi, who is listed as a "prominent maternal ancestor"[29] in Louis's own official biography, likened "the various interpretations offered by the rabbis for a single biblical verse to the sparks that fly when a hammer is struck upon a rock."[30] The metaphor provides another sense of the positive power of fire, but it also implies that interpretation does damage. Something is chipped to make sparks. The rabbis as hammer? The verse as rock? Both? What is damaged, metaphorically, in the attempt to read the white lines through Jewish myths is the accuracy of my former description of the surfaces. Though we might argue that the layering of paint suggests that moments of creation are superimposed on moments of destruction, or that the grids function metaphorically to protect the white lines from the blackness, the surfaces indicate that if Louis wanted to develop suggestions of optimism through his play with Jewish myth, the careful deployment of paint tempered those suggestions. Spectators might know that God's letters escaped destruction on Sinai, but it is clear that, from painting to painting, the white lines do not fly away. They might know that the Torah started as a jumble of incoherence, but then, across the canvases, white lines become no more distinct, no nearer to recognizable letters. Interpretation is also unfixed by the precise transparency of the acrylic. Not only is a spectator unable to see white lines without sensing the blackness around them, but blackness is also always visible below.

Flying sparks disappear as soon as they are seen. What if the same can be said for the interpretations developed in the encounter with the *Charred Journal: Firewritten* paintings? I am not thinking here only of the attempts to read the unreadable white lines, but of all the readings I have described. So many are conditioned by the works' titles, poetic textual fragments indeed, but absent (unlike the unreadable white lines) from the works' surfaces. Addressing the history of titles, the art historian Stephen Bann quotes Proust, for whom a "name sanctioned by memory can become [like] one of those little balloons in which oxygen . . . has been enclosed."[31] Proust's metaphor visualizes the potential of the titling name, but the balloon is pregnant with problems as well as suggestions. What happens to the air when the balloon is popped? Like Rashi's sparks of interpretation, Proust's oxygen disappears, immediately indistinguishable from its surroundings. I am stepping into what earlier I called the space of indeterminacy, for this is what I suggest the *Charred Journal: Firewritten* paintings offer their spectators.

How might we consider this indeterminacy? Why did Louis make these paintings, when he knew that a viewer, in front of abstract canvases, would always necessarily sense all meanings disappear, no matter how he tried to condition them with imposing and extraneous text? Perhaps Louis made these despite their fluctuating failure, despite the doubts he had about the sense of using titles at all, simply because it was inescapably necessary to somehow address the Holocaust, which inescapably addressed him. I want to recall another contemporary intellectual forum to give a sharpened sense of this necessity. The symposium "Under Forty," published in the *Contemporary Jewish Record* in 1944, asked young Jewish writers, "Do you feel you are any different than your Christian colleagues?" A novelist called Albert Halper replied, "Alas, my friends, I am different. Hitler has made me different. . . . When I now sit down to write a story . . . with yesterday's headlines still printed on my brain, I hear the cries of five million expiring Jews outside my window."[32] These words are crude, even vulgar, but maybe the same can be said of Louis's paintings. Perhaps we should stop here, concluding that the paintings never bear the burden imposed by their titles, that the wish for them to do so marks them out as overreaching and desperate, but well-intentioned nonetheless—that the paintings themselves are merely witness to the competing but irreconcilable claims on Louis in 1951—to be an advanced artist and, as a Jew on the left, to address a charged subject. Conceived this way, the paintings seem to concur with Louis's widow's memory of their creation: she recalls that these paintings marked a caesura, a pause in the progress of a career heading toward proper abstraction. In seeking to address a referent, the works were a break—but a necessary one—along a journey.

Instead of reaching this conclusion, it is more interesting to posit that we have here not a momentary abandonment of abstraction, but an intelligent manipulation of its conventions and abilities, and of its impossibilities. We can start by rethinking the manners in which the *Charred Journal: Firewritten* paintings evoke other abstract painting. The grids that cross their surfaces relate to the grids of Modernist painting, the trailed lines to Pollock's practice. Perhaps this relation might mark not just an influence, but an attempt to turn such painting toward the cultural subject matter of the book burnings. However, if there is a kind of use made of Modernist painting, we should also consider that, as much as this use puts a kind of pressure on the normal autonomy of Modernist painting, the conventions associated with abstract painting put a pressure on the kind of readings that might be made of the "writings" on the *Charred Journal: Firewritten* paintings.

As this point, it is appropriate to remind ourselves of aspects of Michael Fried's account. A critic like Fried would not even begin to read the title in order to explore the possible meanings of a work, but neither did he "read" the white lines, not even as unreadable letters. Fried saw the markings in Louis's later paintings as figures against grounds, in those cases as colored figures against the white ground of raw canvas. The *Charred Journal: Firewritten* paintings, in Fried's terms, might embody a tonal reversal—white lines form figures against black grounds—but no essential reversal of significance. The Modernist approach would stop there, and though we have challenged the adequacy of stopping there, it is important now to remember that, as much as the notion of reading and writing can broaden an approach to the paintings, the notion of seeing holds all this in check. As much as they suggest charred pages, the paintings are abstract canvases.

If it is beginning to seem that the Modernist account of seeing puts pressure on the readings that have been explored, I would in fact like to think that this pressure, inasmuch as it unsettles the security of any "meaning" of these paintings, confirms, instead, a kind of indeterminacy of meaning. We can explore the significance of the paintings' indeterminacy, the significance of the fluctuation of meaning and meaninglessness, of the way meanings are suggested and vanish. The significance might be that this dynamic is the way in which the paintings most forcefully—and at the same time most subtly—address the Holocaust.

In *The Writing of Disaster,* Maurice Blanchot wrote that the disaster is at once abstract and specific: at times, it is named simply as "the disaster," but at other times, it is described as "*[t]he holocaust, the* absolute *event of history—which is a date in history—that utter-burn where all history took fire, where the movement of Meaning was swallowed up.*"[33]

As for "the writing of disaster," in the text it seems to refer both to all writing—which, for Blanchot, is always rooted in loss—and to specific writing that addresses the specific disaster. Impossible as it is to untangle the general from the specific, several strands of thought seem suggestive in the context of the discussion of Morris Louis's paintings. The first is Blanchot's concentration on the fragmentary, his understanding that the writing of the disaster is—like the white lines—writing that is ruined, in fragments. "The disaster de-scribes" (7). The second is his concern with etymology—paralleled by Louis's play with roots, with myths, with the origins of writing. But the third strand of Blanchot's thought is what really concerns me here, and that is his contention that the disaster refuses meaning. If the disaster was where "meaning was swallowed up," there is a "danger that the disaster acquire meaning" (41) and a related injunction to "keep watch over absent meaning" (42). The writing of the disaster cannot represent or respect the disaster if it allows it to acquire meaning: the absence of meaning must always be present.

Blanchot's injunction does not specify who or what is to keep watch—the artwork? the author? the reader? In the case of the *Charred Journal: Firewritten* paintings, it seems that the guard is kept through the dynamic I am describing. Louis created objects which cause their viewers to create meanings while constantly forcing these viewers to witness their breakdown. In the encounter, as the paintings offer and retract meaning, the spectator is increasingly aware of the impossibility of fixed meaning, even of the absence of meaning. In this context, then, the failure of the surfaces to cement fixed links to the Holocaust is only a necessary part of the wider success of the series to form a much stronger relationship to the Holocaust. What is represented in the *Charred Journal: Firewritten* paintings is as much the history of the Holocaust and the contemporary significance of that history as its incomprehensibility, its very resistance to representation, the terms of the impossibility of its representation.

After the success of the Workshop exhibition, Louis was delighted. A letter of his wife's exclaims, "it all came out so well that we are more than pleased."[34] But no matter how well it all came out, Louis was, that very week, on the cusp of abandoning the kind of painting he had shown at the Workshop. Seven days before the opening of his exhibition, Louis had made a rare visit to Manhattan where, accompanied by Kenneth Noland and Clement Greenberg, he had seen Helen Frankenthaler's *Mountains and Sea.* According to Greenberg and Michael Fried, this was the moment of breakthrough.[35] The sight of thinned acrylic stained into the very fabric of Frankenthaler's canvas triggered the creation of huge numbers of paintings in a tiny variety of configurations: the *Veils,* the *Unfurleds,* the *Pillars.* If we accept the terms of Modernist theory, this was indeed a pivotal point. But after addressing the *Charred Journal: Firewritten* series, paintings which the Modernists ignored, and whose historical meanings, however we might figure out their workings, they avoided, it is important to reexamine the "breakthrough" moment by probing Louis's apparent abandonment of the strategies at play in the *Charred Journal: Firewritten* series.

Perhaps Louis thought these strategies too frail, and preferred to develop his formal experiments rather than further pursue an impossible task. Perhaps, in taking the continual advice of Clement Greenberg, he also began to agree with his friend's cautions—in a 1950 essay titled "Self-Hatred and Jewish Chauvinism," occasioned by the need to counter a new belligerence in public American Jewish life sparked by reactions to the Holocaust, Greenberg had written, "No matter how necessary it may be to indulge our feelings about Auschwitz, we can do so only temporarily and privately."[36] Perhaps this forty-year-old artist, who had barely sold a work, sensed that the clients of dealers like Samuel Kootz and Andre Emmerich might not tolerate paintings "based on the book burnings." We cannot, and should not, be sure, but hesitantly, we might now revisit later works, finding them not at the end of Modernism's cul-de-sac but at the beginning of a different path. We might exchange the "breakthrough" notion for a more complex formulation of the simultaneous discontinuity and continuity of earlier concerns. Louis's "mature" work manifests the same spirit of hope, the same spirit of a longed-for post-Holocaust Jewish renaissance sometimes suggested by the white lines of the *Charred Journal: Firewritten* paintings. Looking at the *Unfurled* and *Pillar* paintings, we can agree with Michael Fried that the *"firstness of marking"* which they

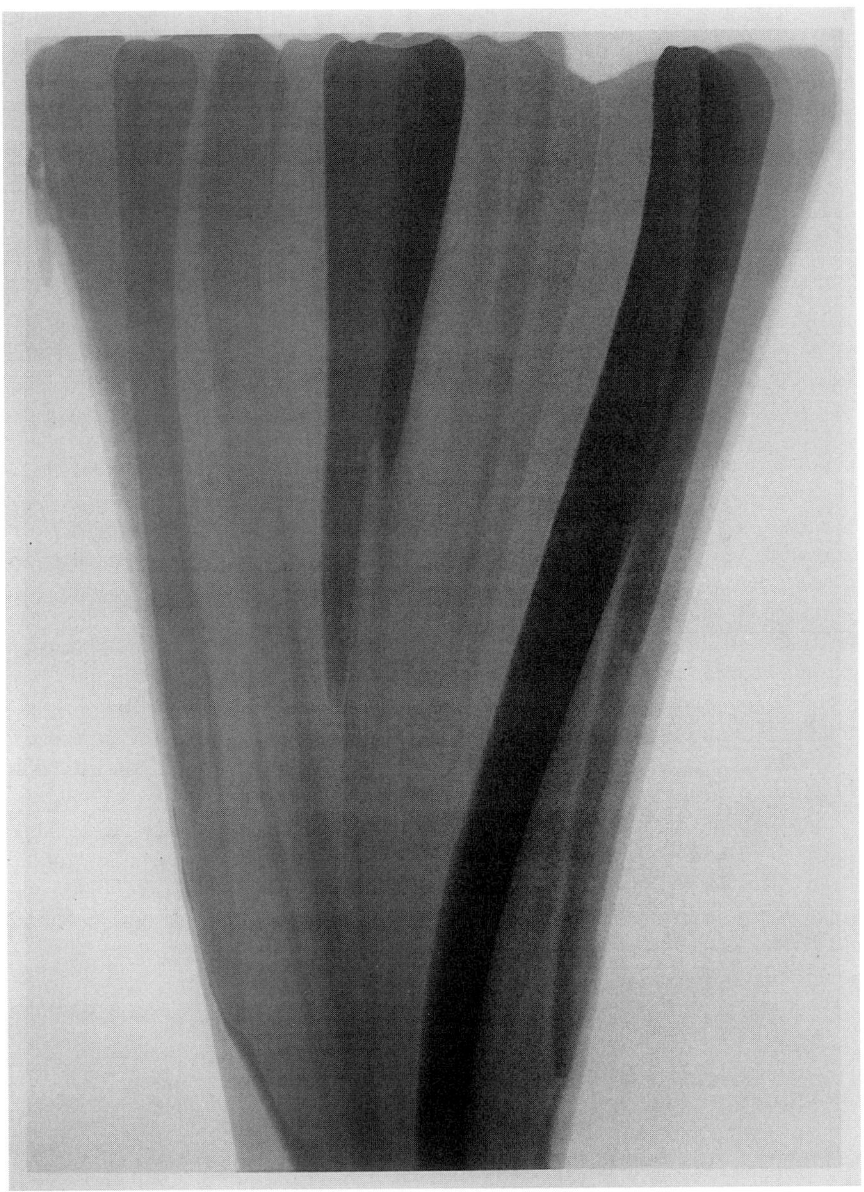

11.8 Morris Louis, *Beth Chaf*, 1959, acrylic on canvas (139" × 102½"). Courtesy National Gallery of Art, Washington, D.C.

dramatize witnesses the "impulse to make one's mark," but suggest that this impulse is not created by some primeval, essential urge, but by the demands of a particular historical moment. Looking at a *Veil* painting such as *Beth Chaf,* we might think that the leap from firewriting to its flame-like washes of pigment is not, perhaps, so great.

Notes

1. Several recent readings of Greenberg's writings in particular should be mentioned, as these problematize the relationship of Modernism and "ethic identity," specifically rethinking the question of Greenberg's "Jewishness." These include Susan Noyes Platt, "Clement Greenberg in the 1930s: A New Perspective on His Criticism," *Art Criticism* 5, no. 3 (1989): 47–64; Lisa Bloom, "Ghosts of Ethnicity: Rethinking Art Discourses of the 1940s and 1980s," *Socialist Review* 24, nos. 1 and 2 (1994): 129–164; Thierry de Duve, "Silences in the Doctrine," in his *Clement Greenberg between the Lines* (Paris: Dis Voir, 1996); Margaret Olin, "C[lement] Hardesh [Greenberg] and Company—Formal Criticism and Jewish Identity" in *Too Jewish? Challenging Traditional Identities,* ed. Norman Kleeblatt (New York and New Brunswick, N.J.: Jewish Museum and Rutgers University Press, 1996), 39–59; Leo Kaplan, "Reframing the Self-criticism: Clement Greenberg's Modernist Painting in the Light of Jewish Identity," in *Jewish Identity in Modern Art History,* ed. Catherine M. Soussloff (Berkeley and Los Angeles: University of California Press, 1999), 180–199; and Juliet Steyn, "The Subliminal Greenberg: Assimilation and the Ideal Other," in her book *The Jew: Assumptions of Identity* (London: Cassell, 1999). Within this fascinating literature, arguments have been made that Jewishness was repressed by Greenberg as he attempted to write a universal art theory, or that notions of "self-criticism" were displaced from his early writings on Jewish themes to become the guiding principle of his aesthetics, a displacement that witnesses the insecurity of his Jewish identity. Many of these essays note the emergence of his writing at the zenith of Nazism. My own interest is in the nuanced effect of the Holocaust on Greenberg's criticism, his silence about artists who, though they gained his support, sought to address the Holocaust in manners which his criticism could not recognize.

2. Michael Fried, *Morris Louis* (New York: H. N. Abrams, 1971), 32.

3. Though rarely discussed, these paintings were the subject of an exhibition organized by Mira Goldfarb Berkowitz at the Jewish Museum in New York in 1998. Goldfarb Berkowitz, a Louis scholar, has also written an M.A. thesis on these paintings ("Sacred Signs and Symbols in Morris Louis: The Charred Journal Series, 1951," City University of New York, 1993). While her research and mine make use of many of the same documentary materials (indeed, her biographical attention to Louis's early career is much greater than mine), our procedures are very different, as are our approaches to questions around identity and abstraction. (Since the submission of this essay for this volume, Goldfarb Berkowitz's work has been published in Matthew Baigell and Milly Heyd, ed., *Complex Identities: Jewish Consciousness and Modern Art* [New Brunswick, N.J.: Rutgers University Press, 2001].)

4. Diane Upright Headley, *The Drawings of Morris Louis* (Washington, D.C.: Smithsonian Institution Press, 1979), 51.

5. Leslie Judd Portner, "Art in Washington: One a Newcomer, One a Veteran," *The Washington Post,* 12 April 1953, L3.

6. Clement Greenberg, "Review of Exhibitions of Adolph Gottlieb, Jackson Pollock, and Joseph Albers," in *The Collected Essays and Criticism,* ed. John O'Brian, vol. 2, *Arrogant Purpose, 1945–1949* (Chicago: University of Chicago Press, 1986), 286 (originally published in *The Nation,* 19 February 1949).

7. James Johnson Sweeney, "Miro: Comment and Interview," *Partisan Review* 15, no. 1 (February 1948): 208.

8. Gershom Scholem, "The Curious History of the Six-Pointed Star," *Commentary* 8, no. 3 (September 1949): 251.

9. Maurice Blanchot, *The Writing of Disaster* (Lincoln: University of Nebraska Press, 1995), 5, 146.

10. Interview with Marcella Louis Brenner, 27 May 1999.

11. Diane Upright, *Morris Louis: The Complete Paintings* (New York: Abrams, 1985), 11.

12. Clement Greenberg, "Review of an Exhibition of Willem de Kooning," in *Collected Essays,* 2:229 (originally published in *The Nation,* 24 April 1948).

13. See "Black or White," in Stephanie Terenzio, ed., *The Collected Writings of Robert Motherwell* (New York: Oxford University Press, 1992), 71–72.

14. "Book-Burning Day," *New York Times,* 11 May 1933, 16.

15. Blanchot, *Writing,* 4.

16. Jean-Paul Sartre, *Anti-Semite and Jew* (New York: Schocken, 1995), 24.

17. Harold Rosenberg, "Does the Jew Exist?" *Commentary* 7, no. 1 (January 1949): 8–18.

18. "The Jewish Writer and the English Tradition, Part II," *Commentary* 8, no. 4 (October 1949): 363.

19. Ibid., 368.

20. Marjorie Fiske, *Book Selection and Censorship: A Study of School and Public Libraries in California* (Berkeley and Los Angeles: University of California Press, 1959), 48.

21. Interview with Marcella Louis Brenner.

22. Louis Strauss, *Persecution and the Art of Writing* (Chicago: University of Chicago Press, 1952), 25.

23. Morris Louis Files, Archives of American Art (Smithsonian Institution), reel 4993, 1434.

24. Mira Goldfarb Berkowitz also used the Heine quotation in the pamphlet produced for the Jewish Museum exhibition to draw attention to the connections between burning books and burning bodies.

25. See Gershom Scholem, *On the Kabbalah and Its Symbolism* (New York: Schocken, 1996), 44–50.

26. Elliot Cohen, "An Act of Affirmation," *Commentary* 1, no. 1 (November 1945): 1.

27. See Scholem, *On the Kabbalah,* 76.

28. Upright Headley, *Drawings,* 52.

29. Morris Louis Files, Archives of American Art, reel 4988, 0021.

30. Jonathan Boyarin, *Storm from Paradise: The Politics of Jewish Memory* (Minneapolis: University of Minnesota Press, 1992), xvii.

31. Stephen Bann, "The Mythical Conception Is the Name: Titles and Names in Modern and Post-modern Painting," *Word and Image* 1 (1985): 178.

32. "Under Forty: A Symposium on American Literature and the Younger Generation of American Jews," *Contemporary Jewish Record* 7, no. 1 (February 1944): 23.

33. Blanchot, *Writing,* 47.

34. Marcella Louis to unspecified person ["You all"], letter dated 15 April 1953, Morris Louis Files, Archives of American Art, reel 4988, 0076.

35. Greenberg, *Collected Essays,* vol. 4, *Modernism with a Vengeance, 1957–1969,* 96, and Fried, *Morris Louis,* 11.

36. Clement Greenberg, "Self-Hatred and Jewish Chauvinism," *Commentary* 10, no. 5 (November 1950): 429. While this does suggest Greenberg's aversion toward public "indulgence" of "feelings" about the Holocaust, it would be wrong to argue too conclusively from this article about Jewish communal politics that Greenberg did not tolerate any art that approached the Holocaust. Though his formal accounts of Chagall's *White Crucifixion* and Picasso's *Charnel House* pass over historical subject matter, in a rare sympathetic passage on Hyman Bloom he recognized that there were things that "as a Jew in the face of recent events [Bloom] may want to say" (*The Nation,* 26 January 1946, 109). Some years later he praised a Jacques Lipchitz sculpture that was "intended to express the feelings of a Jewish refugee from Hitler" (*Commentary* 18, no. 3 [September 1954]: 259). It seems clear, still, that he conceived no space within Modernist abstraction for the address of the "recent events." In the introduction to my Ph.D. thesis ("The Memory of Modernism: Abstract Art and the Holocaust," University College London, 2002) I discuss at length Greenberg's approach to Modernism in relation to his published writing on Jewish culture and on the Holocaust.

12 Emblems of Atrocity

Holocaust Liberation Photographs | CAROL ZEMEL

For Lionel Ziprin

The pictures of Nazi concentration camps by American photographers Lee Miller and Margaret Bourke-White are well-known images of Holocaust atrocity. Taken on journalist assignment—both women traveled with American military units through the liberation of France and Germany—the pictures rely on a presumption of photography's truth to stand as testimony to a catastrophic history. In *Remembering to Forget: Holocaust Memory through the Camera's Eye,* Barbie Zelizer details the documentary impact and history of such photography and its effect on Holocaust memory.[1] My concern here is less with history than with the modes and categories of its representation, the way this history and its memory have been visually defined. The documentary authenticity of the pictures is undisputed. I want instead to consider the iconic power of some of these photographs, their enduring force as emblems that enable memory of the past.

This power has developed over time, and it derives not only from the terrible information the pictures disclose, and from their repeated public display, but also from the pictorial modes that reinforce viewer fascination with—and judgment of—the horror they convey. We may anticipate emotional, moral, and ethical responses to these pictures: their content seemingly demands it. I want here to slow down or complicate the move from emotional to moralized

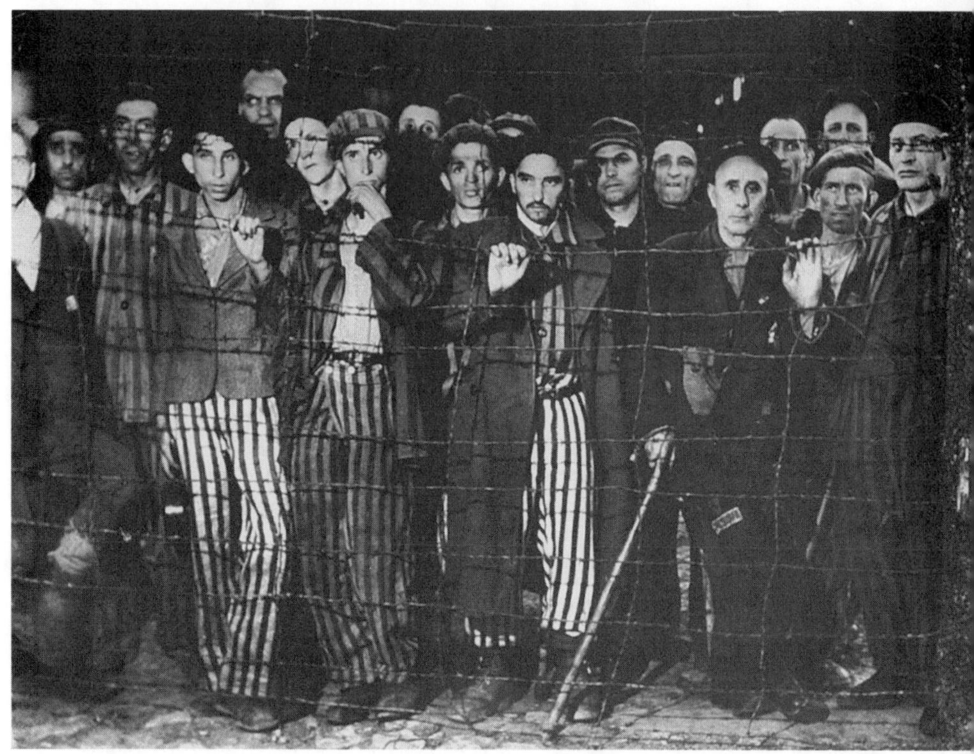

12.1 Margaret Bourke-White, *Prisoners at Fence in Buchenwald,* 1945. Courtesy Margaret Bourke-White/TimePix.

reaction, and to explore instead two other orders of response to the pictures, both of which provoke unsettling and unsettled debate. One is aesthetic, in particular a turn to the category of the Sublime to understand the fascinations and incommensurability of the Event. The other is the tacitly Christological framework for response to the pictures. Despite their representation of a Jewish genocide, these documentary images, like the term Holocaust, are discursively wrapped in Christological symbols and iconographies.

Susan Sontag's reaction sets out both dimensions, when she describes seeing such photographs in July 1945 as "a negative epiphany."

> Nothing I have seen—in photographs or in real life—ever cut me as sharply, deeply, instantaneously. Indeed, it seems plausible to divide my life into two parts, before I saw those photographs (I was twelve) and after, though it was several years before I understood fully what they were about. . . . When I looked at those photographs, something broke. Some limit had been reached, and not only that of horror; I felt irrevocably grieved, wounded, but a part of my feelings started to tighten; something went dead; something is still crying.[2]

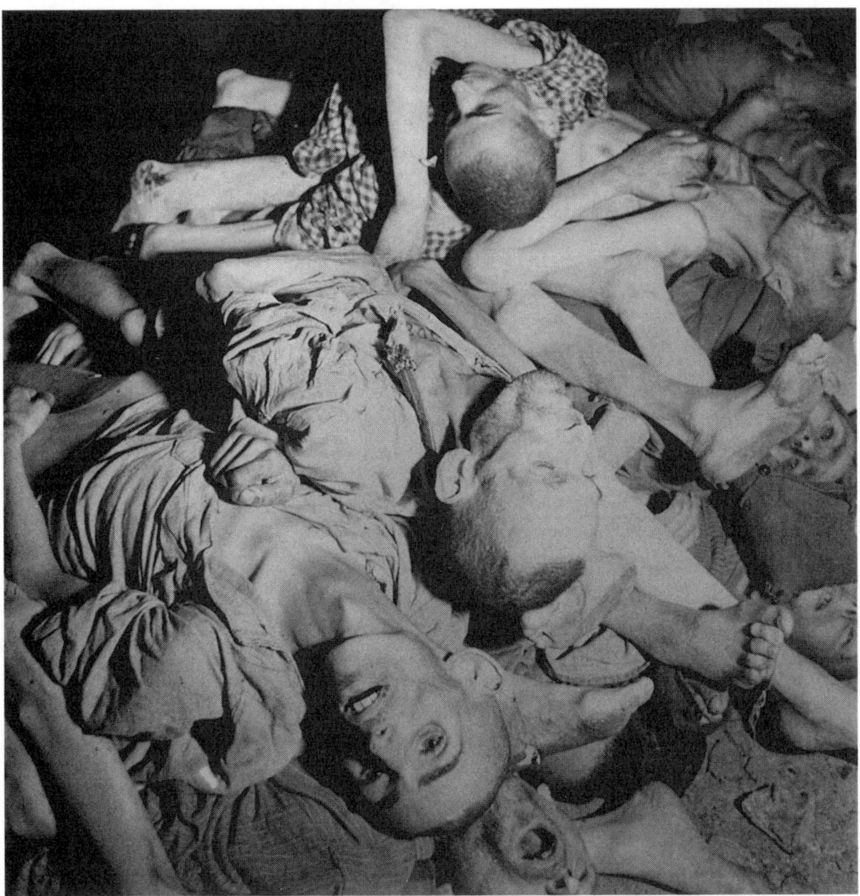

12.2 Lee Miller, *Buchenwald*, 1945. Photograph by Lee Miller, Lee Miller Archives, Chiddingly, England.

The pictures changed Sontag's world in some absolute way: the moment was marked in memory, and time split into before and after their sight. But by labeling her experience "negative epiphany" and thus invoking the language of Christian revelation, Sontag linked the images to an aesthetic and spiritual immensity—horror's breaching of limits, the infinitude of death, endless mourning and grief. As if to underscore Sontag's epiphany, in the six decades since their making, these images have become more than evidence. For many viewers, they invoke the limits of human endurance; they call for moral reflection on human nature and the capacity for evil; for some, they offer an opportunity to mourn. Shocking as they were as historical accounts, several of them are also now icons, that is to say, familiar pictures that emblematically compress or condense the data of events.

From the Greek word *eikon* or image, "icon," for the art historian, means a magical or mystical image, imbued by a community of viewers with an intensified power or force. The label typically designates religious images, pictures of Jesus or Christian saints, installed in churches or shrines where, through figural likeness and symbolic association, their representation is amplified to spiritual presence. This comes about not only through their settings, but through particular formal strategies as well. Time-bound context is expunged from the pictures, and settings are abstract and timeless. Incident and anecdote give way to formality and essence; rather than personality we see presence. In many Russian icons, for example, a solemn-faced saint wears brilliant robes whose pattern of Christian motifs dominates the image far more than his facial features and carries a meditative aura that is much more visually impressive than any bodily likeness or form. The word "icon" is most often associated with religious images, but I use the term also in a more secular sense, closer perhaps to David Freedberg's notion of powerful images whose signifying effects immediately awaken a deep arousal or stirring even in untutored viewers.[3] Indeed, one might say that the photograph's "perpetual now" (what Roland Barthes called its "absolute present"), its seizure and stoppage of time, is uniquely suited to the condition of the icon. Andy Warhol's pictures of Marilyn Monroe (or his Campbell's Soup imagery, for that matter) are secular examples of reality understood as image become icon. Thus, more than a documentary record, an iconic image has contemplative and invocational power: it summons qualities beyond the forms depicted and consideration of those qualities as ideas. Functioning as icons, these pictures of concentration camp liberations evoke more than the moment they depict, and despite their shocking impact, they invite thoughtful scrutiny. Their content acquires symbolic identity. Just as the word "Auschwitz" signifies not one Nazi extermination camp but the camps in general, so do these pictures summon a general history. No matter how specific their features, the people shown here are a special population. They are prisoners, perpetrators, and liberators, but most often, they are victims: literally and emblematically, the six million Jews murdered in the Nazi genocide.

How then do documentary, aesthetic, and spiritual formulations limit or shape the pictures' meaning? Before considering religious or spiritual readings of the pictures, I want first to examine their documentary-aesthetic character. Sontag again sets out the problem. Exempting "photographs of those horrors, like the Nazi camps, that have gained the status of ethical reference points"[4]—she does not say how this has occurred—she nevertheless worries about the long-term dulling effect of atrocity photographs. Just as Walter Benjamin remarked in 1934 on the camera's ability to turn degraded subject matter into beautiful form and an object of enjoyment,[5] Sontag too argues that as the documentary specifics of the photograph fade from memory, formal interests take precedence over historical meaning. "Images transfix. Images anesthetize," she writes, and "[t]ime eventually positions most photographs . . . at the level of art."[6]

This apparently constitutes a danger. Indeed, many scholars—most famously Theodor Adorno, Elie Wiesel, Saul Friedlander—have warned against the aestheticizing dimensions of Holocaust representation, its problematic proximity to visual pleasure, and its immorality in the face of atrocity.[7] The argument voices anxiety about how—morally and ethically—documentary photographs (or perhaps any image) should work. It is easy enough to understand the notion that time dims the power of history to stir outrage or moral concern. Old news is no news. But Sontag's claim that "'concerned' photography has done at least as much to deaden conscience as to arouse it"[8] implies that such repositioning of photo-documents as art bolsters their technical or formal qualities—that is, our attention to skill and artistry—at the expense of their content, producing such misplaced reactions as admiration—"What a beautiful picture"—or distance—"It's only a photograph." In this view, any perceived stylization in Holocaust images, even an analysis centered on stylistic effect, may be an affront to the record of suffering they depict. The argument hinges on several issues: a philosophical debate about the Sublime as an effective category for discussion of the Holocaust, but also, for art historians, the persistence of modernist positions that separate the sensation of formal effects from the moral or ethical meaning of content or subject matter. Such positions would confine to reportage the difficult issue of how to represent the force of what Kant called "radical evil" and the fascinations of our darkest side.

If, then, we reject the silence that defers to the unspeakability of the Event, and if we assume that all histories, even the most documented, are incomplete and fragmentary, can we turn to the aesthetic for better understanding of history's visual or literary accounts? I believe we must. To insist on only the evidentiary status of atrocity pictures obscures the ways in which aesthetic effects deliver historical data, reify fragments of memory, and enable the passage from document to icon. It also sidesteps the ways in which the pictures continue to fascinate. Are these fascinations always inappropriate? Should they be immediately set aside as Holocaust porn or aberrant psychology? To aestheticize, however, need not be to anesthetize. On the contrary, consideration of these effects may help us understand enduring interest in images of terror and atrocity. I want, therefore, to propose another kind of looking and analysis, one that does not forgo the aesthetic, but rather turns to it directly, and through frameworks of the Sublime consider the pictures' fascinations, their presentation of evil and excess, and their cultural force as icons.

Excepting approximately thirty thousand extant prisoner drawings, most images of the Holocaust were made at the liberation by Allied forces—American, British, Russian. The act of witness was central to their mission, but the pictures vary significantly in their designs and emphases. Military file photographs, for example, often took a longer or broader view, showing camp grounds strewn with bodies as liberating armies discharged their work. Journalists' pictures, in contrast, were usually part of some narrative report or story. Like Miller's picture of a dead SS guard floating in a canal, they often come closer to their human subjects, whether suffering prisoner, camp guard, or tangled corpse.

Bourke-White and Miller were experienced professionals whose wartime images are informed by qualities already part of their photographic styles. In the 1930s, Bourke-White pioneered the genre of photo-narrative for *Fortune* and *Life* magazines. Working for Time, Inc., she joined General George Patton's Third Army as it moved across the Rhine and entered Buchenwald in March 1945. Her pictures appeared in Luce publications and in her own book on the liberation of Germany, *Dear Fatherland, Rest Quietly* (1945). Miller developed her photographic approach in Paris, where, as artist and model, she was part of the Surrealist milieu. By the 1930s, she had produced an innovative photographic oeuvre that included gender-bending images of the nude body and destabilizing images of famous sites, such as the Great Pyramid of Giza presented as shadow rather than substance. Living in England during the war, in 1941–42 Miller published pictures of the Blitz in a collection titled *Grim Glory,* and in 1944 she traveled with the American Forty-Second and Forty-Fifth Infantry Divisions through the liberation of France, into Paris, and on to Germany. Her dispatches—text and images—were published in the British *Vogue,* and in what seems a surreal juxtaposition, atrocity photos were set beside the frivolities of high fashion.[9]

In considering their images, I want to proceed from documentary to more iconic forms. Among the characteristic subjects of liberation photography are German civilians summoned by Allied generals to view the camps and "clean-up" operations—prisoners or soldiers moving corpses from trains, wagons, pits. Both types offer information and, in their design, they construct positions of witness, perpetrator, and heroic liberator. But the pictures of civilians also enact a double witnessing: the real spectacle is not the dead, but German citizens photographically designated guilty bystanders to Holocaust atrocity. Indeed, in their written accounts of the war, both Bourke-White and Miller expressed cynicism about civilian claims not to know of the camps' activities.[10] One well-known image by Bourke-White shows well-dressed men and women solemnly filing past the dead. In it, a woman turns her head away and holds a handkerchief to her nose; a man leans forward, possibly perturbed; another stands with hands folded, apparently resolute. With the camera set at a casual observer's angle across from the endless procession, the image invites the viewer to scan the group, to note responses, and then to judge these ordinary men and women from the secure space of victory and difference.

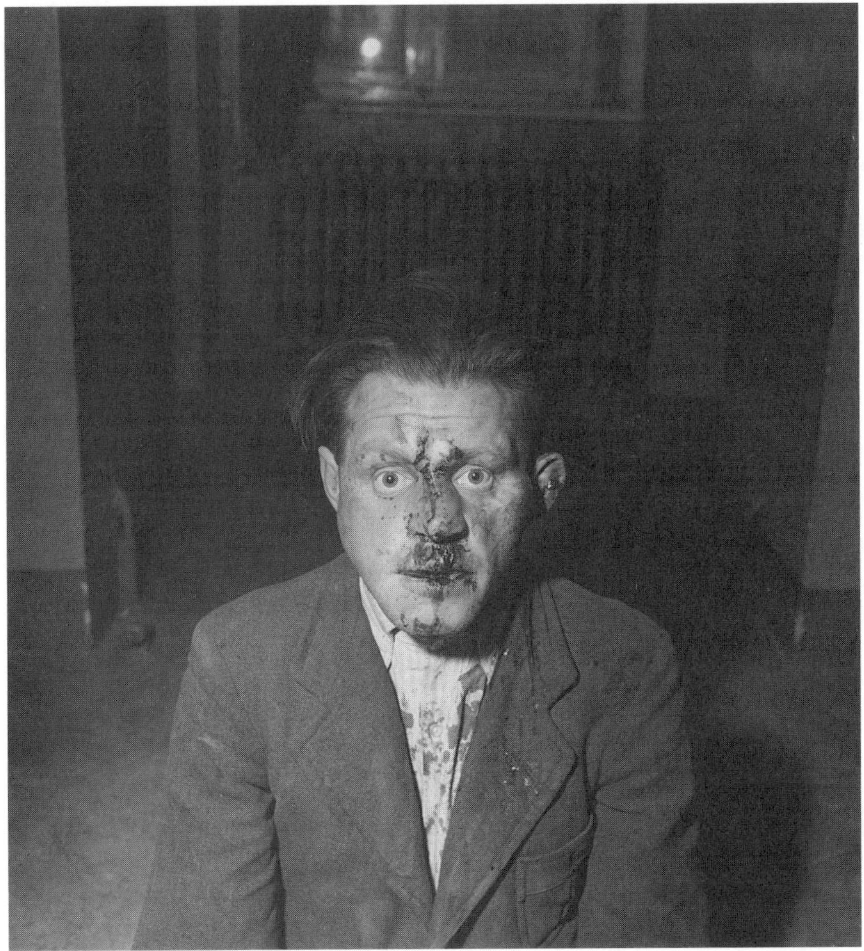

12.3 Lee Miller, *Beaten SS Guard, Buchenwald*, 1945. Photograph by Lee Miller, Lee Miller Archives, Chiddingly, England.

The many pictures of troops disposing of corpses in the camps provide similar certainties. We stand behind and with the uniformed soldiers, cushioned by their backs from the full force of the shocking sight, but at the same time sharing their identity—and heroism—as liberators.

Miller's portraits of captured SS guards and camp personnel are both more formal and more unsettling images. The shift in photo genre from documentary to portrait elicits different conventions, expectations, and meanings. Whether of kings or criminals, portraiture is used to characterize individuals and to specify social place; this is as true of prison mug shots as it is of society portraiture or social genre. This is the mission of German photographer August Sander's vast portrait survey of German citizens in the first half of the century.[11] Central to this practice in its more insidious forms is the notion that character may be read through physiognomic traits and principles, a pseudo-science that, for example, informs Nazi photo-documentation of genetic and racial inferiority. But such premises are often contradicted. Even in "The Face of Germany," the first photo portrait section of Bourke-White's *Dear Fatherland, Rest Quietly,* the ordinary faces of high-placed German citizens, often members of the Nazi party, belie their political or moral choices and exemplify not satanic character but what would be called the "banality of evil." Using the genre to exploit and tumble portrait assumptions and styles, Miller's *Captured SS Guard* and *Beaten SS Guard, Buchenwald* rely on discomfort and paradox. The beaten man is plump and oafish, seen under glaring light with blood trickling down his face and vest; he is marked by someone's rage, and his bug-eyed stare announces his terror to the camera's gaze. His condition is raw and startling for an official presentation, and it confronts the viewer with the war's violence. The same is true for the adolescent guard, his blackened eye worn like a decoration, his arm raised in defiant salute. To specify and enlarge such individuals through portraiture bitterly underscores the very terms of identity wrested from the Nazis' anonymous victims. But the unsettling impact of the images goes further, for in tempting us to scrutinize the face of evil or sadistic character, the portraits capture and objectify the perpetrators and supply occasion for multiple hatreds—theirs and ours.

Still more disturbing than documentary images of witnesses and portraits of perpetrators are the iconic pictures of prisoners and the dead. Everyone who participated in the liberation reported shock at what met their eyes.[12] In 1945, correspondent Edward R. Murrow told American radio listeners, "I pray you to believe what I have said about Buchenwald. I have reported what I saw and heard, but only part of it. For most of it I have no words."[13] Countless soldiers were physically sickened by what they saw, and Bourke-White pulled, as she put it, "a 'veil' over her mind."

> In photographing the murder camps, the protective veil was so tightly drawn that I hardly knew what I had taken until I saw prints of my own photographs. It was as though I was seeing these horrors for the first time. I believe many correspondents worked in the same self-imposed stupor. One has to, or it is impossible to stand it.[14]

Seeing through the protective veil, Burke-White assigned her own affect to the images rather than her experience. She may well have moved through the camp snapping pictures in a "self-imposed stupor," but her well-known image of prisoners in Buchenwald seems carefully thought out and almost staged. Rows of prisoners two or three deep form an impenetrable wall across the foreground; their dark clothing is punctuated by prisoner stripes, and their

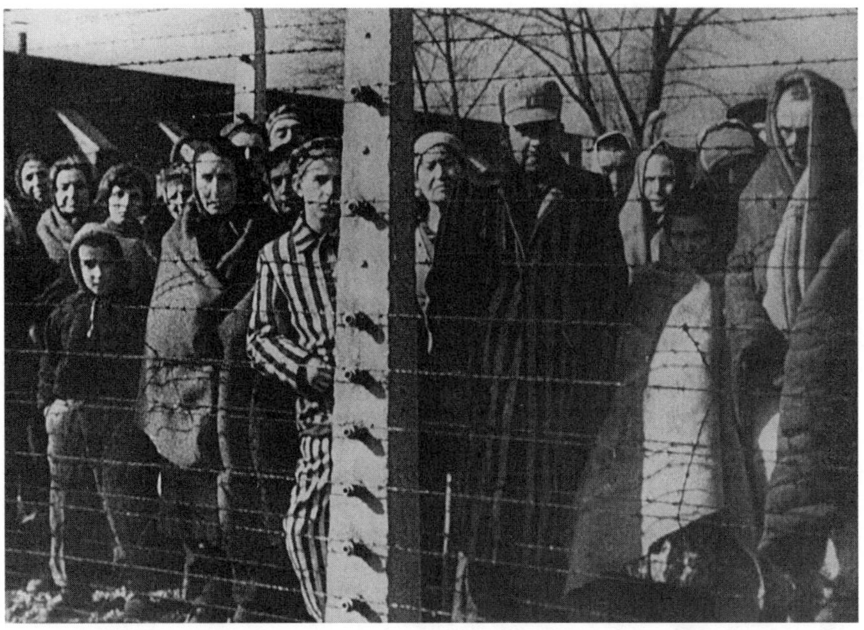

12.4 *Prisoners at Auschwitz after the Liberation,* 1945. Courtesy Yad Vashem, Jerusalem.

pale faces stare solemnly back at the viewer. Arrayed there, their heads almost touching the top of the frame and obscuring the details of the setting, these anonymous men are defined—totalized, one might say—as "prisoners," and the barbed-wire grid underscores that status and identity.

We may contrast this design with a similar picture taken in Auschwitz by a Russian military photographer (Fig. 12.4). The barracks and bare branches behind this prisoner group provide some sense of place and season. The arrangement of figures—men, women, and children, some clutching wraps against the winter cold—seems haphazard, as if these people suddenly moved toward the fence. Heads are ranged at differing heights, faces are obscured or blurred in shadow. And though the camera comes close, the viewer is distracted from the prisoners' faces by the large post that clumsily divides the composition and competes for pride of place. Unlike the regularized scrutiny offered by Bourke-White's design, the viewer's gaze is more dispersed here, momentary and scanning like that of a spectator walking by.

Together, these pictures may illustrate the distinction between document and icon. Both, of course, record historical situations and camp sites, and both establish positions of witness. In both the prisoners are a special population, different from the viewer, fenced off and marked by their uniforms. And in both, they return the viewer's gaze. But prisoner curiosity in the Auschwitz

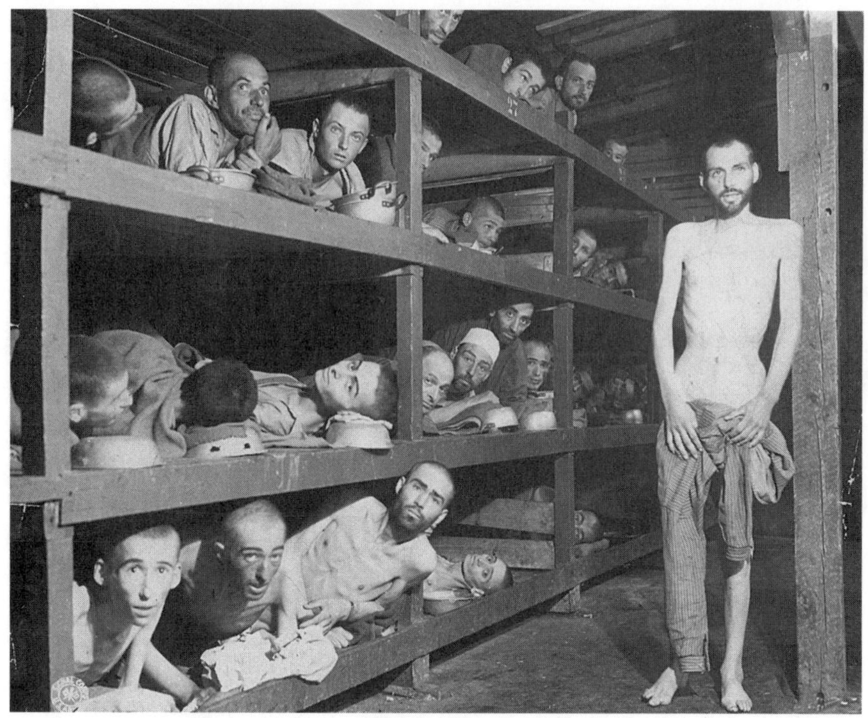

12.5 Margaret Bourke-White, *Inside Dormitories, Buchenwald,* 1945. Courtesy Margaret Bourke-White/TimePix.

image is confrontational in the picture of Buchenwald. The grim expressions, the full-frame density of the group, and, most of all, their regular, frontal alignment binds these individuals into militant unity. We are not simply being greeted as liberators in this picture; we are met by an assertive human force.[15] In contrast, the artlessness of the Auschwitz photograph conveys a sense of moment; it is embedded in the details and conditions of history. Bourke-White's forceful design suppresses irregularity or moment. The image is emphatically presentational; it shows a special assembly of prisoners, and thus formalizes and intensifies their situation from particular record to iconic tableau.

The confrontational energy in this cordoned group slackens in images of barracks at Buchenwald, where prisoners appear so haggard and emaciated that they hover at the border of life and death. Again, as is characteristic of Bourke-White, the image is a dramatic tableau: a human storehouse presented as still-life or nature morte, where men are ranged like goods on shelves. As the men peer out at us as liberators, we stare back with terror and curiosity, noting how the ravaged physiques diminish signs of individual identity.[16] This scrutiny is brought up short by the spectral figure at the right: frontal, naked for no reason, covering his genitals with a bunched up uniform. This is the prisoner-body: less person than specimen and stand-in for the others ranged in the wooden stacks. Beyond this, through the raking light and abrupt shadows, the darkness is impenetrable. Death is but moments or inches away, and the man who blocks our gaze in this modern "harrowing of Hell" (Jesus' descent into Hell to recover damned souls) signals that nothing further could be shown or seen.

In their representation of liminal spaces—the fenced edge of the camp, the barracks' threshold—Bourke-White's pictures bring viewers to the forbidden and unknown. The shared act of witness takes us to the brink of human existence, to a space between life and death. Drawing the viewer to that place, edging us into barely imaginable terrors, the pictures' content and dramatic design summon what I call a "Holocaust Sublime."

Though the term is hardly neutral, it has been used by historians and philosophers to characterize the Holocaust's enormity.[17] Let me review its basic features, in order to clarify my use of it here. In Edmund Burke's eighteenth-century formulation, the Sublime is characterized by intense feelings of terror, danger, and even pain. "Terror," Burke wrote, "is the ruling principle of the Sublime."[18] Burke finds sublimity in shock and suddenness, magnitude and power, infinity, darkness, blinding light—all qualities that suggest danger or death and are bound to an impulse of self-preservation. Attentive to the irrational dimensions of experience, he notes that, rather than avoidance, the emotional intensity of the Sublime sparks attraction and fascination—offering what he calls "delight" or "a sort of delightful horror"[19]—especially when these feelings are modified, as they are in representations, by some degree of safety or escape. In the present case, for example, we are able to confront the terror of the concentration camp through our literal distance and the framed safety of the photograph. We are, after all, neither victims nor perpetrators, only indirect witnesses, and through representation we can indulge our curiosity about and fascination with human behaviors that we cannot explain. If, to some minds, this position seems stranded in sensation or sensational effect, there may nevertheless be more than shock or terror in the experience. In the Kantian formulation, sublimity depends not only on the stirring of the senses but also on the awakening of reason, an awareness of human capacity, and, through this, the possibility of a moral response.[20] Shifting the emphasis from the Sublime object, the viewing/thinking subject becomes the locus of the Sublime. The force of sensation in Burke's position—the tenacity of terror's grip—is overridden by the engagement of reason, so that, in the case of these photographs, shock, terror, and incredulity—perhaps even pleasure—may be followed by moral outrage at such extremes. In his essays on the Sublime—and to the point for this paper—Friedrich Schiller includes human suffering in what he labeled the (Pathetically) Sublime. "The image of another's suffering," Schiller wrote, "combined with emotion and the consciousness of the moral freedom within us, is pathetically Sublime."[21]

Some scholars object, however, that for the representation of Holocaust memory, both the shudder of pleasure and imagined threat afforded by infinite power and, in the second phase of the Sublime, reason's awareness of moral independence from that power summon a heroics of resistance and mastery, and a potential for rhetorical closure inappropriate to the horror and magnitude of the event. Zachary Braiterman writes that the "[t]he Holocaust and its first-memory already belong to the past, contained within a frame, already domesticated. Ironically a rhetoric of sublimity will only increase that domestic character."[22] Braiterman also disputes the "argot of resistance" that pervades the Sublime and ensures its moral uplift. And Lawrence Langer reminds us of the need to "surrender . . . the comforting notion that suffering has meaning—that it strengthens, ennobles, or redeems the human soul."[23] Can Holocaust representation allow such moral uplift to those of us outside the experience? Can it result in anything other than "domestication" through a framing narrative of heroics and redemption?

These are important considerations, and I'm not sure I can settle the matter. But I do believe that the Sublime—Burke's, Kant's, and Schiller's formulations—need not subsume or diminish the magnitude of Holocaust suffering. On the contrary, it is that very magnitude, the measureless extent and detail, the seeming boundlessness of the horror that summons this aesthetic category as an enabling tool of analysis—for only in the Sublime does representation test the mind's limits and attempt to confront what may scarcely be imagined. Thus the Sublime in these pictures does not necessarily lead to transcendence or resolution of the ineffable, but in its picturing of "radical evil" to the contemplation of limitless terror, excess, and death.

Because the most memorable images of the liberation represent human bodies *in extremis* and the dead, I want to situate some of these pictures within established European iconographies of death. Doing so, I turn to the second, spiritual order of iconization and response and the ways in which a sacralizing aura and Christological frame have been set around a transgressive event. The transgression, I want to stress, is not only that of murder; it is also in the act of looking, in the protracted scrutiny of death that Holocaust imagery provides. There is little doubt of death's fascinations. Plato, in *The Republic,* illustrates a conflict of mind when desire wins over reason, with Leontion's impulse to look at the bodies of executed men.

> He wanted to go and look at them, and yet at the same time held himself back in disgust. For a time, he struggled with himself and covered his eyes, but at last his desire got the better of him and he ran up to the corpses, opening his eyes wide and saying to them [to his eyes], "There you are, curse you—a lovely sight! Have a real good look!"[24]

As Leontion's struggle and the blurted satisfactions of his visual desire suggest, the sight of death is never a casual matter. Every culture manages its terrors

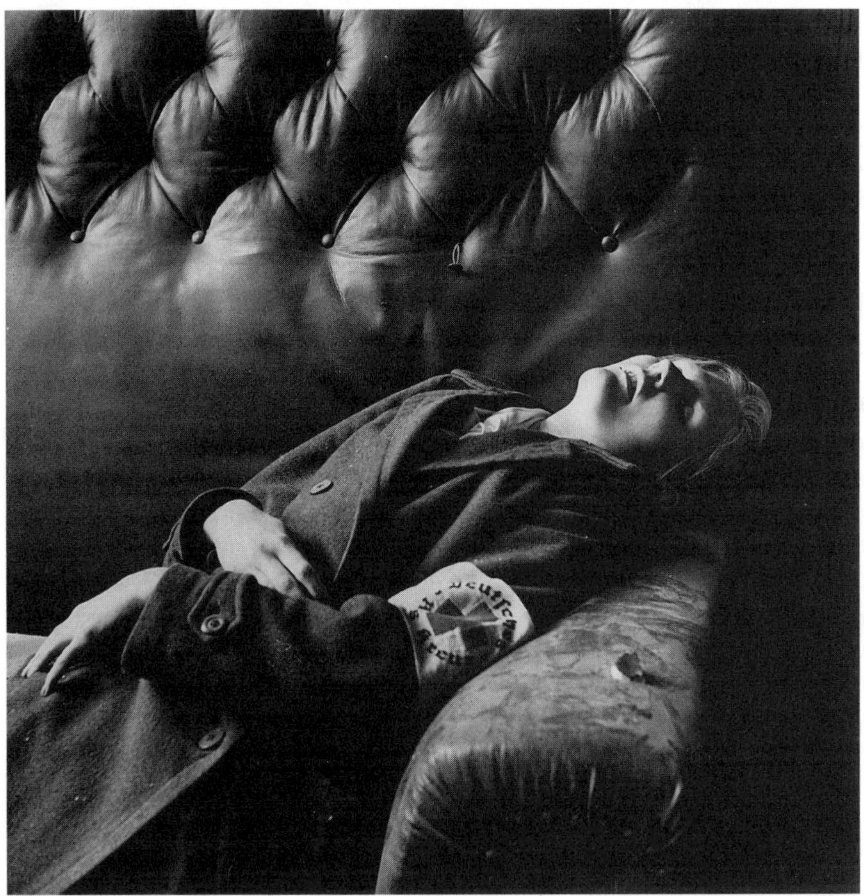

12.6 Lee Miller, *Daughter of the Burgomeister of Leipzig*, 1945. Photograph by Lee Miller, Lee Miller Archives, Chiddingly, England.

through ritual and ceremony. In the case of the liberation photographs, the journalists' mission—or any mission—legitimates the act of looking as the camera masks and mediates the dreadful sight.

Accordingly, two modes of picturing death in western tradition are relevant here: military and, of course, religious imagery.[25] Both subsume the death of a person or group to some noble purpose or higher destiny. This is no more the case for fallen fighters in Meissonier's *Barricades* (1848) than for the family of the burgomeister of Leipzig, suicides in the offices of the town hall on the eve of Allied victory.[26] Both Bourke-White and Miller photographed this scene—possibly within hours of each other. Taken from some height—a balcony or desktop—Bourke-White's pictures confirm the victors' omniscient surveying gaze. But Miller's image comes very close to the daughter draped across the leather sofa. "She had pretty teeth," was Miller's comment, restating her camera's attention to unexpected or intimate detail.[27] The graceful position of the young woman's body recalls the elegiac presentations of funerary sculpture—like Bernini's *Blessed Ludovica Albertoni* (1671–74) in the Altieri Chapel in Rome—and to some extent it moderates the viewer's judging gaze. Does Miller here poeticize this death, pushing it beyond evil politics and ideology? Is death in the name of any cause an ennobling act? Do these suicides of a Nazi official and his family fascinate as a photographic stand-in for the suicides of Hitler and Eva Braun? And how might one relate the sense of family tragedy in this image to the anonymous murder victims of the Nazi regime?

Indeed, the named, placed, and, most important, self-inflicted death in this picture stands in painful contrast to images of tumbled heaps of corpses piled in the camps. Nowhere is the Nazi reduction of persons to despised matter more visible. In some, the disturbing presence of the bodies is alleviated by the view of Allied soldiers—merging the viewer with the rescuer once again, and providing some sense of closure, some end to the tale. Bourke-White's pictures from Erla of prisoners incinerated by the electrified fence is a terrifying tableau, they, like the fence-posts, stretching back into infinity. But Miller characteristically avoids even the pictorial comforts of tableau, and instead proffers intimacy. This overhead shot brings us close to the dead as liberating witness, but also perhaps as perpetrator, as fellow prisoner, or even as Sonderkommando, one of those prisoners forced to load the gassed bodies into ovens. Seen upside-down, with heads poking through tangled limbs, the figures lose any specific identity, though the viewer wants to walk around the pile to find a space where identity will appear. But this is impossible, denied by the raw data and by the picture's design. With only a tiny ledge of visible ground as toehold, the composition is dizzying, and the pinwheeling body parts reinforce the vertiginous effect. They are jammed edge to edge and beyond the camera frame, an impacted mass of bodies, the nameless and numberless victims of the Nazi Holocaust.

To grasp the force of the picture as secular image we may refer to Gericault's 1819 painting *Severed Heads,* in which the heads are nestled together in some indeterminate space. Despite the bloody linen and the agonized face of the head on the right, the picture's design suggests a sleeping pair—a couple, perhaps—their bodies simply covered by a sheet. The sight of violent death—not so long after the terrors of the Revolutionary guillotine—is thus ameliorated by a comforting composition, and the picture's fascinations are driven by this paradox: brutality and death rendered almost peaceful by design. Closer to our history, we may consider Picasso's *Charnel House,* a painting dated 1944–45, presumably based on published photos of liberated camps in Poland, and which Miller might have seen in Paris earlier that year.[28] Avoiding the expressive comforts of color, the painting's somber palette mimes a news media source, and the tangled limbs seen here are muted into a semi-abstract pattern of black, white, and gray. But the jumble of body parts shown in the Buchenwald photograph offer no such compositional comfort. The intimacy of the design holds us hostage, thrusts us powerfully before measureless horror—many viewers cannot bear to look—and into the realm of a Sublime.

To be sure, we do not gaze in any of these images at natural phenomena—sublimity's conventional sites. But as Schiller argued and as Paul Crowther writes in *The Kantian Sublime,* the Sublime is found not only in divine or natural forces but also in human actions and events that, for good or evil, render, in Crowther's words, "the scope of some human capacity—vivid to the senses."[29] Clearly images like this take us beyond documentary data to the human capacity to perform and experience such acts. But it is the picture's form that demands—insists on—surrender to its content, and in surrendering the viewer is not only told of evil through documentary evidence—a mode of representation that may indeed grow tired and fade—but more actively realizes it, is plunged into evil's effects through the spinning sensations of the design.[30]

The unsettling pictorial capture may be underscored as well through the concept of the Abject, a subcategory of the Sublime theorized by Julia Kristeva. Here, too, the limits of self dissolve in infinitude, but with overwhelming sensations of horror and disgust, as the boundaries of body and person threaten to mingle with putrefaction and impurity. As a bitter and tragic realization of the Nazis' racial purification, their maniacal need to render Jews refuse, rags and pieces, hardly worth even the numbered inventory of slave labor, the terrain of the camps was nothing else than a wallowing in abjection, with no access to human order, culminating in the apparatus and revulsive materiality of death—the fence, the gas, the furnace, the corpse. "The corpse," Kristeva writes, "seen without God and outside of science"—that is, outside any theological or epistemological frame—"is the utmost of abjection."[31] The question is, do we insist on theological meaning, and refuse abjection's "without God" for such extreme circumstances? Eliminating context, distance, and the culturally ennobling, Miller's photograph plunges us into that contamination, with hardly a toehold to keep us secure.

As a one-time Surrealist, Miller surely was familiar with and even enjoyed the irrationalities and destabilizing contradictions she encountered and pictured. Indeed, as a liberation witness, her camera delivers a blasphemous and surreal form of intimacy: She napped in Eva Braun's bed, was photographed musing at Hitler's desk and playing nymph in his bathtub. Taken within a day of Miller's photographs of Dachau, when she and other American correspondents were lodged in Hitler's Munich apartment, a carefully staged photograph of her naked body (though cunningly shielded by tub and camera) sitting where once Hitler's naked body sat conjures its own disturbing combinations of viewer voyeurism and disgust. As Melody Davis writes about this picture,

"Who would bathe near his skin cells . . . where his feet and genitals once touched? . . . Dachau's showers become Hitler's bath, and Miller's body was the conduit, the place of meeting."[32] Seen as part of Lee Miller's *War,* this is not a trifling with history through Surrealist juxtaposition or play. It is a considerably more confrontational presentation of the war's horrors and paradox. From the heart of that contradiction, Miller wrote to her London editor,

> Well, alright he [Hitler] was dead. He'd never really been alive for me until today. He'd been an evil machine-monster all these years, until I visited the places he'd made famous, talked to people who knew him, dug into backstairs gossip, and ate and slept in his house. He became less fabulous and therefore more terrible, along with a little evidence of his having some almost human habits; like an ape who embarrasses and humbles you with his gestures, mirroring yourself in caricature. "There, but for the grace of God walk I."[33]

However unsettling Miller's photographic choices, the pictorial fascinations of these images break through the iconoclasm of the "unrepresentable" and bring us as witness to the conditions of abjection, or—refusing abjection's void, the "without God and outside of science"—to the space of the Sublime.

Even as an aesthetic category, it is a pictorial Sublime that has been most effectively comprehended through Christian icon and consciousness. We need only recall the tangled mass of bodies in images of the Massacre of the Innocents or the Last Judgment to find stirring representations of death and suffering. Pictures of martyred saints abound in Christian iconography: the dying St. Sebastian, St. Lawrence, and numerous others exemplify this representation of both suffering and spiritual sublimity. In this cultural frame, the pictures of the dead in Buchenwald and Dachau are more than documents, as the Crucifixion is more than an event on Golgotha Hill. If suffering and death are central icons of Christian culture, if they encourage and abet visual meditation on these themes, then photographs like these—secular images that for many seem to conflate human and divine catastrophe—may supplement that iconography of suffering and install a Christological frame for Holocaust history and remembrance. A pictorial language in which the image of a dying man on a cross is a site of spiritual uplift may readily annex these images of the dead and near-dead as icons of suffering and martyrdom.

In traditional Jewish culture, however, where such iconicity has no place, the images may function differently. The sight of corpses whose deaths are due not to resistance or heroic principle but to identity—to their Jewishness—provokes a double subjectivity for Jewish viewers: the viewer is also called upon to be nearly a victim, a survivor, or an escapee. This is not to suggest that Judaism lacks an elaborate martyrology or even literary images of suffering and death. One need think only of the flaying of Rabbi Akiva by the Romans, images of the sacrifice of Isaac or Akedah, or chronicles of catastrophe. But apart from mass culture images such as photographs of the 1905 Kishinev pogroms, visual references to Jewish martyrology are rare. Tombstone decorations are symbolic plant and animal forms, not figurative effigies. Jews are commanded to remember through prayer and ritual; they do not picture the dead. In a sense, the modern tendency, even among Jewish artists like Chagall, to picture Jesus as a suffering Jew and to depict the excesses of fascism as a modern Christian Passion generalizes Jewish experience and dilutes its Jewishness for a more ecumenical frame.[34] Indeed, depictions of the camp dead as Christian martyrs—bodies pinned against the electrified wire fence, corpses lying with outstretched arms—demonstrate our cultural readiness to locate as Christian the meanings of Holocaust catastrophe. Thus the transcendent force of the Sublime combines with the familiar forms of Christian iconography to provide moral rescue of the images' horrors and fascinations. Like the name commonly used for this history, they draw the Khurbn or Shoah—the Jewish catastrophe—toward the Christian Holocaust or spiritual sacrifice.

To avoid those dangers, we may insist on the overwhelmingly Jewish focus of the event, as well as heed the misgivings of Braiterman and others about sublimity's uplifting character. He suggests we acknowledge that Holocaust-memory is now entirely textual rather than experiential, and that we interrogate and interpret that textualized memory—visual, literary, filmic, etc.—rather than revere the magnitude of the Holocaust. Reconsidering the images by Bourke-White and Miller may lead us, I believe, to that position: Bourke-White with the sublimity of her photographic tableaux, and Miller, more troubling, with her pictures' audacious and dizzying intimacies.

Sontag's claim about atrocity photographs' ultimate deadening impact requires, it would seem, a response that reorients her concerns. Even her own acknowledgment that "something is still crying" in her declares—though hardly explains—these images' enduring impact. More to the point, and what is troublesome as photo-document becomes icon, is not a numbing of conscience, nor even our human fascination with evil, nor even the linking of horror's fascinations with the Sublime. It is the sealing of a murdered Jewish population as a martyred people timelessly, essentially, and reverentially into another's sacralized space.

Notes

I am grateful to Gideon Ofrat and Zachary Braiterman, my colleagues in 2000–2001 at the Center for Advanced Judaic Studies, University of Pennsylvania, for their discussion of and guidance on several issues in this paper.

1. Barbie Zelizer, *Remembering to Forget: Holocaust Memory through the Camera's Eye* (Chicago: University of Chicago Press, 1998).

2. Susan Sontag, *On Photography* (New York: Dell, 1979), 19–20.

3. See David Freedberg, *The Power of Images* (Chicago: University of Chicago Press, 1989), 22. I do not, therefore, use C. S. Peirce's well-known formulation of icon/index/symbol, where "icon" means merely "likeness" and is not imbued with

particular affective presence or power. See Peirce's "What Is a Sign?" in *The Essential Peirce,* vol. 2, ed. Peirce Edition Project (Bloomington: Indiana University Press, 1998), 4–10.

4. Sontag, *On Photography,* 20.

5. Benjamin, quoted in ibid., 107.

6. Ibid., 21.

7. See Theodor W. Adorno, "Cultural Criticism and Society," in *Prisms,* trans. Samuel and Shierry Weber (Cambridge, Mass.: MIT Press, 1990); Elie Wiesel, "Does the Holocaust Lie beyond the Reach of Art?" *New York Times,* Arts and Leisure section, 17 April 1983; Saul Friedlander, *Reflections of Nazism: An Essay on Kitsch and Death* (Bloomington: Indiana University Press, 1993). The issue is also raised by Ziva Amishai-Maisels, *Depiction and Interpretation: The Influence of the Holocaust on the Visual Arts* (Oxford: Pergamon, 1993); Andrea Liss, *Trespassing through Shadows: Memory, Photography, and the Holocaust* (Minneapolis: University of Minnesota Press, 1998); John Taylor, *Body Horror: Photojournalism, Catastrophe, and War* (New York: New York University Press, 1998).

8. Sontag, *On Photography,* 21.

9. These dispatches, with accompanying photographs, are published in Lee Miller, *Lee Miller's War: Photographer and Correspondent with the Allies in Europe, 1944–45,* ed. Antony Penrose (Boston: Little, Brown, 1992). The book does not reproduce *Vogue*'s page layouts or designs.

10. Margaret Bourke-White, *Portrait of Myself* (New York: Simon and Schuster, 1961), 258; Miller, *Lee Miller's War,* 161.

11. See August Sander, *August Sander: Citizens of the Twentieth Century—Portrait Photographs, 1892–1952,* ed. Gunther Sander, text by Ulrich Keller, trans. Linda Keller (Cambridge, Mass.: MIT Press, 1986).

12. Robert H. Abzug, *Inside the Vicious Heart: Americans and the Liberation of the Concentration Camps* (New York: Oxford University Press, 1985).

13. Edward R. Murrow, "Broadcast from Buchenwald," 15 April 1945, reprinted in *1945: The Year of Liberation,* United States Holocaust Memorial Museum, ed. Kevin Mahoney et al. (Washington, D.C.: United States Holocaust Memorial Museum, 1995), 114–115.

14. Bourke-White, *Portrait,* 259.

15. Vicki Goldberg writes that these men so lacked a sense of themselves as subjects that they neither blinked nor flinched (*Margaret Bourke-White: A Biography* [New York: Harper and Row, 1986], 290).

16. Presumably Elie Wiesel is pictured here (Zelizer, *Remembering to Forget,* 186).

17. See Emil Fackenheim, *To Mend the World: Foundations of Jewish Future Thought* (New York: Schocken, 1982); Jean-François Lyotard, *Lessons on the Analytic of the Sublime,* trans. Elizabeth Rottenberg (Stanford, Calif.: Stanford University Press, 1994); Lyotard, *The Differend: Phrases in Dispute,* trans. Georges Van Den Abbeele (Minneapolis: University of Minnesota Press, 1988); Eli Friedlander, "Some Thoughts on Kitsch," *History and Memory* 9, nos. 1–2 (fall 1997): 376–392. For a critical review of these positions, see Zachary Braiterman, "Against Holocaust-Sublime: Naive Reference and the Generation of Memory," *History and Memory* 12, no. 2 (fall/winter 2000): 7–28.

18. Edmund Burke, *A Philosophical Inquiry into the Origins of Our Ideas of the Sublime and Beautiful,* ed. James T. Boulton (Notre Dame: University of Notre Dame Press, 1968), 58.

19. Ibid., 136.

20. Immanuel Kant, "Book II: Analytic of the Sublime," in *Critique of Judgment,* trans. Werner S. Pluhar (Indianapolis: Hackett, 1987), 97–141.

21. Friedrich Schiller, *Essays,* ed. Walter Hinderer and Daniel O. Dahlstrom (New York: Continuum, 1993), "On the Sublime," 42–44, and "On the Pathetic," 45–69.

22. Braiterman, "Against Holocaust-Sublime," 18.

23. Lawrence Langer, "On Writing and Reading Holocaust Literature," in *Art from the Ashes: A Holocaust Anthology,* ed. Lawrence Langer (New York: Oxford University Press, 1995), 5.

24. Plato, *The Republic,* trans. Desmond Lee, 2d ed. (New York: Penguin, 1987), 156. My thanks to Dr. John Hoffmeyer for pointing out this passage to me.

25. Domestic photographic representations of death, common in the nineteenth century, are also ritually framed as devotional memorials. See Linda Nochlin, *Realism* (New York: Penguin, 1971). In shifting the intended audience for their images, publications of police file photographs and texts like Michael Lesy's *Wisconsin Death Trip* (New York: Pantheon, 1973) may result exclusively in sensationalism.

26. Bill Walton, correspondent for Time, Inc., reported the eeriness of this encounter, as each office disclosed another bureaucrat and family suicide (Goldberg, *Margaret Bourke-White,* 293).

27. Miller, *Lee Miller's War,* 176.

28. Amishai-Maisels, "The Charnel House," *in Depiction and Interpretation,* 57–61 and figure 171.

29. Paul Crowther, *The Kantian Sublime: From Morality to Art* (Oxford: Clarendon, 1989), 163.

30. The result may be what Ernst van Alphen calls a "Holocaust effect": in this case, an aesthetic formulation that both informs and actively engages the viewer in the sight and event. See Ernst van Alphen, *Caught by History: Holocaust Effects in Contemporary Art, Literature, and Theory* (Stanford, Calif.: Stanford University Press, 1997).

31. Julia Kristeva, *The Powers of Horror: An Essay on Abjection* (New York: Columbia University Press, 1982), 4.

32. Melody D. Davis, "Lee Miller: Bathing with the Enemy," *History of Photography* 21, no. 4 (winter 1997): 314–318.

33. Miller, *Lee Miller's War,* 188.

34. See Ziva Amishai-Maisels, "Christological Symbolism of the Holocaust," *Holocaust and Genocide Studies* 3, no. 4 (1988): 457–481, and "The Jewish Jesus," *Journal of Jewish Art* 9 (1982): 92–101.

13 The Uses and Abuses of Photography in Holocaust-Related Art | MONICA BOHM-DUCHEN

Photographic images of Nazi atrocities have become one of the negative icons of the twentieth century—and look set to haunt us well into the twenty-first. Photographs taken at the liberation of the concentration camps were first released in the American and British press in a revelatory three-week period in April–May 1945. Public interest in these terrible images, as in the Holocaust generally, has ebbed and flowed. As Barbie Zelizer has pointed out, "first was an initial period of high attention that persisted until the end of the 1940s; then a period of relative amnesia that lingered until the 1970s; and finally a renewed period of intensive memory work that began in the late 1970s and continues until today."[1] Even in 1945, however, little importance was ascribed to factual accuracy in the labeling of the photographs; the tendency to generalize and universalize, render iconic rather than specific, was already underway.

In her seminal work *On Photography,* Susan Sontag spoke for many—if more eloquently than most—when she described her childhood encounter with these images:

> One's first encounter with the photographic inventory of ultimate horror is a kind of revelation, the prototypically modern revelation: a negative epiphany. For me, it was photographs of Bergen-Belsen and Dachau which I came across by chance in a bookstore in Santa Monica in July 1945. . . . When I looked at those photographs, something broke. Some limit had been reached, and not

> only that of horror; I felt irrevocably grieved, wounded, but a part of my feelings started to tighten; something went dead; something is still crying.[2]

Given these photographs' indisputable status as "ethical reference points," it is hardly surprising that many artists have felt compelled, both visually and morally, to make use of them in their own work. Yet, as Sontag herself admits,

> The sense of taboo which makes us indignant and sorrowful is not much sturdier than the sense of taboo that regulates the definition of what is obscene. And both have been sorely tried in recent years. The vast photographic catalogue of misery and injustice throughout the world has given everyone a certain familiarity with atrocity, making the horrible seem more ordinary—making it appear familiar, remote . . . inevitable. At the time of the first photographs of the Nazi camps there was nothing banal about these images. After thirty years [and how much more so, after more than fifty], a saturation point may have been reached. In these last decades, "concerned" photography has done at least as much to deaden conscience as to arouse it.[3]

If, therefore, one concurs with Sontag's view of the matter, it should come as no surprise that artworks that rely too heavily on the iconography of the photographs—especially if the artists are not themselves Holocaust survivors—have a distinct tendency to appear secondhand and inadequate, crude, overexplicit, and predictable. Some, however well-intentioned, even fall into that troubling category of "Holocaust kitsch," adding little or nothing to our perceptions of the Holocaust's meanings except for a note of embarrassment, if not distaste. Clearly, some account has to be taken of the differing levels of sophistication and knowledge in the viewing public. Where ignorance is the issue, explicitness, if not outright didacticism in the form of posters, documentary exhibitions, or educational books may well be appropriate. But art, I would suggest, has other roles to play.

Even the fact that the artist is a Holocaust survivor—as in the case of Zoran Music, Isaac Celnikier, and Ronny Abram, to name but a few—cannot guarantee an appropriate response on the part of the viewer when confronted with painted or drawn images of piles of corpses or near-corpses, images known to most of us only through photographs. The problems of communicating the sheer scale and intensity of the suffering, and of avoiding any hint of aestheticization, let alone voyeurism or dubious eroticism, persist. Many survivor artists would undoubtedly concur with Karol Konieczny's heartfelt assertion that "my drawings ought not to be subjected to scrutiny and aesthetic artistic criticism. . . . I wish them to be considered a living and shocking document of a world of horror and torment."[4]

Yet the situation is by no means as clear-cut or as simple as Konieczny suggests. In contrast, the recollections of Zoran Music, a survivor of Dachau (and an artist of far greater international stature and reputation than Konieczny), make it clear that the relationship between extreme suffering and beauty is necessarily intimate and unsettling:

> I drew in a state of frenzy, morbidly clutching my scraps of paper to me. I was dazzled by the hallucinatory grandeur of these fields of corpses. . . . I was haunted by the desire not to betray these diminished forms, to render them, as precious as I saw them, reduced to bare essentials. And I felt the irresistible urge to draw, so that this tremendous and tragic beauty might not escape me.[5]

In his 1970s series of paintings and prints, pointedly titled *We Are Not the Last,* he returned to the iconography of his camp drawings, which do indeed recapitulate much of the imagery of the photographs—of which, of course, Music himself had no need. The most moving and paradoxically the most troubling of these images are the most understated: those which merely hint at the vast numbers of victims, depicting a few in relative detail and hesitantly sketching in the contours of the rest. Aesthetic and emotional restraint, which compels the viewer's imagination to fill in the empty spaces, can—in the right hands—be far more devastating in its effect than a more explicit rendering of horror.

When the artist is not a survivor, the issue is more problematic still. A series of monumental, luridly colored mixed media works of the late 1980s, all rather disconcertingly titled *Untitled,* by the American Protestant artist Robert Morris (of former Minimalist fame), quite explicitly incorporate silkscreened copies of camp photographs into neo-baroque, apocalyptic compositions that exemplify the pitfalls of such an approach. Not only can such works be accused of a kind of morbid sensationalism; a deeply disturbing eroticism rears its head as well. This is most glaringly evident in a work from this series that makes use of a photograph of the corpse of a beautiful young woman lying partially naked, startlingly reminiscent of Edvard Munch's provocative *Madonna,* from the 1890s. In its original context, this was a photograph taken in Bergen-Belsen of a young mother lying dead alongside the bodies of her two young children. Interestingly, the image of the woman—unlike that of the two children—did not appear in the press immediately, suggesting that its erotic charge made it seem inappropriate for publication.

Other types of archival photographs have lent themselves, less contentiously perhaps but no less problematically, to incorporation into contemporary works of art. If the photographic images of mounds of bodies haunt us, they do so collectively (that is to say, it would be difficult to single out one photograph above all others). In contrast, there are a handful of less explicitly appalling images, which, perhaps precisely for that reason, have acquired the ambivalent status of icons both unforgettable and sanitized. One such is the moving but slightly ambiguous image of the little boy with upstretched arms taken in the Warsaw Ghetto, onto which it thus seems possible to project all manner of emotions. Another is the famous photograph taken by Margaret Bourke-White of recently liberated inmates of Buchenwald standing impassively behind barbed wire. A notable example of the problems attendant on any aesthetic incorporation of such images is American-Jewish artist Audrey Flack's 1976–77 hyper-realist painting titled *World War II (Vanitas),* in which a rather heavy-handed symbolic vocabulary associated with the Vanitas tradition of still-life painting sits uneasily with the photographic element in the work (by Bourke-White), its psychological separateness from the rest of the imagery and its distance from the artist's own life experience implicit in the fact that it features as a black and white reproduction in a book. (The contrast between the black and white documentary image and the garishly colored paint brings to mind a comparable interplay of monochrome and color, monochrome representing the past, color the present—albeit employed to very different effects—in Natan Nuchi's *Book Installation* and Shimon Attie's *Writing on the Wall* series, both discussed later on in this essay. A more famous instance of the use of this device can be found in Spielberg's film *Schindler's List.*) Flack's own claim that her "idea was to tell a story, an allegory of war, of life, the ultimate breakdown of humanity . . . to create a work of violent contrasts of good and evil . . . of opulence and deprivation"[6] reveals a well-meaning naiveté and a tendency to an oversimplistic didacticism that is all too common among artists intent on making a portentous general statement about the Holocaust.

A refreshingly analytical and visually arresting exploration of the ultimately equivocal status of the camp photographs within contemporary culture is to be found in a recent work by Natan Nuchi. To date, Nuchi—the Israeli-born child of a Holocaust survivor, who currently divides his time between Israel and New York—is best known for his haunting paintings of emaciated single figures set against a somber, abstract, and spatially ambiguous backdrop. Although the source of these images is unmistakable and specific, the images themselves become hieratic and emblematic, their implications universal. The Holocaust victim becomes all victims, Christ-like in his suffering, his nakedness the ultimate challenge to the post-Renaissance western tradition of the heroic male nude. Always lucidly self-aware, Nuchi himself has described his "paintings as commentary and the photographs as the scriptures." His more general statement that "I believe that the problem of how not to dilute and domesticate the harshness of the Holocaust by too much restraint, too many symbols, metaphors or recognizable icons on the one hand, and how not to participate in a crude 'horror show' on the other, will render no artist's achievement free from some measure of failure" should stand as a salutary reminder to us all.[7]

A wish to pursue these crucial issues further has recently prompted Nuchi to create a monumental work titled *Book Installation.*[8] This takes the form of a

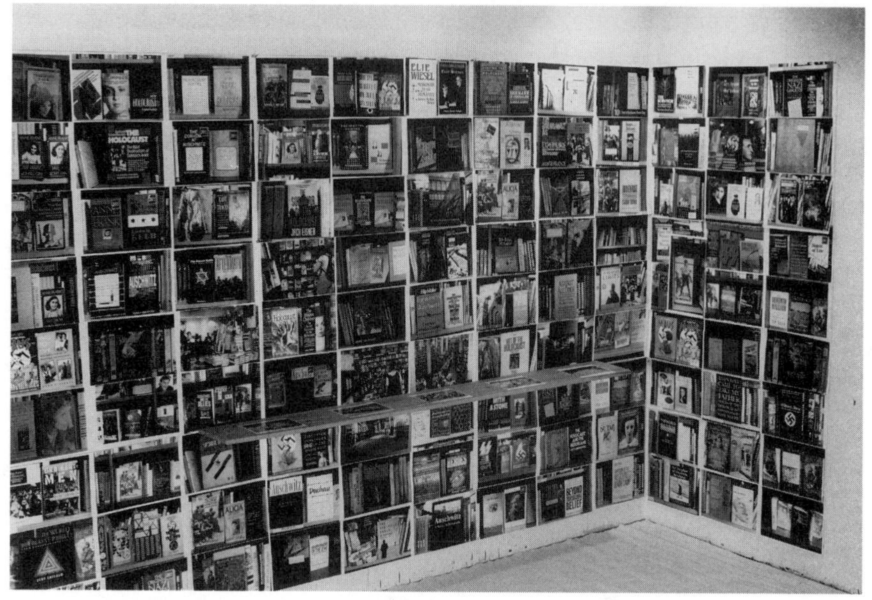

13.1 Natan Nuchi, *The Holocaust in the Market*, 1997, composite color photograph, wooden shelf, 5 b/w documentary photographs (8' × 12' × 4'3"). Courtesy Natan Nuchi.

wall, nine feet by sixteen feet, comprising approximately one hundred color photographs, taken in New York stores, of the covers of books and videos on Holocaust-related subjects. In the midst of all this, on a real shelf jutting out into real space, are exhibited five documentary black and white photographs taken by an American soldier at the liberation of Buchenwald. Unlike the wall, these are only visible from close up. This is clearly a wry but deeply serious commentary on the commercialization, trivialization, and—literally—"packaging" of the Holocaust, in which the role of photography too is subjected to scrutiny.

Nuchi's own heartfelt statement is worth quoting at length:

> The abundance of objects and images in the market and their fast and constant change demand a relation which works by way of fast recognition and fast classification of images. As a result, symbols like the swastika and the Jewish star and icons like the face of Anne Frank, fences with barbed wire, the boy raising his hands in the Warsaw ghetto, the gate at Auschwitz, inmates in striped clothes etc. become substitutes for the experience of slow and deep communion. . . . The needs of the market become the doctrine of what is or is not acceptable to show outside the narrow confines of the specialized Holocaust memorial site. Harsh Holocaust images, which used to be the typical images representing the Holocaust, are rejected as inappropriate, in bad taste, or as

emotional blackmail when they appear unexpectedly in magazines, T.V., on book covers and in other public places. At the same time, seductive, ambiguous, bland images become the norm for Holocaust representation in advertising as well as art.[9]

Certain artists—and their numbers are increasing—have chosen to focus primarily not on images of the victims, but on images of or associated with the perpetrators. In some cases, the intention is overtly didactic: American-born Arnold Trachtman, for example, creates paintings based on a stark juxtaposition of photographically derived images of Nazi (and other) political leaders with the victims of their policies, using many of the graphic devices associated with prewar anti-Nazi propagandists such as John Heartfield. Produced long after, rather than before the event, these seem sincerely meant, but ultimately somewhat pointless.

Far more thought-provoking and subversive in their contemporary implications are the photographic images of fellow Americans Maciej Toporowicz and David Levinthal. The former's series of manipulated black and white photographs titled *Obsession* (displayed in poster form on the streets of Manhattan in 1994) force the viewer to take a critical look at the way the idealized Aryan image of the nude so beloved of Nazism (and embodied by sculptures such as Arno Breker's *Die Wehrmacht*) has survived into our own time and culture, notably in public advertising campaigns. Cryptic and ironic, such works compel us to ponder the intensely problematic relationship between aesthetics and ideology, art and exploitation, both racial and sexual, the cult of the body and the myth of the master race.

In David Levinthal's 1993–94 series of large-scale color photographs collectively—and darkly—titled *Mein Kampf,* deliberately blurred tableaux of Nazi rituals and atrocities recreated by means of toy plastic figurines form a powerful and deeply unsettling meditation both on the dangerous allure of Fascism, then and now, and on the impossibility of unmediated access to the past. For reasons touched on earlier, I would suggest that those works which depict the perpetrators do that job well, while those that depict the victims display a crude grotesqueness that verges on disrespect, even parody. Natan Nuchi's comment that the photographs of the bodies of Holocaust victims are among the very few things in contemporary culture that cannot be treated with irony seems apposite here.[10]

In very different fashion, Arie A. Galles, the son of survivors, also makes powerful use of material appropriated in part from Nazi sources—namely, aerial reconnaissance photographs of the camps—to create a series of spectral drawings in charcoal and white conté crayon, collectively and suggestively titled *Fourteen Stations.* As in the case of Natan Nuchi's paintings, this reference to Christ's suffering coexists with the specifically Jewish concept of the Kaddish or prayer for the dead. Each drawing is named after a concentration camp, in alphabetical order (in accordance with the Hebrew alphabet) from Auschwitz-Birkenau to Stutthof. On another level, these works throw sinister light on the technological efficiency of the Nazi killing machine; on yet another, they explore and exploit the uneasy relationship between attractive, seemingly abstract form and terrifying content.

Between 1988 and 1992, German artist Jochen Gerz, better known for his controversial counter-monuments, created a series of large-scale wall panels incorporating photographs and text titled *It Was Easy.* Part of a politicized conceptual tradition that also, in very different contexts, includes artists such as Victor Burgin and Barbara Kruger, Gerz here juxtaposes seductive monochrome photographs of abstracted fragments of the natural world (branches, clouds, and so on) with blackly ironic and deliberately shocking verbal statements ("It was easy . . . to hate . . . to make soap out of bones . . . to win . . . to plunder the loot . . ."). On one level, Gerz clearly speaks as the conscience of a guilty people; on another (irrespective of whether or not this is morally acceptable), he implicates us all, forcing us to consider the nature of complicity in evil.

Family snapshots and portraits, unbearably poignant reminders of happier times, frequently—and perhaps too readily—become raw material for contemporary artists dealing with the Holocaust. Generically speaking, much of the power of such imagery depends on the paradox that, for all photography's apparent ability to stop time in its tracks, it cannot ultimately fail to smack of mortality. As Susan Sontag confirms,

> All photographs are memento mori. To take a photograph is to participate in another person's (or thing's) mortality, vulnerability, mutability. Precisely by slicing out this moment and freezing it, all photographs testify to time's relentless melt.[11]

If this fact lends a melancholy frisson to our perception of all photographs, how much more cruelly this applies to prewar photographs of Holocaust victims.

The list of (mostly second-generation) artists who incorporate photographs of their own families' past lives into their work, often in the form of ambitious mixed media installations or assemblages, is a long one. Polish-born, Dutch-resident Ania Bien and Americans Gabrielle Rossmer and Grace Graupe-Pillard number among those who use such sources in visually striking, technically inventive, and thought-provoking ways. Although the urge to restore individuality and dignity to the victims of the Holocaust, to remember not just their deaths but their lives, is understandable and utterly justifiable, in the hands of other artists too many of these artworks end up looking more or less the same, relying—however good the artist's intentions—on a fragmented collage technique that exudes a bittersweet nostalgia, a dwelling on the past that often lapses into self-indulgence.

The work of Christian Boltanski stands somewhat apart in this context. Unusual in the late 1980s for being a major international figure dealing with an otherwise unfashionable subject and for publicly admitting his espousal of sentiment, even sentimentality, he has undoubtedly been a major influence on many of these other artists. Significantly, Boltanski has criticized Robert Morris's appropriation of camp photographs as "sacrilegious."[12] His own approach is certainly more oblique—although not, it might be argued, any less presumptuous. Unlike most of the artists who incorporate intimate domestic photographic imagery into their work, Boltanski appropriates photographs of people unrelated to him; his relationship to them is comparatively distanced and detached. His deliberate enlargement, and hence blurring, of the original photographs of groups of Jewish schoolchildren, taken in the 1930s, serves to rob the children of their individuality while enhancing their symbolic power as icons of lost innocence, lost childhood, and lost life.

The poignancy and resonance of works such as *The Festival of Purim* (1988) and *Altar to the Chajes High School* (1987) are hard to deny. Yet the fact that Boltanski used similar photographically based devices in other works both before and after these (*Les enfants de Dijon* of 1973, for example, and *The Archives—"Detective"* of 1988–89), which contain no overt Holocaust references but exploit the smell of mortality endemic to the photograph—and, moreover, in the case of the latter work, blur the visual boundaries between victims and perpetrators—seems problematic. How, then, is one supposed to differentiate between the pathos of childhood, the passing of lives in the natural order of things, and the inconceivable brutality of death during the Holocaust?

To what extent, we are compelled to ask, does the integrity of such artworks depend on the knowledge that the documentary material is indeed what it purports to be? (The recent furor caused by the revelation that Binjamin Wilkomirski, author of *Fragments: Memories of a Wartime Childhood,* is not in fact a Holocaust survivor brought these issues dramatically into the limelight.) My own feeling is that while artists, not being historians or archivists, have the right to take certain liberties, to manipulate their raw material in a way denied to the latter, the moral boundaries can indeed easily become blurred.

A more analytical and cerebral approach to the role of prewar photographs can be found in the work of the American Nancy Ann Coyne. *Sites of Memory* is a politically sensitive installation project which depicts the life stories of thirty Holocaust survivors who have chosen to return to their native Vienna. As Coyne herself writes, "The work is a form of social archeology combining oral history, portrait photographs of individuals in their living rooms and the collection of survivors' personal photographs and documents as a method of excavating Holocaust survivors' buried, hidden and often fragmented memories and narratives."[13] Of particular interest to her is the question of "the photograph as an object of memory"—the historical images for their role as visual evidence and *aide-memoires,* the contemporary portrait photographs for what they reveal about each person's reestablishment of a sense of identity in present-day Austria. Central to the project, therefore, are thirty specially constructed photo albums displayed on reading tables and lecterns, narrating how survivors' photographs were saved.

As already indicated, many of the most thought-provoking artworks produced by artists born since the Second World War are those which do not look backward in mourning or nostalgia (although the need to mourn and to remember, of course, rightly persists), but which grapple instead with the legacy of the Holocaust in the present, "the contemporary reality of the Holocaust," which, as James Young succinctly puts it, "is not the event itself, but *memory* of the event, the great distance between then and now, here and there."[14] Indeed, the whole concept of cultural memory, in which the Holocaust occupies a pivotal position, has become a central issue in much contemporary art practice and theory. Not surprisingly, given the greater sophistication of photographic theory in recent years and the increasingly widespread recognition of the complexity of the photographic image, photography is often a crucial component of such work.

It is precisely the unsettling relationship between present and past, presence and absence, that American artist Shimon Attie seeks to address in his impressive series of photographs titled *Writing on the Wall.* Resident in Berlin in the early 1990s, at a time when the very fabric of the city was undergoing radical transformation, he combed the archives there for photographs of prewar German-Jewish street life in the working-class, orthodox quarter of Scheunenviertel, formerly in East Berlin, which he then slide-projected, wherever possible, onto the very geographical locations where the original photographs had been taken. Once done (and the process itself can be seen as a kind of "happening" or form of installation art), what remains is a haunting series of photographs that people contemporary Berlin, rendered in hallucinatory color, with the black and white ghosts of its murdered population. Past and present collide, fulfilling Attie's aim of "interrupting the collective processes of denial and forgetting."[15]

For some years now, German photographer Henning Langenheim has taken seemingly deadpan, "straight" black and white photographs of sites of Nazi atrocities throughout Europe. Collectively titled *Memorials,* the series quietly alerts the viewer to the complexities and ironies of the ways in which the Holocaust is remembered. Although visually compelling, the images which dwell on the grim and fragmentary physical remains are tinged with a note of romantic melancholy that some might see as inappropriate to the subject. More incisive, and ultimately more devastating, are those which highlight the apparent ordinariness of these places today, the way in which these sites have been rendered banal, anodyne, fit for tourist consumption. English photographer Robin Dance is one of several others who work in a similar mode. So very low-key and understated is his approach, however, that any hint of the irony that makes Langenheim's work so memorable is easy to overlook.

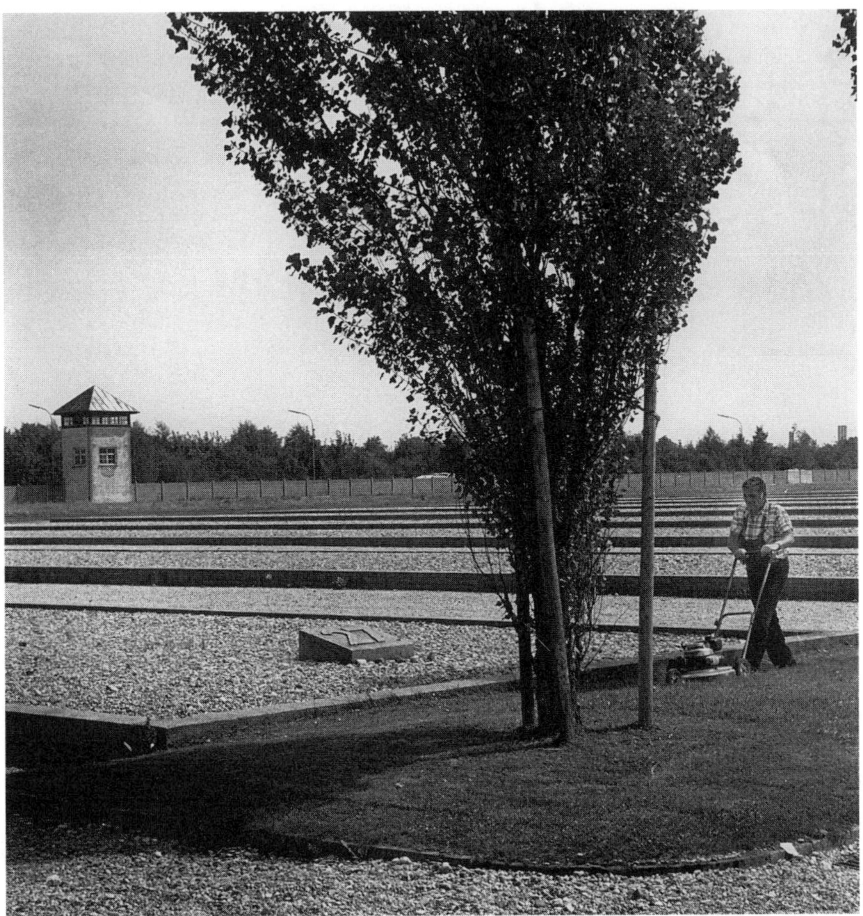

13.2 Henning Langenheim, *Dachau 1987: Grass,* from Memorials series, b/w photograph (30 × 37.5 cm). Courtesy Henning Langenheim.

This unsavory, yet perhaps inevitable, transformation of concentration camps into tourist attractions, and the concomitant fetishization of relics, has not gone unnoticed by artists. Iraqi-born German resident Mona Yahia, for example, went so far as to create a fold-out series of colored, almost "pretty" picture postcards of the death camps, titled *KZ Tours* (1988)—a gesture of breathtakingly bad taste that nonetheless makes an important point. Israeli-born Naomi Salmon takes seemingly matter-of-fact close-up black and white photographs of the artifacts displayed in Holocaust museums around the world, which provide a telling commentary on the way such objects are rendered both unbearably vivid and impossibly distant, simultaneously eloquent and mute.

Another approach favored by certain artists has been to focus on photographic images of everyday objects—trains, chimneys, showers—rendered

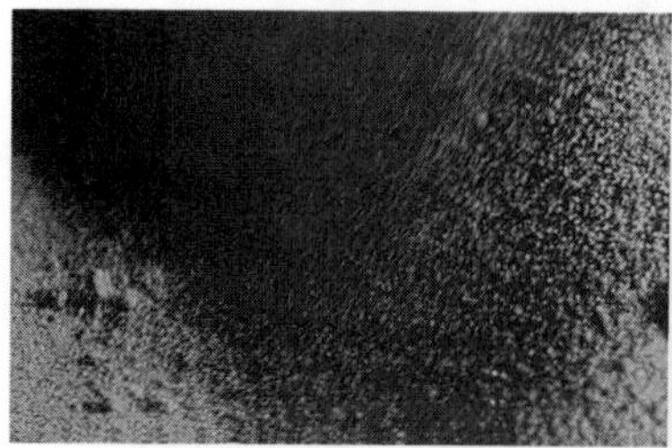
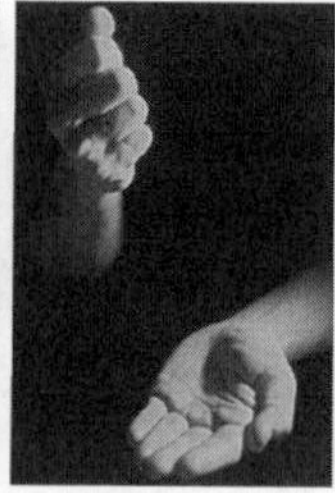
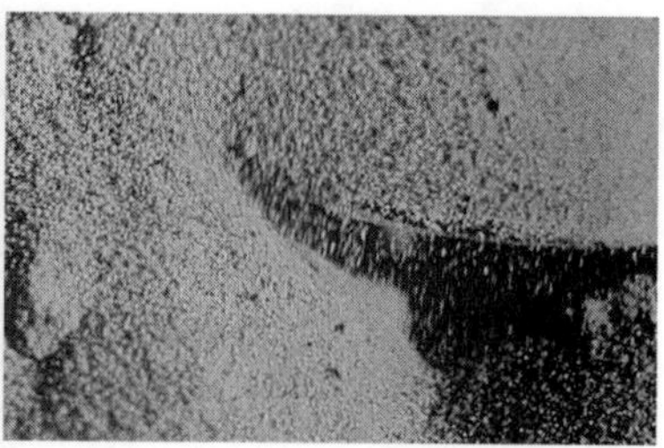

13.3 Lily R. Markiewicz, *Places to Remember 11*, 1995, photo-sound-installation (detail), 2 b/w and 1 color photograph on canvas (120 × 474 cm). Courtesy Lily R. Markiewicz.

sinister in the present by their past association with the Holocaust. *De Natura (Humana)* of 1992, for example, by Canadian artist Peter Krausz, consists of a series of deliberately out-of-focus, unnaturally green color photographs of a naked man in a public shower. In the context of the rest of Krausz's work in other media, much of which concerns itself more explicitly with the Holocaust, the generalized sense of vulnerability and menace evoked by the series takes on more specific implications. Similarly, in her series of tinted and texturally manipulated photographs titled *Prayer by the Wall*, second-generation American artist Debbie Teichholz uses the culturally resonant triptych form to juxtapose photographs of fields, railway lines, and piles of logs taken in Hungary and Israel in the early 1990s:

> As I walk through a field of trees cut for logging, my vision metamorphizes them into discarded corpses. As I smell the freshly turned-over, rich, amber rows of Israeli earth, I think about the rows of train tracks, and I still hear the silent screams.

Her approach to iconography bears out Sontag's thesis:

> I have chosen not to use archival images as symbols because I feel these images, which belong to our collective consciousness, often have a distancing effect on the viewer, because they are so recognizable and therefore emotionally dismissable.[16]

Focusing more overtly on issues of self-definition, Lily R. Markiewicz, the German-born child of survivors, now resident in London, has over the last ten years or so evolved a sophisticated symbolic vocabulary to explore the complex issue of post-Holocaust female identity. Photography is central to her practice, whether in the form of film or video, or of still photographs, often combined with sound, grouped together to create a total environment. In *Places to Remember II* (1995), large, tantalizingly abstracted and fragmented images of sand—contained, spilled, and shifted—are accompanied by a cyclical, ambient recording of her own voice, which for the most part deals in poetic and nonspecific terms with issues of dislocation and alienation; but by the unexpected and abrupt inclusion of the word "Jew" roots the haunting generalities in a highly specific context—that of a member of the "second generation" attempting to come to terms with the legacy of the Holocaust. Her most recent installation is even more allusive. *Promise* (1998–99) incorporates large-scale monochromatic photographs of bodies immersed in water, evoking a state of limbo in which sensations of pleasure and terror, confinement and release, exile and belonging coexist. In Markiewicz's own words:

> Mine is an exploration of an aftermath, of a past which has become a present, of the absence of a traceable reality, which has become the presence of memory. I am not concerned with the Holocaust directly, the event, its causes, reasons and details. I am concerned with the ripples, the ramifications, the consequences and our perceptions of it—our place "in it."[17]

Another less cerebral approach has been to use contemporary photographic imagery of a highly personal, often autobiographical nature. Artists who do this are often less intent on making general statements about the significance of the Holocaust than on exploring, on a symbolic and often allusive level, its emotional and psychological effect on one artist, one family now. Yocheved Weinfeld—notable also for being one of the first artists to concern herself primarily with the suffering of women in the Holocaust—was born in Poland in 1947, the daughter of survivors, and emigrated to Israel at the age of ten. Since the 1970s, much of Weinfeld's work has taken the form of deeply disturbing mixed-media images, in which, by photographing herself reenacting traumatic episodes from her family's past, she problematically casts herself in the role of Holocaust victim. Pesi Girsch, who lives in Israel but was born and raised in Germany until the age of fourteen, also self-consciously creates theatrical photographic scenarios that relate—albeit more obliquely, and with a distinctly surreal touch—to her own experience as a child of survivors. Using family members and friends as her—strikingly sculptural—models, her haunting black and white photographs resonate with a multiplicity of cultural references and archetypes, in which the memory of the Holocaust plays a crucial part.

A 1991 series of carefully staged black and white photographs titled *Parents* by Susanna Pieratzki, also of German-Jewish origin, depicts her parents, both of them survivors, in a sequence of symbolically significant poses, and accompanied by symbolically significant props that relate to their life experiences. Each photograph is given a number and a title—such as *Birth, War, Remembrance*—that allude to a terrible, yet elemental, life cycle. *War,* for example, depicts Pieratzki's father in striped pajamas, facing away from the camera, eight wire hangers dangling behind his back—a reference to the eight siblings he lost in the Holocaust. The series as a whole speaks eloquently of ordinary human beings who have managed to retain a great inner strength

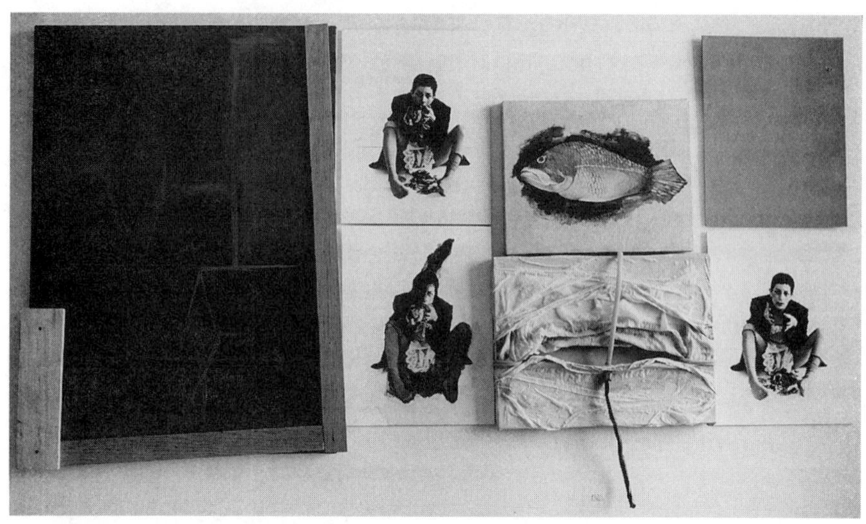

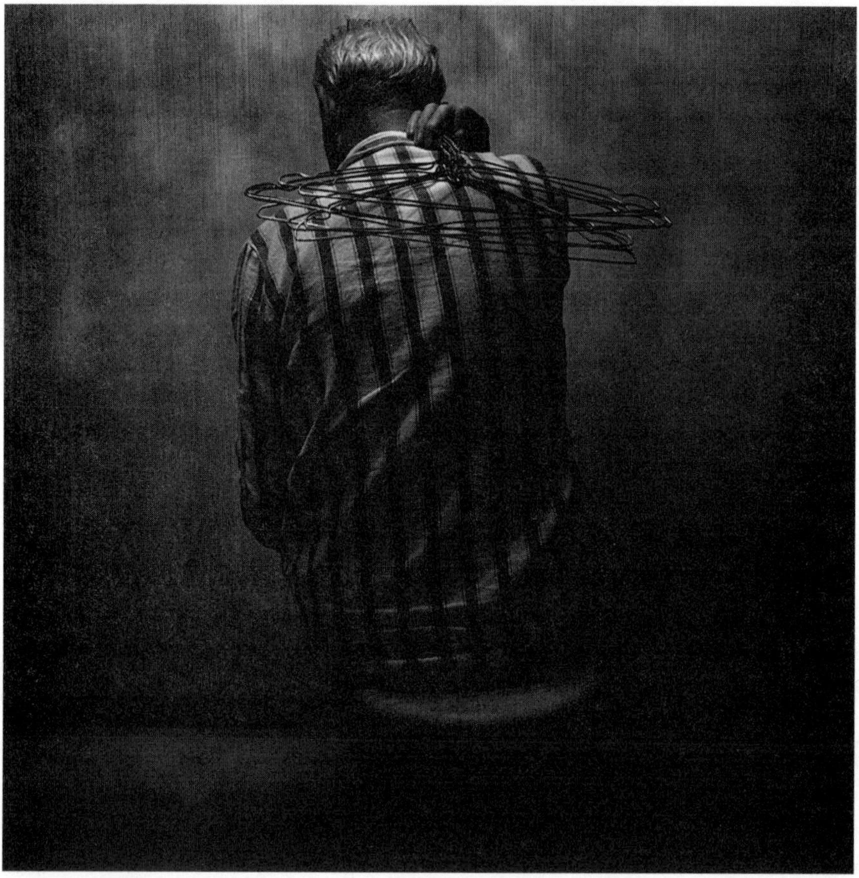

and beauty in spite of—perhaps because of—their great inner sadness; and of a daughter's immense respect and tenderness for the parents she can never hope fully to understand.

Photography, then, is a crucial component in a great deal of serious contemporary art dealing with the Holocaust. There is clearly room for a multiplicity of approaches—some, however, as we have seen, more contentious than others. Works that favor the factual and documentary, over and above the aesthetic, undoubtedly have an important role to play in helping us to remember for the future. Conceptual works that offer, among other things, an intellectual critique of the (formerly unchallenged) testimonial credentials of the photographic medium force us to confront and reflect upon deeply problematic issues. Lastly, works that make use of photography but unashamedly employ the devices of art—symbolism, imagination, fantasy—are, I would suggest, equally valuable for the new and often startling light they cast on aspects of a subject that continues both to haunt and to elude us.

Notes

1. Barbie Zelizer, *Remembering to Forget: Holocaust Memory through the Camera's Eye* (Chicago: University of Chicago Press, 1998), 14.

2. Susan Sontag, *On Photography* (New York: Farrar, Strauss and Giroux, 1973), 19–20.

3. Ibid., 20–21.

4. Letter from Karol Konieczny to Janina Jaworska, quoted in Janet Blatter and Sybil Milton, *Art of the Holocaust* (London: Pan, 1982), 142.

5. Quoted by Michael Gibson in "Tua Res Agitur," in *Zoran Music: We Are Not the Last—The E. B. Birch Collection,* texts by Jean Clair and Michael Gibson (Saint-Thomas, Virgin Islands: Everett B. Birch, 1988).

6. Quoted in Nelly Toll, *When Memory Speaks: The Holocaust in Art* (New York: Praeger, 1998), 65–66.

7. Natan Nuchi, "Artist's Statement," in *After Auschwitz: Responses to the Holocaust in Contemporary Art,* ed. Monica Bohm-Duchen (Sunderland: Northern Centre for Contemporary Art; London: Lund Humphries, 1995), 153–154.

8. This was featured in a group exhibition titled *Veiled Time,* comprising a number of exhibitions of contemporary art on Holocaust-related themes held in five different venues in New Jersey in 1999. A catalogue was published by the New Jersey Commission on Holocaust Education.

(Facing page, top)
13.4 Yocheved Weinfeld, *Eat. Eat. In the war they even ate potato peels,* from Stories for Little Children, 1981, mixed media. Courtesy Yocheved Weinfeld.

(Facing page, bottom)
13.5 Susanna Pieratzki, *War,* from Parents series, 1991, b/w photograph (26.5 × 26.5cm [10½" × 10½"]). Courtesy Susanna Pieratzki.

9. Natan Nuchi, unpublished artist's statement.

10. Bohm-Duchen, *After Auschwitz,* 153–154.

11. Sontag, *On Photography,* 15.

12. Nancy Marmer, interview with Boltanski, 2 November 1988; quoted in Marmer, "Christian Boltanski: The Uses of Contradiction," *Art in America* 77, no. 10 (October 1989): 169–180, 233–235.

13. Nancy Ann Coyne, "Sites of Memory," unpublished project abstract.

14. James Young, *The Texture of Memory: Holocaust Memorials and Meaning* (New Haven, Conn.: Yale University Press, 1993), 344.

15. Bohm-Duchen, *After Auschwitz,* 147.

16. Quoted in Stephen C. Feinstein, "Artistic Responses of the Second Generation," in *Breaking Crystal: Writing and Memory after Auschwitz,* ed. Efraim Sicher (Urbana: University of Illinois Press, 1998), 213; see also Teichholz's artist's statement in *Witness and Legacy: Contemporary Art about the Holocaust,* ed. Stephen C. Feinstein (Minneapolis: Lerner, Minnesota Museum of American Art, 1995), 45.

17. Lily Markiewicz, note accompanying *Silence Woke Me Up Today,* videotape, 1989, quoted in Feinstein, "Artistic Responses," 204.

Part IV

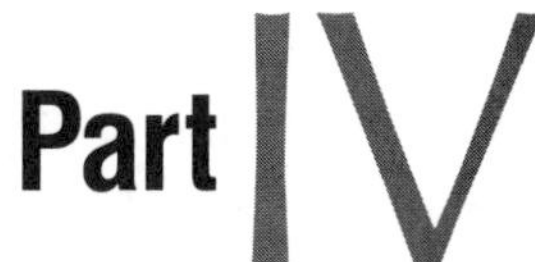

National Expressions of Remembrance

14 The Jewish Museum, Vienna

A Holographic Paradigm for History and the Holocaust

REESA GREENBERG

One of the most pressing issues facing Jewish museums is how to represent the relatively recent murder of millions of Jews and the physical, psychic, and cultural damage to millions more. Unlike Holocaust museums, which are devoted to chronicling and memorializing a constellation of events related only to the Holocaust, Jewish museums recount centuries of Jewish history prior to the Holocaust and an increasingly longer post-Holocaust period. In Jewish museums, should the Holocaust be presented in the same manner as other historical events, or should it be given special treatment?

When the Jewish Museum in Vienna reopened on Dorotheegasse in 1995, its chief curator, Felicitas Heimann-Jelinek, expressed the obvious: "The return to the old classical museum tradition is not possible after Auschwitz."[1] This museum was the first of its kind when it first opened, in 1893. In 1938, when the Nazis forced the museum to close, Vienna's Jewish population numbered 180,000. During World War II, 65,000 were murdered and 100,000 exiled. Of the 12,000 Jews residing in Vienna in 1992, five hundred were native Austrians or Hungarians; the rest, Russian and Iranian refugees or Israelis. In Heimann-Jelinek's words, "Above all, the main interest of a post-1945 European Jewish Museum should be to motivate its visitors to ask themselves the right questions."[2] This essay examines how the Jewish Museum in Vienna uses highly unusual installations and atypical processes of physical interaction with its displays to encourage its visitors to ask "the right questions" about a particularly traumatic time in Jewish history.

Post-Holocaust Jewish museums usually contain exhibits of Jewish ritual objects and some depiction of Jewish history: Biblical, national, local, or Zionist. Both components are present in the Jewish Museum in Vienna. In other Jewish museums, however, the Holocaust as part of Jewish history is usually represented in only one exhibit area and presented as part of a larger chronological sequence,[3] whereas in Vienna the Holocaust is invoked on all three floors of permanent displays. The result is a multitemporal and multidimensional viewing experience. Visitors reencounter the same time period repeatedly in different locations and configurations throughout the museum. Time is multilayered, fluid, metaphoric, reminiscent of the interaction between memory and real time that occurs in non-museal life. As visitors move through the museum, their bodies and their minds continually shift between different time periods, experiencing them from varying vantage points, continually crossing that fine line where past and present intertwine.

The Jewish Museum's all-pervasive presentation of the Holocaust is housed in the eighteenth-century Palais Eskeles. At the Jewish Museum in Berlin, built between 1997 and 2000, Daniel Libeskind envisaged a similarly integrated museum experience, but Libeskind was able to build references to the Holocaust into the architectural fabric of a new building. Libeskind's architectural envelope, with its ripped-apart Star of David ground plan and profile, destabilizing tilted floors, and vast, dark, empty chambers, determines a viewer's experience, making it impossible to forget that his is a post-Holocaust Jewish museum, regardless of what exhibits are installed in the interior. At the Jewish Museum in Vienna, the architecture of the mansion was more or less a given and, in an inversion of what happens in Berlin, it is the permanent displays throughout the museum that gently insist on reminding viewers of the Holocaust and the ephemerality of history.

The displays themselves are based on a twofold temporal strategy. The past and what was lost are materialized on the ground and second floors through the relative emptiness of the galleries and what Heimann-Jelinek identifies as a *pars pro toto* methodology in which a part of the collection represents the whole. Conversely, the use of a design aesthetic based on installation art of the 1970s and '80s in all the permanent displays is a constant reminder that the museum exists in a post-Holocaust culture. The result is a courageous postmodern Gesamtkunstwerk, a hybrid of traditional Jewish museum and Holocaust museum, where visual and kinesthetic means evoke aspects of historical trauma and situate it in the viewer's present.

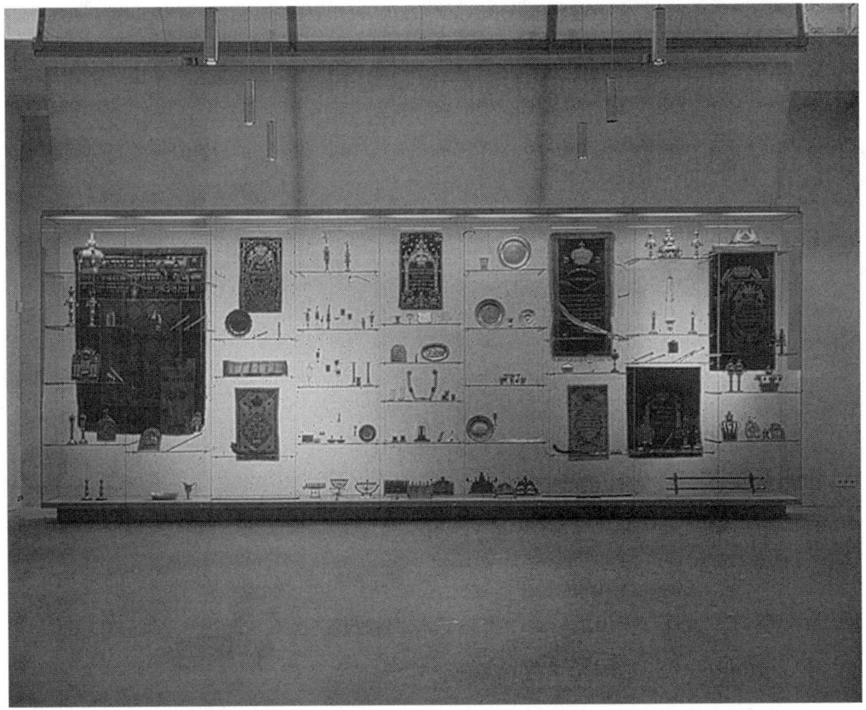

14.1 Max Berger Collection, ground floor, installation view, 1998, Jewish Museum, Vienna, 1995. Courtesy Jewish Museum, Vienna.

What follows is an attempt to reconstruct the experience of visiting the museum floor by floor. What I transmit is only partial and destined to fail, for no account, visual or verbal, can convey the complexity of the experience of constantly changing physical viewpoints, the random order in which the exhibits can be seen, and the continual shifts in inner perceptions unfolding over the time of a visit.

The Viennese firm Eichinger oder Knechtl remodeled the building, which has three floors of permanent displays (ground, second, and third) and one floor for temporary exhibitions (first).

A large inner courtyard, glassed over at the height of the third floor and covered with a velarium, serves as reception hall, auditorium, and main-floor gallery. The courtyard is deep inside the building, beyond the bookstore and café and not immediately visible on entering the museum, easily missed if one does not know it is there. But even if at the start of the visit museum-goers bypass the courtyard, with its vitrine of Judaica collected after 1950 and a related installation by artist Nancy Spero, it is visible from the next two floors. Interior windows, an architectural design which moves visitors along the open

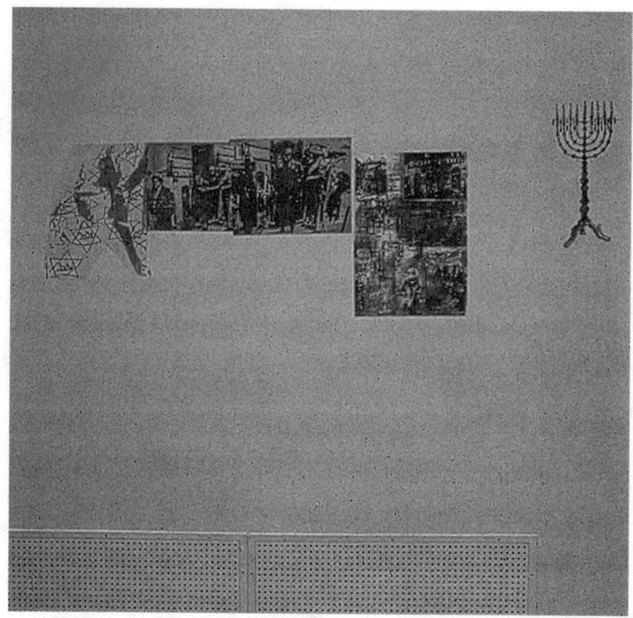

14.2 Nancy Spero, *Remembrance/Renewal,* 1996, ground floor segment with amalgam of images related to the Holocaust, Jewish Museum, Vienna. Courtesy Nancy Spero/Jewish Museum, Vienna.

courtyard wall as they enter galleries on the upper levels, and Spero's multistory installation make it impossible for visitors to escape the themes of liturgy and loss at the center of the building. The courtyard, then, is the literal and metaphoric core of the museum. Its almost hidden placement echoes Vienna's tendency to hide or circumnavigate a Holocaust history the city would prefer to forget; seen from so many perspectives, the courtyard represents the impossibility of forgetting a trauma that so altered the city's life.

From the upper floors, visitors encounter the courtyard displays from afar and at various angles. At ground level, the initial experience of the exhibits is at closer range and frontal. The long vitrine, running almost the full width of the courtyard's far wall, contains approximately a hundred ceremonial objects selected from the ten thousand items which Max Berger, a Polish Jew, collected when he moved to Vienna after World War II. Unlike many displays of Judaica in Jewish museums, which present a number of variations on a theme as testimony to the richness and diversity of pre-Holocaust Jewish ceremonial life, the Berger vitrine is comparatively sparse, with relatively few examples of each type of object.[4]

The sparsely filled, flat-wall, single-vitrine design of the installation responds, to some degree, to the physical demands of its location in a multipurpose

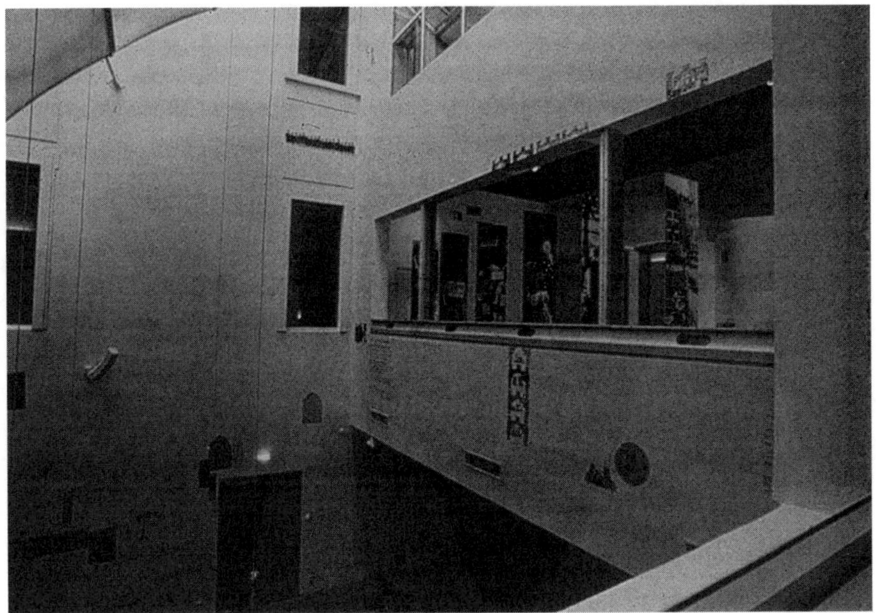

14.3 Nancy Spero, *Remembrance/Renewal,* 1996, installation view, Jewish Museum, Vienna. Courtesy Nancy Spero/Jewish Museum, Vienna.

room. The two-dimensional, uncrowded presentation is functional, the most sensible way of ensuring maximum protection for these jewel-like objects when the space is filled with chairs or people, and an ideal device for teaching about Jewish rituals. At the same time, the frontal display and studied placement of each artifact underscore its emblematic character and nonfunctionality in a post-Holocaust world.

The Berger artifacts are arranged according to the Jewish calendar's highly articulated sense of time. Viewers pace along the vitrine, following the cyclical rhythms of the holidays and festivals. Yet, because of the glass shelves, the objects appear to float in space, suspended, timeless. If their formal, frontal, flat presentation is in keeping with their ceremonial nature, the same aesthetic also connotes the decorum of memorial plaques. An adjacent, unobtrusive wall label connects the collection to the Holocaust: "In memory of my father Roman, my mother Anastasia, my sister Lace, and my brothers Salomon and Jehoshua, who were murdered in Auschwitz and Treblinka." The words of the label are pivotal in ensuring that what might appear to be a benign, didactic display of museum artifacts related to Jewish rituals is read in conjunction with the Holocaust and humanized. The museum corpus stands in for the murdered bodies of those who can no longer use the artifacts. Each object in the vitrine becomes a surrogate for a Holocaust victim and viewers are made to face this reality, literally.

The label for the vitrine, roughly printed directly on the wall in rust red, wraps around the corner and spreads out horizontally on the adjacent wall, where it links with a set of images from Spero's 1996 *Remembrance/Renewal* placed further along the wall to the right. Spero's amalgam consists of found and reworked photographs of a 1938 Gestapo raid on the Viennese Jewish community, Jews forced to wash the streets of Vienna on their knees, the destroyed Leopoldstadter Tempel, anti-Semitic slogans on a coffee house, and yellow cloth for Star of David armbands. The stamped, photographic montage, situated between the inscription on the left and a stenciled image of a candelabrum from the Berger collection on the right, is the only section of Spero's seemingly unstructured composition positioned at eye level, placed there at the insistence of the artist in spite of the museum's concerns about the mural's conservation.[5]

Because the Berger inscription and Spero's images are at the same height, viewers read the two displays as continuous, a single timeline. Yet any sense of fixed temporality, any sense of being fixated in a given time period, is confounded when prewar liturgical art is displayed with a postwar glass wall installation aesthetic, or when prewar photographs are altered and hand-printed so that they can be read as contemporary images. Both the museum and the artist renounce any attempt at reconstructing the time of the trauma, insisting on a contemporary interaction with the past and a face-to-face relationship with the viewer.

Spero further confounds a fixed sense of time in other direct and indirect references to the Holocaust placed higher up in various locations around the courtyard. For example, she sets the words from Albert Drach's (1902–1995) contemporary poem "Ballad of the Race of the Moon" opposite the Berger Collection on the first-floor level, so that as viewers turn away from the vitrine and look up—at the moon?—they are confronted with words that speak of the irrationality of anti-Semitism. To the left of Drach's poem, Spero enlarged an image taken from a fifteenth-century woodcut portraying the 1421 burning of Viennese Jews who refused to be baptized. The juxtaposition functions to break down any Enlightenment notions of progress with regard to the treatment of Jews in Vienna.

In addition to obvious Holocaust references, Spero alludes to what has been lost in Vienna's cultural and social life after 1938 through images of the composer Gustav Mahler; the dancer Hanne Wassermann, who disappeared after emigrating; the dancer/sculptor Gertrud Kraus, who emigrated to Israel in 1935; the opera star Fritzi Massary, who died in 1969 in Hollywood (who wraps around a corner); and the 1935 women's team from the Macabee Sports Club, who are lined up in a row over a side window. These active, secular

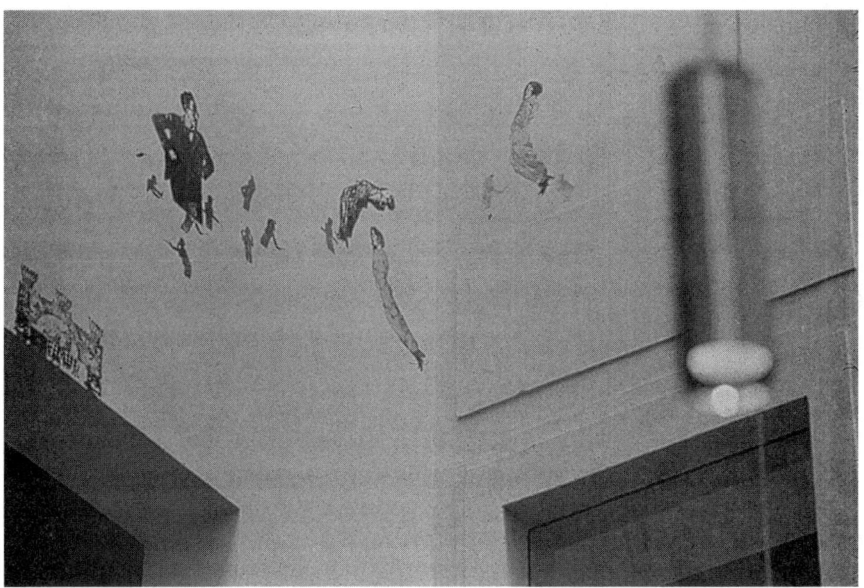

14.4 Nancy Spero, *Remembrance/Renewal,* 1996, installation view, Jewish Museum, Vienna. Courtesy Nancy Spero/Jewish Museum, Vienna.

portraits are juxtaposed with images with a religious theme. For example, to the right of the Drach poem, fifteenth-century German-Jewish women read from the Passover Haggadah and fourteenth-century Jewish women bake matzo.

Spero's spatially complex composition, impossible to grasp in its entirety from any one position, coupled with the isolation of her delicately stamped and overstamped images, underscores her refusal of grand or received narratives. She deals in fragments of time, moments rather than stories, allowing the visitor to piece together meaning. Discussing her earlier use of expansive compositions of intermittent elements, Spero says the forms are "not merely spreading out in space so the viewer couldn't see everything at once, but [for] the possibilities of a peripheral vision as a disruption of a way of looking at art. I was very interested in doing something wild and different—figures that couldn't be caught by the male gaze."[6] Spero understands that a different way of seeing is essential if one is to reconfigure the past, that seeing differently is predicated on a different relationship between the body of art and viewers' bodies.

What Spero didn't know at the time she devised her composition was the importance of varied eye movement as a tool for healing trauma. According to the theories developed in conjunction with EMDR therapy (eye movement desensitization and reprocessing), a person's eyes tend to lock in a given position when experiencing or reexperiencing trauma, freezing the event or events in a neural network. Moving one's eyes in a different pattern while reviewing past trauma breaks the frozen physiological and psychological neurologic connections and allows the trauma to be processed and integrated in the present, though precisely how and why eye movement is so effective in unblocking and transforming trauma is unknown.[7]

Spero's images of active women from many historical periods also help heal trauma. Because of the range of female types included, including Holocaust survivors, the museum space in Vienna functions as a "good enough mother,"[8] able to permit and contain the psychic pain of the Holocaust without producing an aesthetics of victimhood or redemption and without feminizing suffering. What Irit Rogoff calls "the production of pathos" is absent, as is the construction of an image of the forever mourning or mournful daughter.[9]

Some post-Holocaust Jewish museums, notably the Jewish Historical Museum in Amsterdam, attempt to redress the absence of women in their permanent displays in a manner characteristic of first-stage feminism: they insert women into traditional historical accounts. Another strategy is to include expressionist figurative art by women to represent the feminized, symbolic, or emotional component of Holocaust exhibits. Ursula Liebruchs's archetypal sculpture *Prisoners* (1955) in the Frankfurt Jewish Museum and Han Mes's mural-size allegorical painting *The Battle of the Forces of Good and Evil, The Triumph of Justice* in the Jewish Historical Museum in Amsterdam are included to represent nonverbal suffering. By contrast, Spero's Holocaust-related images are not substitutes for women mourners, nor are they isolated from history.

Spero's *Remembrance/Renewal* is the only commissioned art at the Jewish Museum in Vienna.[10] As the title of the cycle suggests, the work fuses processes of remembering and renewal, joining the two in the same physical space either by a slash, which combines separate words into an amalgam, or by sequentially printing and overlapping unrelated images, which then read as inextricably linked. Spero's generic title refers as much to events and erasures which led to the formation of the Berger Collection and its subsequent presentation at the Jewish Museum as to processes which exclude women from and reinsert them into Jewish history.

In Vienna, the museum's integration of the Berger Collection with a visual history of Jewish women reformulates representations of the Holocaust and museal Jewish masculine and feminine spheres. First, the museum's incorporation of the vitrine's liturgical objects traditionally associated with the Jewish masculine sphere into the realm of the feminine and the decorative implies the fungibility of Jewish gendered realms.[11] Second, women are depicted as active agents in religious and secular life. Their bodies are portrayed in movement, at work and at play. Third, there is no history of Jewish men anywhere in the museum. There is only a fragmentary history of Jewish women that takes the form of an artist's construction, a format that draws attention to the constructed character of all histories, including histories of the Holocaust.

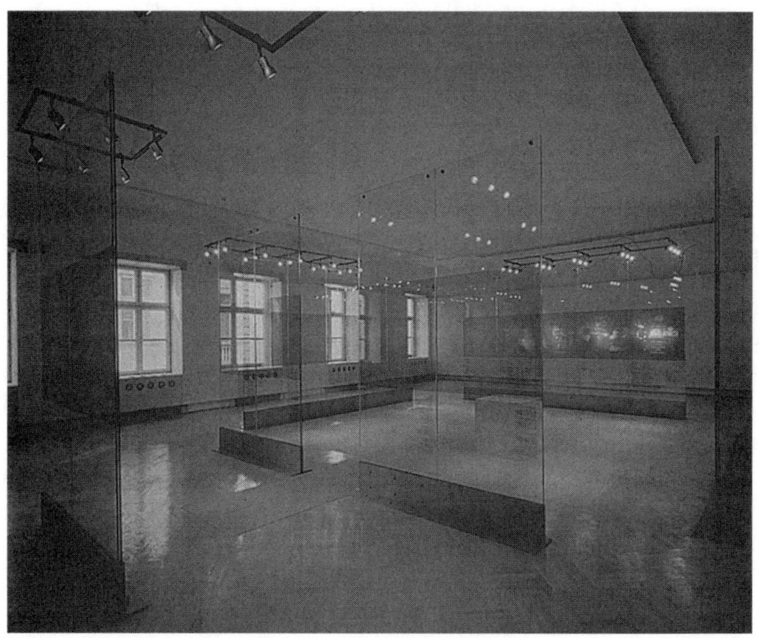

14.5 The historical exhibition, third floor, installation view, 1998, Jewish Museum, Vienna, 1995. Courtesy Jewish Museum, Vienna.

The second-floor permanent display usually takes visitors by surprise. Designed by curator Felicitas Heimann-Jelinek, architect Martin Kohlbauer, and holographer Julian Fischer, the installation consists of a glass-walled chamber placed off-center within a large, otherwise empty renovated space. The transparent room within a room is constructed of twenty-one free-standing transmission hologram plates conveying a synoptic history of Jews in Vienna. On this floor, the only other permanent display component is located outside the main exhibition room, down a corridor and off in a corner. There, in a tiny space, two computer terminals accessible to the public contain data on the history of the Jews since biblical times.

Heimann-Jelinek wanted this display, unlike the others in the museum, to "tell something about history without showing the historical object."[12] Although each hologram pictures objects in the museum's collection and the computers contain images of artifacts in the museum, there are no actual objects on the second floor. For Heimann-Jelinek,

> objects feign to hold some essence of the past, but in fact an object is merely a relic of the past, or even a relic of a certain part of the past. . . . It is just as lost as the past which it once belonged to. . . . In reality, only its empty shell has remained, for its "soul" has disappeared into history. The medium of the transmission hologram confronts this disappearance. It emphasizes history's withdrawal.

> Furthermore, it raises doubts about the absolute expressive value of the historical item and about the concept of "true" historical reconstruction.[13]

Holograms and computers portray objects at one remove. Their nonmaterial images frustrate viewing responses based on nostalgia or connoisseurship, two common responses in a museum. Because both media insist on the physical involvement of the viewer in ways that have not as yet become formulaic in the context of museum visiting, holograms and computers encourage the viewer to interact with history in different ways.

The very visibility of holographic images depends on the position of the viewer. From some angles, it appears as if there is nothing to see, a lack that Shelley Hornstein interprets as a vehicle for representing the enormous losses due to the Holocaust.[14] None of the holographic images are fixed or stable. None can be grasped or held. The holograms vary in size and orientation, present one moment, gone the next, in an analogy to visitors' relationship to history. The physical movement required of viewers, advancing and retreating, changing viewpoint angle, shifting from one side to another, is akin to the mental manipulations required to reformulate history and one's relationship to it.

Brief text labels on the floor provide some historical grounding. Viewers can read around the floor or use the labels as cues to the seemingly unrelated, free-floating, eerie, yellow-greenish apparitions suspended in three-dimensional space. Despite a chronological frame, there is no obvious chronology here. Viewers can enter and exit the hologram room at will through the various openings of the glass-walled repository, just as they do outside the museum when "visiting history" or thinking about the past. Space and time are fluid.

At times, the walls surrounding the hologram panels are used for temporary exhibitions. Sometimes they are painted red or black and appear very different from the photographs in museum publications. During these temporary exhibitions, the color and material on the surrounding walls visually merge with the glass hologram panels, creating a convergence of past and present.

Compositional devices such as isolation, montage, and repetition underscore the necessity for rethinking history. In one panel, a recent model of the seventeenth-century Vienna ghetto hovers ghostlike in the air, dislocated in time and scale from its origins. Throughout the installation, the almost futuristic look of the holograms implies a contemporary, prospective vantage point on the past, an alternative to the retrospective, reconstructive configurations usually used to represent history.

Holograms are more than a new imaging medium. The invention of holograms in 1965 inspired an entirely different way of understanding all matter and life forms. What is radical about holography is that any piece of the image will reconstruct the whole. Holography, a form of lensless plate photography, makes an image by recording the interference pattern of the wave field of light scattered by an object. "When the photographic record—the hologram—is placed in a coherent light beam like a laser, the original wave pattern is regenerated [and a] three-dimensional image appears."[15] In other words, the entire image is reconstituted from a fragment of the wave pattern.

In what has become known as the holographic paradigm or the holographic universe, neurosurgeons, quantum physicists, and mathematicians conceive of the universe as composed of frequencies or waves rather than particles or matter. In 1969, Karl Pribam suggested that the brain worked like a hologram because memory was not confined to any one anatomical part of the organ,[16] and in 1971, David Bohm hypothesized that the universe is organized holographically, with interpenetrating and interconnecting energy patterns, to explain nature's ability to regenerate itself. In the 1990s, holistic health practitioners devised practices of holographic healing, such as holographic memory resolution[17] and holographic repatterning, based on the premise that accessing a fragment of a trauma, usually in the form of a picture "freeze-framed" into our emotional bodies, is sufficient to let us work through the entire traumatic event, because each memory fragment bears the capacity to recreate the whole. A multisensorial process of release based on the visualization of three-dimensional images and the replacement of trauma-associated cues transforms the trauma.

The implications for a museum using holograms and holographic thinking to present the memories and the objects of history are profound, especially when what is displayed is filtered through the trauma of the Holocaust. On the second floor of the Jewish Museum, Vienna, the overall sense that something is missing, that something is different, that something is invisible; the holograms' ghost-like images; the references to earlier periods of intolerance and racial murder; the bolts of material from which the yellow Star of David armbands imposed by the Nazis were cut; the conjoining of the Austrian and Israeli flags are all fragments referring to the Holocaust. Although Heimann-Jelinek says she did not know of the holographic-universe theories or of holographic trauma resolution when she conceived the hologram installation, her incorporation of a *pars pro toto* methodology, the atypical physical engagement necessary to view the holograms, and the repatterning of Holocaust-type cues in a nontraditional aesthetic can be seen and experienced as a holographic museological experience with the potential for releasing some of the Holocaust's legacies.

If the presentation of the Holocaust is allusive and all-pervasive rather than narrative or chronological, the provision of a memorial for Holocaust victims on the second floor is equally so. The holographic plate room-within-a-room functions both as a space for remembering and as a tomb, not unlike the room/tomb designed by Rachel Whiteread in 1996 for Vienna's Holocaust memorial. Although situated outdoors, Whiteread's controversial white cast-concrete "library" also uses the compositional device of a contemporary structure surrounded by the architectural fabric of the past, here the contiguous seventeenth-century facades of the almost completely enclosed Judenplatz, to reference a third time frame, that of the Holocaust.[18] Like Kohlbauer's chamber, Whiteread's inner room is a void; but Whiteread's inside-out walls of inverted books are designed to be read from the exterior, while the holograms are best seen from within. Compared to the solid muteness of Whiteread's Judenplatz monument, Kohlbauer's transparent and fragile-looking glass room/tomb has more in common with I. M. Pei's 1989 Louvre pyramid, where glass walls reflect and mirror the surrounding nineteenth-century courtyard and viewers access the past by entering a contemporary mausoleum-like structure.

While Kohlbauer's glass plates are essential as the ground for the holographic images, the configuration of a glass room within an interior room is similar to a contemporaneous museum display project at Vienna's renovated Museum of Applied Art. There the Viennese architects Eichinger oder Knechtl, the firm responsible for the renovations at the Palais Eskeles, built an interior room to house and display the museum's collection of late-nineteenth-century furniture. In both the Eichinger oder Knechtl and Kohlbauer designs, the highly contemporary use of large, unarticulated walls of glass to form a three-dimensional space updates the museum vitrine, enlarging windows on the past into inner chambers of the mind, rhetorical spaces where memory resides and is activated. Through physical juxtaposition, different periods of time mentally coexist, seen and experienced simultaneously. The radically reduced size of the modern room within the historical room materializes spatial and temporal distance, encouraging viewers to associate the display with a mausoleum.[19]

At the Jewish Museum, Vienna, the museum-mausoleum implications expand to include both objects and people. Viewers enter the memory chamber and become part of the display, either seen by viewers outside the glass walls or reflected on the glass panels alongside the holograms inside the chamber. In the liminal zone created by the tomb/room, screen memories, reflections, and projections create a sense of suspended time in which the living present and dead past merge.

Upstairs, on the third floor, the attic, there is a different room within a room, one that also refers to a tomb. In a viewable storage area accessible to visitors, movable shelves crowded with artifacts from the museum's collection arranged according to object type are jammed together to form an impenetrable chamber in the center of the room. The arrangement, organized by curator Gabriele Kohlbauer-Fritz, while ordered, appears cluttered in what Ernst van Alphen has identified as a "Holocaust effect" and is reminiscent of Christian Boltanski's installations.[20] Presence here is predicated upon absence and archival clutter speaks of the disappeared.

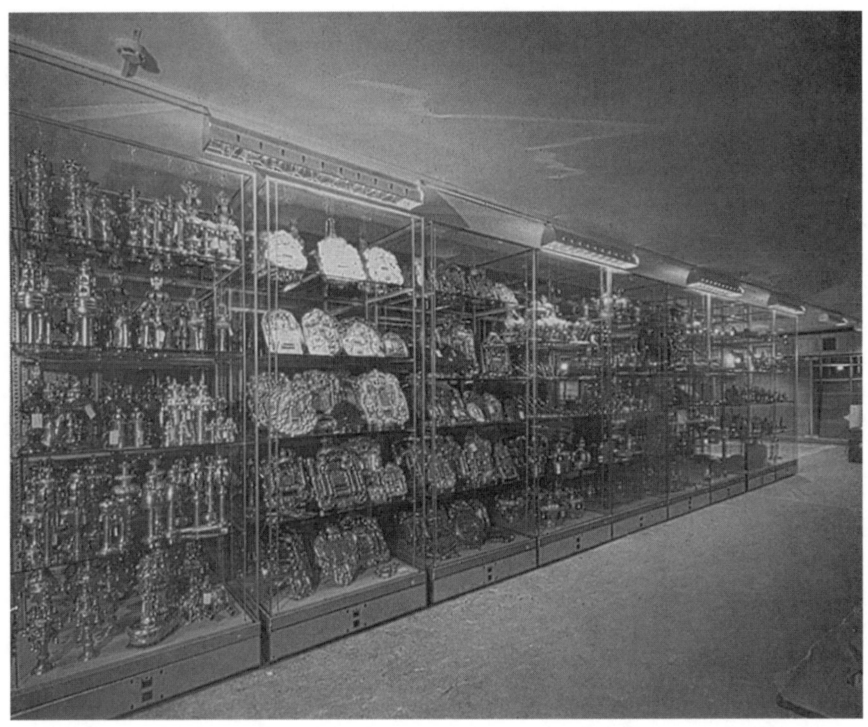

14.6 Viewable storage, fourth floor, installation view, 1998, Jewish Museum, Vienna, 1995. Courtesy Jewish Museum, Vienna.

The display is an unsettling amalgam of Schatzkammer (treasure room) and depot for abandoned objects. Abundance invokes the dispossessed and the dead. Viewers are simultaneously invited in to see what the museum has amassed and are intruders in a mausoleum dedicated to the former owners of what is on display.

Unlike the naturally lit, spacious ground and second floor permanent display areas, where everything exhibited is visible, the third floor is dark, cramped, crowded with layers and layers of partially visible objects. The outer shelves are the "presentation zone," the inner shelves, the "stacking zone" where uncatalogued museum objects are stored. Visitors sense they have entered a different sphere, a paradoxical area in which they are both given and denied access. The moveable shelves do not move. Once again, a sophisticated, highly contemporary approach to display is used as a device for commentary on the museum's relationship to the Holocaust.

Each floor of the museum is distinctly different in appearance yet linked by a minimalist approach to exhibition design and a single broad thematic: a post-Holocaust reexamination of history. The Jewish Museum in Vienna is not a place of nostalgia or celebration. It is not stuffed with artifacts; it does not construct a comprehensive narrative of the Jewish people from biblical times to the present; and it does not explain Jewish rituals in any detail. Instead, the museum radically reduces the number of artifacts on view and rejects a fixed chronological approach. The relative emptiness of the museum functions as a cue to what is not there; the mingling of time frames breaks down conventional notions of historical periods; the use of highly contemporary media and design points more toward the future than the past.

The all-pervasive importance of the Holocaust is implicit, felt throughout the building, as well as seen. Because there is so little text and so few artifacts, the Jewish Museum in Vienna has been criticized as being too dependent on viewers' having prior knowledge about the Holocaust to be effective as a place to learn about what actually happened.[21] The museum has also been criticized for the absence of any overt political content in the displays. At the museum, the underlying assumption is that most visitors do, in fact, know about the Holocaust, that experiential truth is as valid as narrative truth, that the past must be brought into the present, and that doing so does not mean the museum must be a pedagogic site. The extent of the protests against the inclusion of Jörg Haider's Freedom Party in the 2000 Austrian Parliament suggests that Austrians of all ages do know about the Holocaust, corroborating the Jewish Museum's belief that museums and art can work in less explicit ways. At the Jewish Museum in Vienna, the fundamental concepts associated with modernist museums have been jettisoned and a new museum paradigm, more in keeping with the post-Holocaust era, has been created.

Notes

1. Felicitas Heimann-Jelinek, "Memoria, Intelligentia, Providentia," in *Jewish Museum Vienna,* [ed. Felicitas Heimann-Jelinek and Hannes Sulzenbacher] (Vienna: Jewish Museum Vienna, [1996]), 130.

2. Ibid., 129.

3. An exception is the Jewish Historical Museum in Amsterdam, which in 1987 arranged the first section of its displays thematically.

4. At the Jewish Museum in Frankfurt, the Judaica displays designed by Mrs. Feldhammer soon after the museum opened in 1988 also use a limited number of objects. However, this installation—with its series of tableaux for each holiday, culminating in a Schatzkammer or treasury of Hanukah menorahs—is more theatrical in its lighting and spacing. By contrast, at the Jewish Museum, New York, and the Musée d'art et histoire du Judaisme, Paris, opened in 1998, the displays present as many variations of each object type as possible. In relation to the Holocaust, an aesthetics of absence indexes loss and an aesthetics of plenty demonstrates the "wealth" of the pre-Holocaust period.

5. Interview with Werner Hanak, organizing curator of the Jewish Museum Vienna's Spero project, 26 March 1999. Additional information about the project can be found in Werner Hanak and Widrich Mechtild, "Nancy Spero: *Remembrance/Renewal,*" in

Heimann-Jelinek and Sulzenbacher, *Jewish Museum Vienna,* 45–48. For information about other Spero work related to the Holocaust, see Jon Bird, "Survey," 55–60, 82–87, and Sylvère Lotringer, "Focus: Explicit Material, b," 98–109, in *Nancy Spero,* Jon Bird, Jo Anna Isaak, and Sylvère Lotringer (London: Phaidon, 1996).

6. Quoted in Bird, "Survey," 60.

7. See Francine Shapiro, *Eye Movement Desensitization and Reprocessing: Basic Principles, Protocols, and Procedures* (New York: Guilford, 1995). See also Philip Manfield, ed., *Extending EMDR: A Casebook of Innovative Applications* (New York: Norton, 1998), and Laura Parnell, *Transforming Trauma: EMDR* (New York: Norton, 1996). My thanks to Steve Vazquez and Chuck Lustfield, who introduced me to EMDR.

Precedents for using eye movement to affect the mind and body are found in Yoga, Ayurvedic medicine, and the contemporary neurological use of micro-movement to repattern brain activity. Some theories suggest that vertical eye movement is a vehicle for linking the chakras, points or centers of spiritual energy in different places in the body, while horizontal eye movement is a means of connecting the two hemispheres of the brain. There are questions about how EMDR works and doubts that it works at all. Currently, the efficacy of EMDR is under attack because no blind trials have proven that the reported changes are due to EMDR. See Carol Milstone, "The Finger-Wagging Cure" (*Saturday Night,* 18 August 2001, 22–28) for a discussion of the difficulties of accepting the treatment fully.

8. The phrase is D. W. Winnicott's and refers to a mother who can encourage a child's separation without terror during loss and detachment.

9. Irit Rogoff, in conversation with the author.

10. *Remembrance/Renewal* is a departure in Spero's Holocaust iconography. Spero's first Holocaust-related images are part of a 1966–70 gouache cycle protesting American involvement in Vietnam titled *The War Series: Bombs and Helicopters.* After 1974, Spero's war work concentrated exclusively on portrayals of women (*Torture of Women* [1974–76]) which, after 1978, she made with a stamp technique that facilitated her use and reuse of found images.

When Spero returned to Holocaust themes in the 1990s, she created temporary museum installations devoted to a single woman murdered for resisting the Nazis—various versions of the *Ballad of Marie Sanders, the Jew's Whore,* begun in 1991, and *Masha Bruskina,* initially developed for the 1993 Whitney Biennale. Spero's first work in a Jewish museum was a reformulation of *The Ballad of Marie Sanders/Voices: Jewish Women in Time* for the opening of the renovated Jewish Museum in New York in 1993. All of these installations combine text and found image photographs printed and overprinted directly on the wall, spread in what appears to be a random configuration over a vast surface.

At the Jewish Museum Vienna, for the first time, Spero combines Holocaust imagery with other Judaic themes and histories. Spero's isolation of Holocaust imagery from her other war work corresponds to a time when, according to Peter Novick in *The Holocaust in American Life* (Boston: Houghton Mifflin, 1999), American Jews without the ties of a common religion or shared histories increasingly turned to the Holocaust as the primary signifier of their Jewish identity.

Spero has said, "As a secular Jew I have never been very involved with religious objects. But people like me are more aware of this crisis of identity that came with the Holocaust" (Hanak and Mechtild, "Nancy Spero," 47). Spero's recent interest in the Holocaust can be placed in the same context of Jewish identity politics that gave rise to the 1995 American Holocaust Memorial Museum in Washington and the 1998

Museum of Jewish Heritage in New York: her focus on women and the Holocaust, though, introduces other dimensions to current American formulations of Jewish identity.

11. See Daniel Boyarin, *Unheroic Conduct: The Rise of Heterosexuality and the Invention of the Jewish Man* (Berkeley and Los Angeles: University of California Press, 1997) for a discussion of Jewish gender stereotypes.

12. Interview with Felicitas Heimann-Jelinek and Reesa Greenberg, Vienna, 6 October 1998.

13. Felicitas Heimann-Jelinek, "On the Historical Exhibition at the Jewish Museum of the City of Vienna," in Heimann-Jelinek and Sulzenbacher, *Jewish Museum Vienna,* 62–63.

14. See Shelley Hornstein, "Nothing to See: Private Mourning in Public Art," in *Memory and Oblivion* (Dordrecht, The Netherlands: Kluwer Academic Publishers, 1999), 1003–1110, a paper first presented at a session on modern memorials at the Twenty-Ninth International Conference of Art Historians, Amsterdam, 1996.

15. Ken Wilber, introduction to *The Holographic Paradigm and Other Paradoxes: Exploring the Leading Edge of Science,* ed. Ken Wilber (Boulder, Colo.: Shambhala, 1982), 6.

16. Our current understanding of memory is that we have a number of memory systems located in different parts of the brain. The amygdala forms and recalls strong emotion, especially fear; the hippocampus allows us to remember having been afraid; the medial temporal lobe is associated with implicit or nondeclarative memory and associative memory; and the basal ganglia are responsible for explicit memory and for motor skills.

17. Brent Baum, *The Healing Dimensions: Resolving Trauma in Body, Mind, and Spirit* (Tuscon: Healing Dimensions, 1997).

18. After numerous delays, work on Whiteread's Holocaust monument was inaugurated in late autumn 1999. To address one of the controversies about her memorial, the proposed library structure was moved one meter so as not to stand on the site of the bima—the platform from which the Torah is read—of the medieval Or Sarua Synagogue beneath. To satisfy other objections, Whiteread's memorial is to be augmented by a Holocaust museum in the medieval Mizrachi House, located on the Judenplatz, and five hundred square meters of underground archeological exhibition space devoted to the synagogue, which was destroyed in a 1421 pogrom. The resulting constellation constitutes what Shelley Hornstein called a "topography of horror," a term taken from the title of a session that she organized at the annual meeting of the American Society for Aesthetics in 1997 and which I extend to suggest that the mass murder of Vienna's Jews cannot be construed as an aberration. The mausoleum references of Whiteread's Holocaust monument room, contained as it is by the eighteenth-century facade walls of the Judenplatz, expand to include all victims of Viennese anti-Semitism. When the Judenplatz becomes a pedestrian zone, its museal character and affinities with other Viennese rooms within rooms will be more obvious.

19. See Douglas Crimp, *On the Museum's Ruins* (Cambridge, Mass.: MIT Press, 1984).

20. In his *Caught by History: Holocaust Effects in Contemporary Art, Literature, and Theory* (Stanford, Calif.: Stanford University Press, 1997), Ernst van Alphen describes the Holocaust effect of abandoned objects on shelves used with great effect by the artist Christian Boltanski in installations such as *Canada* (1988). It is entirely possible that museum installations using this presentational strategy were inspired by Boltanski's work.

21. Edward van Voolen, curator, Jewish Historical Museum, Amsterdam, in conversation with the author.

15 Memory Block

Rachel Whiteread's Holocaust Memorial In Vienna

REBECCA COMAY

> I am a sculptor: not a person of words, but of images and forms . . .
>
> —Rachel Whiteread

ABSENT INSTALLATION, INSTALLING ABSENCE

In January 1996, following an international competition initiated two years earlier by Simon Wiesenthal, Rachel Whiteread's project for a Holocaust memorial was commissioned by the city of Vienna to be erected on the Judenplatz, in the heart of the old Jewish ghetto. The unveiling was scheduled to take place on 9 November 1996—the fifty-eighth anniversary of Kristallnacht. Whiteread's project would be virtually the first explicit Austrian memorial to the Jewish victims of the Holocaust (with the exception of a notorious sculpture near the Albertinaplatz depicting a Jew scrubbing the pavement)[1] and effectively the first official acknowledgment of Austrian complicity in the genocide. As such, it was to put an end to a fifty-year silence regarding Austria's troubled relationship to its own Nazi past, and transform the terms of public discourse in a country which had, since the war's end, been comfortably accustomed to regarding itself as Hitler's first victim.

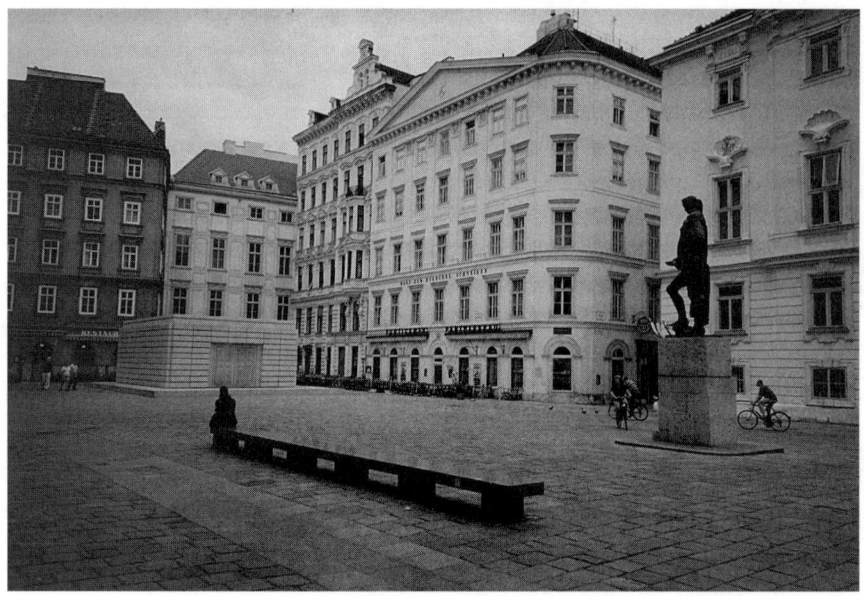

15.1 Rachel Whiteread, *Holocaust Memorial*, 2000, Vienna. Photo by Rebecca Comay.

The memorial—an austere rectangular block thirteen feet high and with sides of thirty-three and twenty-three feet, constructed out of multiple cast slabs of creamy gray concrete—was to resemble an inverted library. Sealed off and inaccessible, its impenetrable double doors would lack both hinges and handles: a hollow recess would display the negative imprint of the two missing doorknobs, whose shape would be accessible only to the hand which groped inside. With the exception of the doorway, the four vertical surfaces of the monument were to consist entirely of evenly mounted rows of tightly stacked modules, each containing the casts of twenty neatly aligned books, every book positioned with its spine turned inward, each nearly identical in height and thickness, with only the most subtle variations in the curvature and buckling of the pages of the individual volumes. The homogeneity of the structure—its internal modular repetition (reminiscent of the serial forms of minimalist sculpture and evocative too, perhaps, of the abstractly statistical nature of the deaths being commemorated), its rectangular regularity (the proportions of which in fact echoed the proportions both of the Judenplatz itself and of the rooms contained within its buildings), and, finally, its material consistency (its emphatic uniformity of color and surface texture, which again resonated chillingly with the creamy stucco of the surrounding buildings and with the freshly laid paving stones of the refurbished square)—would throw into stark relief the minute rhythmic variations which were introduced at the

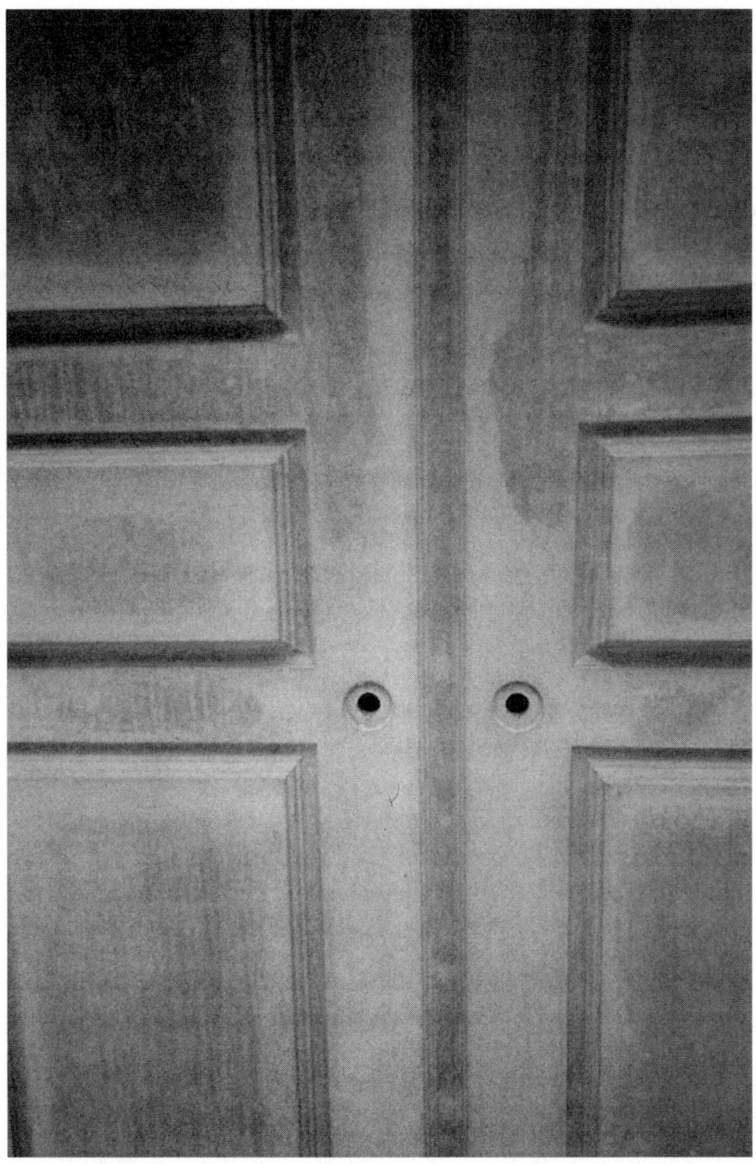

15.2 Rachel Whiteread, *Holocaust Memorial*, detail (door with hollow handle). Photo by Rebecca Comay.

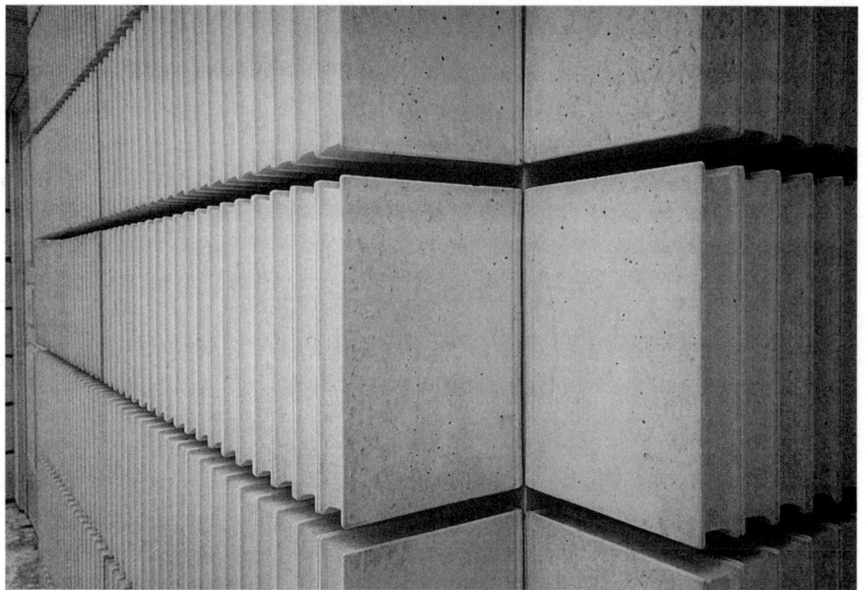

15.3 Rachel Whiteread, *Holocaust Memorial*, detail (rows of books). Photo by Rebecca Comay.

level of pattern (forty slightly different wooden book molds were arranged in varying combinations into individual rows of twenty volumes each, which were then cast in concrete and aligned and stacked in almost imperceptibly varying sequences), as well as the unpredictable effects of aging and weathering to which the porous concrete would be vulnerable. Blankly unreadable in itself, the library would nonetheless become a surface for unpredictable inscriptions—the work of rain and temperature, the spills of food and drink on the plinth—which would open it to a fragile future even while testifying to the frozen historical moment it embodied. (The inevitable vulnerability of the work to vandalism was a separate issue, which the modular construction of the monument—designed for easy dismantling—in part addressed.)

In its stony materialization of an absence—a solid void which evoked the signifying possibilities of the archive only seemingly to revoke them—the memorial continued the trajectory which Whiteread had been exploring from the very beginning of her career, but with a significant twist. Using the medium of casting to create palpable negations of objects through the materialization of the void surrounding them, Whiteread had for a decade been imprinting absence through the eerie presence of a medium which in its very obduracy and opacity evoked the persistence of a loss as intangible as it was insistent. From the various attempts to solidify the phantom spaces lurking around and under familiar domestic objects—the shadowy emptiness of a

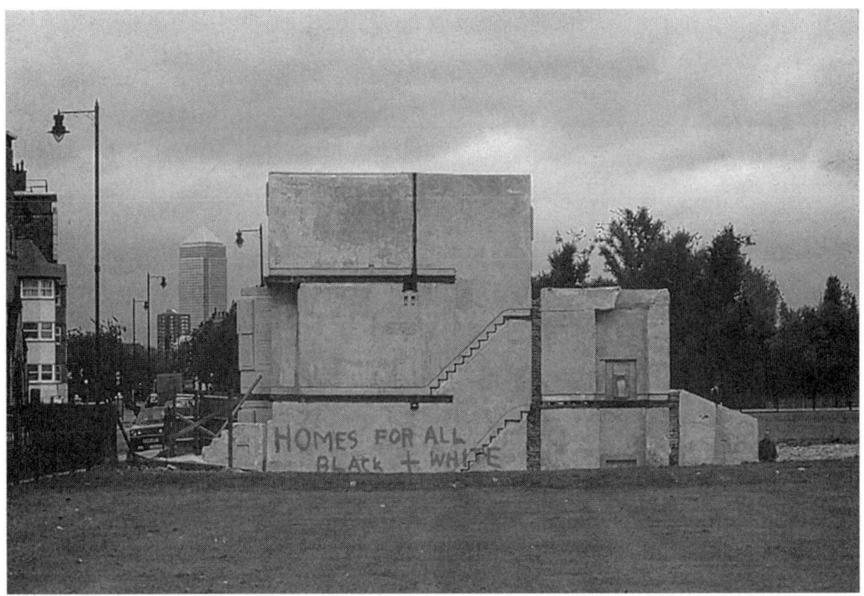

15.4 Rachel Whiteread, *House*, 1994. Courtesy Artangel. Photo by Sue Ormerod.

closet, the underside of a mattress, the hollow space beneath a bathtub, the space beneath the floorboards—to the audacious transformation of the interior vacuum of a condemned house in the East End of London into the congealed density of reinforced concrete (a project which was to win the artist the Turner Prize in 1993, which was in turn condemned to demolition, and which, during the long Thatcher years, was to raise burning questions about the issues of public space, public art, and the right to public housing), Whiteread had been systematically exploring relations between inside and outside, secrecy and disclosure, private and public, loss and reparation. By imprinting the ignored, occult spaces around and within everyday objects which were themselves frequently in the abject position of cast-off detritus—the stained and droopy mattress, the expropriated slum house—her work had seemed to point simultaneously to the persistence of memory and to its ultimate limit. In the context of Austria's perplexing relationship to its own troubled past—the closed book its history had seemingly become—Whiteread's proposed memorial appeared at once enigmatic and strangely literal.

An intense controversy immediately followed the jury's unanimous decision. Shared outrage made strange bedfellows of those from every side of the political and cultural spectrum—Jews and radical right-wingers, liberal democrats and businessmen—as the objections and complications proliferated. Fueled by the archaeological challenges arising from the recent excavations of the medieval synagogue which had been discovered underlying the projected site of the memorial (many argued that the ruin itself was a sufficient memorial to the fate of Austrian Jewry), intensified by the inevitable bureaucratic red tape of city politics, compounded by devastating electoral losses for the Social Democrats (and the upsurge of the extreme right) in the municipal elections of 1996, a cascade of obstacles led to a lengthy suspension of the work's installation. Created offsite, in modular components, the monument languished in a warehouse for some four years while its fate continued to be debated. Inauguration dates were repeatedly announced only to be canceled at the last minute, the complications continued to swirl, until finally, to everyone's surprise—not least the artist's—and in a poorly attended ceremony marked by the conspicuous absence of key national representatives, including Jörg Haider, notorious leader of the Austrian Freedom Party (FPÖ), the monument was unveiled on the Judenplatz on 25 October 2000.

Today, almost a year later, the violent history of the polemics remains largely invisible on the quiet square. Newly laid paving stones cover the once gaping pit of the excavations; a nearby doorway leads without fanfare to a subterranean archaeological museum exposing the charred remains of the medieval synagogue (once thought to contradict the very need for a Holocaust memorial); and an eerie harmony of texture, shape, and color ties together the sculpture and its surroundings. Despite the almost ubiquitous local response to the edifice—"very modern . . ."—what is perhaps most chilling is the extent to which the monument snugly chimes with the locale. In an inner core largely untouched since the fin de siècle—Hans Hollein's notorious mirror-clad Haas Haus (1990), a hideous shopping center facing the Gothic splendor of the Stephansdom, marks the one exception in this somewhat fossilized museum of an inner city—Whiteread's edifice assumes a startling familiarity. Almost demure in its proportions, exquisitely coordinated with its surroundings, the monument seems surprisingly at home. And precisely from this familiarity arises its unexpected power to shock.

Only two inconspicuous signs mounted in the vicinity of the monument give any indication of the nervous circumstances of its installation. On one nearby wall, sandwiched between a furniture shop and a hair salon, an unsigned inscription, dated 29 October 1998, speaks of the history of Christian anti-Semitism in Vienna, praying for salvation through forgiveness. Another wall, next to the archeological museum, displays a bilingual notice, in Hebrew and German, dated April 2001—thus six months after the installation—and signed by the Jewish community of Austria, expressing gratitude to the righteous Austrians who had risked their lives to help Jews escape the genocide. If the monument speaks of an absolute moment of illegibility, its very existence has already produced an anxious accumulation of writing; as I write this, however, no graffiti has come to deface the work itself.

FACE-OFFS

One of the most intriguing proposals to come out of the storm that raged during the five long years leading up to the work's installation was put forward in the summer of 1996 by Johannes Hawlik, the environmental spokesman for the Austrian Peoples' Party (*Volkspartei*). Hawlik did not simply reproduce any of the arguments which had been persistently advanced from every conceivable direction to show just how and why Whiteread's monument would be in the end inappropriate for the Judenplatz: the shopkeepers' arguments (bad for business); the residents' arguments (the loss of parking spaces); the security arguments (the inevitable invitation to neo-Nazi provocation); the archaeological arguments (the risk to the integrity of the recent excavation of the medieval synagogue: the sad irony of burying one memorial in order to erect another); the economic arguments (the escalation of the budget necessary to accommodate both the archaeological site and the proposed memorial); the aesthetic arguments (the alleged incompatibility of the cold concrete cube with the architectural splendor of the site: the predictable "hunk of concrete" [Betonklotz] insult,[2] which in this case, it must be said, had turned rather quickly into the chilling characterization of the "Jewish bunker" as a *Fremdkörper* [foreign body] defacing the organic perfection of the baroque square); even the theological arguments ventured in some quarters (the affront to the Book and the Name posed by this shrine to illegibility and anonymity);[3] the identity-politics arguments (the easy stereotyping of the people-of-the-book, the ignoring of all the doctors, the bankers, the workers, the housewives . . .); and so on. Nor, indeed, as "people's representative," did Hawlik invoke any of the vexing issues which inevitably accompany any discussion of public art—whose monument? which public? which people? Hawlik's objection ostensibly arose simply from the fact that there already was a monument on the square—specifically, a bronze statue of the eighteenth-century dramatist and Enlightenment philosopher Gotthold Ephraim Lessing—leading him to deliver a rather striking one-liner with the distinct ring of a Western: "This square's not big enough for two monuments."[4]

Rather than piling this "environmental" consideration onto the mounting heap of arguments as to why Whiteread's project should be modified, relocated, or, as was usually argued, scrapped altogether, Hawlik proposed, perhaps in jest, that the Lessing monument instead might well be carted off—where? it was, after all, meant to be a "symbol of tolerance"—to the Vienna Rathaus (city hall).

Erected by Siegfried Charoux in 1934, melted down for ammunition by the Nazis in 1939, rebuilt and reinstalled in the Morzinplatz by the same artist in 1968, relocated to the Judenplatz as recently as 1982 after Charoux's death, the Lessing memorial had in any case long since become a simulacrum of itself, had already relinquished all claims to site-specificity, authenticity, and singular originality, and could well stand to function as the displaced remainder and reminder of the by now rather frayed values of civic rationality, consensus, and debate. Much like the self-multiplying ring in the famous parable told by Lessing himself in *Nathan the Wise* (a parable already recycled from Boccaccio), the statue had already forcibly submitted to the logic of mechanical reproduction, mass-production, self-substitution, and was perhaps ready to announce to the world the lesson of Lessing himself in his explication of the paradoxical truth of monotheism as the very undoing of every hierarchy or exclusivity—what Lessing calls the "tyranny of the one."[5]

Whether facetious or not, Hawlik was perhaps on to something. A shortage of space would have been the least of the issues. Nor is the most interesting tension between the two memorials the rather banal opposition between abstract cube and figurative statuary, a contrast which the jury was to note approvingly in their official endorsement of Rachel Whiteread as the winner.[6] And the tension goes beyond the obvious irony of casting Lessing, the seer of the Enlightenment, as the witness to an object which would seem simultaneously to insist on the promise of enlightenment and to spell its ultimate relapse into barbarism. Poised high above the projected monument, the statue had by the summer following the announcement of the competition become a kind of bystander to the growing rubble field as excavations unearthed the charred remains of the medieval synagogue, which had been burnt, along with so many of its members, in the famous pogrom of 1421. The Gesera, a contemporary account, reports that during the atrocities marking the regime of the Habsburg duke Albrecht V, following accusations that Jews had desecrated the Host, hundreds of poorer Jews were sent down the Danube in rudderless barges; 160 Jewish children were sold on the condition that they be converted forcibly to Christianity; almost another hundred Jews hid in the synagogue before eventually committing mass suicide to avoid slaughter or baptism; and six months later the remaining survivors of the Viennese Jewry were burned alive outside the city walls. A fifteenth-century wooden plaque at one end of the square commemorates the event with a depiction of Christ's baptism and a statement comparing the water that cleansed the body of Christ to the fire that cleansed Vienna of its Jews. The stones of the destroyed synagogue were soon enough incorporated into the expansion of Vienna University (whose Catholic faculty had in fact spearheaded the persecution). If the closed doors and silent volumes of Whiteread's inverted library seem to describe the essential relapse of culture from a site of openness and emancipation to one of simultaneous exclusion and confinement, it is worth recalling that for the Haskalah (Enlightenment) Viennese Jews of the late eighteenth century, after the emancipation under Joseph II, it was specifically learning and enlightenment, high German literary culture, which was to break down the barrier or "hedge" of the ghetto, and this precisely by allowing the Jews to assimilate or "melt"—as free rational individuals—into the surrounding populace.[7]

Occupying the highest point on the square and facing the sealed doors of the stony library, the figure of Lessing would also be forcibly in the position of viewing from above what would be strictly invisible to the actual passerby. The inverted ceiling rose, which is exposed to Lessing's eyes alone, would seem to function in a rather overdetermined manner. A mounting for a missing light-fixture, evoking a source that no longer casts a light and which indeed itself recedes from visibility, the rose in the first place suggests a traumatic blind spot at the very origin of enlightenment. A seemingly decorous, decorative moment, a circle and center interrupting the rigid rectangularity of the structure, the rose would appear furthermore to function equally as a secret artist's signature. Here we find the quintessentially inside-out mnemonic index by which Whiteread's work has become known: everything that paradoxically reinstates as "style" the very technique of casting as the "without-style"—everything, indeed, that marks this monument as unmistakably a Whiteread. Such a secret flourish would trace the paradoxical signature to that which speaks of the absolute effacement of every proper name or signature. But the ornament also has a tangible engineering function: drainage. If Whiteread had drilled holes in her earlier bath pieces in order to puncture the suffocating intensity of their coffin-like interior—to provide, in her words, an opening for "release" or "airflow"[8]—what in this context functions literally as a drain-hole cannot fail to evoke a further chilling association between death and hygiene: the showerhead.

But the debate with Lessing goes far deeper. It is not only the spokesman of liberal humanism who is being confronted on the Judenplatz. Lessing is also, famously, the author of the *Laocoön*. The locus classicus of the idealist debate between word and image, Lessing's *Laocoön* stages what will for the next two centuries dominate discussion of both visual art and literature. What is at stake in Lessing's attempt to legislate the boundaries of "painting" and "poetry"? (These charged terms stand in for the entire opposition between visual and verbal forms of production: space versus time, simultaneity versus succession, image versus text.) Lessing's polemic against the ancient thesis of the "sister arts" (Simonides, Horace)—the reciprocal conversion between word and image—is well known and the details need not detain us here. Suffice it to say that his attempt to block the hybridization captured by the oxymorons of "dumb poem" and "speaking picture"[9] directs itself in the final instance against an uncanny disordering of the relations between life and death as such. A theological subtext can be detected here. The segregation of narrative flow and visual stasis—discourse and image—prevents the contamination of living time and the stillness of death, a contamination which would indeed threaten to unsettle the boundaries between the human and the divine. The descriptive poet who tries to paint in words, to depict congealed spatial relations within the temporal medium of language, not only is said to assume the symbolic castration and muteness of the seraglio (59), but, moreover, in his "dry" (83), "cold" (96), and "lifeless" (91) enumerations is found to inflict upon the body he would represent a mortifying fragmentation and deformation (88, 104, 109). The allegorical painter who tries to narrate in images, to display the temporality of events within the parameters of plastic space, is compared to a fetishist or idolater who would feign to animate dead matter by temporalizing it and in this way transgress the monotheistic imperative (55ff.).

BETWEEN WORD AND IMAGE

It is tempting but perhaps hasty simply to transpose the terms of the *Laocoön* debate into the terms of conceptual art movements of the past two decades in an effort to trace the various displacements of the minimalist artwork into text, installation, photography, or architecture—the self-inscription of the image, broadly speaking, into language. Such a trajectory would seem to shift the object from a condition of tautological positivity (minimalism's "what you see is what you see") toward a condition of discursivity epitomized by the conceptualist turn to language, as indeed to architecture—a move which in its defetishizing reflexivity would reaffirm art's repressed utopian promise. If minimalism's positivity had come, by the 1960s, to symptomatize a fundamental lack of reflexivity with respect to its own conditions, the conceptualist response would have been precisely to rupture any such reified satisfaction by inscribing within the artwork itself a critical relation to its own conditions of production and reproduction. (Hence the various interventions in the various channels of presentation, distribution, and consumption—museums, institutions, urban spaces, publications, and so on—by which conceptual art in its first flush distinguished itself.[10]) The conceptual undermining of minimalist visuality would in this sense direct itself in the first place to what would remain the latter's ultimate blind spot and resulting acquiescence to its own context. The apparent mitigation of visuality through the turn to discourse would thus on a deeper level vindicate the latter's promise as the very possibility of enlightenment.

How might such a problematic apply to Whiteread? Her monument would appear to evoke a minimalist object while blocking the conceptualist translation into text or architecture. The object here remains an object: it fails to make that passage toward language which had once appeared to be art's only alternative to positivity. While its very referent evokes a certain synthesis of language and architecture (there is no more perfect mediation than a library), as an object the work seems to renounce the very mediation to which it alludes. Strictly speaking neither sculpture nor text nor architecture, the work rather suspends itself between these as a testimony to a frozen possibility, and bears the essential stigma of its own failure to transcend. Indeed, it exposes the very promise of transcendence as idealism. Hovering between thing and language, the work marks the place where words themselves congeal into stony, meaningless matter.

It is the Proustian library which is here effectively being deconstructed: recall the final epiphany of the *Recherche.* Waiting for the music to end, so he can finally join the party, the narrator casts his eye absently over the magnificent first editions adorning the posh interior of the Guermantes library. If the red cover of the book, in its insistent materiality, haphazardly attracts his attention, such a moment of exteriority will be ultimately recuperated by the interiority it seems most to resist. If the ideal book is for Proust in this respect the unread book, the useless book, the out-of-work book (as Benjamin, Adorno, and Blanchot will, in their own rather different ways, also insist on), if one can and must come to judge a book by its cover, this is because in the end it is the opaque body of the book which, by providing the ultimate resistance to memory as a movement of idealizing interiorization, furnishes the essential obstacle which needs to be posited in order to be overcome. The physicality of the binding thus stands here paradoxically for the very possibility of the "binding" or mastery of trauma (in Proust, a trauma set off, indeed, by overreading), and thus promises an overcoming of the brutal anonymity and stammering idiocy into which the narrator has for the past three thousand pages been cast. Whence the official conversion of the dead letter into living spirit: the transformation of the book as "huge cemetery in which . . . the names are effaced" into the Book as cathedral in which the buried child is to be resurrected.[11]

Whiteread's memorial would seem to inhibit this last move. The reversal of the spines of the books here contains more than the signature of inversion that is by now her trademark. For while the exposure of the normally concealed page edges suggests a kind of "inside on the outside" (compare the exposed stairway of *House,* the stain on the bath, the writing on the underside of the sink, the imprint on the mattress), the very fact of their exposure points equally to the ultimate encrypting not only of the "outside on the inside" (the spines now permanently incarcerated in concrete) but equally of the "inside on the inside": the page surfaces themselves, fused as a block, forever inaccessible. Doubly illegible—stripped of title and irretrievably sealed—the books announce the opacity of an archive impenetrable in its own self-display. If to see the page edges is to see what should have remained hidden (Freud's very definition of the uncanny), the viewer here becomes witness to a secret all the more recalcitrant in being disclosed. Opaque in their exposure, the books dislodge the very opposition of concealment and manifestation—the opposition, too, of burial and resurrection—and announce the endlessness of a mourning without term.

ADVENTURES OF THE ILLEGIBLE

This is not the first time books have materialized themselves to the point of illegibility. A comparison with the rather diametrically opposed projects of Marcel Broodthaers and Anselm Kiefer may be instructive. How, specifically, does Whiteread's concrete library differentiate itself from the plastered book of *Pense-Bête,* on the one hand, and the monumental library of *Zweistromland,* on the other?

With momentous consequences, Broodthaers was to inaugurate his career as artist (and end his previous career as "poet") with the hyper-Mallarméan gamble which would efface the book by materializing the signifier. The experiment took a variety of forms: literally burying his own literary remains in plaster (*Pense-Bête,* 1964, a possible homage to Duchamp's *Tongue in My Cheek* of 1959—the speechless self-parody of the artist); installing his texts as physical objects behind the coffin-like protection of the museum vitrine (*La signature de l'artiste,* 1974); defacing the pages of an edition of Mallarmé's *Coup de dés* with his own adhesive, tomb-like lozenges, visually erasing the semantic power of the poem so as finally to liberate the word to the plasticity of the letter (*Un coup de dés n'abolira le hasard. Image,* 1969); or, finally, producing his own "industrial poems" of 1968—embossed plastic plaques, "paintings" (as he called them) blind-stamped in limited editions which in their monochrome seriality (an effect enhanced by the linguistic repetitions incorporated within the actual inscriptions) are brought to the point of near illegibility, and this by virtue of the very process of reproduction by which they are brought into relief.

It is arguable that in each of these different materializations of the letter Broodthaers reverses the conceptualist transition from image to language, thus announcing art's ineluctable persistence as a "thing of things."[12] In the artwork's very turn to discourse lies its inextricable immersion in the "tautology of reification."[13] What appears at first to blur the line between language and object indeed equally contests any claim to reciprocal permeability or mediation—what Broodthaers mocks as "the shining hand-in-hand of poetry and the visual arts."[14] The object rigorously suspends itself between text and image while negating both. In exposing the ultimate failure of conceptual art to transform seeing into reading, it marks the essential relapse of such a project into the museal resuscitation of pictorial and sculptural form.

Kiefer's *Zweistromland* (1985–89) may well exemplify such a relapse. The ambiguity of these monumental lead books heaped on their massive steel shelving is palpable. On the one hand, these titanic volumes present the specter of absolute illegibility: weighing up to three hundred kilograms each, impossible to handle, they announce absolute ruin both in their substance (encrusted with salt stains, emulsions, ash, the moldering traces of transience) and in their content (incorporating apocalyptic photographs of abandoned factories, decaying cities, archaeological relics, along with overdetermined shots of vanishing railway tracks). On the other hand, redemption glimmers in the very ciphers of destruction. The persistence of heavy matter gestures toward transfiguration—the alchemical potential of lead, together with its protective anti-radioactive properties—just as meaning beckons in the references to the occult knowledge of the Tarot (*The High Priestess*) and to the Mediterranean cradle of civilization.[15] The illegibility of the books is thus here only provisional, an impediment which restricts and forestalls reading so as to vindicate it at a deeper level. The colossal volumes "preclude access by the ordinary mortal,"[16] thus reserving their ultimate significance for those invested with the authority to interpret them. Such a promise is formally inscribed in the very arrangement of the shelves, which are angled like the pages of a book: the sculpture as a whole assumes the shape of an open book which the spectator can walk around so as to peruse both recto and verso in their entirety. Indeed, *Zweistromland* perhaps finds its logical fulfillment in the publication of the lavish, oversized book which bears the same name, and which includes not only the artist's documentary photo-essay of the installation but photographs of a selection of the otherwise inaccessible leaden pages.[17] At this point the blocked promise of a reciprocal conversion of image and text suddenly flares into the Wagnerian phantasm of the Gesamtkunstwerk—the "becoming space of time" (Parzifal)—the ultimate suspension of history within the mythic plenitude of nature.

What dialectic of word and image might be at work in Whiteread's stony library? Neither the conceptual negativity of a Broodthaers nor the monumental positivity of a Kiefer: is there a third possibility between negation and positivity? How are we to understand the strange interplay of seeing and reading in this construction?

NEGATIVES, POSITIVES

Whiteread's memorial also strikes a contrast with the memorial to the burned books at the Bebelplatz in Berlin. Micha Ullman's 1996 *Bibliothek* commemorates destruction with the ciphers of absence: a small sunken pit in the cobblestoned square, a series of painfully empty shelves (built to hold twenty thousand volumes), the whole subterranean structure illuminated and covered over by a thick glass pane on which the spectator is tacitly invited to walk. The glass surface—at once ceiling, floor, and window—reflects back the transient vacancy of the sky, the clouds, the adjacent façade of the Law Faculty of Humboldt University, which had, in fact, in its previous incarnation, enthusiastically organized the Nazi book burning ceremony on 10 May 1933. Also inevitably reflected in the glass is the spectator, who necessarily

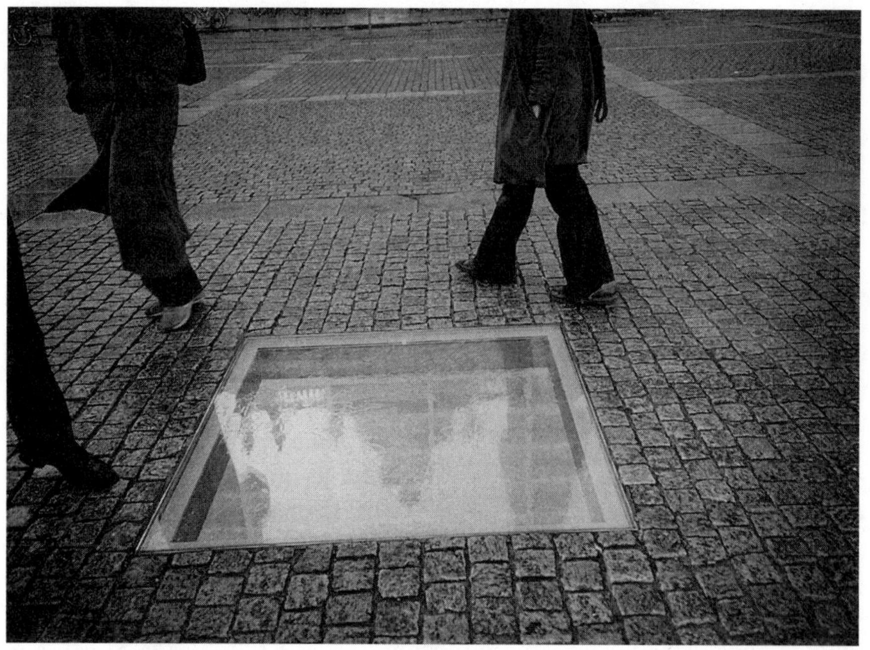

15.5 Micha Ullman, *Bibliothek*, 1996, Bebelplatz, Berlin.
Photo by Shelley Hornstein.

enters the image in order to view it, but does so precisely as stain or blind spot: to approach the pit is inevitably to block the transparency of the window-floor—as shadow, as reflection, and finally as the interference of a solid body—and thus to occult the very ground on which one stands. In its original conception, Whiteread's monument would seem to substitute height for depth, presence for absence, books for shelves, contents for container—indeed to the point where the very frame supporting and enclosing the ensemble here evaporates without a trace.

There is no trace of shelving—not even a negative trace—in the model submitted by Whiteread for the competition. In a startling deviation from Whiteread's habitual practice—and in striking contrast to her extensive recent experiments with book-sculptures (see, for example, *Untitled [Five Shelves]*, 1995)—the model represents the books not only in positive form (not the emptiness surrounding the books but the books themselves), but as lacking any obvious support or context. In the model, the bottom edge of each shelf load is emphatically not flat.[18] As if gravity itself had been eliminated, the uneven, wiggly planes described by the top and bottom edges of each row of books appear to be vertically symmetrical, and thus now register only the absence of even the absence of the missing support or ground. Not even the negative imprint of a shelving system is registered in the sketch for the library, in which the arrays of books, invisibly bolted to the recessed wall, appear to float between the vacant intervals defined solely by the symmetrical intrusion and confrontation of the facing horizontal edges.

One can perceive in Whiteread's trajectory an increasing complexity of incorporation or containment: a movement from casting containers used by human bodies (hot-water bottles) to objects used to contain or support both human bodies and their objects (beds, chairs, baths, tables, floors, cupboards), and in turn a move from containers to containers containing containers (desks with encrypted drawers) and containers of containers (rooms, houses), and so on.[19] At the extreme limit of such a logical trajectory stands the library. A room full of shelves full of books full of pages full of words exemplifies a container of a container of a container of a container of a container. At every stage, what is "inside" presents itself as radically "outside"—exterior to its own exterior—in that it forms a limit to what can be enclosed, contained, or included. Interiorization would in this sense simultaneously reach its apogee and its limit.

It is striking that precisely at this point, where the logic of containment reflexively intensifies itself, there is a sudden reversal in Whiteread's formal strategy: the suggestive power of the cast is seemingly relinquished. Rather than functioning negatively as the materialization of an absence, the library presents us with a pure positive volume with barely a trace of negativity or absence. The ceiling rose and door moldings and fixtures are the only truly negative forms or strict inversions in the entire structure—the negativity of the books is expressed by their literally inside-out position rather than by their negative imprint—and would effectively function here only as the artist's signature. In this respect the memorial would seem to go against the grain of Whiteread's entire practice. Does it not mitigate the subversive promise of the cast—its refusal to reify what can be rendered only as absence or negativity? Does it not threaten to reinstate—indeed, qua monument—a kind of positivity which would in this context be achingly suspect?

THE PARADOXES OF COUNTER-MEMORY

By now the problematic is familiar. In Germany, above all, it has become the essential imperative of the Holocaust memorial to remark on its own impossibility—its inevitable function as alibi, substitute, pacification, absolution—and as such to unmark itself, so as to efface the guilty traces of its own subsistence. A whole genre of anti-monuments has been catalogued: sunken pyramids in Kassel, disappearing obelisks in Harburg, buried inscriptions in Saarbrücken, and so on.[20] Habituated, one might even begin to suspect a certain grandiosity in such self-subversions. Even setting aside the suspicion that the very act of disappearance would inevitably reinstate the prestige and aura of the vanished original, one might question the longing for purity inherent in the work's own self-negation—the secret promise of the tabula rasa.

Indeed, it is arguable that such literalizing strategies of effacement only reinstate the idealization of memory by reintroducing the hierarchy of mind over matter, concept over object: thus the displacement of the locus of commemoration from the tangible exteriority of the body to the spiritual inwardness of the pure (even absent) spectator—and ultimately, indeed, to the inwardness of an imaginary community constituted within the transparency of a public sphere of democratic consensus and dissensus. Jochen Gerz's invisible monument at Saarbrücken (*2,146 Stones,* 1991), for example, was explicitly referred to and relocated within the "interior memorial" of a public both informed and formed by the media debate which was inevitably to follow. A similar rhetoric surrounded the installation of the "sinking monument" of Jochen Gerz and Esther Shalev-Gerz at Harburg (*Monument against Fascism,* 1986–93)—twelve meters high, six years to sink, a transient surface for inscription, fully buried in the end—an anti-monumental monument which, through incorporating both defacement and effacement, both graffiti and self-occlusion, as essential moments of its own erection, ultimately both deferred to and vindicated the prior existence of an enlightened public commissioned to assume the burden of remembrance within the interiority of the heart.

NEGATIONS, REFLECTIONS

Much could be said about the evocative potential of the cast: Pompeii, the death mask, the inscription of a negative space which may or may not—this is the uncertainty—be converted into positivity. The nineteenth-century language of casting paralleled with uncanny rigor the language of speculative philosophy: negation, negation of the negation, the movement whereby a mortified matter reifies and eventually thereby redeems itself in living spirit. Rodin famously referred to the plaster stage of the process as the time of the subject's death (admonishing his sitter, "don't worry . . . life will return"),[21] to be followed by a triumphant resurrection in the final product. Hence the traditional association of casting with photography in every essential respect: negativity, indexicality, reproducibility. Indeed the history of photography is bound up with the history of casting to such an intimate degree that it not only shares the latter's basic vocabulary (negative/positive, editions, enlargements, etc.) but indeed takes the latter as its exemplary subject. As if reflexively registering what is most essential about its own medium, early photography finds in the fossil and in the plaster cast—two favorite props of nineteenth-century studio still-lifes—a specular object for its own self-investigations. The earliest known

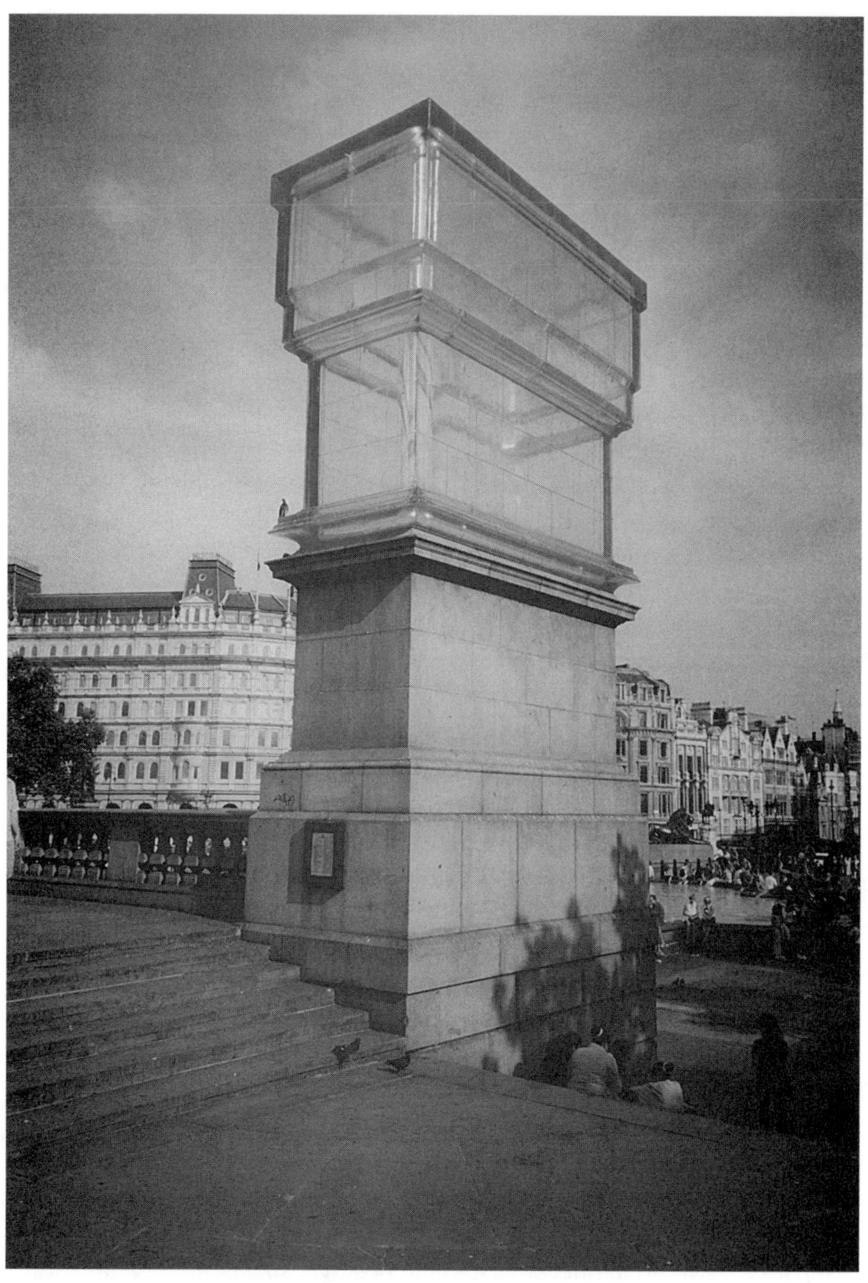

15.6 Rachel Whiteread, *Monument*, 2001, Trafalgar Square, London. Photo by Rebecca Comay

print by Daguerre himself (*Still Life,* 1837) features decapitated plaster cherub heads gazing vacantly into the empty space of the photograph: death confronts the viewer in the most kitschy symbols of resurrection.

Whiteread's work has distinguished itself up to now by its rigorous materialization of an absence: its emphatic arrest of the casting process at the moment of an irrecuperable negativity. Why—and why above all in a Holocaust memorial—this seeming return to figural representation? Why does the "Nameless Library" stage this apparent turn to positivity?

The model presents a rather startling feature which may go some way to complicate the issue. According to the original proposal, the memorial was to be mounted on a glass base on which were to be engraved the two official inscriptions stipulated by the initial terms of the competition, making reference to the more than sixty-five thousand Austrian Jewish victims of the Holocaust and providing a list of the sites of extermination. Thus mirrored, the monument would seem to achieve a kind of weightlessness in being absorbed within its own reflection. Paradoxically lifted by its groundless platform, the monument would in this sense present the perfect antithesis to the "base materialism" of Whiteread's earlier floor pieces, with their gravitational density, their downward pressure. (The experiment with weightlessness is continued in Whiteread's *Monument* of 2001—a "monument" which placed on an empty plinth in Trafalgar Square an inverted, translucent cast of the same plinth, substituting for an absent object the phantom presence of the base itself, at once dematerialized, elevated, and emphatically redoubled.) The model of the Vienna monument suggests that whatever positivity is contained within the monument would be evaporated by the reflected image in the glassy plinth. In the glass the sculpture would find its own specular inversion. It is indeed the mirror which now performs, if only virtually, the negative function of the cast.

The visual multiplication of the bookshelves in the glass evokes a Borgesian repetition suggestive of a Romantic specular regression. Strikingly, the glass would here function simultaneously as a surface for reflection and as a surface for inscription. To look into the glass would be to observe the superimposition of blank book edges upon the traces of an indelible inscription. And, indeed, vice versa. In the mirror, language would return to object, object would return to language—the latter now reduced to its barest abstraction as the empty list of names which marks the utter limit of commemoration.[22] Suspended between the negative and the positive, such a moment might indeed have marked the impossible passage between word and image—the paradox of a redemption that can by this point only arrive too late.

Alas. In the final version now assembled in Vienna, the glass base has been replaced by opaque gray concrete. Already stained and dirty, the list of place names fades beneath a layer of grime.

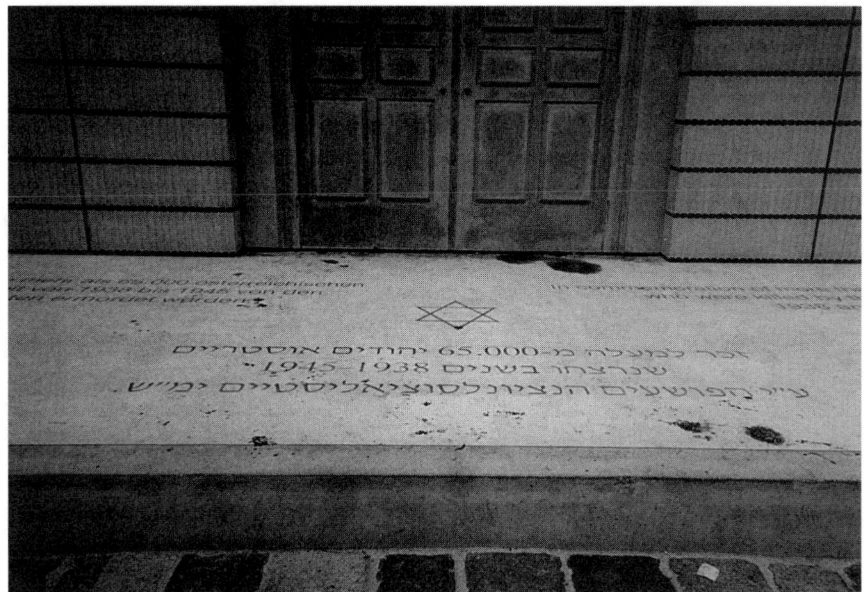

15.7 Rachel Whiteread, *Holocaust Memorial*, detail (plinth with stains, etc., together with inscription and beginning of rows of books). Photo by Rebecca Comay.

Notes

1. The *Monument against War and Fascism*—originally commissioned as a Holocaust memorial, and scheduled to have been unveiled on the fiftieth anniversary of the Anschluss and Kristallnacht—was erected, three years late, after considerable controversy, on the vacant site of the exclusive Jockey Club, a Ringstrasse-style building destroyed during the Allied bombing of 12 March 1945, behind the Staatsoper, and across from the elegant Sacher hotel (home of the original Sachertorte). The sculpture, which makes no direct reference to the Holocaust, refers to the humiliation of the Viennese Jews after the Anschluss, who were forced to clean away anti-Nazi graffiti using acid-soaked brushes, and is widely disliked in Vienna.

2. "Aber was soll denn [der] Betonklotz sein?—ein Mischmasch aus zerreibenen Stein und Eisen . . ." [But what is this hunk of concrete supposed to be? A mishmash of crushed stone and iron . . .] (Alfred Hrdlicka, quoted by Britta Blumencron, "Der Streit um das Mahnmal eskaliert," *Kurier* [Vienna], 30 July 1996, pp. 11f.). Hrdlicka is, significantly, the artist behind the notorious *Monument against War and Fascism* on the Albertinaplatz, the inadequacy of which in fact fueled the efforts to commission a "proper" Holocaust memorial on the Judenplatz.

3. *Die Gemeinde* (Vienna), June 1996.

4. "Der Judenplatz ist zu klein für zwei Denkmäler." See "ÖVP-Hawlik: Lessingsdenkmal soll übersiedeln," *Der Standard* (Vienna), 26 August 1996, p. 6.

5. Gotthold Ephraim Lessing, *Nathan der Weise* (Munich: Goldmann, 1954), 3.7, p. 91.

6. *Judenplatz Wien 1996: Wettbewerb, Mahnmal, und Gedenkstätte für die jüdischen Opfer des Naziregimes in Österreich, 1938–1945,* Kunsthalle Wien (Vienna: Folio Verlag, 1996), 78, 82.

7. Theodor Gomperz, quoted in Steven Beller, *Vienna and the Jews, 1868–1938: A Cultural History* (Cambridge: Cambridge University Press, 1989). See also Gershom Scholem, "Jews and Germans," in *On Jews and Judaism in Crisis: Selected Essays,* ed. Werner J. Dannhauser (New York: Schocken, 1976), 71–92.

8. Interview with Iwona Blazwick, in *Rachel Whiteread: Sculptures,* ed. Jan Debbaut (Eindhoven: Stedelijk Van Abbemuseum, 1992), 12.

9. Gotthold Ephraim Lessing, *Laocoön: An Essay on the Limits of Painting and Poetry,* trans. Edward Allen McCormick (Indianapolis: Bobbs-Merrill, 1962), 5. It is the allegorical painting and the descriptive poem which for Lessing epitomize the problem.

10. For the most influential and sophisticated version of this argument, see Benjamin Buchloh, "From the Aesthetic of Administration to Institutional Critique (Some Aspects of Conceptual Art, 1962–1969)," in *L'art conceptual: une perspective* (Paris: Musée d'art moderne de la ville de Paris, 1990); reprinted in *Conceptual Art: A Critical Anthology,* ed. Alexander Alberro and Blake Stimson (Cambridge, Mass.: MIT Press, 1999), 514–537.

11. Marcel Proust, *Remembrance of Things Past,* trans. C. K. Scott Moncrieff and Terence Kilmartin (New York: Penguin, 1989), vol. 3, 940, 924.

12. Marcel Broodthaers, "Ten Thousand Francs Reward," in *Broodthaers: Writings, Interviews, Photographs,* ed. Benjamin H. D. Buchloh (Cambridge, Mass.: MIT Press, 1987), 45.

13. Quoted in Benjamin H. D. Buchloh, "Open Letters, Industrial Poems," in Buchloh, *Broodthaers,* 84. I am extremely grateful for this entire essay, which demarcates so clearly some of the ideological issues at stake in Broodthaers's encounter with conceptualism. For other excellent readings of the relationship between text and image in Broodthaers, see Dieter Schwartz, "Look! Books in Plaster: On the First Phase of the Work of Marcel Broodthaers," and Birgit Pelzer, "Recourse to the Letter," both in Buchloh, *Broodthaers,* 57–66 and 157–181 respectively.

14. Broodthaers, "Open Letter," Ostend, 7 September 1968 (quoted in Buchloh, "Open Letters, Industrial Poems," 91).

15. *Zweistromland* (Mesopotamia) and *The High Priestess* are, respectively, the German and the English names given to the installation.

16. Anselm Kiefer, *Zweistromland: Mit einem Essay von Armin Zweite* (Cologne: DuMont Buchverlag; London: Anthony d'Offay, 1989).

17. Ibid.

18. Whiteread's notes for the construction of the book units make this clear as well: molds of twenty volumes were to be constructed and bolted to the building in such a way that they could be turned upside down. See notebook pages published in *La Biennale di Venezia. XLVII Esposizione Internazionale d'Arte,* ed. Ann Gallagher (London: British Council, 1997). The actual monument deviates rather crucially from the model. The modular units of books (cast in concrete and fiberglass from carved wooden models) have now been constructed with their bottom edges horizontally aligned, as if, in fact, registering the absent pressure of a supporting shelf. This is not the only discrepancy which is to be noted between the model and the final product, as we shall see.

19. This point has been noted by Mark Cousins in his perceptive essay "Rachel Whiteread: Inside Outcast," *Tate Magazine* 10 (winter 1996): 37.

20. For an excellent overview of the phenomenon, see James Young, ed., *The Art of Memory: Holocaust Memorials in History* (New York and Munich: Prestel, 1994), as well as Young, *The Texture of Memory: Holocaust Memorials and Meaning* (New Haven, Conn.: Yale University Press, 1993).

21. Albert Elsen, "When the Sculptures Were White: Rodin's Work in Plaster," in *Rodin Rediscovered,* ed. Albert Elsen (Washington, D.C.: National Gallery of Art, 1981), 132.

22. See Hegel's *Encyclopaedia* account of an expropriated or "mechanical" memory [*Gedächtnis*], epitomized by the serial list of proper names held together by the "empty link" or "empty volume" [*leeres Band*] of an abstract subjectivity. Proper remembrance would require the interiorization of such externality within the fullness of the living (no longer machinelike or corpselike) subject. G. W. F. Hegel, *Philosophy of Mind,* trans. William Wallace (Oxford: Oxford University Press, 1971), §462–463.

16 Turning the Places of Holocaust History into Places of Holocaust Memory

Holocaust Memorials in Budapest, Hungary, 1945–95

TIM COLE

Walking through a city's streets, we stumble, before long, upon monuments and memorials. By their very nature, these objects of metal and stone invite us to look beyond their form. As James Young notes, "where contemporary art invites viewers and critics to contemplate its own materiality, or its relationship to other works before and after itself, the aim of memorials is not to call attention to their own presence so much as to past events *because* they are no longer present."[1] This implies that memorialization is more than simply a question of aesthetics.

Memorials therefore force us to look beyond the immediate agency of the memorial artist to the event or person being remembered, and also to those doing the remembering. Indeed, Arthur Danto's words—"*we* erect monuments so that we shall always remember and build memorials so that *we* shall never forget"[2]—suggest that stumbling upon a memorial forces us to look at ourselves. Constructing a memorial is a conscious act of choosing to remember certain people and events, and by implication choosing not to remember other people and events. And that conscious act is a "political" one, "political" in the sense that it is about power over memory, power over the past, and power over the present.

Art in public places is "almost always the product of some instrumental purpose outside the domain of pure aesthetics" and thus art with "political resonance."[3] In some cases, the erection (or destruction) of memorials is explicitly an act of the central state. This was true in the immediate postwar period in Eastern Europe, where Holocaust memorials "were usually seen as forms of symbolic politics under the direction and patronage of the central government." In Western Europe, by contrast, Holocaust memorialization tended to be "left to private and local initiative and thus developed in an ad hoc and piecemeal fashion."[4] However, whether planned by central government or private initiative, the act of remembering is essentially political. After all,

> To commemorate is to take a stand, to declare the reality of heroes (or heroic events) worthy of emulation or, less frequently, that an event that occurred at a particular place was indeed so terrible that it must be remembered forever after as a cautionary note.[5]

Whilst the history of the Holocaust would at first glance seem to be of the latter type—"an event . . . so terrible that it must be remembered forever after as a cautionary note"—there has been—and is—a tendency to commemorate it through the lens of heroism. Israel was not alone in the 1950s in using the languages of both "martyrdom" and "heroism" to refer to the Holocaust.[6] As I wish to explore more fully in this essay, the option of choosing to remember this event through heroism is one which has been—and is—important also in Hungary.

There is, after all, not one monolithic history of the Holocaust, but rather, as Michael Berenbaum suggests, "three separate but intersecting histories of the Holocaust that bear commemoration: those of the perpetrators, the bystanders and the victims."[7] This triad of actors also forms the basis for much of the historiography of the Holocaust, perhaps nowhere more explicitly than in the work of Raul Hilberg.[8] However, I think that Tony Kushner is right to add another major actor into the equation and to highlight the contestation—rather than simply intersection—of these strands of commemoration.

Writing specifically about the memory of Bergen-Belsen, Kushner stresses that Holocaust memory is contested rather than unitary. Thus he describes the concentration camp Bergen-Belsen as "saturated" with "complex, diverse, contradictory and dynamic" memory, "a place of contested memory between those who experienced it as victim, perpetrator, bystander and liberator as well as differentiated experience within those groups."[9] These four categories —"victim," "perpetrator," "bystander," and "liberator"—provide four rather different, and potentially conflicting, strategies for remembering the Holocaust.

As well as recognizing diverse, and competing, strategies of remembering, we must also reflect upon the diversity of sites which have been chosen for Holocaust commemoration. Historians and geographers have pointed to the need to examine the meaning which the siting of the memorial more generally attaches to the memorial itself. For example, Nuala Johnson has rightly criticized Pierre Nora's suggestion that "statues or monuments to the dead, for instance, owe their meaning to their intrinsic existence; even though their location is far from arbitrary, one could justify relocating them without altering their meaning."[10] As Johnson points out, "the space which . . . monuments occupy is not just an incidental material backdrop but in fact inscribes the statues with meaning."[11] Thus—as both Johnson and Levinson have noted—the removal of Communist statues from the public places of Budapest to a kitsch "Statue Park" for tourists on the outskirts of the city has imbued these same monuments with radically different meanings.[12]

A number of competing (and potentially conflicting) priorities may determine the physical location of Holocaust memorials, ranging from the pragmatic (ownership) through a concern with visibility (or hidden-ness). In Europe, unlike in the United States or Israel, a further consideration is the choice of a site specifically because of (a selective focus upon) what happened there in the Holocaust past. This is something which remains relatively under-studied by historians and geographers alike, and yet worth further investigation.

Ironically, whilst Holocaust memorials are relatively common within both the United States and Israel, they are surprisingly uncommon in the places where this terrible event occurred—Europe. And yet those places appear to be the most "natural" of places to erect memorials—more natural, it would seem, than Boston or San Francisco or one of the countless other American cities which has its own Holocaust memorial. However, as James Young notes,

> when the killing stopped, only the sites remained, blood-soaked but otherwise mute. While in operation, the death camps and the destruction of people wrought in them were one and the same: sites and events were bound to each other in their contemporaneity. But with the passage of time, sites and events were gradually estranged. While the sites of killing remained ever-present, all too real in their physical setting, time subtly interposed itself between them and their past. Events that occurred in another time seemed increasingly to belong to another world altogether. Only a deliberate act of memory could reconnect them, reinfuse the sites with a sense of their historical past.[13]

Developing the work of Pierre Nora, Young draws a distinction between places of history—the places of past events—and places of memory—the places of present remembrance of past events. For sites of historical events to be turned into sites of memory, there must be a "will to remember" on the part of individuals, institutions, or communities. Where there is that will to remember, sites of Holocaust memory do—in Europe—draw upon sites of Holocaust history, albeit in often selective ways. However, the opposite is also true. Where there has been—and is—a will to forget or erase, then the sites of Holocaust history have been silenced. As Kenneth Foote has suggested, "obliteration" is an alternative strategy to "sanctification" in dealing with sites of traumatic history.[14]

As my comments so far suggest, examining Holocaust memorials—in Europe in particular—involves a number of layers of analysis. It involves consideration of the form (the poetics), consideration of who or what is being remembered by whom, together with how and why (the politics), and consideration of where that remembering is taking place (the place). In the remainder of this essay, I wish to take the Holocaust memorials in Budapest, Hungary, as a case study to explore those three themes of poetics, politics, and place. I wish to ask the questions: how has the Holocaust been remembered (and forgotten), why has the Holocaust been remembered (and forgotten), and where has the Holocaust been remembered (and forgotten)?

BUDAPEST: PLACE OF HOLOCAUST HISTORY, PLACE OF HOLOCAUST MEMORY

Throughout 1944 and into early 1945, the Holocaust was enacted in—and through—the physical, urban spaces of Budapest. In mid-June, the city's Jews were ordered into "yellow-star houses": a form of dispersed ghettoization across the entire city. In November—after the successful coup of the fascist Nyilas Party—Jews were forced into two ghettos. The larger Pest ghetto—located in the traditional "Jewish" VII district—was home to almost seventy thousand "unprotected Jews." The smaller international ghetto, located on the banks of the Danube in the north of Pest, was home to approximately seventeen thousand "protected Jews." These Jews had come under the protection of a number of foreign powers, including the Swedish legation and the "heroic" Raoul Wallenberg. However, even these so-called "protected Jews" were vulnerable to the attacks made upon Jews by armed Nyilas gangs. In the winter of 1944–45, these gangs marched hundreds of Jews to the edge of the Danube and shot them, letting their bodies fall into the freezing water. When the Red Army entered Budapest in January 1945, around 120,000 Budapest Jews remained alive.[15]

In postwar Budapest, therefore, three major sites of Holocaust history presented themselves as potential sites of Holocaust memory: the site of the closed Pest ghetto in the center of the city, the site of the more loosely designated international ghetto to the north of the city, and the site of the mass shootings along the Pest embankment of the Danube. These sites of Holocaust history have, to some extent at least, been transformed into sites of Holocaust memory by a "will to remember." However, on the one hand that transformation has been selective, and on the other hand it has universalized the historical events which took place there. Moreover, the process of creating sites of Holocaust memory has not been restricted to building upon these sites of Holocaust history alone.

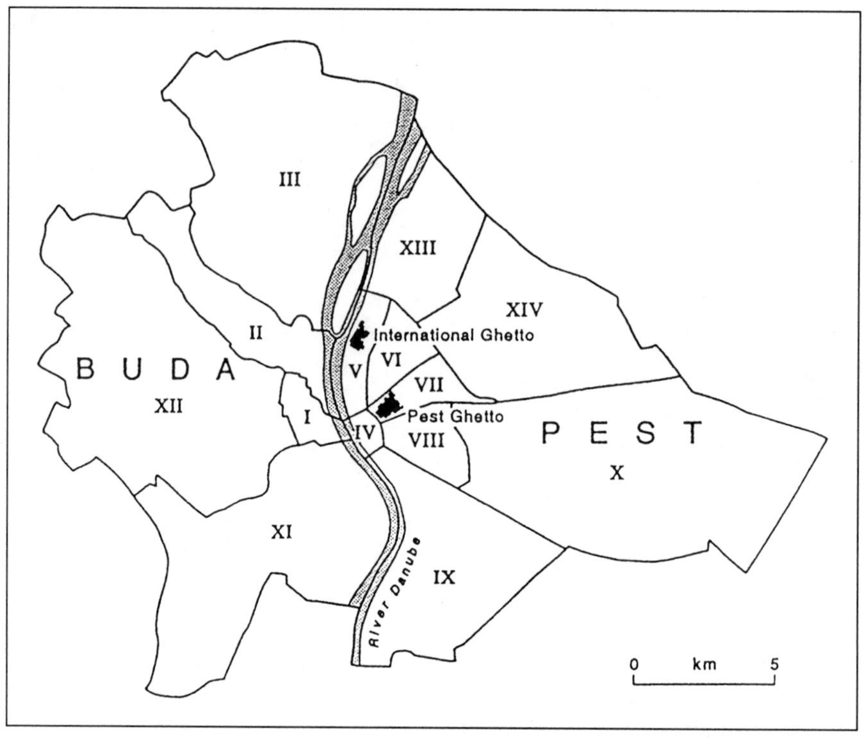

16.1 Map of Budapest showing the location of the Pest and international ghettos. Reprinted from *Journal of Historical Geography* 21, no. 3 (1995), by permission of the publisher, Academic Press.

REMEMBERING THE LIBERATOR IN BUDAPEST: 1945–85

The historical places of the two Budapest ghettos were the sites of the first postwar attempts at memorializing the Holocaust in the center of the city. In the Pest ghetto area, a small wall plaque was erected where one of the gates into the ghetto had been situated. In the international ghetto area, a street was renamed and a small wall plaque erected. However, both places were remembered primarily as the place of the liberator rather than the place of the victim.

The simple wall plaque in the Pest ghetto area was effectively a memorial to the Soviet liberation of the ghetto rather than a memorial to the ghetto itself. That the event being remembered was the Red Army's entrance into the ghetto was implicit in the memorial's being sited at the very edge of the ghetto rather than in its heart, and explicit in the text of the plaque itself: "In the Fascist period one of the gates to the Budapest ghetto stood here. The liberating Soviet Army broke down the ghetto walls on 18 January, 1945." Any notions of "Jewish" specificity were squeezed out by the juxtaposition of the Fascists—the creators of ghettos—and the Soviets—the liberators of ghettos.

In the international ghetto area, the creation of a place of memory was again tied up with the liberator rather than the Jewish victim. In this case the liberator being remembered was not the Soviet Army but the Swedish embassy official Raoul Wallenberg. In 1945, the city council renamed Phõnix Street, in the former international ghetto area, "Raoul Wallenberg Street"[16] and erected a small plaque underneath the new street sign. However, the choice of street amounted to a marginalizing of Wallenberg's memory. Phõnix Street, though within the international ghetto area, had not included any Swedish-protected houses, unlike the nearby Tátra Street, which seemed to Lévai Jenö to be a more appropriate choice, as the majority of houses there had been under Swedish protection. The city authorities, Lévai concluded diplomatically, had made, "no doubt, a well-intentioned error."[17] However, this decision pointed to a marginalizing of Wallenberg's memory. Phõnix Street was a small side street, well away from the main Pest thoroughfare, Szent István Boulevard. Tátra Street, on the other hand, joins this boulevard, which forms the outer ring of central Pest. It was thus too visible. Wallenberg was restricted to a side street rather than being given a place of great visibility.

However, his memory was there. Indeed, in one sense renaming the street amounted to condensing the complex history and geography of the international ghetto into the person of Raoul Wallenberg. In effect the place of history was being "Wallenberg-ized" as it was transformed into a place of memory. Thus it was Wallenberg who was remembered by name in a street sign and wall plaque within the rough area which had been the international ghetto. The ghetto itself was not remembered, but simply formed the place within which Wallenberg was remembered as the heroic figure "who saved ten thousand lives during the Nyilas Terror with his courageous actions and his zealous self-sacrifice" and "vanished during the siege of Pest."[18] The text of the original wall plaque—like the plaque in the Pest ghetto—denied the Jewish specificity of those Wallenberg "saved."

This absence reflected the wider trend within the Soviet bloc of erasing the Jewish specificity of the Holocaust.[19] During the Communist period in Hungary, the Jewishness of the Holocaust was quite literally pushed to the periphery, with the only memorial to the Jewish victims of the Holocaust being sited on the outskirts of Budapest. The *Memorial for Jewish Martyrs* was erected in 1949 within the "Jewish" space of the Central Jewish Cemetery in Pestlôrinc—the largest Jewish cemetery in the country.[20] With the memorial's location here—rather than in the center of Pest—the Holocaust was not simply marginalized and hidden from view, but incorporated within a site of explicitly Jewish rather than explicitly Holocaust history.[21]

In front of an L-shaped wall, a simple black marble sarcophagus acts as a symbolic grave for those whose names are listed on the memory wall—in a memorial where "individual destiny becomes mass destiny."[22] The majority were from communities outside of Budapest, and yet the entire Hungarian Holocaust is concentrated within this burial site of the capital's Jewry. Above the tomb there is text in both Hungarian and Hebrew, with the latter expressing explicitly religious sentiments. The Hungarian text reads, "Murdered by hatred—May love cherish their memory" whilst the Hebrew text reads, "God be mindful of the souls of our Jewish brothers who gave their lives for the hallowing of God's name."[23] This memorial is a place of mourning which is constantly being reinterpreted and reconstructed through the actions and meanings of those who visit. Flowers and stones are placed both on the black sarcophagus and along the bottom of the memory wall. On the memory wall itself, many of the names engraved into the stone have been painted in for emphasis, and added to in pen and pencil. These actions reflect what James Young has called "the constant give and take between memorials and viewers."[24] That process of interpretation and reinterpretation is common to all memorials, and here physical evidence of it remains.

REMEMBERING WALLENBERG, FORGETTING THE HOLOCAUST: 1948–89

The dynamic nature of memorials, which Young has pointed to, can also be seen—albeit in a rather different form—in the contesting of the memorialization of Raoul Wallenberg.

Given Wallenberg's wartime disappearance and his unknown fate in the Soviet Union, remembering (and forgetting) Wallenberg in Budapest was about much more than simply remembering (and forgetting) the Holocaust.

In the immediate postwar period, plans were made to erect a memorial to Wallenberg in Szent István Park, close to the international ghetto area. Commissioned by the Budapest "Wallenberg Memorial Committee," the sculptor Patzay Pál created a statue which showed a bronze figure fighting a serpent. The symbolism of Wallenberg's fight against Nazism was made explicit through the etching of a swastika on the head of the snake. The memorial was erected in 1948 with the agreement of Budapest city officials. However, on the eve of its unveiling in April 1948, it was removed by Soviet troops. Some years later, the bronze statue of the figure and serpent—now minus the swastika—reappeared in front of a pharmaceutical factory in Debrecen, where it symbolized "the triumph of medical science over disease"[25] rather than the triumph of Wallenberg over Nazism.

In the context of the Cold War, the disappearance of this memorial symbolized the disappearance of Wallenberg himself. Protests about Wallenberg's

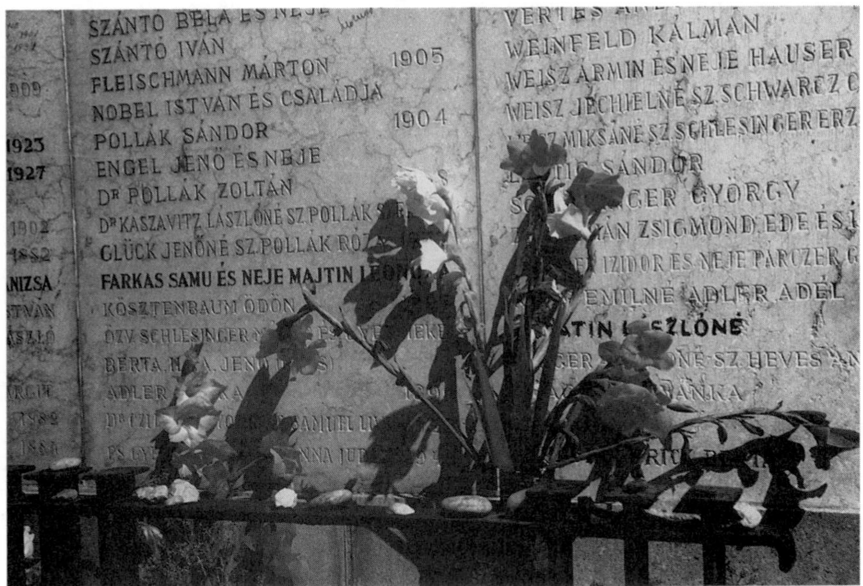

16.2 Detail of the wall of names at the *Memorial for Jewish Martyrs*, Budapest. Photo by Tim Cole.

fate and the fate of his statue were joined as Wallenberg's disappearance was linked with the perceived erasure of his memory in Budapest. This can be seen perhaps most explicitly—outside of Hungary—in the decision of the Wallenberg Committee of New York to install a copy of the 1948 statue honoring Wallenberg on the grounds of the Soviet dacha in Glen Cove, New York, as an act of protest on the fortieth anniversary of Wallenberg's disappearance.[26] During the Cold War, remembering Wallenberg was as much about remembering him as a victim of Soviet "totalitarianism" as it was about remembering him as a victor over Nazi "totalitarianism."

When in 1987 a statue of Wallenberg was erected in Budapest, it did not draw upon the places of Holocaust history in Pest (specifically, the international ghetto) but was located in Buda at the place where Wallenberg's abandoned car was discovered. Although for Rosenfeld it was a "sheer coincidence [that] the site chosen for the monument was the spot where Wallenberg's Studebaker was found abandoned in February 1945,"[27] it is clear from the memorial itself—as well as its location—that it was Wallenberg's disappearance which was being remembered.

Quite self-consciously, the statue replaces that removed the night before its unveiling in 1948. Donated by Nicolas Salgo, the former American ambassador to Hungary, the memorial echoes Patzay's earlier sculpture. On the pillars—of

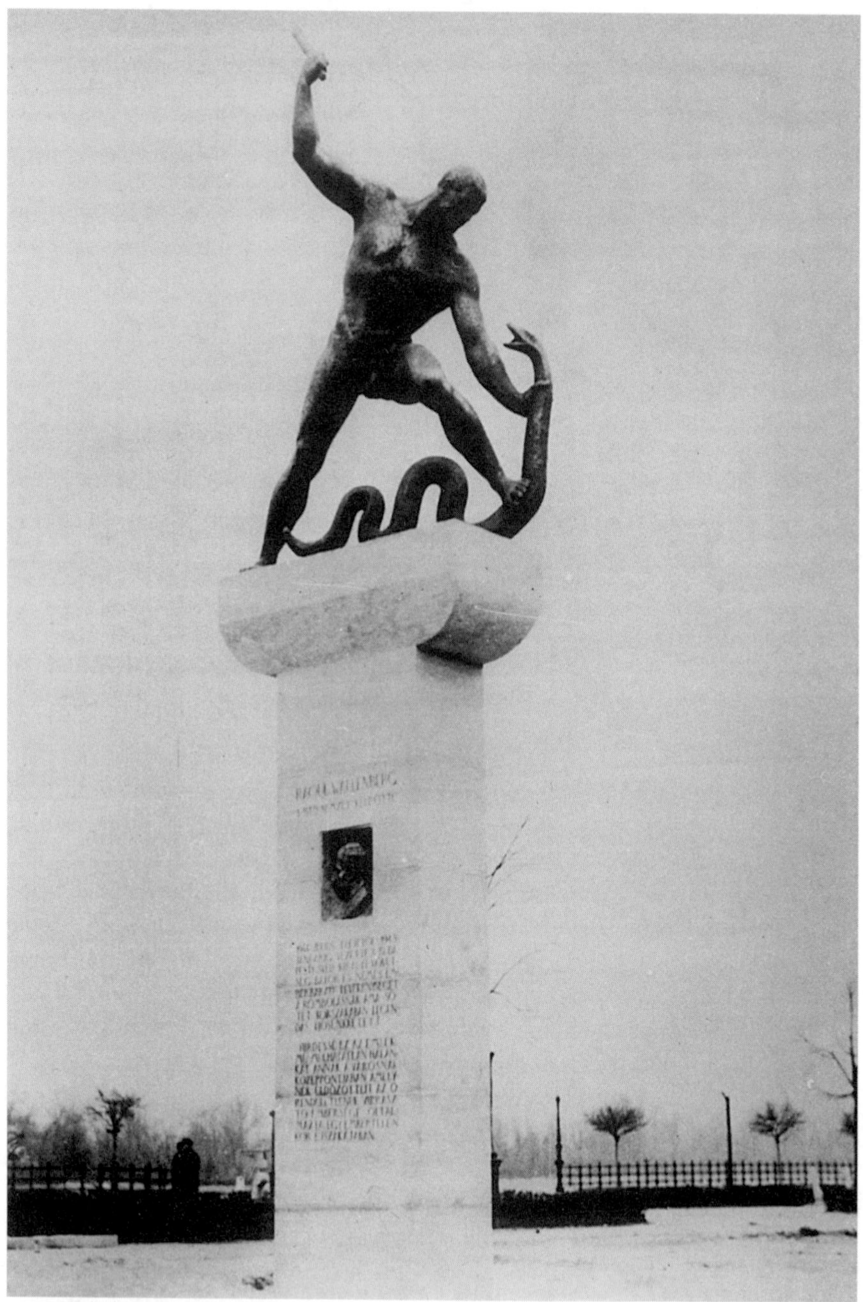

16.3 Pál Patzay's short-lived *Wallenberg Memorial*, Budapest. Magyar Nemzeti Múzeum Történeti Fényképtar, courtesy of USHMM Photo Archives.

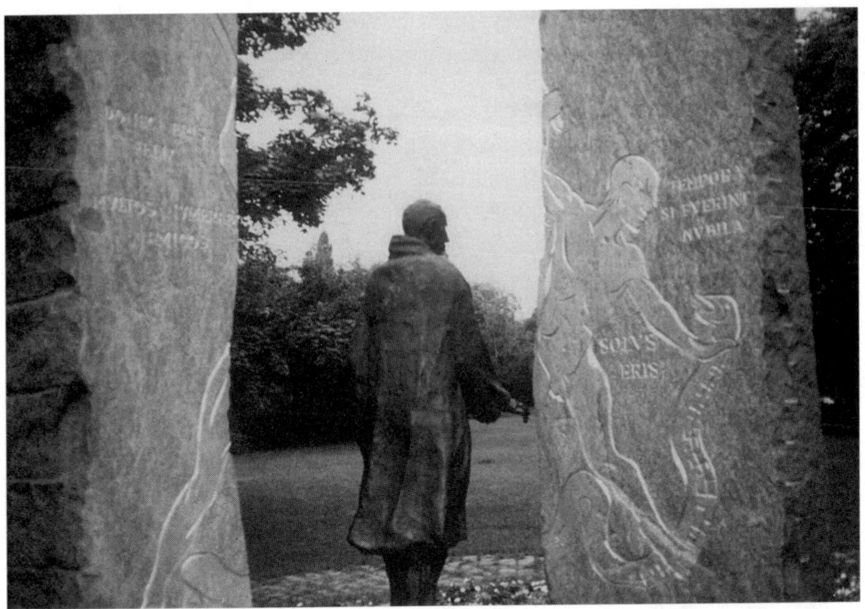

16.4 Rear of Imre Varga's *Wallenberg Memorial,* Budapest. Photo by Tim Cole.

Swedish marble—that stand on either side of the figure of Wallenberg, the sculptor (Varga Imre) has etched in gold a man striking a serpent covered in swastikas.[28] Unlike the earlier plaque in the international ghetto, the Latin text beside Varga's statue—"While good fortune stands by your side friends are plentiful. But should gray clouds gather, you are alone to withstand the storm"[29]—does not mention Wallenberg's wartime activities. Rather, it makes clear that it is Wallenberg who is being remembered, not Budapest's Jews.

This statue sought to reverse the Soviet erasure of Wallenberg's memory and pointed, in part, to the increased freedom being exercised by the Hungarian government vis-à-vis Moscow. After all, the 1987 erection of the statue was authorized by Budapest city officials, and came a year after the admission by the Hungarian ambassador to Britain that the statue outside the pharmaceutical factory in Debrecen had been created as a tribute to Wallenberg.[30] However, this increasing official sanctioning of Wallenberg's memory in the late 1980s should not be overstated. As John Bierman notes, the unveiling ceremony of Varga's statue, on 2 May 1987, was a "small and discreet" affair which was not attended by any senior members of the Hungarian government.[31] Yet in the context of Hungary's increasing independence from Moscow, Wallenberg became a man through whose disappearance Soviet aggression could start to be remembered.

REMEMBERING THE VICTIMS: 1987–95

However, at the same time that Soviet influence in Hungary lessened, there were also moves to remember the Jewish victims of the Holocaust in the symbolic space of central Budapest. While in 1985, the fortieth anniversary of the liberation of the Pest ghetto had been remembered in another memorial plaque—on a reconstructed ghetto wall—as the triumph of the Soviet army, by the late 1980s, official permission was given to erect a specifically "Jewish" memorial in the courtyard of the Dohány Street synagogue.[32] This *Memorial of the Hungarian Jewish Martyrs* was unveiled on 8 July 1990, and its location within the area of the 1944 ghetto signaled a transformation of this site of Holocaust history into a site of specifically Jewish Holocaust memory.

And yet, while self-consciously drawing upon a site of Holocaust history, this memorial also drew upon the earlier history of Budapest Jewish life. The precise siting of the memorial is justified in terms of both the site's Holocaust and pre-Holocaust significance:

> That spot is hallowed ground—*Admath Kodesh*—to all of us, the place where our next of kin, our relatives came to a miserable end, whose common grave still is there. It is the one common grave in Hungary in which solely those massacred in the Holocaust are buried. It is the site, therefore, where a memorial that befittingly proclaims their memory should be erected. At that very place, too, Raoul Wallenberg and his associates did their utmost to save people who were being persecuted, fighting desperately to frustrate the murderers' plans.
>
> That very spot, close by the gate of the ghetto . . . was the daily scene in times past of a considerable proportion of Jewish life.
>
> There, from synagogues and meeting-houses prayers would go up and rise heavenward, and *bokhers,* Talmud Torah pupils would hurry to seminaries and schools.
>
> This memorial must be erected on that spot, site of the World War II horrors.[33]

Thus the memorial is perceived to be about both Jewish and Holocaust memory, located within the multilayered place of both Budapest Jewish religious history (the synagogue) and Budapest Holocaust history (the ghetto). Indeed, the sculpture itself, which is both an upturned menorah and a weeping willow, tries to link these two memories, Jewish and Holocaust.

As with the earlier memory wall and symbolic grave in the Jewish cemetery, this memorial transforms a site of Budapest Jewish history into a site of memory for all "600,000 Hungarian Jewish Martyrs." (However, unlike the earlier memory wall, adding a name costs $125.) While very few of those "600,000" worshipped in this place of Budapest Jewish history, or died in this place of Budapest Holocaust history, the national history of Hungarian Jewish life and death is telescoped into the memorial space of the courtyard of the

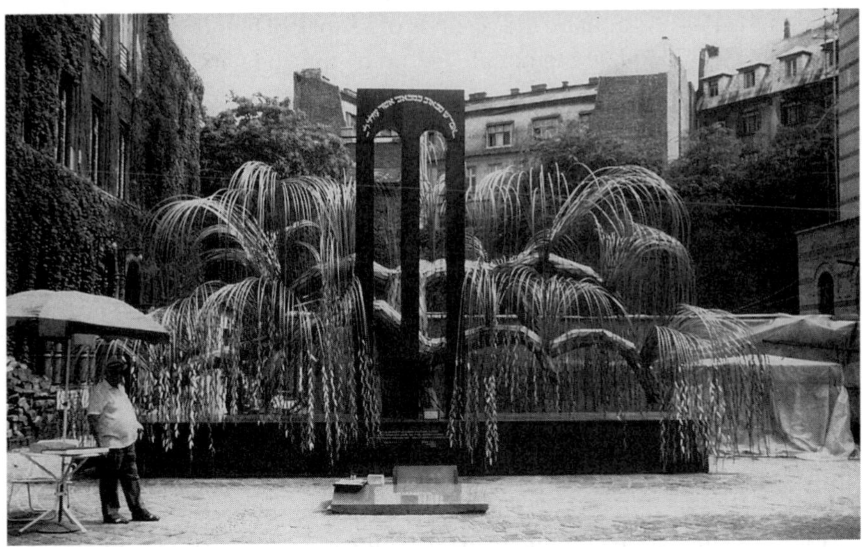

16.5 *Memorial of the Hungarian Jewish Martyrs,* Dohány street synagogue courtyard, Budapest. Photo by Tim Cole.

synagogue that stood just inside the Pest ghetto walls. The majority of the "600,000 Hungarian Jewish Martyrs" were taken from their homes in provincial Hungary to Auschwitz in summer 1944 and murdered there. Yet they are remembered inside the ghetto wall in Budapest, which was one of only two Hungarian ghettos—the international one being the other—to be liberated rather than liquidated. The much older wall plaque a few yards from the memorial is a reminder of that aspect of "Holocaust" history.

In many ways this earlier plaque—which remembers Soviet liberation rather than the Jewish victims—is more visible. While the martyrs' monument—a steel tree mounted on a red granite slab—does dwarf the nearby wall plaque to the Soviet liberators, it is "hidden" behind a fence in the private "Jewish" space of the synagogue rather than being in the public space of the city's streets and squares. On the one hand, the synagogue fence provides protection for this memorial (from antisemitic protesters), but on the other hand, the fence serves to distance and marginalize this memory.

In the post-Communist era, however, memorials to the victims have been erected in public spaces, as something approaching a free market of memorialization has emerged. Thus, while it is the first memorial to the "Jewish" victims of the Holocaust in central Budapest, this memorial just inside the Pest ghetto wall is not the only memorial to the "Jewish" victims. The upturned menorah/weeping willow memorial in the synagogue courtyard contrasts markedly with the small *gal-ed*—a witness heap of stones, as in

Genesis 31:45–48—built on the grounds of a block of flats on the Pest bank of the Danube. This simple memorial, "set up by the Hungarian Zionist Federation and the Hungarian Office of the Jewish Agency for Israel" in April 1994, is "in memory of those sacrificed and the heroes of the Zionist resistance." It is therefore not a memorial of Jewish "martyrs" alone—as the Dohány Street synagogue memorial is—but a memorial of Jewish "heroes" as much as Jewish victims. In this, it remembers the Holocaust in typically Zionist and Israeli terms.[34] Such Israeli Zionist memory is removed from the American Diasporic memory of the Holocaust, which characterizes the *Martyrs' Memorial* erected by the New York–based Emanuel Foundation. In some ways, therefore, the Israeli Zionist memory of "heroes and martyrs" and the American Diasporic memory of only "martyrs" contest the memorial space of Budapest.

The location of the Zionist memorial is a part of the recent process of transforming the Danube river bank into a place of memory. In the winter of 1944, Budapest "Jews" were shot and thrown into the river by Nyilas gangs, and this history—of Hungarian complicity in the Holocaust—has started to be remembered. However, the Zionist memorial is in many ways in the "wrong" place. The major sites of execution were to the south of where the memorial has been placed, and yet in some ways the specific site of history has been replaced by a more general sense of the whole Pest Danube bank as a site of memory. The memorial located closest to the historical site of the shootings is a series of tiles by the artist Anna Stein. Set into the ground in the middle of a road junction just on the northern side of the Margit bridge in 1990, it is dedicated "as a token of remembrance to those Hungarians who in the winter of 1944–45 fell victim to the Nyilas terror," and thus is marked by a lack of Jewish specificity. There is a nationalizing—a "Magyarization"—of memory at work here, whereby the victims of the Holocaust cease to be the "victims of Fascism" of Soviet Communist memory, and become instead the "Hungarian" victims of post-Communist Hungarian memory. In both the Soviet and post-Soviet periods, therefore, the "Jewishness" of the victims has been downplayed and denied in the city's streets.

REMEMBERING THE LIBERATORS, FORGETTING THE VICTIMS?

Whilst the Soviet liberation is not remembered in these post-Communist memorials, the role of the non-Soviet liberator continues to dominate the memorial landscape. Indeed, the transformation of the site of the Pest ghetto into the site of Soviet liberation, which characterized the wall plaque set up immediately after the war, is mirrored in some ways by the transformation of the Pest ghetto into the site of memory of the Swiss diplomat Carl Lutz. In 1991, the Swiss Carl Lutz Board, with the support of the city council, erected a sculpture by Szabó Tamás in the heart of the Pest ghetto's eighth district.[35] It is a monument to Lutz as "savior" rather than a memorial to the Jewish victims of the Holocaust. Indeed, the Jewish specificity of those "saved" by Lutz in 1944 is suppressed in a text which speaks only of "those thousands of Nazi persecuted saved through the leadership of Swiss Consul Carl Lutz in 1944."

Lutz, along with Wallenberg and the consular officials of a number of other neutral countries, did act to protect thousands of Budapest Jews in the latter half of 1944, but he didn't do it here. The attention of the neutral legations was focused on the international ghetto area in northern Pest—which, as I have suggested, has been "Wallenberg-ized," and hence there is no room for Lutz there—rather than the Pest ghetto. But in the case of Lutz, the so-called "Glass House" at 29 Vadász Street, where the Swiss legation sheltered Jews, suggests itself as an alternative site of memory. And yet the site of history of the Pest ghetto—which had little to do with Lutz—has been transformed into a site of memory of Lutz (and those he saved). In many ways this amounts to a form of colonization of the Pest ghetto. It is about the erecting of monuments to liberators, rather than memorials to victims.

At the end of the twentieth century, perhaps it is easier to remember Holocaust heroes than it is to remember Holocaust victims. It is, after all, more comfortable to give the Holocaust a happy ending. This preference for heroic liberators over victims is not limited to the Communist period alone. Rather, political changes have created new heroes. Wallenberg and Lutz have replaced the Red Army.[36] This concern with (male) heroism of course stretches back well beyond the Communist period, and further afield than Hungary. As Janice Monks says of memorial sculpture more generally, "conveyed to us in the urban landscapes of Western societies is a heritage of masculine power, accomplishment, and heroism."[37] However, choosing to remember the Holocaust in Budapest through the common trope of the heroic male (specifically Wallenberg) may actually amount to forgetting the Holocaust.

Notes

1. James E. Young, *The Texture of Memory: Holocaust Memorials and Meaning* (New Haven, Conn.: Yale University Press, 1993), 12 (emphasis in original).

2. A. Danto, "The Vietnam Veterans Memorial," *The Nation,* 31 August 1986, 152, cited in Young, *Texture of Memory,* 3 (emphasis mine).

3. Sanford Levinson, *Written in Stone: Public Monuments in Changing Societies* (Durham, N.C.: Duke University Press, 1998), 39.

4. Sybil Milton, *In Fitting Memory: The Art and Politics of Holocaust Memorials* (Detroit, Mich.: Wayne State University Press, 1991), 10.

5. Levinson, *Written in Stone,* 137.

6. Tim Cole, *Selling the Holocaust: From Auschwitz to Schindler—How History Is Bought, Packaged, and Sold* (New York: Routledge, 1999), 122.

7. Michael Berenbaum, *After Tragedy and Triumph: Essays in Modern Jewish Thought and the American Experience* (New York: Cambridge University Press, 1990), 33.

8. Raul Hilberg, *Perpetrators, Victims, Bystanders: The Jewish Catastrophe, 1933–1945* (London: Lime Tree, 1993).

9. Tony Kushner, "The Memory of Belsen," *New Formations* 30 (winter 1996–97): 18 (emphasis mine).

10. Pierre Nora, "Between Memory and History: *Les lieux de mémoire,*" trans. Marc Rousebush, *Representations,* no. 26 (1989): 22; criticized in Nuala Johnson, "Cast in Stone: Monuments, Geography, and Nationalism," *Environment and Planning D: Society and Space* 13 (1995): 51–65.

11. Johnson, "Cast in Stone," 51.

12. Ibid., and Levinson, *Written in Stone,* 71–73.

13. Young, *Texture of Memory,* 119.

14. Kenneth E. Foote, *Shadowed Ground: America's Landscapes of Violence and Tragedy* (Austin: University of Texas Press, 1997), 24–25. Foote notes that "whereas sanctification leads to the permanent marking of a site and its consecration to a cause, martyr, or hero, effacement demands that all evidence of an event be removed and that consecration never take place. Whereas sanctification is spurred by the wish to remember an event, obliteration stems from a desire to forget."

15. Tim Cole and Graham Smith, "Ghettoization and the Holocaust: Budapest, 1944," *Journal of Historical Geography* 21, no. 3 (1995): 300–316.

16. Géza Komoróczy, ed., *Jewish Budapest: Monuments, Rites, History* (New York: Central European University Press, 1999), 400. Komoróczy notes that the street was initially named Wallenberg Street, but its name was changed again to Raoul Wallenberg Street in 1946.

17. Lévai Jenö, *Raoul Wallenberg: Regényes élete, hõsi küzdelmei, rejtélyes eltûnésének titka* (Budapest: Magyar Téka, 1948), 260.

18. A photograph of the original wall plaque is reproduced between pages 169 and 170 of Agnes Adachi, *"Child of the Winds": My Mission with Raoul Wallenberg* (Chicago: Adams, 1989). This plaque was replaced in 1989 with a new one.

19. See Andrew Charlesworth, "Contesting Places of Memory: The Case of Auschwitz," *Environment and Planning D: Society and Space* 12 (1994), 579–593, and William Korey, "Anti-Semitism and the Treatment of the Holocaust in the USSR/CIS," in *Anti-Semitism and the Treatment of the Holocaust in Postcommunist Eastern Europe,* ed. Randolph L. Braham (New York: Columbia University Press, 1994), 207–224.

20. Komoróczy, *Jewish Budapest,* 442, although Adolf Rieth, *Monuments to the Victims of Tyranny* (New York: Praeger, 1969), 82, gives the date as 1948.

21. A similar marginalizing of memory, in this case of the Chicago Haymarket Riot of 1886, is noted in Foote, *Shadowed Ground,* 11–14: "The business community claimed the site of the bombing to erect a policemen's monument and prevented labor from memorializing its martyrs within the city limit. The memorial to the labor martyrs was placed at their grave in Waldheim Cemetery, across the city line in Forest Park."

22. Rieth, *Monuments,* 23.

23. Ibid., 24.

24. Young, *Texture of Memory,* ix.

25. Harvey Rosenfeld, *Raoul Wallenberg,* rev. ed. (New York: Holmes and Meier, 1995), 122.

26. Ibid., xv.

27. Ibid., xxii.

28. Henry Kamm, "Wallenberg: Statue Rises in Budapest," *New York Times,* 15 April 1987, Section A, 2.

29. Translation in John Eisenhammer, "The Search Goes Back to Moscow for the Truth about Wallenberg," *The Independent,* 12 October 1989, 12.

30. Rosenfeld, *Wallenberg,* xxii.

31. John Bierman, *Righteous Gentile: The Story of Raoul Wallenberg, Missing Hero of the Holocaust* (Harmondsworth: Penguin, 1995), 201.

32. László Keller, *Küldestésem: A zsidó tradíciók szolgálatában* (Budapest: Távlat Kiadás, 1994), 146–147.

33. *Don't Forget the Victims!* pamphlet (New York: The Emanuel Foundation, n.p., n.d.).

34. See Cole, *Selling the Holocaust,* 121–127.

35. Komoróczy, *Jewish Budapest,* 396.

36. With the recent creation of a "Raoul Wallenberg Emlékpark" [memory park] in the courtyard of the Dohány Street synagogue that holds the *Memorial of the Hungarian Jewish Martyrs,* this Wallenberg-ization is all the more marked.

37. Janice Monk, "Gender in the Landscape: Expressions of Power and Meaning," in *Inventing Places: Studies in Cultural Geography,* ed. Kay Anderson and Fay Gale (Melbourne: Longman Cheshire, 1992), 126.

17 Berlin Elegies

Absence, Postmemory, and Art after Auschwitz

LESLIE MORRIS

In 1992 the city of Berlin produced a tourist map of Jewish "places." It is a map of the absence of the lost object of Jewish life, a map of places that are no longer there but at the same time are "there" as they are marked by that absence. On the back is the familiar U- and S-Bahn guide provided by the city, enabling the tourist to reach these sites that are no longer "there." Jewish life in Germany is lost but not forgotten. It even comes complete with a map—of mourning, of memory, of absence—to get you "there."

The "there" indicated by the Berlin map—which is, paradoxically, *not* there—the lacuna that marks a place of mourning, memory, postmemory, and nostalgia, is the "imprint" of the Shoah in Germany today. Andrea Liss formulates "postmemory" as consisting of "the imprints that photographic imagery of the Shoah [has] created within the post-Auschwitz generation."[1] The Berlin map of absence encapsulates the project of commemoration and postmemory: it is not solely the memory of the Shoah, but the memory of the layers of representation as they have accrued, in the public imagination, over the past decades. Holocaust remembrance in post-1989 Germany is a postmemory that cannot be traced back to an originary moment of the Holocaust itself, but that circulates endlessly as representation, as melancholia, as the elegy for Berlin that still echoes in the ruins of the city that is in a constant state of (re)construction.

Yet ironically, or perhaps fittingly, this absence has never been more fully enacted; in the years since the appearance of the map of Jewish absence in 1992, German culture has been saturated with plays, films, concerts, lectures, newspaper articles, symposia, and art exhibits that thematize and explore the current obsession with Jewish culture—both with the vanished Jewish culture as represented by the map of Jewish places in Berlin and with the resurgence of Jewish life as it has been taking shape in Germany since Unification a decade ago. Despite the current preoccupation with Jewish life in Berlin, there is simultaneously, and perhaps paradoxically, a preoccupation with Jewish death and dying, and both preoccupations circulate endlessly in a cultural maelstrom that moves, inexorably, back to the United States. Furthermore, the current German preoccupation with Jewish culture and remembrance of the Shoah is dependent on and mediates the forms Holocaust remembrance has taken in the United States. In Thomas Mitscherlich's 1996 film *Reisen ins Leben* [Travel into life], Daniel Libeskind's Jewish Museum, Anselm Kiefer's recent paintings that allude to poems by Ingeborg Bachmann, and the New York rock opera *Hedwig and the Angry Inch,* Jewish memory—its absence and presence—in Germany foregrounds its own mediation.

Calling into question the viability and possibility of history, knowledge, and subjectivity, these post-Holocaust texts are all marked by meta-reflection about the Holocaust and memory. Furthermore, all these texts, in attempting to problematize the limits of representing the Holocaust, become themselves elegies to the past viability of Holocaust representation. The notion of postmemory is tied to this. Postmemory takes as a given that the nature of memory itself is mediated, never transparent, an "imprint," as Liss terms it, of its prior representations. This notion of postmemory insists on the impossibility of a transparent relationship to the past and to language, announcing itself instead as artifact, as mediated between the various layers and levels of memory, experiential and textual. Postmemory, as I am using the term, is memory that cannot be traced back to the Ur-text of experience but rather unfolds as part of an ongoing process of intertextuality and translation and a constant interrogation of the nature of the original.

I turn to the idea of postmemory as a way to think about the visual proliferation of Holocaust remembrance work in Germany; the constant, indeed, some would say, compulsive, acts of remembrance and commemoration in Germany in the past decade are as concerned with the mediated nature of memory as they are with both uncovering and challenging an "authentic" experience of the Holocaust which can then be represented through art or literature.[2] This obsession with Jewishness in Germany has not gone unnoticed; the nearly constant hum of klezmer music in the background of this feverish cultural production in Berlin is hard to miss. At the center of the "new" Berlin is the rebuilt Potsdamer Platz, with its newly opened "Arcades"—

a dizzying shopping mall that constitutes its center, and that contains Berlin's first bagel shop, Salomon Bagels. Salomon Bagels in Berlin—which has as its logo "Salomon Bagels: wisdom that you can eat"—is a visible, commercial marker on the map of Jewish absences and the landscape of memory and postmemory that defined Berlin in the late 1990s.

Furthermore, the placement of Salomon Bagels in the Arcades adds another layer to the rich figuration of the Potsdamer Platz in the historical, cultural, and political dimensions of Berlin from the turn of the century through the fall of the wall in 1989 and the recent rebuilding of the city. More than a mere shopping mall in an urban center, the Potsdamer Platz Arcades carry the echo and the weight of past city spaces—by the invocation of Walter Benjamin's *Arcades Project,* his vast but unfinished memorial to the primacy of consumption among the nineteenth-century Parisian bourgeoisie—and exist as a cultural site where mourning, consumerism, and spectatorship collide. In contrast to the Potsdamer Platz Arcades, whose excessive consumerism provides (or seeks to provide) a reprieve from the weight of the past that marks public spaces in Berlin, the Potsdamer Platz was for years a construction site, filled with cranes and the rubble of the past and future, yet a construction site announcing itself as museum space. During the late 1990s, for example, a passenger leaving the subway to enter the Arcades moved through a large anteroom that had three cut-out windows framing the construction site. The frame that the subway passenger, en route to the Arcades, was invited to look through was marked by motion and change; as the construction proceeded, the picture through the frame changed weekly, perhaps daily. The existence of the frame depended on a constantly shifting body of spectators: subway passengers on their way to the Arcades who became, through the audible citation of Walter Benjamin and his *Arcades Project,* the city-dwellers who are the museum-goers of modernity.

In this new "museum" of the Potsdamer Platz, even the bagel—displayed behind glass at Salomon Bagels—becomes an object to be scrutinized and then consumed by passers-by. The mixture of consumer pleasure and historical myth is found, too, in the bagel shop's menu. On the front is an abstract drawing of a chess game, next to the list of drinks and bagel varieties a new-age elaboration of the meaning of chess, and on the back cover a "history of the bagel seen from a Salomonic viewpoint." Here various "origins" of the bagel are put forth, ending with a reflection on "the nourishing" and "the nourished." What seems at first glance to be a parody of academic discourse quickly proves instead to be an attempt to have the new "immigrant," as the brochure calls the bagel, serve as a unifying cultural force, which is described in the passage as bringing together, in its roundness, "that which have always been separated—yin and yang, male and female, mind and soul, East and West. . . . Salomon joins again mother and child, Germans and Jews, America and Russia."

I begin with this point on the map of contemporary Berlin to suggest the complex ways in which remembrance, nostalgia, and melancholy for the lost Jewish world of Berlin shape the landscape of the city, and how this remembrance inevitably pivots around and returns to, or echoes, the United States. Yet the nearly obsessive fervor for anything Jewish in Germany underscores the fact that at the core of German culture there is an absence of Jewishness, or at least of the vibrant Jewish culture that existed before the Shoah. While the presence of Jewish markers in Berlin (such as bagels and the ubiquitous, melancholic strains of klezmer music) suggests that this absence can be filled, contemporary artists and cultural critics focus not on filling "the void" but rather on highlighting it. While the bagels in the Arcades depend on the illusion of filling the gap—the gap, perhaps, that the construction site of the Potsdamer Platz still underscores—Daniel Libeskind's Jewish Museum in Berlin is constructed around his concept of "voids," and voids punctuate the museum. In fact, the city of Berlin has come a long way toward acknowledging the absence of Jewish life in Germany since it launched its monumental exhibition on cultural history *Jüdische Lebenswelten* [Patterns of Jewish life] in 1992, to mark the fiftieth anniversary of the Wannsee Conference. On the one hand, the *Jüdische Lebenswelten* exhibit paid tribute to the contribution of Jewish life in Germany while on the other hand it failed to reflect on the very fact that Jewish "life" in Germany has become the object of a museum exhibit. In contrast to this landmark exhibition, Libeskind's Jewish Museum evokes the absence of what was once a vibrant Jewish culture: the "voids" create a distinct rupture in the function and meaning of architectural and museum space in Germany.

This preoccupation with inscribing absence and blank space onto sites in Berlin is not something that Libeskind has invented. Christian Boltanski's *Missing House* installation in the Grosse Hamburger Strasse in Berlin, for instance, and Shimon Attie's installation *Writing on the Wall* in the Scheunenviertel both foreground the interplay between Jewish absence and presence in Berlin, using the public spaces of the city to explore the relationships between contemporary life in Germany and the memory of a Jewish culture. Yet Libeskind's conception of the museum goes a long way toward acknowledging the fiction of wholeness that lies behind any attempt at portraying the void. Libeskind inscribes the discussions about memory and history into the voids that punctuate the building, creating out of the museum space a repository, not of art, but of memory and postmemory. Libeskind's museum serves as a testament to the absence of Jewish life in Germany; its architectural design stands as a counterpoint to the pervasive nostalgia and fetish of Jewishness of present-day Berlin. The *Jüdische Lebenswelten* exhibit of 1992, which sought to recreate and evoke the richness of Jewish life in Berlin through art, artifacts, music, dance, and literature, preserved instead a statically absent Jewish life in Germany, a Jewish life of remnants, artifacts, memento mori kept "under glass."[3]

If the *Jüdische Lebenswelten* exhibit put Jewish experience under glass, Libeskind's museum is devoted to the absence of that traditional model of a collection; instead, he posits a collection which he has described as "reducible to archival and archeological material since its physicality has disappeared."[4] *The Jüdische Lebenswelten* exhibit concerned itself with the resurrection and redemption of this physicality, evoking pathos and nostalgia as it placed its objects—a physical presence that is now a trace—under glass. In contrast, Libeskind is concerned not only with this absent trace of Jewishness in Berlin, but also with what he describes as an "invisible matrix or anamnesis of connections . . . between figures of Germans and Jews; between the particular history of Berlin, and between the Jewish history of Germany and of Berlin."[5] The elliptical and elusive connections he draws all circle around Jewish Berlin culture, including Schönberg's *Moses und Aron,* Walter Benjamin's *One-Way Street,* and the Berlin Jews deported during the war. Libeskind has created a piece of conceptual art, a reflection on the role of art and the role of the museum in Berlin; his anti-museum, as some have called it, challenges the notion of the museum as a repository for objects.[6] The presence of the voids is a way of questioning the feasibility of that kind of representation: the void cannot be filled with real or mimetic objects, it can only point to its own status as void.[7]

Another text that, like Libeskind's museum, foregrounds its own status as text and insists on the highly mediated nature of memory is Thomas Mitscherlich's 1996 film *Reisen ins Leben.* As a hybrid film that weaves together memoir literature, survivor testimonies, and documentary footage (albeit with a fictive cameraman), Mitscherlich's film bears some resemblance to another recent, well-received film about Jewish memory in Germany, *Herr Zwilling und Frau Zuckermann.*[8] Yet Mitscherlich's insistence on the mediated nature of memory and his interest in exploring the borders and limits of geographical space and memory constitute an important step away from the kind of nostalgic memorializing of Jewish culture that has shaped much of Holocaust remembrance in Germany—i.e., away from the absent "there" in the Berlin map that is filled with such insurmountable pathos. As he explores the interplay between memory and place, Mitscherlich—the son of Margarete and Alexander Mitscherlich, the authors of the 1967 text *Die Unfähigkeit zu trauern* [The inability to mourn]—inserts himself into the discourse about mourning after the Shoah which was begun by his parents and taken up with renewed energy in Germany in the 1980s. By presenting his trip "into life" as, at the same time, a trip into highly mediated landscapes of memory and history, Mitscherlich avoids slipping into the discourse of death and nostalgia that characterizes much of Holocaust remembrance in Germany; *Reisen ins Leben* represents, I believe, a new moment in German Holocaust remembrance and film.

Reisen ins Leben weaves together the testimonials of Gerhard Durlacher, Jehuda Bacon, and Ruth Klüger, all of whom survived Auschwitz as teenagers. Yet Mitscherlich does not simply tell the stories of these three survivors, but rather concerns himself with the difficulties of representation, narrative, and image. Durlacher, Bacon, and Klüger are all, significantly, artists who have explored the limits and the viability of Holocaust representation in the visual arts and in literature. Mitscherlich begins his film with documentary footage, shot by the Allies right after the war, of Germans walking past the mounds of dead bodies at Dachau, holding handkerchiefs to their noses. The footage is authentic, recognizable because it is now part of the corpus of images of the Holocaust that have made their "imprint," as Liss asserts, on the visual imagination that shapes Holocaust discourse. Liss insists on not reading documentary photographs only as objective documents: "on a deeper psychic level, they set up the shock of the unimaginable made visible." The shock value of these images, their extremity, and the ways in which they challenge and test the viewer's empathy, Liss argues, create out of the Holocaust documentary photograph a medium that "challenges and expands the limits of the documentary."[9]

Mitscherlich's film concerns itself with precisely these limits and with the questions of authenticity, authorship, reciprocity, and transparence or opacity that the documentary photograph raises. The documentary footage shown at the beginning and periodically throughout the film, however, is attributed to the eager, zealous filmmaking of a fictive American soldier, Sergeant Mayflower, a sort of Everyman/American GI cameraman, who was, as we learn from the voice-over, under orders from General Eisenhower to film the end of the war and the atrocities committed by the Nazis. Sergeant Mayflower is now returning to Germany to revisit the sites he once filmed, in particular the camp at Ohrdruf, where he once captured General Eisenhower on film. This journey back to Ohrdruf by the fictive Sergeant Mayflower is one of several that the film evokes. By mixing documentary footage with the voice-over of Sergeant Mayflower, Mitscherlich problematizes the acts of narration and remembering as he highlights the difficulties of separating fact from fiction. Furthermore, the introduction of a fictionalized narrator named Mayflower grafts American history onto the tableau of German history, creating another slippage in a text that is already marked by the frame of a wet, and thus not fully transparent, windshield. The recurrent shot from inside a car, often in the rain, presents the spectator with the view of a rain-soaked windshield, with the windshield wipers moving at irregular intervals. Thus the insistence on the arbitrary and filtered view of the past that suffuses the entire film recurs, again and again, as we are led into the landscapes that punctuate it, and into the lives of the three survivors. In filming the recurrent image of the rainy windshield, where images are blurred and then suddenly become clear, only to become blurred again, Mitscherlich suggests the mediated nature of the testimonies that make up the bulk of the film. Furthermore, the fact that these testimonies are interspersed with the other narratives he inserts into the film (such as the documentary footage shot by the fictive Sergeant Mayflower) raises the question of their authenticity and transparency, of whether they can be taken at face value or if they too participate in a similar slippage between fact and fiction, like the real footage ostensibly taken by the not-so-real Sergeant Mayflower.

Mitscherlich's central concern in highlighting the medium of filmmaking and of images in general is underscored further by the voice-over of Mayflower narrating Eisenhower's orders to the cameramen not to create propaganda. We hear Eisenhower's words repeated—"We're not Nazis"—and are reminded yet again of the role of filmmaking under the Nazis, presented with another layer of slippage and self-reflexivity. Mayflower, an American who nonetheless speaks in German without a trace of an American accent, becomes the moral voice for the film and for the act of filming atrocity. The subject position of the photographer—our fictive Sergeant Mayflower—underscores the intervention and agency of the photographer that lie behind the putatively objective and factual status of these photographs. For instance, we learn how Eisenhower wanted close-up shots "worthy of Hollywood"; in another segment of the film, Sergeant Mayflower narrates his failed attempt to film German refugees with a long-range telephoto lens, and his consequent need to mingle with them. Mayflower is disturbed by the fact that his distance from the perpetrators is shattered, that he has gone to the Germans in order to film them. Finally, as he is filming the Jewish refugees boarding the ship at Bremerhaven for the United States, the voice-over adds that it was a pleasure to film this "happy event."

The suggestion that the documentary is by nature opaque is reinforced by the camera shots taken from a car window as it moves through Holland, Israel, and California, each geographical location corresponding to the testimony of a survivor. Yet despite the differences between the geographical places Mitscherlich films, he joins these landscapes visually through images of the desert and of wandering, creating images that do not correspond to any transparent reality. Thus the borderland between Holland and Germany which introduces the testimony of Durlacher is shot so that it is reminiscent of the desert, of a no-man's-land of blank, indeterminate, illegible spaces. Similarly, the shots of the California beach that are interspersed with Ruth Klüger's testimony look like desert scenes as well, evoking the trope of the Jew as wanderer, as nomad, as citizen of a perennially indeterminate nation-state. The indeterminacy of the landscapes of the film is reinforced by the fact that we do not know who is in the car, who is driving, where we are going, and when or if the windshield wiper will clear the glass of the rain that is accumulating. The movement of the car gliding almost blindly through the various landscapes creates an almost hypnotic state that is meant to suggest, by analogy, the process of memory that unfolds in the three testimonies.

Reisen ins Leben is, finally, a poetic meditation on the meaning and viability of memory. Mitscherlich does not attempt to articulate the meaning of memory and testimony, but instead allows the film to be evocative, suggestive, allusive and elusive, relying on the principle of repetition and refrain, placing each survivor's testimony alongside the Sergeant Mayflower sequences and the drives through varied landscapes. The film is more concerned with evocation than it is with establishing historical facticity, yet the testimonials captured do follow the convention of survivor testimonies, where the interviewer remains off-camera and we are given static, close-up shots of the survivor, often overcome with emotion, telling his or her story, pausing, making the viewer aware of all that is not being said alongside what is actually said.

Yet, beyond the actual enterprise of narrating the testimonies of the three survivors, it becomes clear in the first minutes of the film that Mitscherlich is concerned not only with the project of narration, but even more with the relationship between image and memory. The opening shots of streams of Germans forced to look at the mountains of bodies in Buchenwald contrasts with the footage Mitscherlich inserts, introduced by Sergeant Mayflower telling of an amateur cameraman who was supposed to film the Ebensee concentration camp in Austria, but who instead filmed gorgeous scenes in the Alps, in color, cinematically beautiful and historically timeless. The film is framed, in many respects, by this ongoing discussion about the uses and abuses of image. At the end of the film, Ruth Klüger asks whether photographs possess a different kind of memory than experience; she then asserts that "reality only comes into being when it is photographed." With this observation, the film ends.

By thus raising questions about photography, memory, representation, and art after Auschwitz, Mitscherlich's film participates in the corpus of films and art installations in Germany that have, since the late 1980s, created and fostered a fascination not only with the Holocaust but also with the question of whether representations of the Holocaust are even viable. Perhaps the artist who has concerned himself most directly with this uncertainty of representation—both of the traces of Jewish history in this decidedly German landscape and, more controversially, of a mythological Germanic past—is Anselm Kiefer. The Hamburger Bahnhof Museum[10] in Berlin contains a painting by Anselm Kiefer, an enormous canvas with the opening of a poem (unattributed) by Ingeborg Bachmann as a standard Kiefer "signature"—"Wohin wir uns wenden im Gewitter der Rosen, ist die Nacht von Dornen erhellt"—scrawled at its top. The poem appeared in Bachmann's first volume of collected poetry, *Die gestundete Zeit* [Mortgaged time] (1953); in 1957 Hans Werner Henze set it to music after Bachmann added a second stanza for him. The first and original stanza, whose opening Kiefer inscribes into his painting, is

> Wherever we turn in the storm of roses,
> The night is lit up by thorns, and the thunder
> of leaves, once so quiet within the bushes,
> rumbling at our heels.[11]

Bachmann was accused, when she published this first volume, of a kind of timelessness and ahistoricity and of failing to name the specific fascist past. Yet more recent critics, such as Marjorie Perloff and Sigrid Weigel, have demonstrated the ways in which Bachmann's poetry grapples not only with the inadequacy of language in the aftermath of the Shoah, but also with the project of inscribing history into the literary text.[12] Bachmann's poem is packed densely with alliteration, assonance, and internal rhyme, all of which move the poem forward just as the "thunder of leaves" which follows at "our heels" moves forward. Yet the space into which "we" move is marked with the indeterminate "wherever" and the genitive metaphor "in the storm of roses," both of which create a space of indeterminacy and what Perloff has termed a poeticity in which poet, speaker, and reader all dwell.[13]

It is precisely this indeterminate space that Kiefer captures. Kiefer's painting, with "Wherever we turn in the storm of roses" scrawled at the top of the canvas, takes up Bachmann's challenge to find a way to preserve art and beauty in what she termed, in the poem "Psalm," the "afterbirth of terror."[14] Below the Bachmann text Kiefer has placed pink shapes that suggest fields of poppies, and long sequences of letters and numbers. On the surface of the canvas are strewn actual barbed wire and sand, which evoke the image of a map delineating the former concentration camps. Equally significant, the barbed wire and sand break the "frame" of the painting as limited, two-dimensional space; here the canvas intrudes into our space and plays with the idea of the "real." There is, in this Kiefer painting, no longer pure representation, but rather a fusion of abstract and real components. Yet, instead of names, the various sites are indicated by numbers, suggesting the numbers assigned to stars by astronomers and also evoking the memory of the numbers tattooed onto the skin of the inmates. At the same time, however, Kiefer skews that memory, calling it into question and creating both certainty and uncertainty in the viewer, as the numbers on the canvas are longer than concentration camp inmate numbers and often hard to decipher. These numbers, placed in the field of poppies (that are perhaps not poppies but the roses, however indeterminate, of the Bachmann poem, or the poppies of Kiefer's depictions of Celan's "Mohn und Gedächtnis" [poppy and recollection] in his poem "Corona," thus poppies which carry such excess of signification that they become indeterminate), become, in the context of this canvas, metonymic for the process of remembering the camps; the epic size of the canvas and the barbed wire inscribe the poem into another textual and metaphorical landscape, "re-membering" and refiguring the storm of roses as poppies and Bachmann's indeterminate "wohin" (wherever) as a recognizable Holocaust site—or perhaps, to quote "Früher Mittag" [Early noon], another early poem from *Die gestundete Zeit,* a place "where Germany's earth blackens the sky / where Germany's sky blackens the earth."

Kiefer's recent canvas *Lichtzwang* (1999), a reading of Celan's poem "We were lying" from his collection *Lichtzwang* (1970), is an iteration of this one, and a visual translation of the lines from "Früher Mittag." The canvas, about the same size as *Im Gewitter der Rosen,* consists of a similar panorama of sites, this time more unequivocally depicted as constellations (with Orion the only word spelled out), and tiny lead garments (identified as pieces of Lilith's clothing, thus establishing the Jewish context of the canvas). In *Lichtzwang,* however, there is no longer a suggestion of poppies or roses, just darkness, the darkness of the first line of Celan's poem, "Wir lagen schon tief in der Macchia" [We were lying / deep in the macchia].[15] The "Macchia," the stain, the darkened space that recalls the burnt-out topography of "Früher Mittag," is contrasted to Kiefer's evocation of constellations in his poem "Soviel Gestirne" and Bachmann's own preoccupation with stars in *Anrufung des großen Bären* [Invocation of the Great Bear]. But what—to bring this back down to earth—does this have to do with history and memory and poetry? Let me answer that by turning to Anne Carson's suggestion that Celan's use of the asterisk in many of his poems signifies that which cannot be said:

> Asterisk, that perfectly economical sign. A star in any language. A mark on the page that pulls its own sound in after itself and disappears. A meaning that refuses to waste a single word in order to write itself on the world. For stars, as you know, exist in their own time. Depending on your coordinates, you may be gazing at a star in the night sky whose actual fire ceased to exist millennia ago. Depending on your alphabet, you may be looking at a word in a poem that has already ended.[16]

The resuscitation of "a word in a poem that has already ended" is the trope that generates an earlier Kiefer painting (1993) bearing the title of Bachmann's poem "Böhmen liegt am Meer" [Bohemia lies by the sea], in which Kiefer transforms the Bachmann poem, with its intertextual reference (to Shakespeare's *A Winter's Tale,* act 3), into what is arguably a Holocaust landscape. Bachmann's Bohemia poem—written in 1964 and published in 1968—recreates textual memory, evoking Bohemia lying on the seacoast as a place that exists only as text, as postmemory that is of necessity mediated, opaque, and not transparent. Kiefer's painting, on the other hand, seeks to "translate" Bachmann's Bohemia with Holocaust signifiers that can be traced back to an originary moment, thus suggesting, as he does in much of his work, that "all roads lead to Auschwitz." This is precisely what might explain Kiefer's strong reception in the United States and, as a result, what brings Bachmann to an American audience. In a strange but penetrating way, Kiefer thus both defamiliarizes and Americanizes Bachmann, inscribing her texts into the landscape of European concentration camps familiar to an American audience and, in an odd twist, refiguring her as a Holocaust—if not Jewish—author.[17]

The two Bohemia texts—Bachmann's poem and Kiefer's painting—evoke memory not as something real but as a place that only exists as text and as intertextuality (Shakespeare's Bohemia), memory that comes into being only through the opaque medium of language. Kiefer's painting is a translation, into another medium, of the already mediated textual memory of Bachmann. Kiefer inscribes and transforms Bachmann's imaginary landscape into the familiar landscape of the concentration camp and the map of Europe, yet defamiliarizes both the Bachmann text and, finally, the "map" that is barely visible in the dizzying visual expanse of the painting. The Böhmen of Bachmann's poem becomes a trace, a textual memory that carries with it the weight of other textual memories (most significantly, Shakespeare) and that then becomes absorbed onto the canvas of Kiefer's painting, and from there back to the text. Thus the circulation of signifiers between the Bachmann poem and the Kiefer painting can be seen as demonstrative of the circulation of memory and postmemory in post-Holocaust texts.

This chain, or circulation, of signification is also, I argue, what constitutes the melancholic, elegiac quality of both Kiefer's paintings and Bachmann's poems. By bringing Bachmann onto the canvas, Kiefer participates in the act of painting as mourning and as melancholic repetition. That his painting *Im Gewitter der Rosen* hangs in the Berlin Hamburger Bahnhof Museum is another link in this chain of signification, where the museum space stands in the memory of the ruins of Germany after Hitler. Both these paintings of Kiefer's not only evoke a Bachmann text but show the trace, or imprint, of the Holocaust as it is inscribed, however elusively and elliptically, in the poem. The roses of Bachmann's poem carry the weight of signification, as Romantic symbols, but then exceed this signification through the indeterminate "wohin" that pulls the reader into the poem; Bachmann's roses reappear, in Kiefer's painting, as elliptical memories of roses, or perhaps poppies, as flashes of color that are as indistinct and illegible as Bachmann's night illuminated by thorns.[18] By reaching into the repository of image and metaphor, Kiefer shapes and then remembers the Bachmann texts as Holocaust texts, yet, like Bachmann, in a way that is elusive, evocative, poetic. Both Bachmann and Kiefer have shattered familiar tropes of poetry and memory and produced texts that, while legible, both exceed and probe the limits of representation. As Lisa Saltzman has aptly noted, "Kiefer gives us representation, but representation as ruin."[19]

The figuration of the Holocaust in these two Kiefer paintings is mediated through Kiefer's strong reception in the United States—a critical acclaim that stands in stark contrast to the ambivalence and discomfort he arouses in his

German audience.[20] Kiefer, a German-born artist who no longer lives in Germany, has become *the* German artist for the American museum public, bringing to the United States works of art that explore the viability and persistence of historical memory.[21] That Kiefer would be so well received in the United States is both predictable and puzzling, especially given his contested status in Germany.[22] Yet it is his popularity among American Jews that merits further reflection. While Saltzman offers a plausible explanation of how Kiefer's problematic reception in Germany is due to his association with neo-Expressionism, seen by the German left as bearing the trace of fascist appropriations of German Expressionism before the war, this does not, however, explain his popularity with American Jews.[23]

To do so, I return to the idea that post-Holocaust art in Germany and the United States emerges from the reservoir of memory, or postmemory, that circulates between America and Germany, a shared memory of the Holocaust that perhaps situates the "origin" as Auschwitz but that has created a chain of signification that moves beyond the borders—metaphorical and geographic—of Auschwitz. The "Americanization" of Kiefer is a crucial component of his popularity among American Jews—he is the German who dares to challenge the postwar stance of a sanitized, denazified Germany, the German willing to place himself as a German, in settings which recall Italian fascism, with one hand raised in salute to Hitler. His transgression, perhaps disturbing and unsettling to a German audience, consists not only in exposing the layers of historical memory, but in creating new layers of figuration and signification, burying that memory and then evoking it again.[24]

Similarly, the rock opera *Hedwig and the Angry Inch* also creates a new layer in the figuration of the Holocaust as it points to the ways in which historical and cultural memory are shared between America and Germany; more precisely, it is the American rendition of German memory that comes to the stage in *Hedwig.* The opera tells the story of an East Berlin would-be male-to-female transsexual, Hansel/Hedwig, who spends his childhood in East Berlin putting his head and his radio in the oven so that he can listen uninterrupted to American rock music. In an attempt to escape East Berlin, Hansel decides to marry Luther, a Black American GI, but he must first undergo a sex-change operation, becoming Hedwig. The operation does not quite work; an "angry inch" remains of the former Hansel's penis. Hedwig, whose angry inch keeps her forever split between male and female, East and West, appears as a drag queen and, in the performances in which Ally Sheedy played the lead, as a drag king, that is, as a female performing as a male-to-female transsexual. The main marker of her femaleness is her wig, which is simultaneously a play on words with "Hedwig," thus suggesting the ways in which femaleness may—like Germanness in this opera—exist solely in the realm of language, of representation, of artifice.

Hedwig and the Angry Inch is filled with references to divided Germany, the memory of the Holocaust, and the Cold War. Furthermore, as a rock opera that carries with it the trace of American rock operas such as *Jesus Christ Superstar,* and *The Rocky Horror Show,*[25] *Hedwig and the Angry Inch* asserts a uniquely American voice, yet one that is dependent on the interplay among Germany, America, and the Holocaust. After living with Luther in a trailer park in Kansas, Hedwig is abandoned by him and becomes involved with Tommy Gnosis, the son of the commander at Luther's base. After Tommy Gnosis also leaves her, she meets Kristal Nacht, the most famous drag queen in Zagreb. Hedwig takes Kristal Nacht back to the United States to join the band "The Angry Inch," but then threatens to report her to the Immigration and Naturalization Service if she continues to wear drag and perform as Kristal Nacht.

As the opera progresses, Hedwig displays a rather stereotypically Germanic cultural despair: she appears on the stage as a melancholic trying to make sense of the world, of the past, of German history, sexual identity, and memory. Thus, as a text that mediates between German memory (displaced memory of the Holocaust and now the memory of a divided Germany, through the figure of the drag queen Kristal Nacht), *Hedwig and the Angry Inch* presents the memory of the Holocaust as displaced and inscribed into the divided Germany. This split is suggested through the body of Hedwig as she is incompletely transgendered (the angry inch), split between male and female, East and West Berlin, Germany and America, prose and song. The opening song thematizes the splits that join Berlin and Hedwig:

> On August 12, 1961, / a wall was erected / down the middle of the city of Berlin. / The world was divided by a Cold War / and the Berlin wall / was the most hated symbol of that divide. / Reviled. Graffitied. Spit upon. / We thought the wall would stand forever, / and now that it's gone, / we don't know who we are anymore. / Ladies and gentlemen, / Hedwig is like that wall, / standing before you in the divide / between East and West, / Slavery and Freedom, / Man and Woman, / Top and Bottom.

The insertion of a decidedly American opposition—slavery and freedom—and the mention, at the end of the passage, of sexual roles expand on the central theme of the divided city and the divided self.

The split self that forms the basis of the opera can also be seen as a Derridean slippage; the splitting is never finite and does not lead back to any notion of originary wholeness. Hedwig, after all, sings of her transformation in terms that call to mind Frankenstein and the Bible as much as a contemporary discourse about sexual identity and transgender: "I rose from off of the doctor's slab / like Lazarus from the pit." The opera adamantly rejects the idea that changing one's gender renders the subject whole; Hansel's process of becoming Hedwig, for instance, is evoked again and again in the opera with the metaphors of edifice and (potential) ruin: "Try and tear me down!" In the song

"Sugar Daddy," Hedwig croons to Luther, her "sugar daddy," in lyrics in which sexual and national identities collide:

> Oh the thrill of control / like a Blitzkrieg on the roll. . . . It's our tradition to control / like Erich Honecker and Helmut Kohl, / from the Ukraine to the Rhone. / Sweet home über alles, / Lord I'm coming home.

The opening chords of "Sugar Daddy" are a twist on the first chords of "Deutschland über alles," thus invoking in a camp-like way Nazi Germany, but also Jimi Hendrix's rendition of the Star Spangled Banner. The displaced "quotation" of Jimi Hendrix and that era of American rock—the rock that Hedwig, still at that time Hansel, would listen to in East Berlin by sticking his head in the oven—creates a nostalgia for the American rock opera, evoking it as an elegiac moment that belongs to the past and that is irretrievable except as quotation. Furthermore, the mention of the oven—metonymic, perhaps, for the Holocaust—into which Hansel once put his head in order to listen to American rock, serves as the opera's link between the Holocaust and American rock; most significant, however, is the way in which the Holocaust is always present—displaced, allusive, sly, and comic, the camp as camp (the oven, Kristal Nacht).

Later in the opera, Hedwig sings a lament, a reworking of the opening song "Tear Me Down," thus moving the opera from its defiant opening line ("Ladies and gentlemen: Whether you like it or not: Hedwig!") to the elegiac mode in the song "Hedwig's Lament." In this reworking of "Tear Me Down," Hedwig appears no longer as a Lazarus who has risen from her slab, but instead simply as Hedwig, "cut up into parts." This mode casts a nostalgic eye back to the history of rock operas in America and to the earlier parts of *Hedwig* itself. The opera then moves on to the final scene, in which Hedwig reveals herself as a muscular woman—that is, as a drag king beneath the drag queen—and Kristal Nacht similarly reveals herself as a woman. The lament, if in fact there is one in *Hedwig and the Angry Inch,* is for all lost certainties—sexual, historical, textual, and, most significantly, epistemological.

Like the Mitscherlich film, Libeskind's museum, and Kiefer's paintings, *Hedwig and the Angry Inch* draws on the shared memory of the Holocaust, a memory that has migrated beyond the borders of national memory and identity, a memory that is suspended between America and Germany. The first lines of *Hedwig* establish the opera's central concern with knowledge and identity, as Hedwig addresses the audience before starting her song: "Don't you know me, baby, I'm the new Berlin wall, try to tear me down!" This is, I believe, what constitutes the elegiac in these "Berlin elegies," which, like the map to the Jewish sites that are no longer there, mourns not only the murder of the Jews but the viability of art in the aftermath of the Holocaust, while also, paradoxically, celebrating indeterminacy, self-reflexivity, and ambiguity of representation.

Notes

1. Andrea Liss, *Trespassing through Shadows: Memory, Photography, and the Holocaust* (Minneapolis: University of Minnesota Press, 1998), 86. Also see Marianne Hirsch's use of the term in *Family Frames: Photography, Narrative, and Postmemory* (Cambridge, Mass.: Harvard University Press, 1997).

2. One conceptual artist who challenges the ability of art to represent the Holocaust is Zbigniew Libera, particularly with his *LEGO Concentration Camp* series, an installation that consists of seven boxed LEGO sets depicting such things as crematoria and experiments on inmates. See Stephen Feinstein, ed., *Absence/Presence: The Artistic Memory of the Holocaust and Genocide* (Minneapolis: Center for Holocaust and Genocide Studies, 1998), 44.

3. The museal aspect is underscored by the glossary of "Jewish words" provided at the back of the exhibition program available at the museum, which includes words such as "Kaschrut," "matzah," and "Torah." There, for instance, the word "Holocaust"—found in the glossary between "Diaspora" and "ivrit," stands as a singularly "Jewish" word, despite its transformation into a German noun, "der Holocaust."

4. Daniel Libeskind, *Countersign,* Architectural Monographs no. 16 (London: Academy Editions, 1991), 86.

5. Ibid.

6. I want to ask whether Libeskind's voids—an architectural "intervention" in the process of spectatorship—alter the spectator's role in any way, or if the voids still adhere to modernist demands of spectatorship. In *Modern Art in the Common Culture,* Thomas Crow makes a similar point in his discussion of Gordon Matta-Clark's site-specific art *Window Blowout,* which was intended to make a political point about housing in New York: in each window casement at the Institute for Architecture, he placed a photograph of a new housing project in the Bronx in which the windows had already been broken, and then he blew the rest of them out with an air rifle. Eisenmann criticized this for recalling Kristallnacht. Crow points out that it also secured Matta-Clark's modernist stance, as it made him into an "artist as romantic outlaw." See Thomas Crow, *Modern Art in the Common Culture* (New Haven, Conn.: Yale University Press, 1998), 135.

7. Libeskind is also playing with what Umberto Eco has defined as *hyperreality:* "Everything looks real, and therefore it is real; in any case the fact that it seems real is real, and the thing is real even if, like Alice in Wonderland, it never existed." See Umberto Eco, "Travels in Hyperreality," in *Faith in Fakes* (London: Vintage, 1983), 16. As a postmodern architect, Libeskind is aware of the paradox about reality that Eco describes; as someone who has designed a museum in Berlin, he is consciously alluding to the city's status as one of the world capitals of the traditional museum, exemplified in particular by the Pergamon Museum, with the reassembled Ishtar gate, the Pergamon Altar, and the full market gate to Miletus inside the museum space.

8. *Herr Zwilling und Frau Zuckermann* (dir. Wolfgang Koepp, 1998) makes evident the museal aspect of Jewish life—the preoccupation with a Jewish past while focusing on the German present. Like Mitscherlich's *Reisen ins Leben,* Koepp's film constitutes a fundamentally elegiac encounter, in its use of repetition and the proscribed act of witnessing, with the history and memory of the Holocaust. Koepp's film is as much the tale of its two witnesses, Frau Zuckermann and Herr Zwilling, as it is about the vanished world of Czernowitz. Koepp shot the film in the now mythical city of Czernowitz, a city that is recalled by Paul Celan in his Meridian speech as being forever irretrievable and lost, as an elusive place marked by a finger on a map of a

place that no longer exists. Koepp draws on this nostalgia while keeping the film rooted in the present. He insists on countering the nostalgic memorializing of Czernowitz and the lost world of Eastern European Jewry, by making a film that centers on two Jews living in Czernowitz today.

9. Liss, *Trespassing through Shadows,* 1.

10. It is interesting that Kiefer's painting is displayed in the Hamburger Bahnhof Museum, which opened in 1996 as the "Museum für Gegenwart" and for contemporary art. Built in the mid–nineteenth century as a train station, in 1906 it had become the "Verkehrs- und Baumuseum." Shortly before the Third Reich, the museum caved to National Socialist aesthetics, exhibiting larger-than-life marble statues of Prussian ministers in the form of dying warriors. The building was damaged in 1943 in air raids and in the final days of the war, because of its strategic location, was wrecked further. After the war, the museum was caught between East and West: situated in West Berlin, but administered de facto by the East German Reichsbahn as railway property. The GDR officials, however, could not reopen it as a museum because the laws set up by the allies limited the operations of the East German Reichsbahn to transportation. The museum was spared the fate of many damaged buildings, which were often destroyed so that they would not serve as reminders of the war.

11. Ingeborg Bachmann, *Songs in Flight: The Collected Poems of Ingeborg Bachmann,* trans. Peter Filkins (New York: Marsilio, 1994), 61.

12. See Sigrid Weigel, *Ingeborg Bachmann: Hinterlassenschaften unter Wahrung des Briefgeheimnisses* (Vienna: Paul Zsolnay, 1999), and Marjorie Perloff, *Wittgenstein's Ladder: Poetic Language and the Strangeness of the Ordinary* (Chicago: University of Chicago Press, 1996).

13. Perloff also points to the poem's indeterminacy, which exists alongside the formal, structured verse (*Wittgenstein's Ladder,* 148).

14. Bachmann, *Songs in Flight,* 57.

15. *Poems of Paul Celan,* trans. Michael Hamburger (New York: Persea, 1972), 289.

16. Anne Carson, *Economy of the Unlost* (Princeton, N.J.: Princeton University Press, 1999), 119.

17. This more recent work by Kiefer comes after two decades of his oedipal struggle as a German son on German soil, where he refigures himself, quite controversially, as Nazi—in his "Occupations" series, for instance.

18. Perloff suggests that the "storm of roses" and the mention of thorns point not only to sexual love, but also to the Passion of Christ (*Wittgenstein's Ladder,* 148).

19. Lisa Saltzman, *Anselm Kiefer and Art after Auschwitz* (Cambridge: Cambridge University Press, 1999), 96.

20. See Saltzman, *Anselm Kiefer,* 101–105 for an excellent discussion of Kiefer's problematic reception in Germany. See also Sabine Schütz, *Anselm Kiefer: Geschichte als Material: Arbeiten, 1969–1983* (Köhn: Dumont, 1999). Schütz points out that Kiefer's enthusiasts in the United States are, for the most part, Jewish collectors and gallery owners. Kiefer himself asserted, "Ninety-five percent of the American collectors who own paintings of mine are Jewish. That is certainly only one aspect of America, but a very important one" (my translation). See Schütz, *Anselm Kiefer,* 69, n. 64.

21. Sabine Schütz chronicles Kiefer's reception in the United States, citing in particular John Russell's *New York Times* piece in which he proclaimed, "Nobody noticed at the time—how could they, when so much else was happening?—but one of the best things that happened to Germany in 1945 was that Anselm Kiefer got born." See Schütz, *Anselm Kiefer,* 78 n. 20. Alongside this sort of panegyric to Kiefer can

also be found more temperate assessments of his success in the United States, notably by the Germanist Frank Trommler, who has speculated that Kiefer fulfils the American public's desire for an artistic genius in the aftermath of the deaths of artists such as Picasso, Duchamp, and Warhol. See Schütz, *Anselm Kiefer,* 69.

22. We can also ask whether the figuration and invocation of the Holocaust in Kiefer's work enables an American audience to displace its own historical, shared memory in the wake of, for instance, the Vietnam War.

23. Saltzman, *Anselm Kiefer,* 103. Saltzman, however, also challenges the notion that Kiefer is to be aligned with neo-Expressionism.

24. Lisa Saltzman makes a similar argument. She suggests that Kiefer is less concerned with the archaeological project of uncovering the buried, hidden secrets of the German past than with creating layers, covering and burying this past, entombing it. See Saltzman, *Anselm Kiefer,* 90–91.

25. I would even add to this list Laurie Anderson's evocation of Benjamin's Angel of History in her song "The Dream Before" on her *Strange Angels* album. I am grateful to Roni Shapira for pointing out to me that David Bowie, Iggy Pop, and Lou Reed lived and recorded in Berlin in the 1970s, and for alerting me to the acoustic and narrative affinities between *Hedwig* and *The Rocky Horror Show.*

18 Invisible Topographies

Looking for the Mémorial de la déportation *in Paris*

SHELLEY HORNSTEIN

> True space makes architecture into substance, thought makes architectural space an abstraction.[1]

I

In all the frames of the 350 hours of footage from which the 9½-hour film *Shoah* was made, we do not see one image of the Holocaust. Instead we have impressions, details, and silence. Claude Lanzmann, director of the magisterial project, says, "One has to talk and be silent at the same time. I have much silence in *Shoah*."[2]

And so begins the unending and contentious debate over whether or not to represent the Holocaust, and over what might very well be the limits of representation. The question has been all too well discussed, from Theodor Adorno's comment on writing poetry after Auschwitz, to Elie Wiesel's refusal to endorse representation of the Holocaust, to Primo Levi's plea for "a language 'of this other world,' a language born here."[3]

The question needs to shift, however, to what we must make of work that is being produced, work that carries as its theme reflections on the long-term effects of the Holocaust, particularly on children of survivors, and what criteria must be used to consider such work. Indeed, we must ask what language needs to be created to allow this kind of work (whether created immediately following the war or as contemporary as this moment) to be understood. And moreover, is understanding the work something we should even aim for, in the light of the incomprehensibility of such history?

Still, Lanzmann did make *Shoah.* As a collection of visual testimonies in film, it found an enormous and still expanding audience. Making art that provokes thought in the viewer or remembrance in the artist is unavoidable. But to what degree and how should it be done? These are questions anyone must grapple with who steps into this difficult terrain. A benchmark in this debate is *Probing the Limits of Representation,* edited by Saul Friedlander, in which he postulates,

> If one adds the fact that the perpetrators invested considerable effort not only in camouflage, but in effacement of all traces of their deeds, the obligation to bear witness and record this past seems even more compelling. Such a postulate implies . . . the imprecise but no less self-evident notion that this record should not be distorted or banalized by grossly inadequate representations. Some claim to 'truth' appears particularly imperative. It suggests, in other words, that there are limits to representation that should not be but can easily be transgressed. What the characteristics of such a transgression are, however, is far more intractable than our definitions have so far been able to encompass.[4]

Representation should not and cannot be a totalization or full presence of what might be conceived of as the Holocaust. I emphasize "conceived of" because the problem we face is its magnitude of beastliness, beyond any concept of beastliness that has come before, and "notwithstanding all the usual acts of beastliness of human history, the integrity of this common layer had been taken for granted. . . . Auschwitz has changed the basis for the continuity of the conditions of life within history."[5] Any attempt, therefore, to represent wholeness or closure strips the event of truth, in that its wholeness can only be told in fragments, and will continue to be told in fragments, in parts abstracted from any image of the whole. To tell a master narrative, thereby assuming that the complete story is known, is to deny the importance of the objective's massive scale. This plan, this "thing" ("la chose," as Lanzmann calls it), is limitless, and our imagination must recognize this fact. It is even echoed by those murdered. Maurice Blanchot recounts that the wish of everyone at Auschwitz was to declare, "Know what happened, never forget, and at the same time never will you know."[6]

Rather, representation might be a relationship of past, present, and future, where a past is constructed with traces. A trace is an abstraction, but even figuration is technically an abstraction of something even larger, abstracted, that is, from the larger whole. This whole, or a totalization, is the same as fullness, or "full presence." To avoid presenting the whole, and really the impossibility to conceive of what it might mean to present or represent the whole, abstraction, according to some, is fundamental. In 1962, the era of abstract art, abstraction must be seen as opposed to figuration, where a strategy of figuration must be seen as representation.

Dominick LaCapra identifies the absurdity of attempting to represent (as representation is equated with figuration):

> On an epistemological level, there is positivism in the idea that an objectifying notational system can ideally represent, transparently render, or capture the essence of an object. On a psychological level, there is what might be seen as the reversal of positivism in the reliving or reincarnation of a past that is experienced as fully present.[7]

The contemporary literary theory concept of intertextuality is therefore critical: no totalization—only parts and traces—but always in combination. To understand or even begin to understand (in the abortive attempt to understand—an attempt that is always, inevitably, doomed), one must read, see, know this and this and this. And later, one must add to this and this: that. Because of the impossibility of knowing all ("jamais vous ne saurez") and indeed because of our limited recognition that we will never have enough knowledge to know it all, pieces of the past, pieces of the present, and the relationship of those "abstracted" representations can give us the power to begin a reading (that will go nowhere but always begin again), as if knowing may even have an end. This quality of constitutive and limited knowledge, this abstraction from completeness, is the only possible "knowledge" of the *Shoah.* Lanzmann tells us,

> One must know and see, and one must see and know. Indissolubly. If you go to Auschwitz without knowing anything about Auschwitz and the history of this camp, you will not see anything, you will understand nothing. Similarly, if you know without having been, you will not understand anything either. There must therefore be a conjunction of the two. This is why the problem of places or sites is capital. It is not an idealist film that I made, not a film with grand metaphysical and theological reflections on why all this happened to the Jews, why one killed them. It's a film on the ground level, a film of topography, of geography.[8]

And so, to discuss the complexities of abstraction and why it makes no more sense than figuration as a way to represent the past, it is to topography that I turn, for there is a very strong link between the place where history is recorded, abstracted from the larger locality and even nation-state, and the larger area of ground upon which we build or dig. And while Lanzmann suggests the ground as a place whence we begin, which is different from how I will use it in this essay, still, the ground as metaphoric reference to beginnings is quite useful as an act of underpinning and representing the past in the present.

II

> The stones of remembrance of the Second World War . . . make up a piecemeal, scattered, shattered collection of tens of thousands of steles, plaques, and monuments. Yet in spite of their extreme diversity, the separate, tightly-packed memories, coexisting while unaware of each other, have common threads among them.[9]

In what Pierre Birnbaum describes as a "profoundly Catholic" country dotted with abbeys and churches, traces of Jewish memory are, as Barcellini and Wieviorka suggest above, "piecemeal, scattered, shattered" ("emietté, disperse, atomisé") to the point that there exist thousands of plaques and monuments commemorating the tragedies of the Second World War without coherent links between them, yet assembled as if part of a homogeneous whole. As a result, Birnbaum contends, time is steadfastly erasing symbols of this history.

Common to many of these monuments is the phrase "mort pour la France," inherited from the First World War and entered into law on 2 July 1915. This law stipulated that one was authorized to inscribe these words only if the monument was communal, unless special authorization was granted in order to honor a particular individual. Among the many thousands of memorials, only four in France—three of which are located in Paris—are national monuments and thus part of a collective initiative to remember: the Chapel of the Deportation in the Church of Saint-Roch, the two memorials of the concentration camps in the Père-Lachaise cemetery, and, in Alsace, the memorial at Struthof, the only concentration camp built on what was and now is again French soil, fifty kilometers from Strasbourg. Saint-Roch has a forthright Christian agenda to commemorate within the precincts of the church. In each one of these memorials, Jewish loss is either absent or merely referenced. Many of these sites have an aura of contemplation and silence, and one wonders whose collective voice is speaking; they underscore the eclipsing of Jewish memory by French (national) memory. As Birnbaum notes,

> Absent from the memory of the kingdom and of the nation, French Jews themselves often behave as if suffering from amnesia. Their memory is almost entirely identified with that of France. They have forgotten the events of their own history.[10]

If Jews have forgotten the events of their own history, it must be remembered that this forms an essential part of what Ernst Renan, in his "What is a Nation?" (1882), claimed we must do in order to meld with, to align with, indeed to surrender to, a national, collective whole. The illusion of universalism in the 1789 Declaration of the Rights of Man and of the Citizen is created by a politics of humankind and a series of assumptions based on Enlightenment values such as progress, rationalism, justice, and tolerance. Renan served to provide a model of constructed harmony and equality while ensuring that we disregard difference:

> Forgetting, I would even go so far as to say historical error, is a crucial factor in the creation of a nation. . . . [T]he essence of a nation is that all individuals have many things in common, and also that they have forgotten many things. No French citizen knows whether he is a Burgundian, an Alan, a Taifale, or a Visigoth, yet every French citizen has to have forgotten the massacre of Saint Bartholomew, or the massacres that took place in the Midi in the thirteenth century.[11]

The indeterminacy of French Judaism in postwar France results from a fundamental need to forget and mourn collectively and to recall Renan's words, but has given rise to a younger generation of Jews in France who struggle with a need to understand their "Frenchness" and "Jewishness." The postwar generation seeks a unified whole to represent history.

Alain Finkielkraut, one of France's towering cultural figures and author of—among many notable titles—*Le juif imaginaire* (1980), outlines the French and Jewish paradox as he sees it: how does one affirm a Jewish identity without resorting to essentialism? One must call for the right to cultural differences, he affirms, yet never make them absolute; they must always be subject to international human rights laws. Furthermore, he reviles cultural relativism and moves in the direction of a commitment to universalism as expressed in the spirit of the French Revolution, seeing such a commitment as a protection against slipping or being tempted toward totalitarianism. This stance emerges, as Natalie Rachlin suggests, from the postwar experiences of Finkielkraut and other French Jews, who see themselves

> belonging to a particular imagined community of French Jews, the generation of Ashkenazi Jews born immediately following World War II, whose parents escaped the Nazi genocide. These parent-survivors have asked, says Finkielkraut, two contradictory things of their children: that they assimilate, so as not to resemble those who were killed, and at the same time that they live in the shadow of the dead, in the shadow of the Holocaust. Loss and the prescription not to lose are, then, at the heart of this generation's collective identity. . . . The genocide thus has broken a certain symbolic filiation on which Jewish identity is traditionally based. For Finkielkraut, the memory of what preceded the Holocaust, because it was never transmitted, can never give his Jewishness the plenitude his parents' had. His Judaism was emptied by the Holocaust.[12]

One memorial coalesces in stunningly abstract architectural forms these modern ideas of assimilated oneness, of a history that may have wanted to speak to all and blend identities. At the eastern tip of the Île de la Cité in Paris, directly behind the gardens of Notre Dame Cathedral, lies the *Mémorial des Martyrs de la Déportation* [Memorial to the Martyrs of the Deportation], built in 1962 by Georges-Henri Pingusson (1894–1978), an architect and professor at the École des Beaux-Arts. The choice of Pingusson as architect was no accident. He had been an emblematic figure in the architectural community for many years already, having made his mark in the modern movement with important projects built between the wars, in particular the Hôtel Latitude 43° (1929–32), cascading over the bay of St. Tropez. He collaborated with Frantz-Philippe Jourdain, architect of La Samaritaine department store in Paris, and André Louis for the Union des Artistes Modernes (UAM) Pavilion at the World's Fair of 1937 and the reconstruction of the village of Waldwisse in 1948 after the Allied bombings, as well as various other towns in the Moselle. Between 1950 and 1959, he served as director of the Groupements d'urbanisme des bassins sidérurgique et houiller Lorraines [Urban association of the Lorraine metal and carbon mines] and eventually became known for a vast array of reconstructions and new urban schemes for communities in eastern France. He was also known for his churches, which were begun in the 1930s, revisited after the war, and realized after his death in 1978, such as the Église Saint-Antoine in Boust-Usselskirsch, Église de la Nativité in Fleury, or the Église Saint-Martin Evêque in Corny.[13]

The memorial project was initiated in 1953 by the Réseau du souvenir [Network of Remembrance], founded the year before as an association of "deportees," as they called themselves, survivors of the German concentration camps. Thanks to the Réseau, the law of 14 April 1954 was voted in; it declared the last Sunday in April to be dedicated to victims of the deportation and survivors of the death camps. The Réseau asked the municipal council of Paris to obtain an appropriate site for a memorial. Although the project was authorized to proceed (the council unanimously voted in favor of building a monument to the Martyrs of the Deportation on Parisian soil), the site was not officially designated until 1956, when a lot was allocated by the municipal council "on the point of the Île de la Cité, upriver of the Seine, in the Archbishop's Square."[14] More bureaucracy followed: in 1958 the Ministry of the Interior authorized the building of the memorial, but in December 1960 the prime minister launched a public campaign, followed by an order from the Ministry of War Veterans, for the creation of a national committee for the building of a monument in Paris to the memory of the heroes and martyrs of the deportation. The project was finally realized and inaugurated in 1962 by President Charles de Gaulle.

These dates are important because a parallel project with much publicity began in 1957, when the International Auschwitz Committee, an association of survivors, announced an international competition, presided over by Henry Moore, to build a monument to commemorate the victims of National Socialism. While the competition, according to Moore's later statement to the press, was doomed from the start because the outcome could never satisfy all those concerned, it is crucial to note the terms in which the first and greatest proposal, in the opinion of the artists and architects on the committee, was rejected. The project was not in keeping, so the other committee members stated, with the jury's rule concerning the altering of the ruins of the site at Birkenau, and it would have been too expensive. Perhaps most important of all, the survivors on the committee commented that it was too abstract. For them, abstraction diffused a focal point for commemoration; the literalness of their experiences could not be conveyed by an abstract remembrance.[15] The monument was finally constructed in 1967 and titled *International Monument to the Victims of Fascism.* Clearly survivors wished to retain some expression of figuration, and yet other monuments with similar objectives opted for abstract, modernist forms expressive of the time.

In Paris alone, two independent monuments were proposed to commemorate the dead victims of the Holocaust. It appears, after some consideration of what is implicit in the documents, that the Île de la Cité memorial was designed as a parallel project to the *Monument du martyr juif inconnu* [Monument to the unknown Jewish martyr] at the site of the Centre de Documentation Juive Contemporaine, rue Geoffroy-l'Aisnier. The latter honors the memory of all six million Jews murdered during the Holocaust, whereas the Pingusson memorial singles out the French losses exclusively and highlights that these losses are neither Jewish nor belonging to any other religious, racial, or cultural denomination; rather, the lives lost were those of French patriots, "mort pour la France." The *Monument du martyr juif inconnu,* proposed in 1951, was inaugurated in 1956.[16] When the memorial on the Île de la Cité was proposed in 1953, it was important that it be considered a separate expression from the former. While the former was created as a Jewish site of mourning and remembrance, the latter was intentionally free of any connection to religion, culture, race. What the memorial on the Île de la Cité attempted to represent was French suffering; it was to be a site of national identity.

The artistic consultant chosen by the Réseau was Jean Cassou, at that time chief curator of the Musée national d'art moderne.[17] While three teams of paired architects and sculptors were invited to contribute proposals in the spring of 1953, it was Georges-Henri Pingusson who was asked to elaborate further.[18] Cassou was probably instrumental in selecting Pingusson; although there is no documentation to support this conclusion, it seems likely given the minutes of the general assembly of the Réseau du souvenir, in which we can read that Cassou stated,

> We agreed on the forms, the aspects that should make up this monument. It should not be built like ordinary statues or monuments, but instead should consider the site, whose lines present a harmony that is characteristic: it should not break away from the horizontality of the river and the point of the island . . . it should invite the passerby to . . . feel as though he should be welcomed into this space at once intimate and collective. . . . [T]his is a project in which the architectural spirit, organization of space, construction, are more important than the sculpture.[19]

Early sketches show that Pingusson's sculptor-partner on the project, Raymond Veysset, proposed various sculptures in the form of steles to be placed within the second, open-air triangular space of the monument. However, Veysset was not involved with either the final drawings or the finished project, and although the documentation is scant, it seems that Cassou's wish for a monument "more important than the sculpture" was ultimately respected.[20]

Financed partly by the state, with other funds from various additional sources including a national campaign that accepted donations even from schoolchildren, the memorial is built on a site donated by the city on the condition that no part of the memorial be visible above ground.[21] Indeed, the symbolic liaison between the Notre Dame Cathedral and the *Mémorial* is marked by the way that the crypt of the church is extended topographically and spiritually by the crypt of the memorial.[22] The initial brochure published by the Réseau du souvenir captures this relationship as follows:

> It was important that the site itself should express the Spirit of Remembrance. Its place, therefore, was in the ground of our time-honored capital, within the precincts of the old Paris of Philippe-Auguste, at the foremost point of the Île de la Cité, in the thousand year old shadow of Notre-Dame. It was here that the Crypt was hollowed out of the sacred isle, the cradle of our nation, which incarnates the soul of France—a place where its spirit dwells. For was it not around this core, this "twin vessel" sung by the poet Charles Péguy, that our country came into being?[23]

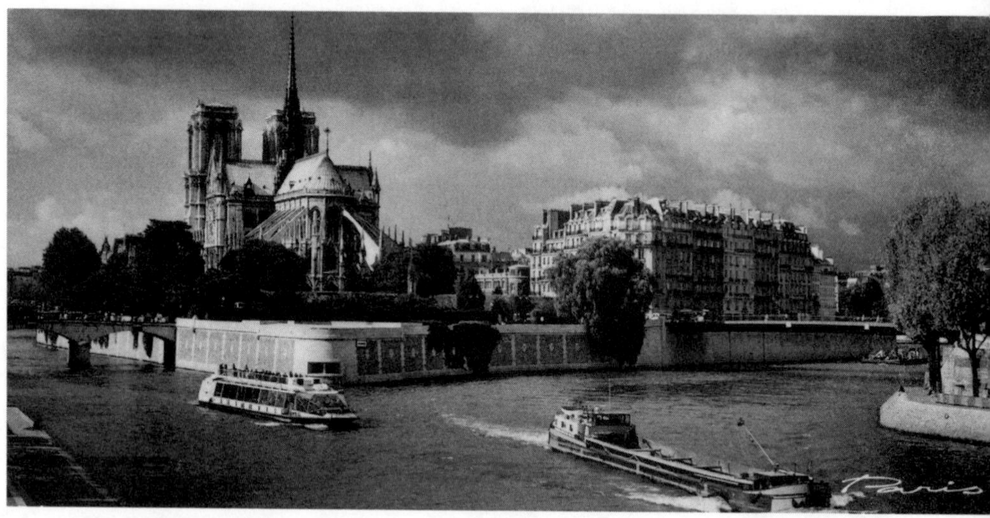

18.1 *Paris, Notre-Dame et l'île de la Cité,* n.d. Rectangular "window" of monument is seen behind the bateau-mouche (tourist river-boat). Thierry Colin, Aquarupella, La Rochelle, France. Reprinted by permission.

The rhetoric is clear: from Notre Dame Cathedral to the poetry and philosophy of Christian advocate Charles Péguy (the "twin vessel" recalls the towers of Notre Dame). This only serves to confirm that the civic objective was to maintain this monument (and others in France and elsewhere) within the precincts of a national place of mourning devoid of individuals and their communities, in spite of recognizing what at the time was calculated at two hundred thousand lives lost.

The space of the *Mémorial* begins at street level. In order to find the monument, and you must be determined to do so, you must walk behind Notre Dame Cathedral and begin to search. All you will find is a fenced property with high Hicks yew hedges that restrict any view beyond. A very small sign indicates that the memorial is beyond the gate, and it is only at this moment, if you are fortunate enough to find that sign, that you realize you are there and that the hunt is over. Inside the gate a lawn rolls out to the river, but inland it is halted at a short concrete wall that bears the name of the memorial. This space might be read as a preliminary space of abstraction, almost a tabula rasa, a site that cleans the slate of the chaos outside the gates and permits a meditative aura to displace any previous congestion of the mind and spirit. In addition, it is helpful to read this space as marking time in a way that helps us to somehow slow down so that we can rest our thoughts and prepare for what follows. Indeed, this important space, which doubles as an entrance and exit, devoid of figuration and alternative references, forces us to take the time to walk from the gate to the entrance, or the exit to the gate: this orchestrated space takes careful measure of time.

Two narrow punctures in the wall indicate entrances and it is at this point that the steep descent leads you into the majesty of a contemplative space that the memorial holds below. Each step down creates a rhythm calculated in the architecture to mark time in perfect syncopation with what happens before our eyes: our careful movement down a very steep and narrow staircase with unusually high risers is calculated to progressively cancel the Parisian facades until they disappear altogether and all that is left for us to view is the geometrically square-tiled white floor enveloped by the whitewashed solid walls of this empty and penned, somewhat triangular, space. The striking austerity is relieved by a sculptural grille that leads the eye to the tip of the space, which is sliced off and left open with a view of the Seine River, reminding us that we are level with the water. This is perhaps the singular most aesthetic bind: the heightened beauty of the space is further enhanced by the drama of the water smacking the space in which we are located. Pingusson bars the opening with a sharply angular sculptural black grille he designed, which sets the tone: we feel a sense of entrapment and are never relieved by any simulation or redemption of the past. We are in a monument that reverses any sense of the past and aims to see the present and the future. Because of an aesthetic

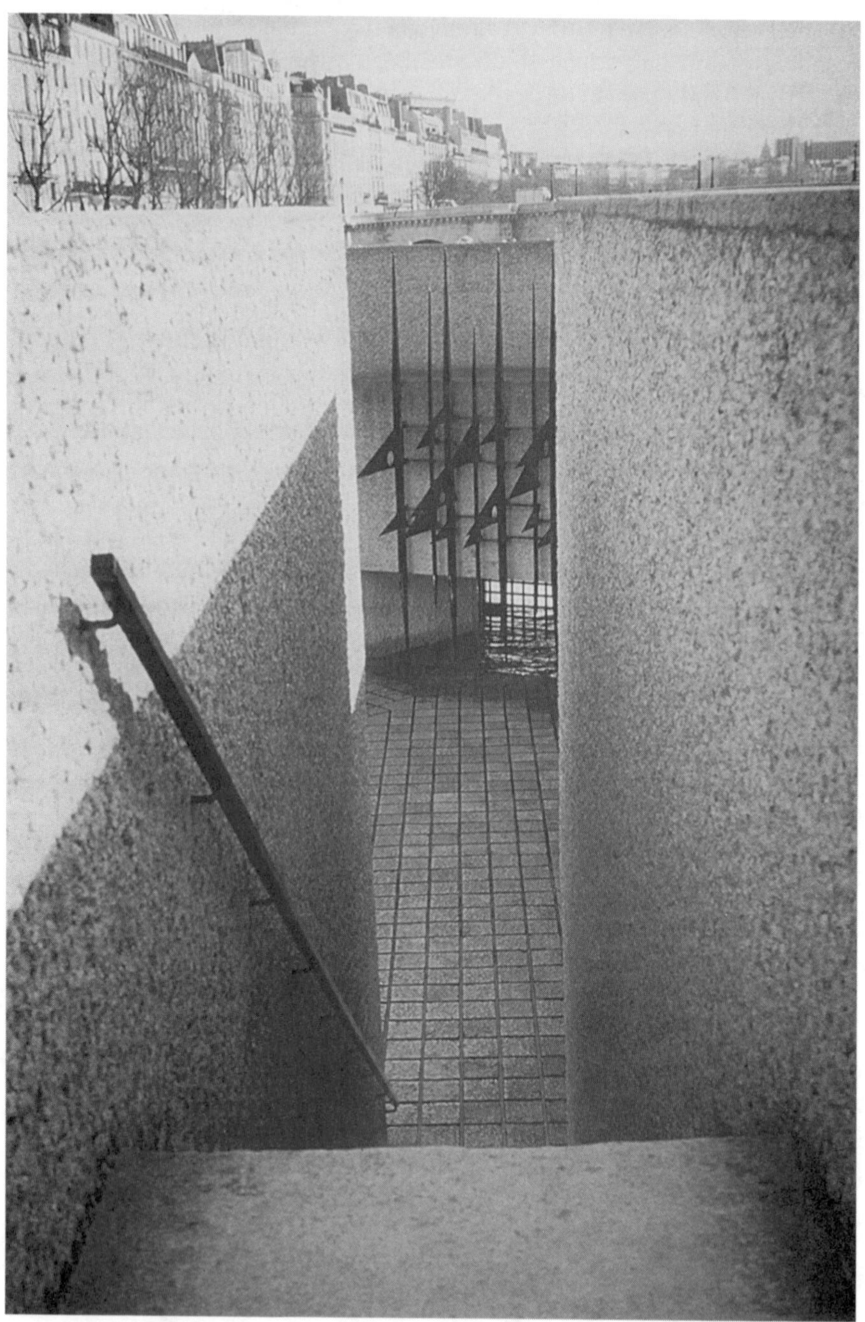

18.2 Georges-Henri Pingusson, *Mémorial aux Martyrs de la Déportation*, descending stairwell to second space. Photo by Shelley Hornstein.

awareness within the space, it is impossible to re-present any semblance of the brutality and trauma of the past. Pingusson clearly understood this impossibility: that is, rather than create a monument that reflects on a recreation of the past, he encourages our reflection in the present by making us first and foremost admire the solemnity of the space and its evocation of silence. He does this by slowing down our pace and monitoring our ambulatory visit through the monument, carefully considering the timeframe, as if he were manipulating grains of sand in an hourglass. Without that clean separation from the past, without that desire to be seen as independent from it with nothing more than subtle aesthetic footnotes, it would not be possible to observe the horror of that past. Pingusson frames the past under an opaque surface. The past is there but impossible to see. He wrote,

> The expression of this monument is purely architectural, no sculpture was judged necessary, only the complete bareness speaks, as well as the only elements, air, water, earth and fire.[24]

Within this second space, we are infused with the awareness of where we are, our physical place on the Île de la Cité at the "mouth" of the island. We feel our precariousness sharply in this site, where being below ground and flush with the river suggests that this memorial can be consumed, submerged by the river. This chilling sensation reminds us of our own fragility.

The final space is an internal, crypt-like interior space, again accessed by an acutely constricting pair of pylons. Here, natural light is restricted and limited and artificial light is strategic. We enter into a hexagonal space, a memorial space by virtue of what often connotes such a space: a tomb to an unknown deportee. A very long and narrow corridor inaccessible to visitors—almost like a crawl space—exhibits 200,000 lighted glass beads on the facing walls. This refers to the custom in Jewish synagogues of placing a light on the memorial board in memory of deceased relatives. Across the entrance and above, etched deeply into the stone, read the following words: "Deux cent mille français sombrés exterminés dans les camps nazis" [Two hundred thousand French citizens lost, exterminated in the Nazi death camps]. Two galleries traverse the central space: to the left and right are niches with the names of the camps engraved on triangular copper plaques and embedded deep in the concrete marking the urns placed within, which contain ashes of concentration camp victims. Each niche reveals an empty, symbolic prison cell and outside it, on the walls, are writings by Eluard, Maydieu, Saint-Exupéry, Aragon, and Sartre, among others.

III

The idea that Paris, the center of France and the capital of the revolution, the Commune, and the Liberation, would be selected for the site of the *Monument*

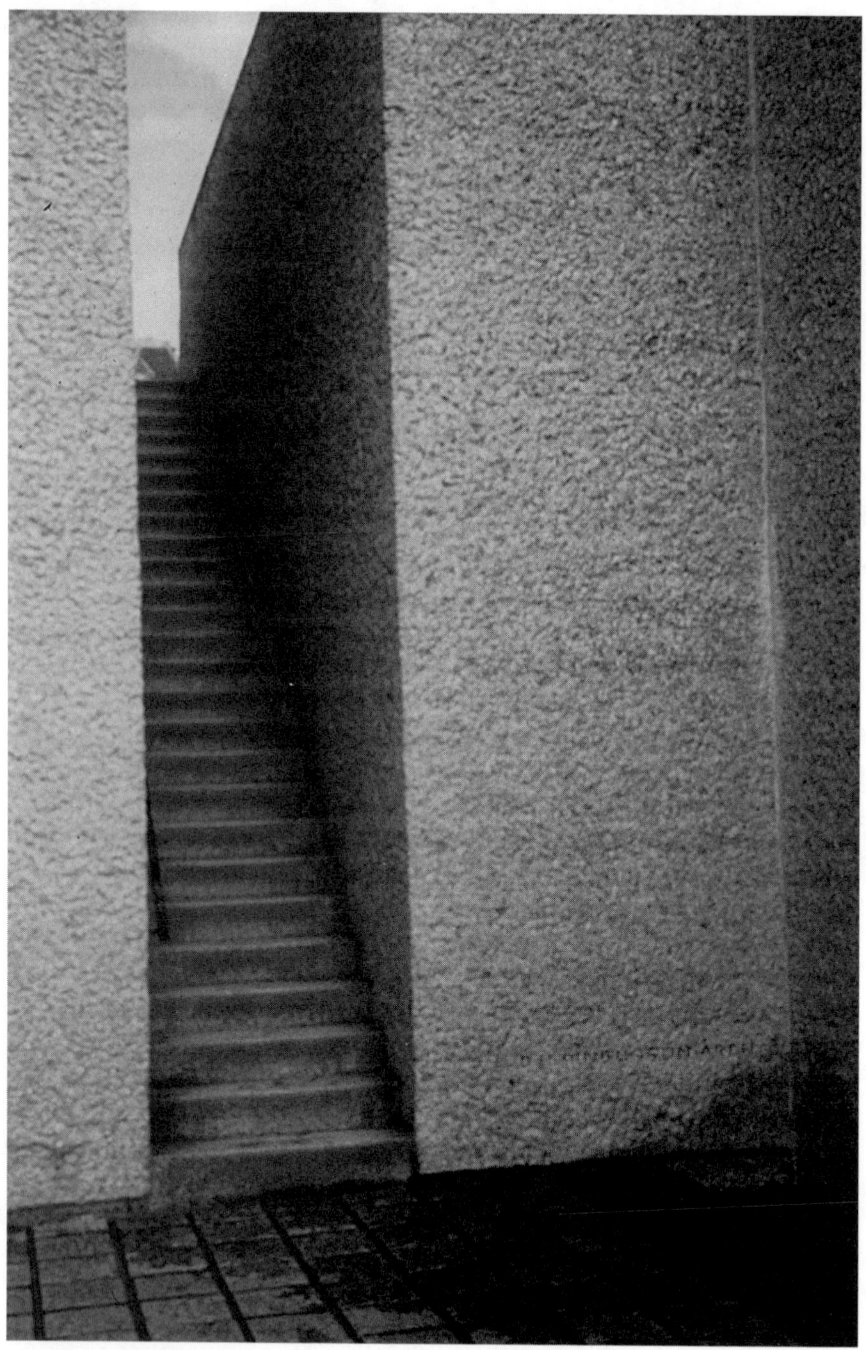

18.3 Georges-Henri Pingusson, *Mémorial aux Martyrs de la Déportation,* north entrance and exit seen from inside the memorial. Photo by Shelley Hornstein.

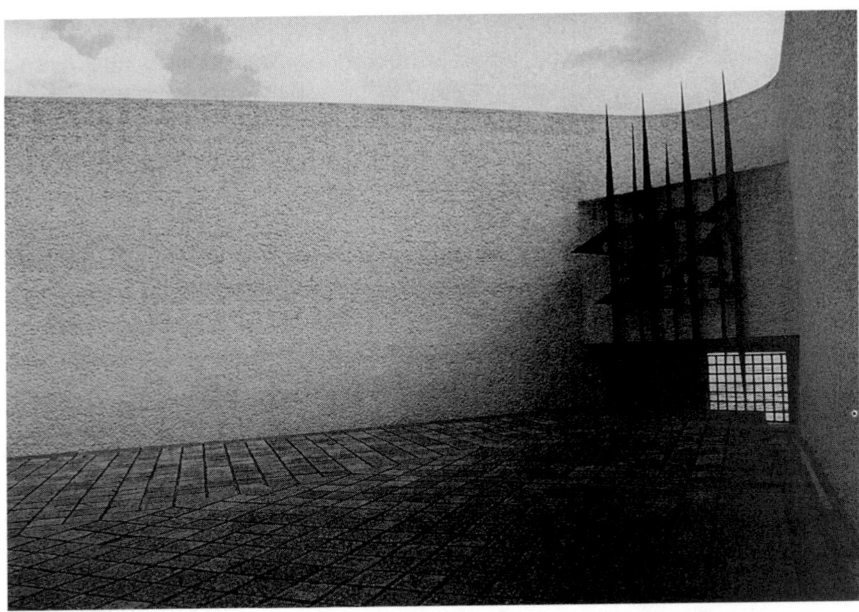

18.4 Georges-Henri Pingusson, *Mémorial aux Martyrs de la Déportation*, somewhat triangular second space, view of grille and river beyond. Photo by Shelley Hornstein.

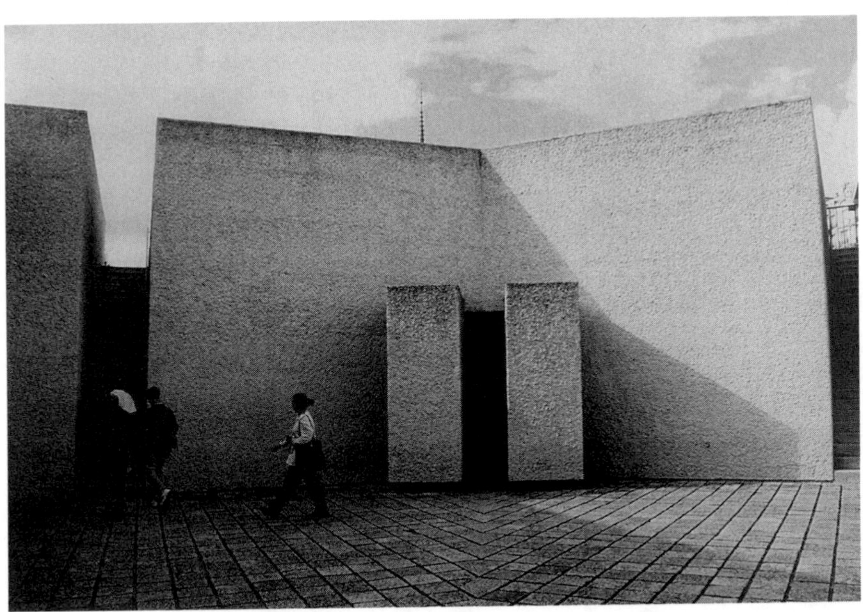

18.5 Georges-Henri Pingusson, *Mémorial aux Martyrs de la Déportation*, view from entrance to memorial space toward courtyard, showing the constricted space of the entryway to the memorial space. Photo by Shelley Hornstein.

du martyr juif inconnu was at the heart of a dispute within Jewish communities from the time the monument was first proposed in 1951 until its inauguration in 1956, on the grounds of the Centre de Documentation Juive Contemporaine (CDJC). This was not to be a monument for French Jews exclusively but rather a monument for all Jews, a singular site for the commemoration of those murdered during the Holocaust. Isaac Schneersohn, an activist and the initiator of the project, had founded the CDJC in 1943 in Grenoble, clandestinely, since the city was occupied by the Italians. Later, after the war, the documents were moved to Paris. Schneersohn defended the site of the memorial with these words:

> France, which, within the scope of one century, experienced three German aggressions, is most certainly the country least likely to forget the crimes of Teutonic barbarism, and is uncontestably the one country that will remain consistently faithful to humanitarian and democratic ideals.[25]

But this was not the view of all, and as Jews tried to piece together their lives in postwar France, they wanted, above all, to forget. Daniel Mayer, who in the end would support the project, was hostile at the outset and insisted that France makes no distinctions amongst its citizens; if a monument were erected to Jewish victims of Nazi crimes, as he framed it, would this not mean that Jews would be singled out?[26] Even André Blumel, another leader within the Jewish community, asked why a monument should be erected in Paris when it was not in Paris that the "martyrs" were assassinated; if Germany wanted to repudiate its past, it should be taking the initiative, and Warsaw should be the most important site of remembrance. And if all these sites failed to initiate such projects, then Jerusalem was where this symbol should be erected.[27]

Let me return to the rights of those killed in the line of national and civic duty. The phrase "Mort pour la France" is frequently inscribed on plaques, steles, and monuments, in accordance with the law of 2 July 1915, which mandates, "in the name of this person who has given his life for the nation, a clear and imperishable title of gratitude and respect from every French citizen." The *Mémorial des Martyrs de la Déportation* never utters a syllable to recognize the cultural identities of those murdered or, furthermore, to acknowledge that the overwhelming majority of lives lost by deportation to death camps during the Second World War were Jewish. Instead, this memorial and this topographic site read as a stunning erasure of Jewish presence and Jewish identity, and in the end an erasure of any Jewish topography of France, while highlighting French national martyrdom. If I am signaling this point it is because of the clear move from the indeterminacy of multiple cultural identities (and Renan's push to forget difference) toward a recovery of Jewish memory palpable in contemporary French writing, preeminently in the work of Finkielkraut.[28] The Simon Wiesenthal Center recently acted on many letters it had received from visitors to the *Mémorial des Martyrs.* Shimon Samuels, director of international relations at the center, requested that the proclamation at the memorial be rectified to read as follows: "to the 200,000 unknown martyrs deported from France, of which more than 70,000 were Jews—men, women, and children."[29] The response from the director of the Bureau des monuments historiques et des lieux de mémoire (at the Ministry of Defense) is telling: the Constitution of 1958 states in Article 1 that "France is an indivisible republic, laic, democratic, and social. France assures the equality before the law of all citizens without distinction of origin, race, or religion. France respects all beliefs." This tradition, the director continues, dates back to the French Revolution and more precisely to the Declaration of the Rights of Man and of the Citizen. Therefore, he concludes, his office is opposed to all changes of the wording at the *Mémorial*.[30]

In spite of these comments today, earlier sketches of the memorial clearly indicate direct references to the Jewish losses. In these images, Pingusson inscribes the Star of David as a central symbol placed on the flat surface of the upper "frame" of the *Mémorial* and at the entrance to it.[31] Yet the actual memorial, and the final phases of the drawings, no longer contain the image. It disappears without an archival trace and it can only be assumed from this that there was a desire to recognize Jewish losses but that over time, it was decided to eliminate any reference to those losses. How curious it is, then, and almost destined, that some interpretations of the monument are convinced of its "Jewish" references. For example, Brian Brace Taylor, then curator at the Museum of Modern Art, New York, and Arthur Drexler, then director of architecture and design at the same museum, asked Pingusson in 1978 to include photographs of the *Mémorial* in a show the museum was preparing titled "Transformations in Modern Architecture" (24 January–27 March 1979). But Taylor erred in naming the memorial, calling it the "Mémorial aux Juifs Martyrs, Île de la Cité" [Memorial to Jewish Martyrdom, Île de la Cité].[32] More surprising still is a 1999 publication on the architect-decorator Jean-Charles Moreux (1889–1956), one of the architects initially invited to work on the memorial in 1953, in which the project is referred to as the "mémorial des Martyrs juifs de la deportation" [Memorial to the Jewish Martyrs of the Deportation].[33]

Hauntingly absent—more precisely, invisible, since we know the history all too well—is what is hiding from us and what is not being told; here, abstraction as an operative strategy takes us the extra distance, beyond the painful and poetic aesthetic impact. Truths are being masked by an abstraction that succeeds at sanitizing the past. Here, a magnificent aesthetic modernism, in keeping with the whitewashed surfaces utilized by an entire generation of colleagues (Le Corbusier, Mallet-Stevens, and others), continues to administer an aesthetic credo that is much adored and respected. The choice of Pingusson expressed the desire for a memorial that was reductionist and abstract, white-

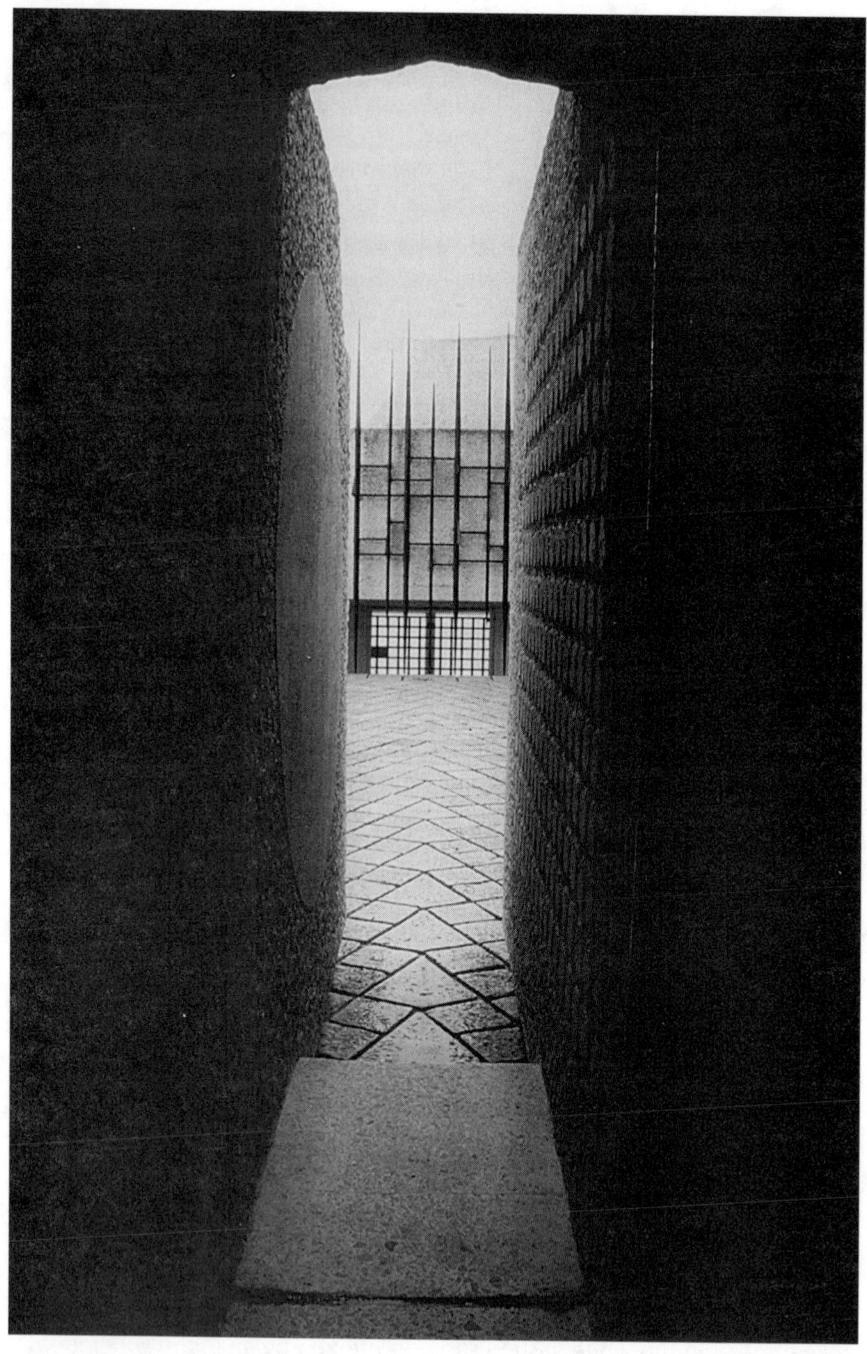

18.6 Georges-Henri Pingusson, *Mémorial aux Martyrs de la Déportation*, Paris, exiting (or entering) the inner memorial chamber to (or from) the second space (as seen from inside the third, inner chamber). Photo by Shelley Hornstein.

washed and sober; a desire to conform to a currency, a currency that was no different from any other elementary school or church that Pingusson designed in Lorraine, or Latitude 43, on the Côte d'Azur. This is not to say that figuration is desirable regardless. It simply must be understood that the strategy of abstraction was imposed to its extreme and reveals the material presence of the principles of universalism.

In the end, the solemn beauty that beckons us to participate in this space also invites our curiosity about the notion of absence and abstraction that is not remedied, alas, by figuration. If, as quoted earlier, "thought makes architectural space an abstraction," then it reminds us to be vigilant in the face of beauty and, in the summary excerpt—or abstraction—that the memorial is, to see what it should yet cannot be. In fact, what seems to play out, especially today, in the spaces of this memorial as an abstracted whole—with an absence of didactic imagery and text, yet with sparse symbols of concentration camps, memorial lights, and a rotunda that evokes the Star of David by its hexagonal shape—is that visitors, who are now free to celebrate cultural particularism and difference, tend to exit from the spaces imbued with a sense of "Jewish" loss. It is a poetic turn. With strident efforts to erase difference and to secure wholeness of French—national—loss through a campaign of harmony in an abstracted idea of universal tragedy, the *Mémorial* particularizes and designates those losses. The very Constitutional requirements of indivisibility, met in a space of abstraction, leave traces of openness that allow for the wholeness never to be understood. As the theoretical place where abstraction from figuration is also a withdrawal from identification and where choosing symbols over a choice not to name Jewish losses is abstraction of another order, Jewish identity, in this site of symbolic forms that aims to suggest wholeness, has been declared.

Notes

1. "L'espace vrai fait de l'architecture une substance, la pensée fait de l'espace architectural une abstraction" (quoted in J. P. Betegnie, "Gestion de l'espace: Visite au *Mémorial des Martyrs de la Déportation,* Enseignement sur l'espace architectural," Archives of the Institut français d'architecture, Fonds Pingusson [hereafter AIFA]).

2. Marc Fisher, "The Truth That Can Only Hurt," interview with Claude Lanzmann, *Washington Post,* 25 June 1999, C2, C8.

3. *Rivistando I Lager,* exhibition catalogue (Milan: Galleria San Fedele, 1985).

4. Saul Friedlander, ed., *Probing the Limits of Representation: Nazism and the "Final Solution"* (Cambridge, Mass.: Harvard University Press, [1992] 1996), 3.

5. Jürgen Habermas, *Eine Art Schadensabwicklung: Kleine politische Schriften 6* (Frankfurt-am-Main: Suhrkamp, 1987), 163, quoted in Friedlander, *Probing the Limits,* 3.

6. "Sachez ce qui s'est passé, n'oubliez pas, et en même temps jamais vous ne saurez" (Maurice Blanchot, *L'Écriture du désastre* [Paris: Gallimard, 1980], 131).

7. Dominick LaCapra, "Lanzmann's *Shoah:* 'Here There Is No Why,'" *Critical Inquiry* 23, no. 2 (winter 1997): 239.

8. "Il faut savoir et voir, et il faut voir et savoir. Indissolublement. Si vous allez à Auschwitz sans rien savoir sur Auschwitz et l'histoire de ce camp, vous ne voyez rien, vous ne comprenez rien. De même, si vous savez sans y avoir été, vous ne comprenez pas non plus. Il fallait donc une conjonction des deux. C'est pourquoi le problème des lieux est capital. Ce n'est pas un film idéaliste que j'ai fait, ce n'est pas un film avec des grandes réflexions métaphysiques ou théologiques sur pourquoi toute cette histoire est arrivée aux Juifs, pourquoi on les a tués. C'est un film à tas de terre, un film de topographie, de géographie" (Claude Lanzmann, "Le lieu et la parole," in *Au sujet de* Shoah: *Le film de Claude Lanzmann,* Bernard Cuau et al. [Paris: Belin, 1990], 294).

9. "Les pierres du souvenir de la Seconde Guerre mondiale . . . constituent un ensemble emietté, dispers, atomisé, de plusieurs dizaines de milliers de steles, plaques et monuments. Pourtant, malgré l'impression d'extrême diversité, de mémoires étanches les unes aux autres, coexistant en s'ignorant, des traits communs demeurent entre les différents souvenirs" (Serge Barcellini and Annette Wieviorka, *Passant, souviens-toi! Les lieux du souvenir de la Seconde Guerre mondiale en France* [Paris: Plon, 1995], 11).

10. P. Birnbaum, "Grégoire, Dreyfus, Drancy, and the Rue Copernic: Jews at the Heart of French History," in *Realms of Memory: Rethinking the French Past,* ed. Pierre Nora, trans. Arthur Goldhammer, vol. 1 (New York: Columbia University Press, 1996), 381.

11. Ernst Renan, "What Is a Nation?," translated and annotated by Martin Thom, in *Nation and Narration,* ed. Homi K. Bhabha (New York: Routledge, 1990), 11.

12. N. Rachlin, "Alain Finkielkraut and the Politics of Cultural Identity," *Substance* 24, nos. 1 and 2 (1976–77).

13. *Georges-Henri Pingusson, architecte; l'oeuvre lorraine,* Paris, Inventaire general, Itinéraires du patrimoine, Archives modernes de l'architecture et la Direction régionale des affaires culturelles, 1997.

14. Barcellini and Wieviorka, *Passant, souviens-toi,* 413.

15. James Young, *The Texture of Memory: Holocaust Memorials and Meaning* (New Haven, Conn.: Yale University Press, 1993), 135–136.

16. For details concerning the conception and building of this memorial, see A. Wieviorka, "Un lieu de mémoire: Le Mémorial du martyr juif inconnu," *Pardès,* no. 2 (1985): 80–98.

17. Jean Cassou also wrote *Le pillage par les Allemandes des oeuvres d'art et des bibliothèques appartenant à des Juifs en France* (Paris: Editions du Centre de Documentation Juive Contemporaine, 1947).

18. The three teams were Pingusson and Raymond Veysset, André Arbus and Robert Couturier, and Jean-Charles Moreux and Emmanuel Auricoste. Each presented significantly different stylistic approaches to the monument. For details, see S. Texier, "Georges-Henri Pingusson, architecte, 1894–1978: L'architecture comme 'transcendance poétique du concret,' ou 'l'impossible doctrine'" (doctoral dissertation, Université de Paris IV-Sorbonne, September 1998), 402.

19. Ibid.

20. These drawings are held by the AIFA.

21. "War Memorial, Paris: A Monument to the French Victims of Nazi Concentration Camps," *Architectural Review* 133 (March 1963): 186–190.

22. See the only detailed article on the monument itself: Elizabeth Vitou, "Paris, Mémorial de la Déportation: Georges-Henri Pingusson (1894–1978)," *Architecture Mouvement Continuité,* no. 19 (February 1988): 68–88.

23. *Memorial to the Martyrs of Deportation,* brochure published by Le réseau du souvenir, n.d.

24. Letter from Pingusson to Arthur Drexler, director of architecture and design, The Museum of Modern Art, New York, dated 17 May 1978, regarding an exhibition titled *Transformations in Modern Architecture* (1979), in which Pingusson's work was included (AIFA).

25. "La France qui, en l'espace d'un siècle, a eu l'expérience de trois agressions allemandes est certainement le pays du monde le moins enclin à oublier les crimes de la barbarie teutonne. Elle est incontestablement le pays du monde qui restera le plus longtemps fidèle à l'idéal humanitaire et démocratique" (Letter from Isaac Schneersohn to Nahum Goldmann, 9 September 1953, CDJC archives, quoted in Wieviorka, "Un lieu de mémoire," 84).

26. Wieviorka, "Un lieu de mémoire," 84.

27. A. Blumel, "Le choix de Paris se justifie-t-il," *La terre retrouvée,* 1 December 1951, 4.

28. Rachlin states,

> Given Finkielkraut's flight back to the fold of Judaism at the end of *The Imaginary Jew,* one might think he would advocate that Judaism take its place in the mosaic of a new French cultural diversity, and thrive on its newly found post-assimilation cohesion and solidarity. But for Finkielkraut, neither the anti-particularistic tendencies of the spirit of the French Revolution nor the notion of culture inherited from Herder's *Volkgeist*—the belief in the absolute uniqueness and genius of each culture—is devoid of danger for Judaism. During the French Revolution, French Jews were the first European Jews to obtain emancipation. But this emancipation and the civil rights it guaranteed were granted under the assumption, on the part of the grantors, that the Jewish particularism, including their semiautonomous communal institutions and the use of Yiddish, would disappear. Integration would eventually ensue, and transform the members of the different French Jewish communities into Frenchmen, albeit of a different religious persuasion. Cultural differences and religious practices were to be matters of private life, according to the universalist ideology of assimilation. This universalist ideology, the French version of the "white man's burden," as Etienne Balibar calls it, justified and guided the French colonial enterprise . . . by presenting its own concept of civilization as a model for all people. In this context, the universalist conception of culture inherited from the Enlightenment may have threatened Jewish identity with progressive disintegration and disappearance. (Rachlin, "Alain Finkielkraut.")

29. Letter from Samuels to Alain Richard, Minister of Defense, 10 September 1999, archives of the Ministère de la Défense, Direction de la mémoire, du patrimoine et des archives, Bureau des monuments historiques et des lieux de mémoire (hereafter MHLM).

30. MHLM, internal memo from Jean-Loup Bonté, 20 September 1999.

31. Some early studies and sketches can be found in the AIFA and at the Archives nationales, in the Fonds du Réseau du Souvenir. Unfortunately, many have been lost, and neither archive contains complete holdings.

32. See correspondence in the AIFA.

33. Susan Day, *Jean-Charles Moreux: architecte-décorateur-paysagiste* (Paris: Norma, 1999), 356.

Contributors

Ernst van Alphen is Professor of Comparative Literature at Leiden University. His publications include *Francis Bacon and the Loss of Self* (1992), *Caught by History: Holocaust Effects in Contemporary Art, Literature, and Theory* (1997), and *Armando: Shaping Memory* (2000).

Monica Bohm-Duchen is an independent writer, lecturer, and exhibition organizer, based in London. She holds an M.A. from the Courtauld Institute. She was contributing editor of *After Auschwitz: Responses to the Holocaust in Contemporary Art,* which was published to accompany a touring exhibition of the same name, which she curated, in 1995. She co-curated *Life? Or Theatre? The Work of Charlotte Salomon,* shown at the Royal Academy of Arts in London in 1998, which toured North America in 2000. She is co-editor of a forthcoming critical anthology of essays, *Charlotte Salomon: Gender, Trauma, Creativity.*

Tim Cole is a lecturer in European social history at the University of Bristol, U.K. His research interests focus on the geographies of ghettoization in Hungary and on the representation of the Holocaust. He is the author of *Selling the Holocaust: From Auschwitz to Schindler—How History is Bought, Packaged, and Sold* (1999) and is currently completing a book on the spatiality of the Holocaust in Budapest.

Rebecca Comay teaches philosophy and literary studies at the University of Toronto. She is currently working on three books: *Mourning Sickness: Hegel and the Impossibility of Memory; Proustian Impressions: Trauma, Technology, Theory;* and *Walter Benjamin: Between Melancholia and Fetishism.* She has recently edited an anthology called *Lost in the Archives* (2002).

Mark Godfrey is Lecturer in History and Theory of Art at the Slade School of Fine Art, University College, London, and has recently completed his Ph.D. in art history (University College, London), on American abstraction and Holocaust memorial. His art criticism has appeared in *Contemporary Visual Arts* and *Frieze.* His published work includes "The Gates of Remembrance: An Oblique Look at Frank Stella's Polish Villages," in *Object,* and "A Space for Public Memory: Rereading Louis Kahn's 'Memorial to the Six Million Jewish Martyrs,'" in *New Voices in Jewish Thought.* He curated a show by the British artist Catherine Yass, called "Synagogue," in 2000, and is working on an exhibition of the work of the American conceptual artist Douglas Huebler.

Reesa Greenberg is an independent scholar and museum consultant whose research focuses on exhibitions and display. Her recent work examines the use of art in museum exhibitions about the Holocaust. Currently, she is expanding an article that appeared in *Jong Holland* 1 (2000) into a book titled *Peggy Guggenheim, Philip Johnson, and Ydessa Hendeles: Private Collectors, Museums, Display—A Post-Holocaust Perspective.* She is co-editor of *Thinking about Exhibitions* (1996) and is an adjunct professor at both Concordia University, Montréal, and York University, Toronto.

Marianne Hirsch is Professor of French and Comparative Literature at Dartmouth College in Hanover, New Hampshire. Her recent books are *The Mother/Daughter Plot: Narrative, Psychoanalysis, Feminism* (1989) and *Family Frames: Photography, Narrative, and Postmemory* (1997). She also co-edited *The Voyage In: Fictions of Female Development* (1983), *Conflicts in Feminism* (1991), and *Écritures de femmes: Nouvelles cartographies* (1996), and is the editor of *The Familial Gaze* (1998). She has published numerous articles on Holocaust memory and representation, especially in photography, and has worked on the memory of the second generation. With Leo Spitzer she is writing a book titled *Czernowitz Album: Four Jewish Families and the Idea of a City Before, During, and After the Holocaust.*

Shelley Hornstein is Associate Professor of Art History and Visual Culture, York University, Toronto. She specializes in examining concepts of architecture, place, and spatial politics. She co-edited *Capital Culture: A Reader on Modernist Legacies, State Institutions, and the Value(s) of Art* (2000) and is currently writing a book titled *Losing Site: The Power of Architecture, Memory, and Place* and co-editing a collection of essays titled *Transforming Memory.* Along with Carol Zemel and Reesa Greenberg, she will be launching *Project Mosaica,* an online Jewish museum of art, heritage, and culture.

Florence Jacobowitz teaches film studies at York University and is a founding editor of and regular contributor to *CinéAction*. She has published articles on a number of European émigré artists working in Hollywood between the 1930s and the 1950s, on melodrama, and on postwar narrative films that address history and memory. She is presently co-authoring a book with Richard Lippe on star images and their iconic meaning in still photography and film.

Berel Lang is Professor of Humanities at Trinity College, Connecticut, and formerly professor of philosophy at SUNY Albany and the University of Colorado and visiting professor at the Hebrew University of Jerusalem, Wesleyan University, and the University of Connecticut. He has written or edited eighteen books, including *Writing and the Holocaust* (1988), *Act and Idea in the Nazi Genocide* (1990), *Heidegger's Silence* (1996), *The Future of the Holocaust* (1999), and *Holocaust Representation* (2000).

Daniel Libeskind is an architect of international standing. In 1989 he won the competition to design the Jewish Museum in Berlin, which recently received the German Architecture Prize. His current projects include the Felix Nussbaum

Museum, Osnabrück (completed); the Imperial War Museum North, Manchester; the "Spiral" extension to the Victoria and Albert Museum, London; the Jewish Museum, San Francisco; and the JVC University, Guadalajara. He has taught at universities around the world. Currently he is the Louis Kahn Professor at Yale University, the Paul Cret Chair professor at the University of Pennsylvania, and a professor at Hochschule für Gestaltung, Karlsruhe. He has received the Berlin Cultural Prize and the Deutscher Architektur Preis, and is a member of the Akademie der Künst in Berlin and the European Academy of Sciences and Arts.

Andrea Liss is a contemporary art historian and cultural theorist in the Visual and Performing Arts Department at California State University, San Marcos. She has published *Trespassing through Shadows: Memory, Photography, and the Holocaust* (1998), a study of contemporary artistic and museum employments of documentary photographs and artifacts in representations of the Shoah. Dr. Liss is currently writing *Maternal Conceptions,* a book on feminist motherhood and contemporary visual culture.

Leslie Morris is an Associate Professor of German at the University of Minnesota, Twin Cities. She is the author of the forthcoming book *Ich suche ein unschuldiges Land: Reading History in the Poetry of Ingeborg Bachmann* (2000) and is co-editing (with Karen Remmler) a volume titled *Contemporary Jewish Writing in Germany.* She has written articles on the poetics of exile, diaspora, translation, and the border, and on artistic and theoretical approaches to memory and the Holocaust. She is currently working on a book on elegy and postmemory in German, American, and French poetry.

Leo Spitzer is the Kathe Tappe Vernon Professor of History at Dartmouth College and Chair of the Jewish Studies Program. His most recent book is *Hotel Bolivia: The Culture of Memory in a Refuge from Nazism* (1998). He is also the author of *Lives in Between: Assimilation and Marginality in Austria, Brazil, West Africa, 1780–1945* (1990, 1999) and *The Creoles of Sierra Leone: Responses to Colonialism* (1974), and is co-editor, with Mieke Bal and Jonathan Crewe, *of Acts of Memory: Cultural Recall in the Present* (1999). He was the Lucius Littauer Fellow at the National Humanities Center (1992–93) and has been the recipient of John Simon Guggenheim, Ford, Social Science Research Council, Whiting, N.E.H., and Rockefeller Foundation awards and fellowships. In 1996–98, he was a National Humanities Center Distinguished Lecturer. He is currently working in collaboration with Marianne Hirsch on a book titled *Czernowitz Album: Four Jewish Families and the Idea of a City Before, During, and After the Holocaust.*

Susan Rubin Suleiman is the C. Douglas Dillon Professor of the Civilization of France and Professor of Comparative Literature at Harvard University. Her major publications include *Authoritarian Fictions: The Ideological Novel as a Literary Genre* (1983; reprinted with new preface, 1993), *Subversive Intent: Gender, Politics, and the Avant-Garde* (1990), *Risking Who One Is: Encounters with Contemporary Art and*

Literature (1994), *Budapest Diary: In Search of the Motherbook* (1996), and the edited volumes *The Female Body in Western Culture: Contemporary Perspectives* (1986) and *Exile and Creativity: Signposts, Travelers, Outsiders, Backward Glances* (1998). Among the courses she teaches are "War and Memory: Representations of World War II in Postwar French Literature and Film" and "The Holocaust and Problems of Representation." She is currently at work on a book titled *Crises of Memory and the Second World War.*

Janet Wolff is Associate Dean for Academic Affairs in the School of the Arts at Columbia University. From 1991 to 2001 she directed the Program in Visual and Cultural Studies at the University of Rochester, and before that she taught for several years at the University of Leeds, where she was Reader in the Sociology of Culture. Her books include *The Social Production of Art* (1981), *Aesthetics and the Sociology of Art* (1983), *Feminine Sentences: Essays on Women and Culture* (1990), and *Resident Alien: Feminist Cultural Criticism* (1995). Her latest book is *AngloModern: Painting and Modernity in England and the United States* (2003).

Robin Wood is Professor Emeritus of Film Studies at York University. He is a noted critic and author of numerous books on film. His work includes *Hitchcock's Films* (1965), *Howard Hawks* (1971, 1981), *Hollywood from Vietnam to Reagan* (1988), *Hitchcock's Films Revisited* (1990), and, most recently, *Sexual Politics and Narrative Film: Hollywood and Beyond* (1998).

James Young is Professor of English and Judaic Studies and Chair of the Department of Judaic and Near Eastern Studies at the University of Massachusetts at Amherst. His published work includes *Writing and Rewriting the Holocaust* (1988); the highly influential *The Texture of Memory* (1993), which won the National Jewish Book Award in 1994; and the edited catalogue *The Art of Memory: Holocaust Memorials in History* (1994). He also curated the exhibit of the same name. His most recent book is *At Memory's Edge* (2000). He is the recipient of numerous awards and fellowships, including a Guggenheim Fellowship, an ACLS Fellowship, and an American Philosophical Society Grant. In 1997 he was appointed by the Berlin Senate to the Findungskommission that chose the design for Germany's national *Memorial for the Murdered Jews of Europe,* now under construction in Berlin.

Carol Zemel is Professor and Chair of the Department of Visual Arts at York University, Toronto. Her most recent book is *Van Gogh's Progress: Utopia and Modernity in Late-Nineteenth-Century Art* (1997). Her current work centers on issues of culture in diaspora. During 2000–2001, she was a Fellow at the Center for Advanced Judaic Studies at the University of Pennsylvania, Philadelphia, where she completed studies for a book titled *Graven Images: Visual Culture and Modern Jewish History.*

Index

Page numbers in *italics* refer to illustrations.